RAISING THEIR VOICES

RAISING THEIR VOICES

British Women Writers, 1650–1750

Marilyn L. Williamson

Wayne State University Press   Detroit   1990

8

20013327
DLC

3-22-90

Library of Congress Cataloging-in-Publication Data

Williamson, Marilyn L., 1927–
    Raising their voices, 1650–1750 / Marilyn L. Williamson.
        p.   cm.
    Includes bibliographical references.
    ISBN 0–8143–2209–3
    1. English literature–Women authors–History and criticism.
2. English literature–Early modern, 1500–1700–History and
criticism.   3. English literature–18th century–History and
criticism.   4. Women authors, English–Biography.   I. Title.
PR113.W55 1990
820.9′9287–dc20   89–36296
                                                    CIP

To the Memory of My Mother

Contents

CONTENTS

Preface

Every approach to literature has its limitations, and it is useful for the author to acknowledge them. My method has been to read literature as it performs social work in a historical context. My interest has been to display the first English women who were aware of their own oppression, how they defined it, and how they represented it in the discourses available to them. I do not therefore make aesthetic judgments the goal of my reading, and some readers will doubtless find much of the writing covered in this study deficient in quality and therefore not worth attention. My work and that of other feminist critics offers the possibility of breaking out of the cycle of assuming that what is unknown or obscure deserves to be so. I do not claim to have discovered inglorious Miltons among the score of writers in this study, but I believe their work deserves attention nonetheless. The neglect is historical: most were well-known, some quite famous, in their own times. Just as historians are beginning to read popular pamphlets along with Hobbes and Locke, or study the family in addition to military campaigns, so literary historians are reading far beyond the canon and the taste and values it forms.

I also insist that a context is not a prior reality reflected in the text. Instead, representations within the text perform complex social work as they endorse, interrogate, or subvert the cultural ideologies that produce them and are produced by them. My work focuses on these questions, rather than offering the reader extended and detailed analyses of individual texts. Ann Messenger's *His and Hers* provides such readings for several of the writers included here.

Knowledge of the writers of this early time may also contribute to the developing controversy about the relation of feminist criticism to post-structural theories. Feminist theory claims that women are a group with accepted attributes and activities, whereas the post-structuralist theorists attack the essentialist concept of woman and see all subjectivity as constructed by discourse that weaves together power and knowledge. My stance throughout this work, though I did not know it during the writing, coincides with that of Linda Alcoff and Teresa de Lauretis, who claim that the construction of subjectivity is a continuous process, produced not only by external social patterns and discourses but through the individual's interaction with such discourses and cultural practices. Such thinking does not compel a choice between the extremes of the essentialist feminine subject and the genderless subject produced by discourse. This approach describes a self-analyzing practice that engages the horizons of meanings and practices at a given historical moment in order to position one's self to assume one's feminine identity as a point of departure in political analysis.[1] This theory helps explain the emergence of an identifiable women's subjectivity in the seventeenth century, as described by Catherine Belsey in *The Subject of Tragedy*. It also explains why Margaret Cavendish could not find a discourse from which to write, and how the two models for the woman poet, Katherine Philips and Aphra Behn, used current discourses—namely, the retirement tradition and the libertine ideology—to forge identities as writers that would form models for their successors. They showed women how to use cultural codes and discourses to become writers and to comment on their own predicament, and their successors immediately created a female literary tradition from the models in order to lend authority to women's writing. That the two traditions soon became labeled with sexual stereotypes should not prevent literary historians from appreciating the process by which Orinda and Behn were used by early women writers to solve their taking the privilege of authorship and publication.[2]

Because of the broad scope of my subject and the emphasis on literature and society, I have omitted all the religious poetry written by women in the period, as well as poets, like Trapnel, who are almost exclusively religious poets, or the poetry of writers included here, such as Astell, if their poetry is religious. I admit that in seventeenth-century England, religious values are social and political, but the issues are so complex that they would have required another framework besides that of gender ideology, which I have used. That would be another study, and one does what one can. The large amount of secular writing produced by women is further evidence of the secularization of life in an era when women were still expected to be extremely pious and many were. Women with the courage to raise their voices about gender relations give us a partial view of what all women were thinking, and this bias must be acknowledged.

My emphasis has also been placed on charting a relatively unknown territory and making connections among the writers wherever possible. Although there have been studies of individual writers, or of groups like the dramatists or the fiction writers, no study has brought together most of the seventeenth- and early eighteenth-century English women writers and shown the connections among them and the traditions they created. The existence of several new anthologies of these writers forms a welcome context in which this study may be read, and my work both supplements or disputes conclusions drawn in Hilda Smith's *Reason's Disciples* (1982), Antonia Fraser's *The Weaker Vessel* (1984), and Ann Messenger's *His and Hers* (1986). When works to which I refer in this study are included in new anthologies, I have used abbreviations in the text, so that the interested reader may refer to original works without having to resort to research libraries or films. The anthologies and abbreviations are as follows: *The Female Wits: Women Playwrights of the Restoration*, ed. Fidelis Morgan (*FW*); *First Feminists: British Women Writers, 1578–1799*, ed. Moira Ferguson (*FF*); *The Whole Duty of a Woman: Female Writers in Seventeenth-Century England*, ed. Angeline Goreau (*WD*). These books also have extensive bibliographies that will be helpful to the interested reader. The appearance of such work attests to the growing interest in the women of this era. Welcome also is the increasing number of historians who are interested in social history and take seriously topics like the family, lineage, sexuality, and the history of gender. Sophistication about the complexities of seventeenth-century England has been greatly increased by the scrutiny, under the leadership of Christopher Hill, of the various revolutions of the period. Valuable knowledge and conclusions have come from these investigations, and their guidance to primary sources is invaluable. For the inspiration to look back to early women writers, all feminist critics are indebted to Virginia Woolf, who may be forgiven her scorn for Eliza Haywood because of her praise of Aphra Behn and her sympathetic reading of the works of Margaret Cavendish.

This book will have two audiences: the general reader and the specialist. For the general reader, I imagine the field as an uncharted territory, and I have sketched its outlines in the hope of inspiring more interest in one or another of the writers represented here. I have tried to accommodate the general reader by presenting a full table of contents and frequent section headings so that the reader may keep his or her bearings in the material. This is especially important because several writers appear in more than one place in the text. The specialist reader, on the other hand, may find some material presented here familiar and may know more about one or another figure than can be included in a work of this scope. This book offers the specialist a context in which to place his or her knowledge in order to confirm or dispute patterns and hypotheses developed here.

Inevitably, too, during the writing of a complex overview of many relatively obscure figures, errors creep into the text, however careful one may be to verify facts, many of which have not yet stood the test of scholarly scrutiny. I have checked biographical facts with *A Dictionary of British and American Women Writers, 1660–1800* (1985), edited by Janet Todd, and therefore I hope I have not perpetuated many errors of the past. The anonymous readers of the manuscript saved me from several mistakes, but I am certain that other errors or misimpressions remain. For these I beg the reader's indulgence.

The making of a book creates many kinds of debts. Long in process, this study has been made possible by several leaves from teaching responsibilities. One year, 1983–84, was supported by the Michigan Fellowship from the Educational Foundation of the American Association of University Women and a sabbatical leave from Wayne State University; another fifteen months of leave in 1985–86 was supported by the Josephine Nevins Keal Chair, awarded by the Department of English at Wayne State University. I am deeply grateful for this confirmation of my scholarly purposes. For generous subsidies to support the publication of *Raising Their Voices,* I wish to thank Garrett T. Heberlein, Vice President for Research and Dean of the Graduate School, and Dalmas A. Taylor, Dean of the College of Liberal Arts, at Wayne State University. I would like to thank Robert Demorest for editing the manuscript and especially to acknowledge the thoughtful help of Anne Adamus throughout the process of publication.

The works of the writers in this study are for the most part not readily available except on film and in research libraries. I am therefore indebted to the following libraries for materials: Hatcher Graduate Library at the University of Michigan, the Newberry Library, the Huntington Library, the Center for Studies in Women's Literature at the University of Tulsa, the Houghton Library at Harvard University, and the Library of Wellesley College. I quote from the Wellesley Manuscript of the poems of Anne Kingsmill Finch, the countess of Winchilsea, by permission. Elizabeth Hampsten has described the Wellesley Manuscript and published several poems from it in "Poems by Ann Finch," *Women's Studies* 7 (1980): 5–19. When I have quoted from poems Hampsten presents, I have acknowledged her in the text. I quote from *The Parliament of Women* (1684) and from *The Female Advocate* (1700) by permission of the Librarian of the Huntington Library, San Marino, California.

Among people, I wish to thank Bernard Goldman for inviting me to edit Rowton's *Female Poets of Great Britain* for the Wayne State University Press, a project that led directly to this one. I am also grateful to Judith K. Gardiner, Carolyn Heilbrun, Arthur F. Marotti, and Carol T. Neely, for their support of the project in its initial stage, and to the anonymous reviewers for the Keal Chair at a later stage. I wish to thank the anonymous readers for the Wayne State University Press, who generously saw the book in the manuscript, made valuable suggestions, and saved me from many errors. For patience with endless ramblings about details, scope, hypotheses, I wish to thank friends—Mary Bolton, Carole Herhold, Pearl Warn, and, especially, Jeanne Flood. My son Timothy has been a better feminist longer than I have. James H. McKay has been patient about computer crises and, as always, kept the faith. My greatest debt is recorded in the dedication. My mother's legacy was twofold: the freedom to write books she never understood and the desire for equality she would have vehemently denied.

Introduction

Man might consider that women were not created to be
their slaves or vassals; for as they had not their Original out of
his head (thereby to command him), so it was not out of his foot
to be trod upon, but in a *medium* out of his side to be his fellow
feeler, his equal, and companion. –*The Women's Sharp Revenge* (1640)

That since we are assured of our Creation in the image of God, and
of interest in Christ, equal unto men, as also of a proportionable share
in the Freedoms of this Commonwealth, we cannot but wonder and
grieve that we should appear so despicable in your eyes, as to be
thought unworthy to Petition or represent our Grievances to this
Honourable House. –*To the supreme authority,* 5 May 1649

The major purposes of this study are two. First, to inform the reader, especially the feminist reader, of the great scope of literary work – poetry, drama, fiction – that was created by women during the latter half of the seventeenth century and the first decades of the eighteenth, to demonstrate the traditions these writers created, and to show the continuities between the neglected and little known seventeenth-century writers and their eighteenth-century successors. In dwelling on these connections, I am not, however, assuming that women's literature is a special category with a unique language, but rather simply tracing out historical facts: women writers saw one another as models and inspirations, they were quick to create traditions to lend authority to their writing, they looked to one another for support, and they frequently wrote for other women. All students of literature – feminist or not – need to reclaim this neglected and obscure portion of literary history in order to possess knowledge of all that was being written while Milton, Cowley, and Swift were active, the better to understand all literature and its context.

Second, I hope to demonstrate that feminist commentary about the condition of women has a continuous history from the early seventeenth century to the present, although our knowledge of the outstanding texts has been more ample for the eighteenth and nineteenth centuries. Here I owe the reader a definition of the term *feminist* as I will be using it in this study. As the epigraphs show, there existed in seventeenth-century England the concept of equality between the genders, the central principle of modern feminism. Yet to limit the description *feminist* to those few writers who claim equality does not do justice to women's thinking about their predicament in its seventeeth-century context. I will therefore call feminist those writers who advocate better conditions of life for women as a social group. The vision of women as a group is important, as Hilda Smith has taught us, and more important than claims of equality in a time when a married woman was still the property of her husband.[1] The advocacy on behalf of women, then, produces a widespread critique of women's social roles, especially with regard to marriage and education. Many of the writers prove to be much before their time, as we shall see, in their resistance to the essentialist formulations about women in the Judeo-Christian tradition and the Western social structures based on its assumptions.

My claim of a continuous feminist history disputes the conclusion of Hilda Smith's excellent study, *Reason's Disciples,* which observes that because many of the writers covered here did not translate their ideas into political agendas, but held private notions about women's lives, their ideas were "truncated," only to be revived now.[2] My argument is that although there may have been short periods in which little overtly feminist work emerged, there is writing about woman's condition almost constantly from the early seventeenth century to the present. The arguments put forward change from era to era, depending on the thinking of the time. The largest gap in our knowledge is understandably at the beginning, and part of my purpose is to augment Hilda Smith's study by exhibiting the variety of writing by women about their condition from 1650 to 1750. Moira Ferguson's collection, *First Feminists: British Women Writers, 1578–1799* demonstrates one kind of continuity.[3] Another is the use of literature by society to reaffirm, interrogate, or subvert its dominant values. For the contextual critic, literature is one means by which individuals and groups deal with their society and in turn are socialized by their culture. Literature is not an artifact formed by a prior socioeconomic reality but an integral part of that reality in forming values and endorsing or questioning ideologies. This effect is apparent in the way in which the pre-Richardsonian fiction deals with parental marriage choices for their children. Although most of the fiction approves filial obedience in the selection of a mate, many stories inspire the reader's doubt about the wisdom of the parents in making such choices. One can observe the novels leading the contemporary reader to question arranged matches and accept those based on the child's inclination.

The amatory fiction written in the late seventeenth and early eighteenth centuries has a similar social role. In the central fantasy of this fiction, a predatory male aristocrat seduces and abandons an innocent woman. After reviewing many of the pre-Richardsonian fictions, already studied incisively by Richetti, I suggest that these texts mediate a massive social change: the late seventeenth century and early eighteenth century gradually had produced an English economy that was centered in trade and commerce, had its roots in self-interest, and encouraged male risk for individual gain rather than hereditary privilege.[4] The male of such a world is represented in fiction written by women for women as a predator, motivated entirely by self-interest, and her challenge is to cope with his behavior. My claim is, then, that the fiction mediates women's problems in dealing with the new commercial world, which held no place for them but encouraged men to think largely in terms of their own interest. These representations need to be added both to Laurence Stone's ideas about companionate marriages in the eighteenth century and to the gloomier picture that after the eighteenth century women retreat into a saccharine domesticity from which they barely emerge to author their great fiction of the eighteenth and nineteenth centuries.[5]

If women produced a continuous critique of their condition from the seventeenth century on, we need only to understand its many forms in order to chronicle it accurately. We now understand most of the genres produced by the "woman" controversy of the sixteenth and seventeenth centuries, thanks to Linda Woodbridge's *Women and the English Renaissance* and Katherine Henderson and Barbara McManus's *Half Humankind*, both of which analyze and make available to the modern reader the many kinds of writing produced by the long controversy over the status and condition of women in the English Renaissance.[6] For the period covered by this study, the controversial material is well represented in Ferguson's *First Feminists*, mentioned earlier. *Raising Their Voices* provides the history of feminist thought with insights into the range and variety of literary genres, themes, conventions, and fantasies women used to deal with their predicament, an understanding of how a convention, like the pastoral, takes on special meaning in women's hands.

The seventeenth century was an extraordinary time for women writers: their genuine literary output begins in 1640, never to diminish again. In this era we have Katherine Philips, the first English woman to publish a volume of poetry; Aphra Behn, the first English woman to live by publishing; the first group of genuine women playwrights, who wrote to be produced; Delariviere Manley, England's first female political journalist. At this time women began to write fiction in great quantities, a fiction that

16

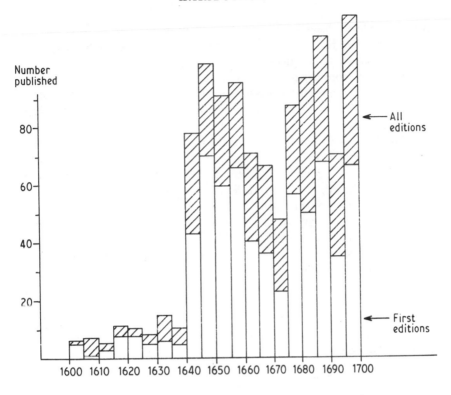

Fig. 1. Frequency distribution of first editions and all editions of women's works published by half-decades. Taken from Patricia Crawford, "Women's Published Writings, 1600–1700," in *Women in English Society, 1500–1800,* ed. Mary Prior (London: Methuen, 1985), p. 212. Used with the permission of Methuen and Company.

eventuated in the English novel, which from its inception carried on the themes they had begun. In general, women wrote unprecedented quantities of books, as shown in figure 1.[7]

In this time women become subjects, in the terms defined by Catherine Belsey: they have a perspective from which they write that is theirs. Instead of being the objects of male perception and expression, women write from a position that they define, a distinct place within the discourses, as we shall see.[8] Women's poetry before the seventeenth century—specifically before Aemelia Lanier (ca. 1570–ca. 1640)—is hardly distinguishable from that of men. But, beginning with the poets studied here, a definite female voice begins to be heard: women take female pseudonyms, turn discourse to their needs, create distinctive themes and conventions.

About 1640 the controversy over women also begins to hear both male and female voices that are different. The change begins with *The Women's Sharp Revenge.*[9] In this era the feminist polemic, as defined by Moira Ferguson, takes shape. To be sure, some of these are written by men, but the polemic, as the successor to the defenses of women, conveys an assertive approach to woman's condition and creates a set of terms that are used to define women's major problems and the solutions to them.[10] Controversial texts of the period include not only parodic writing about the women petitioners but also essays about the condition of women and the state of marriage. Writing of these documents never ceased: for example, Sophia's feminist pamphlets in 1739 are indebted to *The Woman as Good as the Man* (1677), a translation of the work by Poulain de La Barre.[11] If one has the knowledge to trace the continuity, it is there.

As the post-structuralists have taught us, subjectivity does not grow from the air: it is socially inspired, through, as we saw in the preface, taking a stance within the discourses available in one's culture. A vivid example of that theory is the first writer in this study, Margaret Cavendish, duchess of Newcastle. Although she asserted her right to an intellectual life and the privilege of writing, she lacked a discourse in which to frame the terms of her predicament, just as she rejected knowledge of scientific and philosophical discourse within which to fit her cosmological speculations. The result is that she alternated between fantasies of women's omnipotence and rage at her contemporaries for their frivolous lives. She dreamed of a female academy, but ended by saying women who lack education cannot teach one another. She remained Mad Madge, a deviant who has no heirs, though she was frequently cited as a woman of achievement by later advocates of women's education. Cavendish illustrates the difficulty a female subject can have in finding a position within the hegemonic, male discourses.[12]

Fortunately, in the middle of the seventeenth century there were two women writers who found a stance within prominent discourses of their time and therefore could serve as models and examples of a female literary

18

tradition their self-acknowledged successors were quick to create. Katherine Philips, the Matchless Orinda (1631–64), used the retirement discourse, which evolves from the *beatus vir,* the Horatian tradition of the Happy Man.[13] The themes of this discourse are especially compatible with women's ideological situation because they exalt a private sphere in which the poet finds self-sufficient contentment. Whether the writer lived out this vision, as Orinda herself did not, it offered a set of terms to critique the public world from a woman's perspective; but it was also politically conservative. Aphra Behn (1640–89), on the other hand, was strongly male-identified, and thus she found the libertine ideology of the cavaliers compatible with her vision of female sexuality and abilities.[14] Like the cavaliers she was sexually radical and politically conservative: she wrote of a love that was free of concerns on which aristocrats frown: property and ambition. Still, as male-identified, she claimed equality with men as a writer and wrote for money in drama, fiction, and poetry.

In order to establish their authority to take the privilege of writing, the women writers who followed Orinda and Behn immediately looked to them as models and exemplars, along with Sappho, of a woman's literary tradition. To cope with cultural prohibitions against women's writing, which was epitomized in the Salic Law of Wit (see chapter 3, below), the women who wrote in the late seventeenth and early eighteenth centuries allude to Orinda and Astrea (Behn) at the beginning of their first works: "None characterizes herself as an innovator or groundbreaker. Rather, as their verses suggest, they seem obsessed with creating precursors, with legitimizing female art by establishing a lineage that stretches back to the Greek poetess Sappho, through Katherine Phillips (Chaste Orinda) and Aphra Behn (Fair Astrea), to themselves."[15] As we shall see, virtually every writer in this study ties herself firmly to one or both models in their instant literary heritage. The result is that several of the successors quite overgo their models, especially in the case of Orinda, who died at thirty-two having authored one volume of verse, another of letters, and translated two plays. Followers like Mary Astell and Lady Mary Chudleigh, who were far more gifted and learned than Orinda, much exceed their model, though they, like other female writers of their time, begin with her. Creating their own literary heritage is part of the achievement of these early writers, and in this endeavor they enjoyed the help of many male contemporaries, such as Cowley, Dryden, and less significant reviewers.

At first, writers made little distinction between Orinda and Behn. Poems of the eighties compare Behn to Orinda and Sappho, or sometimes Behn is seen as successor to Orinda. Behn expressed her own desire to be immortal with Orinda and Sappho. In the nineties the author of *An Essay in Defence of the Female Sex* hopes the example of Philips and Behn will inspire women to write, and in a tribute to Catherine Trotter's *Agnes de Castro,*

Delariviere Manley salutes Trotter as filling the vacant throne of Orinda and Astrea. In the meantime, however, Behn was being villified by misogynist satirists for her loose morals while Orinda was being praised as chaste.[16] Robert Gould, whose *Love Given O're* (1682) is one of the most important antifeminist satires of the time, was one of the first writers to draw the contrast between Astrea and Orinda. Gould attacked Behn in "The Play-house. A Satyr" (1689) and *A Satyrical Epistle to the Female Author of a Poem call'd Silvia's Revenge* (1691), and in 1689 he wrote "To Madam G. with Mrs Philips's Poems," which defines the invidious comparison between Philips and Behn that endures into the eighteenth century:

> But O! when thou hast read this matchlesse Book,
> And from it's excellence a Judgment took,
> What the fair Sex was then, thou, sure, wilt mourn
> To see how justly *now* they're branded with our scorn.
> Farces and Songs obscene, remote from Wit,
> (Such as our *Sappho* to Lisander writ)
> Employs their time; so far th'abuse prevails,
> Their Verses are as vitious as their Tails;
> Both are expos'd, alike, to publick view,
> And both of 'em have their Admirers too.
> With just abhorrence look upon these Crimes,
> And by thy chast Example fix the Times;
> Right the wrong'd Age, redeem thy Sex from shame,
> 'Twas so *Orinda* got her deathless Name;
> Thou art as fair, hast the like skill in Song,
> And all that thou dost write will last as long.[17]

"Our Sappho" is, of course, Aphra Behn, who wrote memorably of female sexuality. Gradually, as Nancy Cotton has shown, the stereotypes that define all women according to their sexual behavior dominate the reputations of Philips and Behn as well as the writers who use them for models.[18] Although John Dunton listed Behn among the chief English poets in *The Young Students Library* in 1692, the rift between the groups of poets widened in the nineties: Delariviere Manley calls an affected poetess Orinda in her play *The Lost Lover* (1696), and the countess of Winchilsea, a self-conscious daughter of Orinda, represents Apollo lamenting that though Behn had no superior in fancy, language, or wit, she wrote "a little too loosly." [19] By the middle of the eighteenth century, not a single representative of the Behn tradition is admitted to George Ballard's *Memoirs of Several*

Ladies of Great Britain (1752), but Cavendish, Philips, and several of her followers are represented. In a fulsome eulogy of women's abilities, *The Feminiad* (1754), the Reverend John Duncombe praises one of Aphra Behn's followers, Catherine Trotter Cockburn, presumably forgetting about her early novel and the plays she wrote as one of the Female Wits; her reputation was probably helped by marriage to a minister. Yet Duncombe is careful to label Behn and her followers as foes to virtue:

> The modest muse a veil of pity throws
> O'er Vice's friends and Virtue's female foes
> Abashed she views the bold unblushing mien
> Of modern Manley, Centlivre, and Behn.[20]

Although the modern reader may reject—and lament—the sexual stereotypes that divide the two groups of descendents of Orinda and Behn, the differences among them are more than superficial: they relate to genres, themes, audiences, conventions—in short, the varied aspects that give distinction to an artistic voice. Yet at the same time, the modern reader, for whom many of the writers here are obscure figures, should not see the groups presented here as static or rigid. Some writers who employ more than a single genre are represented in differing patterns, depending on the genre. Several writers claim both Orinda and Behn as models. The challenge for the modern reader is to disregard the sexual stereotype and to understand that the models and traditions were useful to the women writers and are useful to literary historians, at least in charting an unknown territory. Undoubtedly later work will refine, revise, modify, or possibly erase distinctions made here. But these provide a beginning.

As a model for a woman writer, Orinda had many self-acknowledged followers: they were Anne Killigrew (1660–85), Mary Lee Chudleigh (1656–1710), Mary Astell (1668–1731), Anne Finch, countess of Winchilsea (1661–1720), Jane Barker (1652–1727?), Elizabeth Singer Rowe (1674–1737), Mary Barber (1690–1757), and Mary Masters (fl. 1733). The fiction of Penelope Aubin (fl. 1720s) and Mary Davys (1674–1727?) shows some of Orinda's characteristics. These writers are politically, socially, and artistically conservative. They are sometimes married to a supportive husband but usually without children. They are reserved about sexuality and often retreat to a special community where their putative audience is a coterie. Most of their writing is poetry, with occasional plays, novels, essays, or autobiographical letters. They seldom write for money, hesitate to publish or call attention to themselves; they frequently use undoing to excuse their assertion in writing or publishing.[21] They develop a woman's perspective on their experience, and from the retirement tradition they develop a series of meaningful themes: their ideal is self-sufficiency, a stoic hold on a tranquil integrity that depends on private virtue and cultivates the self in solitude. Their feminism is concentrated on changes in women's attitudes and choices in the marriage relationship and in women's opportunities for better education. These writers find authority in taking Orinda as a model. Their conservatism does not allow them to advocate radical change in marriage, but they want better lives for women as a group. They see the values of the retirement tradition as presenting their readers with ways to live better lives in social confines that cannot be changed.

As we have seen, Aphra Behn began a second tradition of women writers with a distinctive perspective. Among the tribe of Behn are the Female Wits: Delariviere Manley (1672–1724), Catherine Trotter Cockburn (1679–1749), and Mary Pix (1666–1709), as well as Sarah Fige Field Egerton (1669–1723), Mary Hearne (fl. 1718–19), Eliza Haywood (1693–1756), and Susanna Centlivre (1669–1723). "Ephelia," whose identity is not yet clear, calls herself Behn's heir and follows her in writing largely about female sexuality. These women tend to be assertive about their capacities; despite male condescension to them, they believe women can write as well as men. They compete with men in the city scene, writing plays and fiction as well as poetry. They frequently write for money and seldom apologize for publishing their work. They are also eager for recognition and see both men and women as their audience. These writers use the current discourses in fiction and drama, yet they often turn them to special feminist purposes. They deal with fantasies in which property is the enemy of desire, in which males are frequently predatory, and in which women acknowledge their sexuality. The relationship sometimes idealized in their fiction and drama is the stable extramarital affair or the tolerant marriage, in which the woman is not treated as property and where she enjoys some independence. Their fiction and poetry are haunted by the theme of abandonment, yet they consistently demonstrate ways of surviving abandonment and the other disasters that plague women.

Although each group of writers may have distinctive qualities, these authors were all women writing in common cultural conditions, and so they also share many other characteristics. Both groups were obliged to justify their privilege in writing, the major reason they sought authority in a model. They feel constrained by their lack of education. They sought freedom, but community too, especially with other women, often in intimate relationships. They frequently used autobiographical forms, made distinctive uses of the pastoral, and wrote extensively on political themes. Lawrence Lipking's definition of a woman's poetics is useful in approaching

22

their work: "Poetry is the expression of a life, personal and incomplete, and proportioned to the self; employing whatever language and conventions one has been allowed to acquire; presented in fragments; and achieving, through sharing the emotions of loneliness and abandonment, a momentary sense of not being alone."[22] Useful as it is, Lipking's formulation needs to be amplified because we find all these writers working out ways of surviving loss and writing to show other women means for survival of their individual predicaments, and for coping with the condition of women in general. Ann Messenger's description of Eliza Haywood's *Female Spectator* as the art of the survivor shows a way of modifying Lipking's formulation.[23] Women may begin writing to deal with loss, but they end writing to survive it. Because poetry is more public than private expression in the seventeenth century, we can also observe the degree to which contemporary discourse shapes women's writing, just as it does men's, but also the degree to which women transform the discourse to their purposes as a group.

If this period produced so much for women, a legacy that endured in a variety of forms, our question must be, Why then? Why did women begin to raise their voices in unprecedented ways and numbers at this particular time in England? A great part of the answer lies in the conditions narrated by Antonia Fraser in *The Weaker Vessel*.[24] The period from 1640 to 1689 was one of enormous turmoil in England, of constitutional, religious, political, socioeconomic, and sexual unrest:

> The great divide between early and modern England is not 1640 or 1660 or even 1688. The divide is the half century from 1640–89. It was during this half century that the foundations were laid for the constitutional, political, religious, and socioeconomic structures of modern England, structures that were stable until the great reforms of the nineteenth century, and structures that in fact were changed less by these nineteenth-century reforms than the earlier structures had been changed by the revolutions of the seventeenth century.[25]

We know that periods of unrest are liberating for women, who may try new opportunities in roles usually denied them, and the civil war showed the mettle of countless Englishwomen. *The Weaker Vessel* may be augmented by diaries and autobiographies of women, which demonstrate an impressive ability to cope with the challenges of war, exile, imprisonment, frequently while bearing and rearing fragile children.[26] More important than the fact of revolution, however, was the profound challenge to authority that inspired it. If the subject did not have to be passively obedient to his king, even if the king proved a tyrant, was his wife under that obligation to obey her husband? A popular poem betrays the anxieties resulting from general unrest; all powerless groups were expected to rebel, and many of them did:

> Come clownes and boyes, come hobbledehoys,
> Come Females of each degree
> Stretch your throats, bring in your Votes,
> And make good Anarchy.
>
> . . . .
>
> We're fourscore Religions strong
> Then take your choice, the major voice
> Shall carry it right or wrong;
>
> . . . .
>
> Then let's ha' King Charles, sayes George
> Nay we'll have his son, sayes Hugh
> Nay then let's ha' none says jabbering Joan,
> Nay lets be all Kings, sayes Prue.[27]

Indeed, some groups of radical women took political action. In the dozen years from 1641 on, women petitioned Parliament and demonstrated for the resumption of trade, for peace, for the release of political prisoners, for changes in laws about indebtedness.[28] (For more about the petitioners, see chapter 5, below.) The actions of the petitioners inspired only scorn in an aristocrat like Margaret Cavendish, and they were just a small part of enormous social unrest:

> In the 1640s especially there was much instability and dislocation. Most obviously, many people simply left the homes their families had lived in for generations. Soldiers who had never in their lives been further than the nearest market town went treking over the country under officers who were sometimes forced to dismiss their troops after they had led them hundreds of miles from home. Soldiers deserting or disbanded because there was no more money to pay them wandered over the countryside trying to get back to their homes. Wage laborers, no longer under restrictive laws keeping them in their own parishes, traveled about more or less freely looking for work. When the tide of battle ebbed and flowed, parliamentary sympathizers and royalists in turn found their property being confiscated and their estates occupied by troops. As the defeat of the king appeared increasingly inevitable, more and more of the royalist gentry and aristocracy fled the country. Not only were many of their estates sequestered

and sold in their absence, but physical damage was done as well. Occupied or abandoned estates were plundered.[29]

There remained many divisions within English religious and political thought during the revolutionary decades. Both the political propaganda and the religious pamphlet wars reveal the diversity of opinion. Among the "honest radicals," who brought about the revolution of 1648–49, there were deep divisions, which meant that they could not survive as a force in the Commonwealth: they became separated into the Independent gentry and the Levellers, who stood for greater social equality. As the social ideals of radical sects, such as the Diggers and the Levellers, became more apparent to the old families, the divisions among the "party" became severe. Soon the Levellers wanted to organize nationally, but outside London they had little support, as the gentry protected its social privilege. By 1649 the Diggers and the Levellers were defeated because, to the majority of the decision-makers, any government was better than none, and the Commonwealth, though far from perfect, was the best government all the factions had.[30]

The pamphlet wars trace out a history of divided religious opinion, too. In 1640–41 pamphlets debated the question of the bishops. Should they be destroyed, root and branch, or should their powers be curtailed? Political or religious liberty was never an issue for the writers. Later, in the period from 1644 to 1646, various brands of Calvinists struggled to define the problems of defining the elect and the disciplinary powers of the clergy. In the last years of the revolution, the pamphlets refine the differences between the Levellers and the Independents, alluded to above. They struggle to reconcile concepts of the elect and the vile with notions of social and political equality. These conflicts are resolved with acceptance of social distinctions and the defeat of the radical social ideas of the Diggers and the Levellers. The outcome of the political turmoil and the pamphlet wars is greater freedom of controversy, greater religious toleration, and, most of all, greater secularization of society: "The pursuit of freedom may have been an unintended consequence of the activities of revolutionary Puritans; it was neither their cause nor their inspiration."[31] Conservative women writers may not have approved of radical action or values, but they flourished in the greater intellectual and religious freedom fostered by turmoil.

Within a decade the Commonwealth faltered and then failed: "Among the most striking paradoxes of the English Revolution is the fact that a parliament which could win a civil war against the King was unable to establish a stable regime without him."[32] The Restoration brought an obsessive spirit of sexual freedom and political conservatism. The aristocratic libertine philosophy, however, had little to do with freedom and much to do with the assertion of will by an elite that was rapidly being displaced by a commercial and political world where increased social mobility gradually produced a stable society, one in which women were continually objects of exchange in male aggrandizement through property and alliance arrangements within marriage.[33] The movement of younger sons into trade was required to maintain primogeniture and the coherence of the landed classes, and the parallel movement of merchants and their children into landed society depended on both wealth and marriage. The amount of social mobility in England contributed both to economic growth and to the stability of a society able to change without further revolution:

> Free movement within the social hierarchy allowed for individual merit without endangering social order. Because of this process of assimilation, no powerful and hostile social order arose to challenge the gentry, and new business wealth did not create a self-conscious class, but a functional group. The ambivalence towards business created by the identification, in some quarters, of mobility with original sin and with the repudiation of an inherited calling, fortified the acquisitive spirit. The merchants imitated the values, attitudes, and habits of landed society, but in return the gentry were exposed to the cosmopolitan ideas and behaviour of urban society.[34]

The work of Aphra Behn and Delariviere Manley dramatizes the predicament of aristocratic rakes and their female victims as both adjust to new social conditions. In the plays of Mary Pix and Susanna Centlivre, aristocrats are gradually replaced by London "cits," and Eliza Haywood's later fiction concentrates on ambitious and mercenary males and their female victims.

Once relative stability in the monarchy was also achieved in 1688, centralization of governmental functions meant that women faced another world, like that of commerce and industry, in which they had little place, but middle-class males had an increasingly important part to play. Women did not share in the parliamentary gains and were, in fact, more excluded than before from political life, which now became a centralized public sphere in which men moved, while women remained retired in domesticity. In fact, the political power of women, such as it was, lay in local affairs, where their influence or intrusion might be tolerated.[35] As centralization slowly eroded the last of the feudal structures, women lost ground: "Gradually the net of government tightened, however, and between 1500 and 1750 continuing economic and political changes broke down decentralized rule and the relative autarchy of local communities. Public affairs of all kinds intruded more aggressively into the private world of the family, robbed it of half its sphere of influence, broke its unity, and deprived the women of half their functions. It carried male members away to rule more flamboyantly in the public world."[36]

Although they were gradually bereft of economic and political power toward the end of the seventeenth century and into the eighteenth (despite the reign of Queen Anne), women gradually became more important than ever before as writers and as an audience. This may be seen in the number of plays, novels, and poems they wrote, not to mention their journalism and polemic. Both women writers and more famous male authors address women as a significant audience, and women's influence on the stage reform movement in the nineties may be attributed to their numbers in audiences. Women could read, and write, and act on the stage; these were all sources of limited but public power outside the economic and political spheres.[37]

Despite the religious turmoil of the era, there were certain fundamental Protestant ideas that changed thinking about women in the period, whatever the specific persuasion of the thinker. One such idea is the equality of souls in Christ. This notion may be found in the radical thinkers and in the writings of Margaret Cavendish, Mary Chudleigh, Sarah Egerton, and Mary Astell, all of whom are extremely conservative. Because this idea postpones the achievement of equality to the hereafter, its effect in several feminist works is complex, as we shall see; yet the basic idea of equality is also inspiring. The second and more liberating idea is that women, like men, have rational souls, given them by God to discover the way to salvation. From this kernel idea springs a crucial advocacy for women's education.

The call for better education of women rings from humanist theorists in the Renaissance through the seventeenth, eighteenth, nineteenth centuries, and into our own. Writers of the seventeenth century could look back to a definite tradition in feminist polemic about women's education, stretching back to the Renaissance, in works like Hyrde's translation of Vives's *Instruction of a Christian Woman* (1536). A major inspiration in the seventeenth century was Anna Maria à Schurman's work translated by Clement Barksdale in 1659 as *The Learned Maid; or, Whether a Maid may be a Scholar?* Schurman restricted her interest to gifted single women of leisure, usually of high rank. She defended learning as giving idle women "serious and constant employment." She defended women as capable of learning because they have rational souls: "Whatsoever *perfects* and *adorns* the intellect of Man, that is fit and decent for a Christian woman."[38] Most of the results of learning she envisioned as moral: learning teaches love of God, prudence, magnanimity, courage, honest delight. In short, women's private virtues are enhanced by learning, and privileged women will be kept from vanities by serious work.

Bathsua Makin also defended educating women in *An essay to revive the antient education of gentlewomen* (1673). Makin posed as a male writer and used a familiar rhetorical strategy of male defenses of women: the citing of numerous examples of excellent, educated women in the Bible, in Greek and Roman antiquity, in English history, and in the recent past, including

Anne Bradstreet in America, Katherine Philips, the duchess of Newcastle, the countess of Huntington, and Princess Elizabeth, the last two pupils of Bathsua Makin.

Makin's essay did not seek education to make women equal to men but to make them better helpmates to the husbands whom they will obey. She believed that education would help women think better of themselves and live up to their souls, which are as good as those of men. She also gave a characteristic formulation of why women have been kept from good education:

> Custom, when it is inveterate, hath a mighty influence: it hath the force of Nature itself. The barbarous custom to breed women low, is grown general amongst us, and hath prevailed so far, that it is verily believed (especially amongst a sort of debauched sots) that women are not endued with such reason as men; nor capable of improvement by education, as they are. It is looked upon as a monstrous thing, to pretend the contrary. A learned woman is thought to be a comet, that bodes mischief whenever it appears. To offer to the world the liberal education of women is to deface the image of God in Man; it will make women so high, and men so low, like fire in the house-top, it will set the whole world in flame.[39]

In *The Gentlewoman's Companion: or a Guide to the Female Sex* (1675), Hannah Wooley continued the advocacy of women's education, which she combined with other practical guides to manners, courtships, recipes, medical and pharmaceutical matters, the principles of preserving and distilling, and appropriate model letters for various occasions. In 1705 Lady Damaris Masham echoed Makin's arguments in *Occasional Thoughts in Reference to a Vertuous or Christian Life.* She acknowledged that most parents were afraid to educate their daughters because they might not find husbands who would tolerate accomplished wives and that most women did not pursue education because they had been socialized by their families and their potential mates to fear an interest in study.[40]

In 1709 Elizabeth Elstob, the great Anglo-Saxon scholar, used a preface to *An English-Saxon Homily, on the birth-day of St. Gregory* to defend the right to learning for all women, not just herself: "For if Women may be said to have Souls, and that their Souls are their best Part, and that what is Best deserves our greatest Care for its Improvement." Men would deny women learning, Elstob said, because women may become impertinent or neglect their households. She replied that learning will lead not to impertinence but to dicipline and a more polished nature. Moreover, she observes caustically, no one thinks women's trivial diversions distract them from household chores. Like her forerunners Elstob was convinced that men were afraid to educate women, "but I shall not enter into any more of the Reasons why some Gentlemen are so eager to deny us this Privilege."[41]

Almost unanimously these writers believed women's educational deprivation was a conscious decision on the part of men to oppress them out of fear of what they might do if as fully skilled as men. This idea was grafted upon another from the Cartesian tradition: that custom, and not reason, was the source of their oppression. The translation of a feminist text by a French Cartesian, Poulain de La Barre, *The Woman as Good as the Man* (1677), was an excellent support for this way of thinking because Poulain traced all the ancient exclusions of women from educational opportunity to male jealousies and decisions.[42] The important feature of all these arguments is that they explain women's inferior achievements as a cultural, socialized phenomenon. Custom, not nature or religious authority, accounts for women's oppression. These notions were powerful because we see them overcoming other important traditions in seventeenth-century thought about women: arguments from nature and arguments from biblical and ancient authority. Mary Astell's exposition of this line of reasoning is stunning.

As seventeenth-century women thought about their educational deprivation, they developed a cultural explanation for their own subordination and oppression. The arguments about the authority of nature are subjected to the rigors of logical examination: if oxen are stronger than men, should men be subordinate to them? All other species in nature treat male and female equally. Why do not humans? Biblical and antique texts are discovered to be historically contingent, as they are for Locke. God's statement to Eve was a prediction, not a punishment. A lack of education thus became a cultural explanation for women's lack of achievement from ancient times to the present. It also became a means of women's criticizing other women's lives without being antifeminist: their lives were trivialized and wasted because they were never given the intellectual resources to make them otherwise. To an amazing degree, writers like Egerton and Chudleigh understood that women's internalizing degrading social images was personally destructive. Although some writers were coy and ironic about their lack of education, a self-consciousness about the deprivation kept them from internalizing some of the negative cultural representations of women. Because their lack of education could be a crucial instance of their oppression without being directed personally at father or husband, it became a good focus for social critique of their predicament: they were "Education's, more then Nature's fools."[43]

The range and variety of attitudes toward male and female sexuality in seventeenth-century England was very great. A Rump Parliament that passed the death penalty for adultery in 1650 was succeeded eleven years later by a Restoration court that celebrated the rake, whose personal aggrandizement through sexuality was cosmic. Yet the act of 1650 was not an anomaly, but the result of a long-standing Reformation attempt to install love in marriage and to reform traditional attitudes toward the relation between sex and marriage:

> Although owing its final passage to the special circumstances of the newly established republic, anxious to conciliate the Presbyterians and fearful of sectarian licence, it represented the culmination of more than a century's legislative pressure. It was also part of a wider, though partly unachieved, programme of reform, intended to redefine the prohibited degrees, to introduce divorce, to raise the age of consent, and to punish clandestine marriage. Its ideals were not forgotten after 1660. To many it continued to seem wrong that wealth should be "a privilege for lewdness" and nobody punished "but those who have no money in their pocket." . . . In 1689 William III, in a letter to the Bishop of London, referred ominously to the absence, "as yet," of "sufficient provision made by any statute law for the punishing of adultery and fornication." The societies for the Reformation of Manners emphasized the common-law right of local justices to proceed against sexual offenders, while many later Evangelicals favoured severe penalties for adultery."[44]

In contrast, the cavaliers were not the only group that believed in a radical sexuality during the century. Revolutionary Puritan groups also espoused sexual codes that seem to us today distinctly not Puritan. For example, Christopher Hill has shown that in the eyes of the Ranters sexual intercourse outside marriage was not sinful. That leaders of the Ranters believed in a form of free love, depending on one's intentions, does not seem to have made them especially protective of women's interests, however. This was occasionally compensated by a concern about marriage. Although various stripes of radical thought advocated sexual freedom, the Puritan emphasis on marriage arose, according to Hill, out of a sense that "sexual freedom, in fact, tended to be freedom for men only, so long as there was no effective birth control."[45] The spectrum of sexual ideology extends, then, from the license of the cavaliers and the radical sects to the strictness of Roman Catholicism, with many variations of sexual and religious persuasion in the middle. The gradual shift from religious to secular control of sexuality is part of the social and ideological complexity of the period.[46] Little care was given to the interests or welfare of women in the male thinking about sexuality at the time, and some of the women's critique of sexual ideology may be seen as a response to that indifference.

The writers included in this study represent all colors of this spectrum: from the pious Mary Astell, who wrote as if the body and desire hardly exist, to Aphra Behn whose central theme was sexuality or Delariviere Manley whose gospel was sexual love. The variety of attitudes expressed by the women writers corresponds to the variety of male attitudes, though because of the double standard and the absence of birth control marriage and sexuality were a greater problem for women than for men. Yet the range of attitudes—or sexualities, as some theorists would call them—did have a liberating effect upon the women's ideas about their own sexuality and allow the tribe of Behn, especially, to be creative in their use of the cavalier ideology to develop a critique of marriage and to represent women in astonishingly free heterosexual and lesbian relationships. We should especially note that the spectrum of preferences portrayed by Behn, Manley, Egerton, and Rowe includes lesbian relationships, whereas Orinda eroticizes female friendships in a decorous way. Although women's fantasies, especially in fiction, include the fact that women may become pregnant in love affairs, they emulate men in making this a relatively minor consideration in the relationship, *except* in marriage, where, of course, the child of one man may be taken for that of another. Although women's fictions frequently deal with a resultant pregnancy, they do not advocate women's interests in their art, seeking instead to demonstrate how women may survive in a male universe, largely through bonding to other women. They do not seek to change male indifference, but, taking it for granted, seek to compensate for it.

Within this diversity of thinking about sexuality, certain massive changes were taking place. One was that the genders were becoming more polarized, so that male and female sexuality were assumed to be very different. Women were increasingly assumed to be passive and relatively low in affect, unless they were aroused by a powerful experience, and then they might become insatiable, as numbers of the women in amatory fiction and misogynous satires become. Thus society needed to protect them from such an experience, which might turn them into disruptive persons.[47] Yet Behn and her followers represent women who experience transforming passions and do not lead the reader to assume that the woman should have been kept from her experience. The writers of amatory fiction accept the fantasy of the overwhelming passion, but they also write to counteract its consequences: in their narratives innocent women are victims, but they survive. The authors accept the sexual ideology, but their characters accept responsibility to cope with its consequences alone. These writers represent abandonment, and they make the double bind inherent in the sexuality represented in the fantasy clear to their female audience. Then they demonstrate the means by which the woman may control her life after the experience.

Ideas about marriage were in a similar state of flux, involving a great number of basic changes in attitudes, in theory, in social customs, in religious ideas, and in legal formulations. From the Glorious Revolution of 1688, a number of consequences for marriage flowed. The secularization of the kingship ratified the Reformation tendency to see marriage as a secular contract rather than a sacrament. Reformation thinking that divorce and remarriage were tolerable on certain grounds also developed during the Restoration, when separate maintenance decreed or enforced in chancery and parliamentary divorce became possible. Although women were still held to the double standard for adultery and waited until the nineteenth century for parliamentary divorce, separate maintenance allowed many women to escape unbearable unions.[48]

Legal authority changed gradually. There were crucial cases decided about the marriage relationship in the courts of the seventeenth century: *Manby v. Scott* was the most important. A minority opinion in the suit became the basis on which married women, separated from their husbands and not citizens under the law, could make valid contracts. *James v. Warren* in 1707 found for the wife in a case where the man deserted his wife and was held responsible for her necessitites. Gradually also the temporal or secular courts began to take cases about marriage and other matters that previously had been dealt with in the ecclesiatical courts. A second consequence of *Manby v. Scott* was that the courts were willing to treat certain classes of women as if they had autonomy. Most of these women were wives who had worked out separate maintenance agreements, but they were a precedent for treating married women as legally autonomous, rather than as *feme covert*.[49] One cannot escape the sense that these changes, which seem small to us, would not have occurred but for the crisis of authority in the seventeenth century.

Another gradual change that took place in ideals about marriage also represents a culmination of a century of thought and controversy: marriage for love became increasingly the norm during the period, and, as a consequence, children are supported by literature and practice in making their own matches. Marriage for profit is despised, and the parents are almost always assumed to have mercenary or ambitious motives in arranging matches. Married happiness becomes a social ideal. Heartening in the women's diaries of the era is evidence of marital happiness of the great majority, though we must allow for the possible destruction of records of unhappiness by surviving spouses and children.[50] But with this evidence of good will and even passion between husband and wife, our writers assemble a genuine protest about the married state, one that reflected and contributed to the companionate ideology of eighteenth-century marriage.[51]

As with sexuality the range of criticism of marriage is varied: Orinda's daughters begin by hoping for respect and consideration for the wife, but they foresee equality only in friendship; they end by understanding that women's choices in marriage must be extremely careful because they are accepting monarchs for life. Behn and her followers see marriage as the enemy of love because marriage is a matter of property and interest. For these writers, as for the cavaliers, marriage destroys desire. Yet in contrast to their male colleagues, the women writers make this idea a critique of marriage, which is held up to the ideal of a love that is free, especially from motives identified as male interest. The range of ideas of marriage forged by all these writers is impressive, and it shows how they were able to use current discourses to protest their own oppression.

By the end of the century, despite changes in law and custom, there were still defenders of the subjection of women in works like the Reverend Sprint's "The Brides-Woman's Counsellor (1699), which was forcibly answered by Eugenia and by Chudleigh. The controversy about marriage continued into the eighteenth century, of course, when Mary Astell's *Reflections on Marriage* (1700) was joined by Defoe's *Good Advice to the Ladies: that as the World goes & is Like to Go, the best Way for them is to remain Unmarried* (1702). Eliza Haywood's *Female Spectator* (1744–46) was written in the same vein and explored the nature of women's choices, their happiness in marriage, and their alternatives in separation and divorce.[52]

The change in parent-child relationships also ratified long-held concerns. Elizabethan and Jacobean writers had inveighed against forced marriage, and a whole literature developed around the question during the Renaissance.[53] Yet parents, especially aristocrats, continued to marry very young children out of concerns for property and inheritance. Gradually, however, the primacy of interest gave way to affection or inclination as a motive for marriage, and at the same time the choices of the children were ever more respected in matchmaking:

> By 1660 the shift from the first [parental choice] to the second option [child's right of veto] in the distribution of power over decision-making had already taken place in all but the highest ranks of the aristocracy: it had been conceded, in the interests of "holy matrimony," that children of both sexes should be given the right of veto over a future spouse proposed to them by their parents. Between 1660 and 1800, however, there took place the far more radical shift from the second [child's veto] to the third option, with the children now normally making their own choices, and the parents being left with no more than the right of veto over socially or economically unsuitable candidates. At the same time there was inevitably a marked shift of emphasis on motives away from family interest and towards well-tried personal affection. Almost everyone agreed, however, that both physical desire and romantic love were unsafe bases for an enduring marriage, since both were violent mental disturbances which would inevitably be of only short duration. . . . It is obvious that at the root of these changes in the power to make decisions about marriage, and in the motives that guided these decisions, there lie a deep

shift of consciousness, a new recognition of the need for personal autonomy, and a new respect for the individual pursuit of happiness.[54]

We may observe the representation of these changes in the women's fiction studied in Chapter 4. Coercion of children's choices invariably has disastrous results, sometimes even with providential retribution. Parental judgment with regard to marriage choices is frequently shown to be badly flawed, and the text therefore leads the reader to doubt its efficacy. Once the parents cease to be totally the enemy of their children's wishes, the characteristic fantasies identify interest with men who frequently abandon the heroine and pursue an inferior rival out of ambition.[55] Women's writing shows a high degree of anxiety about making marriage choices as a result of the growing autonomy they could exercise. Much of the fiction is cautionary about the outcomes of various choices that women may make, but it just as frequently demonstrates how to survive in a unkind world.

Finally, a fundamental change in the way Restoration culture conceptualized nature and natural law contributed to a greater sense of personal autonomy that was important for the assertiveness of women taking the privilege of writing. Again turmoil disturbed relatively stable ideas. Laws of nature retained their authority, but they were used to justify such a variety of religious belief, such a variety of libertine social behavior and personal aggrandizement, that the single concept lost much of its stability. The dizzying religious changes brought to England by the Reformation and the English revolution could be unsettling in their effect on belief, as G.E. Aylmer observes in quoting a quatrain from a parish register in Eckington, Darbyshire in 1686–87:

> Our Grandfathers were Papists,
> Our Fathers Oliverians,
> We their Sons are Athiests
> Sure our Sons will be queer ones.[56]

Prominent philosophers, Hobbes and Locke as well as the Cambridge Platonists, problematized the idea of natural law, seeking to rid it of a theological base or any theory of obligation:

> Nature and natural law retained their authority, but by the beginning of the eighteenth century nature and natural law were very differently understood than they had been before the Civil War. Older ideas of natural law were bound – perhaps inextricably bound – to a vision of a divinely created and managed hierarchical universe. The precepts of

the law were determined by the end God had intended for man; its obligatory character depended on its being God's command. Natural man, after the fall, lacked the resources to fulfill the law without supernatural aid. Partly because political experience had made a law dependent on God's will seem so untrustworthy and partly because nature itself began to seem less divine, less hierarchical, and less teleological, the later seventeenth century looked for a more secular idea of natural law. Philosophers tried to show how natural law could exist independently of the will of God and generally attacked the utopian character of the older tradition. Parliament struck out at the powers of the ecclesiastical courts, while the secular courts declared themselves the interpreters and defenders of morality.[57]

Both Hobbes and Locke insist that parent-child and husband-wife relationships are secular contracts, not givens of nature, as the patriarchal theorists had held.[58] Nature without hierarchy and without obligation made way for the gradual development of a new set of relationships for women, not only to men and other women, through greater autonomy, but to themselves. They begin to look within themselves, to define themselves as subjects, rather than objects with obligations in a predetermined hierarchy, subjects who must exercise choice and endure the consequences, subjects whose ideas and dreams are worth recording not just in private pages of diaries but in publications for an audience beyond themselves or their immediate circles.

Women began to write from an acknowledged female persona, often represented to the reader by a classical female pseudonym. Therefore, although we do not know the certain identity of Ephelia, we know her female perspective on a love affair with Strephon, her relationships with other men, and her sense of herself as a writer, even if her creator was a man. If her book was discovered isolated from its context, any reader would know that it was written by a woman or someone pretending to be a woman. A woman tells her love story. If a male writer can pretend to be a woman, women have developed a discourse, and this is another achievement of seventeenth-century women. They put to their own use the cavalier ideology, the pastoral mode, and amatory fiction. Their stories have distinct markers that are easy to detect, even when they use, as they constantly do, mainstream, male discourses. When the ideology of naturally determined gender differences reasserts itself in the eighteenth century, the polarization of the genders is sufficiently great so that female subjectivity does not disappear.

These writers not only acknowledge but insist on the fact that they are women, and so they deal, in individual ways, with their having taken the privilege of writing in a time when such gestures were not socially sanctioned. This study traces the strategies they adopt to cope with classical and biblical injunctions to silence. The most important part of their achievement, however, is to create a widespread consciousness among women themselves—and some men—of the extent of their oppression, as we will see; for they invent a critique of society that never again disappears, even if its full realization awaits our own time: "To be a subject is to be able to claim rights, to protest, and to be capable, therefore, of devising a mode of resistance more sharply focused than prophesying, witchcraft or murder. It is to be in a position to identify and analyse the nature of women's oppression."[59] To raise their voices meant to defend their privilege of writing as women, to identify themes important to women and adapt current discourse to their purposes, and, most difficult of all, to protest their own oppression.

Chapter One

Margaret the First

Reader, I have a little *Tract* of Philosophicall *Fancies* in *Prose*, which
will not be long before it appear in the world.[1]

Margaret Lucas Cavendish, Duchess of Newcastle (1623–73)

Margaret Lucas Cavendish is the first Englishwoman to write a substantial
body of literature intentionally for publication. In her lifetime she published
fourteen works, of which five had second editions and one was translated into
Latin.[2] Most of these appeared in handsome folios. When one first reads her
work, Cavendish seems a mass of contradictions, but her attitudes make sense
because she was the first woman to write for publication in England. Wife to
one of the most important figures of the civil war, she still aspired to fame for
herself as an individual. Self-conscious about her predicament, she helped invent woman's autobiography. Although she lacked an education, she challenged the leading thinkers of her time and dreamed of having her works of
natural philosophy taught at Oxford and Cambridge. Although she deemed
public life "out of the *Sphear* of our *Sex*," she wrote repeatedly on political and
even military subjects and composed a biography of her general husband that
amounts to a defense of his public career.[3] Cavendish's plays, her *Sociable Letters*, and her fiction are full of vivid descriptions of the lamentable conditions
of women's lives, especially their need for education, their frequent suffering
in marriage and childbearing, and the emptiness of their shallow, wasted lives.

However radical or latently feminist many of these gestures may seem, Cavendish had little desire to change her society or the roles it assigned to women. Raised by a strong, widowed mother in a large, happy family, she seems to have learned early that a woman could be distinctive within accepted social roles. Bashful and unworldly as she was when a maid-in-waiting to Henrietta-Maria, her brilliant marriage to William Cavendish did little to shake that confidence. Like her mother, she was extraordinary, and she knew it. Yet that very confidence was a limitation; for although it led her to assume that she could be all, or almost all, that she wanted to be within the restricted scope of a seventeenth-century woman, she never understood the arduous discipline needed for real achievement. She wanted to be a genuine philosopher, but she made a virtue of her ignorance. Because she was first, Cavendish anticipated many actions and attitudes of women writers later in the century, but she looked back for her values. Nature was the center of her imagination in poetry and prose, and so she saw gender differences as unalterably defined by nature. Happily married to an indulgent husband, she repeatedly endorsed the double standard in marriage and tended to blame women for their restricted lives. She portrayed Newcastle as her teacher and superior in all things, despite the fact that he was often content to subordinate his gifts to hers. She assumed that she was exceptional to her gender, and, far from feeling bonds with all women, showed a genuine misogyny upon occasion, especially about radical women. She lamented her poor education and bought quantities of books, yet seems to have read few of them and never studied seriously the works of the philosophers she challenged. She longed for recognition and praise from the learned, but denigrated learning in favor of originality, which in her case was largely fanciful. She wrote a play about a female academy, but confessed in the middle of it that women who generally lack education are poor teachers for one another. She constantly alluded to her gender in prefaces to her works, but often wrote with a male voice within the texts themselves.

Because she was first, she lacked a discourse, even though the word was one of her favorites. That is, she lacked a consistent authoritative set of terms with which to describe her predicament. Just as she gloried in being unconventional with regard to form and disorderly with regard to genre and organization, she neglected the discipline that values a consistent mode of addressing a subject. For Cavendish, "fecundity and originality are the gifts of true wit."[4] This is surely one of the reasons her contemporaries called her Mad Madge. The frustrations of her predicament account for the anger she expressed in her autobiography and elsewhere, anger at women, which from the perspective of centuries seems rage at her own failures and limitations displaced on other women.

Let us examine these characteristics in detail before defining Cavendish's contributions to the traditions of women's writing in the seventeenth century. Her ambitions for lasting fame were expressed throughout her writing: "All I desire, is Fame," she said in a dedication to *Poems and Fancies*. In her autobiography she said, "I repine not at the gifts that Nature or Fortune bestows upon others, yet I am a great emulator; for, though I wish none worse then they are, yet it is lawful for me to wish myself the best, and to do my honest endeavour thereto. . . . But I fear my ambition inclines to vain glory, for I am very ambitious; yet 'tis neither for beauty, wit, titles, or power, but as they are steps to raise me to Fame's tower, which is to live by remembrance in after-ages."[5] As here, thoughts about fame were almost always linked to emulation of great men, for women models never seemed to occur to her: "And of all the Men I read of, I Emulate *Julius Caesar* most, because he was a man that had all these Excellencies as Courage, Prudence, Wit and Eloquence, in great Perfection, insomuch as when I read of *Julius Caesar,* I cannot but wish that Nature and Fate had made me such a one as he was; and sometimes I have that Courage, as to think I should not be afraid of his Destiny, so I might have as great a Fame."[6]

Emulation of Caesar and being remembered occur in concert again at the end of her autobiography: "But I hope my readers will not think me vain for writing my life, since there have been many that have done the like, as Caesar, Ovid, and many more, both men and women, and I know no reason why I may not do it as well as they" (p. 178). Aware of how entirely relational is a women's life, Cavendish confessed that she wrote for herself so that she would not be taken for another, "especially if I should die and my Lord marry again" (p. 178). Earlier in *Nature's Pictures,* to which the autobiography was appended, she was more blunt: "That my ambition of extraordinary Fame, restless, and not ordinary, I cannot deny: and since all Heroick Actions, Public Employments, as well Civil as Military, and Eloquent Pleadings are deni'd my Sex in this Age, I may be excused for writing so much" (sig. C). As Dolores Paloma has suggested, Cavendish would have liked to rule the world, or, at least, to be a victorious conquerer, but "literature was the only 'Heroick Action' not totally forbidden her."[7]

What she could not do, she could write about. In her fantasies she allowed herself greatness, and some women have absolute power. In one of her *Sociable Letters,* for example, she imagined herself as the only woman at a banquet Nature gives for the great poets of all time. In *Nature's Pictures* she presented a She-Ancoret as a prophet to whom representatives of eighteen groups of the world's population resort for her wisdom. The groups include natural philosophers, father of the church, and statesmen, as well as soldiers, virgins, and married folk. The image of the ancoret is a marked echo of one of Cavendish's self-descriptions: "And though I desire to appear to the best advantage, whilst I live in the view of the public world, yet I could most willingly exclude myself, so as never to see the face of any creature but my Lord as long as I live, inclosing myself like an anchorite, wearing a frieze gown, tied with a core about my waist."[8]

The most impressive example of Cavendish's fantasies of women's power is her science fiction, *The Description of a New World, called the Blazing World* (1668). In the Epilogue to this work, she said, "By this Poetical Description, you may perceive, that my ambition is not onely to be Empress, but Authoress of a whole World." This fiction presents a merchant who kidnaps a noble lady, and a storm drives their ship to the North Pole and hence to the Blazing World. Only the lady is preserved by her youth and beauty, and the emperor of the New World instantly loves her, marries her, and gives her "absolute power to rule and govern all that World as she pleased."[9] The empress establishes many learned societies to make observations of the natural world, but soon she becomes concerned about her native country and wants to recruit a learned soul to be her scribe. The spirits inform her that the antique philosophers are too wedded to their own opinions, and modern thinkers (DesCartes, Helmont, Hobbes) are too conceited to be scribes to a woman. So the Spirits suggest the duchess of Newcastle, "one of the most learned, eloquent, witty and ingenious, yet she is a plain and rational Writer" (p. 89). Cavendish's soul is recruited, and she and the empress become loving friends. On one visit Cavendish's soul confesses to the empress that she too wishes to be empress of a world. The spirits suggest that Cavendish create a world, all the others being occupied: "by creating a world within your self, you may enjoy all both in whole and in parts, without controle or opposition; and may make what World you please, and alter it when you please, and enjoy as much pleasure and delight as a World can afford you" (p. 97). The duchess then begins to use the cosmologies of Thales, Pythagoras, Plato, Epicurus, Aristotle, Descartes, and Hobbes, but "at last, when the Duchess saw that no patterns would do her any good in the framing of her World; she was resolved to make a World of her own Invention" (p. 100).

The empress and the duchess visit the duchess's native world to observe the customs, the royal family, and to visit the duke of Newcastle. At Welbeck the empress learns of the civil war and delights in the duke's witty conversation. Back in the Blazing World with the duchess, the empress tries to intervene for the duke with his enemy Fortune, but the duchess learns from Honesty and Prudence not to rely on Fortune's favors The empress seeks the duchess's advice about maintaining order in the Blazing World, and they part with promises of regular visits. This delightfully narcissistic tale reveals more about Cavendish than almost anything she wrote, as utopian fantasies frequently do. In her plays and fiction, she was much more open about giving power to women than when addressing a contemporary audience in her own voice. The fantasies allowed her to compensate for the way in which the world had treated both her and Newcastle, though their problems were different in kind and scope.

In her plays Cavendish said, "I do not keep strictly to the Masculine and Feminine Genders, as they call them,"[10] and indeed she could imagine women ruling in *The Unnatural Tragedy,* where one of the Virgins says, "If women were imploy'd in the Affairs of State, the World would live more happily" (p. 332). *Bell in Campo* presents women fighting battles equally with men under the command of Lady Victoria. In *A Comedy of the Apocriphal Ladies,* Cavendish created a situation where the true heir to the realm is a discreet, wise, and virtuous woman, but her husband, who actually rules, is wild and inconstant. In *The Female Academy,* she envisioned a school for girls, conducted by women, a fact that makes the men in the play very anxious. Although women's dificient education is alluded to, the matrons give elaborate orations on a variety of subjects. The aim of the school, however, is to prepare young women for marriage, and men will have to win them through merit, not parental profit or flattering courtship. Even in her fictions, Cavendish did not stray too far from the status quo for the average woman, to whom she, the empress, and her correspondent in *Sociable Letters* all would be superior. *The Female Wits* represents the women as smart and the men as fools; the women are also given a variety of satiric statements about old men, though the young men seem to have the worst of it; the women's prayer reads as follows: "From Young Mans ignorance and follies, from their pride, vanity, and prodigality, their gaming, quareling, drinking and whoring, their pocky and diseased bodies, their Mortgages, Debts and Serjeants, their Whores and Bastards, and from all such sorts of Vices and Miseries that are frequent amongst Young Men, Good Lord deliver us."[11]

Cavendish frequently criticized male behavior and she sometimes saw male attitudes as a cause of women's oppression, as her successors are certainly to do; but unlike many of them, she defended marriage and the status quo. We find in *The Bridals* that Lady Vertue loves her husband and wants to please him, whereas Lady Amorous seeks liberty, mirth, and good company. The play assures us, "A good husband is a light to a Woman's life, a friend to a Woman's Vertue, and a Crown to a Woman's honour," (p. 69). Steadfast in her devotion to Newcastle, even though she realized his treatment of her was extraordinary, she made occasions to celebrate their good marriage: it was another way in which she was superior to most women.

Yet she was not without an understanding of the trials many marriages presented to women. These she portrayed in the subplot of *The Convent of Pleasure,* in which twenty ladies decide to retire to their own company and live apart from men. Their leader, Lady Happy, says, "Those Women, where Fortune, Nature, and the Gods are joined to make them happy, were mad to live with Men, who make the Female sex their slaves; but I will not be so enslaved, but will live retired from their Company" (p. 7). Later

41

Lady Happy falls in love with a princess who turns out to be a prince in disguise; their love is one indication of how strongly Cavendish believed in the bias of nature, as we shall see. It is a measure of the liberty Cavendish felt in her plays that she has men disguise themselves as women or low-caste sailors, believing as she did that one should never emulate an inferior. In *Youth's Glory and Death's Banquet,* male characters debate the issue of wanting to be a woman like Lady Sans Pareille, but this awesome personage, educated by her father, enjoys most of the privileges and achievements of men.

Although she was an eloquent critic of ordinary women, Cavendish was ambitious for other exceptional women, like her fictional audience in *Sociable Letters:*

> But womens Minds or Souls are like Shops of small-wares, wherein some have pretty toyes, but nothing of any great value. I imagine you will chide me for this opinion, and I should deserve to be chidden, if all Women were like to you; but you are but one, and I speak of Women, not of One woman; and thus I am neither injurious to You, nor partial to our Sex; but I wish with all my heart, our whole Sex were like you, so I might hope to be one of your copies, and though you are an example not to be pattern'd, yet I will endeavour to imitate you as much as I can. (P. 14–15)

In *Poems and Fancies,* Cavendish addresses a statement "To all Writing Ladies," where she defines the spirit of certain ages, how people tend to behave similarly in given historical periods. She goes on to observe,

> There will be many Heroick Women in some Ages, in others very Propheticall; in some Ages very pious, and devout: For our Sex is wonderfully addicted to the spirits. But this Age hath produced many effeminate Writers, as well as Preachers, and many effeminate Rulers, as well as Actors. And if it be an Age when the effeminate spirits rule, as most visible they doe in every Kingdome, let us take the advantage, and make the best of our time, for feare their reigne should not last long; whether it be in the Amazonian Government, or in the Politick Common-wealth, or in flourishing Monarchy, or in Schooles of Divinity, or in Lectures of Philosophy, or in witty Poetry, or anything that may bring honour to our Sex: for they are poore, dejected spirits, that are not ambitious of Fame. And though we be inferior to Men, let us shew our selves a degree above Beasts; and not eate, and drink, and sleep away our time as they doe. (P. 162)

In writing one preface after another, addresses to readers, epistles to readers or to professors or to the universities, always defending her privilege of writing and frequently introducing her folios with long poems of tribute by Newcastle, Cavendish seemed to offer herself and her mate as examples of a woman of letters with an approving husband—a distinguished woman who does not offend male prerogatives. As Elizabeth Toppe asserts in her prefatory letter to *Poems and Fancies,* Cavendish is an audacious example, original but a pattern for writers to come: "You are not only the first English Poet of your Sex, but the first that ever wrote this way: therefore whosoever that writes afterwards, must own you for their Pattern, from whence they take their Sample; and a Line by which they measure their Conceits and Fancies. For whatsoever is written afterwards, it will be but a Copy of your Originall" (sig. A5ᵛ). Unfortunately for Cavendish's aspirations, her example was too eccentric for the gentle but not highborn ladies who succeeded her as writing women, though she was occasionally admired for her learning. Repeatedly, as Cavendish defended her choice of writing in preference to housewifery, needlework, cookery, gaming, dancing, or reveling, she might invoke Newcastle's sanction in poems praising her and her writing. Thus she presented herself as original and yet did not oppose the status quo: she told the reader in *Poems and Fancies* that she had no children, no estate to look after, and that she wrote her verses to distract her mind from her troubles while she was separated from her husband. Her book, she said, was her child. This sort of undoing became characteristic of one tradition in seventeenth-century women's writing, but because she was first and very ambitious, Cavendish employed the defense in rather larger doses than did most of her successors.

Yet for all her apologies about assuming the privilege of writing and for all her early assertions that she chose verse to write "because I thought Errours might better passe there, then in *Prose;* since *Poets* write most *Fiction* and *Fiction* is not given for Truth," Cavendish sought recognition from professional scholars, wrote natural philosophy, and answered the greatest thinkers of her time. She also wrote a book of orations on forbidden public subjects. In these gestures Cavendish was far more intellectually aggressive than any of her successors among conservative women writers. She dealt with her own assertiveness through psychological strategies that we may observe.

The author of *Sociable Letters* informs her female correspondent that women are wrong to be ambitious "to be State-Ladies." She fears that by meddling in statecraft women will prove themselves fools because although they can cause disorder in a state, they cannot cure its ills: "Women in State-affairs can do as they do with themselves, they can, and do often make themselves sick, but when they are sick, not well again: So they can disorder a State, as they do their Bodies, but neither can give Peace to th' one, nor Health to th' other" (p. 13). An interesting simile in light of Margaret's life-long habit of doctoring herself, but evidence that Cavendish has created a persona as author of *Sociable Letters*. Yet the sentiment echoes an outburst at the women petitioners to Parliament in her autobiography:

> But the customs of England being changed as well as the laws, where women become pleaders, attornies, petitioners, and the like, running about with their several causes, complaining of their several griev-ances, exclaiming against their several enemies, bragging of their seve-ral favours they receive from the powerful, thus trafficking with idle words bring in false reports and vain discourse. For the truth is, our sex doth nothing but jostle for the pre-eminence of words (I mean not for speaking well, but speaking much) as they do for the pre-eminence of place, words rushing against words, thwarting and cross-ing each other, and pulling with reproaches, striving to throw each other down with disgrace, thinking to advance themselves thereby. But if our sex would but well consider, and rationally ponder, they will perceive and find, that it is neither words nor place that can ad-vance them, but worth and merit. Nor can words or place disgrace them, but inconstancy and boldness: for an honest heart, a noble soul, a chaste life, and a true speaking tongue, is the throne, sceptre, crown, and footstool that advances them to an honorable renown.[12]

Why are these women forbidden what Margaret did all her life? Because they are not exceptional individuals, but a radical group that would alter the status quo. We will return to our radical women petitioners in chapter 5, below.

If we look further in *Sociable Letters,* we soon discover that the author is persuaded by her correspondent to write a book of orations on public sub-jects over the author's protests that she has neither the training nor the knowledge to write about such topics: "for Orations for the most part, are concerning War, Peace, and Matters of State, and Business in the Com-monwealth, all of which I am not Capable of, as being a Woman, who hath neither Knowledg, Ability, nor Capacity in State Affairs, and to Speak in Writing of that I Understand not, will not be Acceptable to my Reading Auditors" (p. 367). Yet, the author says, her friend has persuaded her to attempt the forbidden, and so she has produced "two or three Orations." We know, of course, that Cavendish in fact had written an entire book, *Ora-tions of Divers Sorts* (1662), and most of the subjects are indeed male: war and peace, the field of war, citizens in the marketplace after a long time of war, causes pleaded in courts of law, speeches to a king in council, a king's speeches to his subjects, funeral orations, marriage orations, orations on an unsettled state, scholastic orations—all subjects alien to a woman of Caven-dish's time. The only subject within her socially assigned sphere is the set of "Femal Orations"; but they are written with a male voice, and they end with keeping women in their place according to nature. They acknowledge some of women's grievances, but endorse woman's natural inferiority to man. Cavendish also accompanied this book with an address to her readers that echoes her words at the end of her autobiography: "But this Age is so Censorious, that the Best Poets are found Fault with, wherefore it is an Honour to my Writings, which are so much Inferior to theirs; Neither can their Dislikes Deterr me from Writing, for I Write to Please my Self, rather than to please such Crabbed Readers."[13] Before we draw conclusions from these varied gestures, we should acknowledge Cavendish's other transgressive texts, her works of natural philosophy.

Douglas Grant, to whom every student of Cavendish is deeply indebted, tells us that her longing for immortal fame took her into the realm of natural philosophy, for there in her time she knew lasting reputations were made. Grant's excellent chapter on Cavendish's pursuit of nature describes in detail how her aspirations to natural philosophy were limited by her lack of education, which might have been mitigated by self-study, had not her independence and social standing kept her from admitting when she could not comprehend the thought of another writer. Yet these very qualities were the ones that allowed her to criticize Hobbes and Descartes in *Philosophical Letters* and *The Blazing World* and to invade the Royal Society. Some of Cavendish's activity was serious: for example, her correspondence with Huygens about Rupert's Drops.[14] But her scientific activity was limited by social boundaries that discouraged experimentation or dissection, and excluded her from membership in the Royal Society, where such activities were then being encouraged and carried on. Some of her speculations are no more fanciful than those of many male contemporaries: for example, the duchess's atomism "is not very different from the corpuscular philosophies advocated by Descartes, Hobbes, and Gassendi."[15] Cavendish espoused a skepticism compounded of her lack of learning and exclusion from the mainstream of scientific endeavor. About her skepticism, Lisa Sarasohn makes this trenchant observation: "The inherent ambivalence of skepticism toward tradition, seeing it as both destroyer and conservative apologist, was reflected in Cavendish's ambivalent attitude toward traditional institutions. She fervently defended the superiority of monarchy and hierarchy, reflecting class rather than gender solidarity, but realized all forms of political association were a tyranny of men over women" (p. 293). Anything Margaret was prohibited she discounted, and so she pooh-poohs the value of the microscope, for example, despite the fact that she and the duke were given good ones by the leaders of scientific thought. That she understood the value of systematic observation was betrayed in her confession that she had seen dissection only in the kitchen. Yet her scorn of experimentation is also conveyed by her assigning it to women because they make puddings.

By 1661, largely because of the political implications of atomism, and certain that her speculations were just as valuable as anyone else's, Cavendish adopted a new model for properties of matter:

> According to her theory the universe is composed of matter and motion, which are inseparable. There are three kinds of matter, differing in figure and type of motion, but inextricably integrated in composed forms of matter: rational matter, the most excellent, which is self-moving, the seat of conception, and the director of the rest of matter; sensible matter, which carries out the commands of rational matter, and is the vehicle for sensual perception; and inanimate matter, which it the least excellent because it lacks perception, although it is self-conscious and the material substratum of all being. All of matter is to some degree animate, but this does not cause divisive or natural anarchy because all types of matter are essentially one; diversity is resolved in unity. Self-moving matter is the principle of the world. This materialism is no less extreme than the duchess's atomism, because in it matter remains eternal and infinite, and the soul is considered material. (P. 294)

Nature was the center of Cavendish's imagination and the key impediment to her advocacy for changes in women's lot. In her assumption of an organic nature that has ordered the cosmos so that moral and spiritual values may be based on that order, Cavendish looks back to Elizabethan times: "I bend myself to study nature; and though nature is too spacious to be known, yet she is so free as to teach, for every straw, or grain of dust, is a natural tutor, to instruct my sense and reason, and every particular rational creature, is a sufficient School to study in, and our own passions and affections, appetites and desires, are moral Doctors to learn us . . . for nature is the chief master; art and education but the underushers, in the School of life."[16] For Cavendish, Nature was a real, active presence in everyday life. In *Sociable Letters* she said, "Since Nature Rules the Bodily Life, and we cannot live Always, nor the Bounds of Nature be Inlarged, I am industrious to Gain so much of Nature's Favour, as to enable me to do some Work, wherein I may leave my *Idea*, or Live in an *Idea*, or my *Idea* may Live in Many Brains, for then I shall Live as Nature lives amongst her Creatures, which onely Lives in her Works, and is not otherwise Known but by her Works, we cannot say, she lives Personally amongst her Works, but Spiritually within her Works" (p. 178).

In *Poems and Fancies* she represents nature as a great housewife with keys at her side to unlock the cabinets of the brain and the senses. In a series of similitudes, Cavendish describes nature as a matron who cooks breakfast, dinner, bisque, hodgepodge, brains, heart, and a charming dessert:

Sweet *Marmalade* of *Kisses* new gathered,
Preserv'd *Children* that are not *Fathered:*
Sugar of *Beauty* which melts away soon,
Marchpane of *Youth*, and *Childish Macaroon*.
(P. 132)

At the beginning of *Poems and Fancies,* Nature calls a council of Motion, Life, Form, and Matter to advise her about making the world. The first section of the book then details an atomic theory of the composition of the world; how the four elements are composed; how natural phenomena, such as disease and aging or vacuum and the motion of the sea occur. The entire first section of the book is a versification of Cavendish's natural philosophy. In the second section, composed of moral dialogues, nature is the architect of all human actions:

What Ill man doth, Nature did make him do,
For he by *Nature* is prompt thereunto.
For it was in great Natures *power,* and Will,
To make him as *she* pleased, either *good* or *ill*.
(P. 59)

Many of the dialogues take place between natural objects or phenomena or between humans and natural objects, such as an oak and a woodsman. "Earth's Complaint" illustrates the degree to which Cavendish holds to the Renaissance notion of a sentient earth that suffers from mining and cultivation.[17] The hunting poems in the next section of *Poems and Fancies* are among the better known in this volume, and they illustrate her sympathy with, and acute observation of, nature's creatures. These were sentiments that reached across time to Virginia Woolf. The section devoted to poems about fairies also allows Cavendish to indulge her natural imagination. To sum up, the book is largely dedicated to nature poetry of one sort or another; and when it is added to Cavendish's works of natural philosophy, the corpus demonstrates the centrality of nature in her thought.

Cavendish's attitude toward women's intellectual limitations and the scorn with which her own scientific speculations were received also changed over time. Early in her career, Cavendish longed for recognition from professional scholars, and her epistle to the universities at the beginning of her earliest work of natural philosophy, *The Philosophical and Physical Opinions* (1655), pleads with the "most famously learned" not to reject the work of women,

lest in time we should grow irrational as idiots, by the dejectednesse
of our spirits, through the carelesse neglects, and despisements of the
masculine sex to the effeminate, thinking it impossible we should
have either learning or understanding, wit or judgment, as if we had
not rational souls as well as men, and we out of a custom of dejectednesse think so too, which makes us quit all industry towards profit-
able knowledge being imployed onely in love, and pettie imployments,
which takes away not onely our abilities towards arts, but higher
capacities in speculations.[18]

Here Cavendish clearly envisioned women with mental endowments similar
to those of men, but internalizing the negative evaluation of their own
abilities until they grow as irrational as idiots. She also saw the limitations
on women's abilities as socially constructed: "Thus by an opinion,
which I hope is but an erronious one in man, we are shut out of all power,
and Authority by reason we are never imployed either in civil nor marshall
affaires, our counsels are despised, and laught at, the best of our actions
are troden down with scorn, but the over-weaning conceit men have of
themselves and through a despisement of us." If scholars could not praise
her work, she hoped they would entomb it so that her thought might
"have a glorious resurrection in following ages." For the development of
Cavendish's thinking about women, it is important to realize that she never
reprinted this now famous epistle in the second edition of *Philosophical and
Physical Opinions* (1663) or the later revision of the work, *Grounds of Natural
Philosophy* (1668); and if one looks at her later views, the reason becomes
clear. In the sixties Cavendish's views about the status of women changed
from being socially based to being biologically based.

Our first indication of this change comes in *Orations of Divers Sort* (1662),
where the social interpretation of women's inferiority is answered by arguments from nature: "But we have more Reason to Murmur against Nature
than against Man, who hath made Men more Ingenious, Witty, and Wise
than Women, more Strong, Industrious, and Laborious than Women."[19]
Because the *Orations* is a quasi-dramatic work, one might infer that Cavendish did not herself hold the opinions expressed in the *Orations,* but we
have unhappy confirmation that she did in a late work of natural philosophy.

Her extended commentary on, and reply to, Robert Hooke's *Micro-
graphia* (1665), *Observations upon Experimental Philosophy* (1666), contains
prefaces in which she indicated her doubts about telescopes and micro-
scopes, but, most important for our purposes, a long preface to the reader
where Cavendish explained why she could not be expected to write as well
as a man, "being of the Effeminate Sex, whose Brains Nature hath mix'd
with the coldest and softest Elements."[20] She continued to argue against
the sociocultural explanation of woman's inferiority ("that men from their

first Creation usurped a Supremacy to themselves, although we were made equal by Nature") using natural terms: "There is a great difference betwixt the Masculine Brain and the Feminine, the Masculine Strength and the Feminine." Men are like oaks, she said, and women like willows. "So Man is made to Govern Common Wealths, and Women their privat Families." Men are like the sun and women like the moon: "This is the Reason why we are not Mathematicians, Arithmeticians, Logicians, Geometricians, Cosmographers, and the like; This is the reason we are not Witty Poets, Eloquent Orators, Subtill Schoolmen, Substracting Chimists, Rare Musicians, Curious Limners; This is the reason we are not Navigators, Architactures, Exact Surveyers, Inventive Artisans; This is the reason why we are not Skilful Souldiers, Politick Statists, Dispatchfull Secretaries, or Conquering Caesars." She went on to argue that women's weak constitution and brain unalterably limit their temperaments and achievements: "Besides, the Education, and the libertie of Conversation which Men have, is both unfit and dangerous to our Sex, knowing, that we may bear and bring forth Branches from the wrong Stock, by which every man would come to lose the property of their own Children, but Nature, out of love to the Generation of Men, hath made Women to be governed by Men, giving them Strength to rule, and Power to use their Authority."

Cavendish softened her indictment slightly by admitting at the end of her preface that some women are more gifted than some men and may develop their talents through education. But the total effect of this preface is to reverse the impression made by "To the Writing Ladies" and the Epistle to the Universities in *Philosophical and Physical Opinions* (655). If we stand back from these changes, a pattern emerges. Cavendish's views about women's inferiority seem to change in the works of the sixties if they are compared with those of the fifties (*Poems and Fancies, The World's Olio, Opinions* of 1655); but if we examine *Sociable Letters* (1664), we find in a dedication to "All Professors of Learning and Art," some strictures about women's role in public life, as we have seen. But generally the criticisms of women are socially based, women's trivial pastimes are rehearsed and their neglect of study condemned. It is the woman friend of the author who encourages her to write orations, and the author reads history to emulate Caesar. Women get their share of criticism, to be sure, but for not achieving more than they do: "Our sex is more apt to Read than to Write, and most commonly when any of our Sex doth Write, they Write some Devotions, or Romances, or Receits of Medicines, for Cookery or Confectioners, or Complemental Letters, or a Copy or two of Verses."[21] The author, a woman, does not expect her philosophical works to be understandable to a male friend of the correspondent.

In short, *Sociable Letters* does not assume the natural inferiority of women, no matter how critical the author may be about women's trivial lives and

49

lack of wit. Yet it separates by two years the two works that set the doctrine out most clearly. I suggest that the difference lies in the kind of work Cavendish was writing. In her more transgressive works, *Orations* and *Observations,* she was using a strategy she had used earlier with elaborate commendatory verses from Newcastle: she was undoing her transgressions into male territory, science and public life, by allaying the reader's fear that she advocated social change for women. When she presented her more private books, such as *Sociable Letters,* Cavendish did not need to undo as much social transgression and so the tone is more relaxed and the comments on women social in character. We should also recall that her plays, which are full of radical women and ideas about them, come from the sixties (1662; 1668), and in those she had the protection of the dramatic genre as well as Newcastle's acknowledged collaboration. In *Observations* the harsh tone conveys anger which resembles that in her autobiography where, after telling of her failure to recover Newcastle's lands, she lashed out at the women petitioners. A similar frustration at her own lack of scientific achievement and acceptance by the scientific community results in anger at all women whom nature has given inferior minds and bodies.

So it is on natural differences that Cavendish's advocacy of women founders: or inequality established by nature cannot be changed. She is eloquently critical of women's lives in *Sociable Letters* (xxi, xxxvi, l, li, lxii, cxii, and cl, among others). Her remedy for women's trivial lives is for them not to change their status but to emulate men, their natural betters, although she also acknowledges that masculine women may be thought unnatural. In both *The World's Olio* and *Observations on Natural Philosophy,* she emphasizes natural differences between the genders, which may appear to us social in character. *The World's Olio* says:

> It is not so great a Fault for a Woman to be Masculine, as for a Man to be Effeminat: for it is a Defect in Nature to decline, as to see Men like women; but to see a Masculine Woman, is but onely as if Nature had mistook, and had placed a Mans Spirit in a Womans Body; but Nature hath both her Mistakes and Weaknesses; but when she works perfectly, she gives Man a gentle and sweet Disposition, a generous Mind, a valiant Heart, a wise Head, a voluble Tongue, a healthfull Body, and strong and active Limbs: To Woman she gives a chast Mind, a sober Disposition, a silent Tongue, a fair and modest Face, a neat Shape, and a graceful Motion. (P. 84)

Not much in that assignment that would make women philosophers! Cavendish seems almost Victorian when in *Orations* she flatters women by claiming that "we Women are much more Favour'd by Nature than Men, in Giving us such Beauties, Features, Shapes . . . as Men are Forc'd to Admire us . . . inslaving themselves to our Will and Pleasures" (p. 232). Honest Margaret Newcastle may not herself have used manipulation to get her way, but as a maid-in-waiting she could have observed it and is worldly enough to make it and the specious sense of power it creates in the weak a part of her picture of relations between the genders.

Cavendish's own imagination is almost never drawn to erotic love. She remarks in *A True Relation,* "I never was infected therewith, it is a disease, or a passion, or both, I only know by relation, not by experience" (p. 162). Instead, her thought centered in marriage of two faithful, loyal, just, honorable persons. Her own marriage to the extraordinary Newcastle she sees as a model relationship. Throughout her works she is clearly aware of the trials of marriage for seventeenth-century Englishwomen, yet she supports the prerogative of husbands in marriage, "which Rights and Privileges they receiv'd from Nature, God and Morality" (*Orations,* p. 93). In *Sociable Letters* she says, "there being no Life I approve so well of as a Married Life, where as much Sympathy Joyns Souls, and Affection Hearts, as Ceremony Joyns Hands; but to live with Antipathy must needs be very Unhappy, and if you be So, there is no way to Help your self" (p. 425). To avoid this predicament from which there was no relief, one had to be very careful in selecting a mate. Possibly because her own marriage was very happy, Cavendish was skeptical about matches that depended largely on sexual attraction ("The Marriage-bed proves the Grave of Love."). She believed in marrying discreetly and letting love grow: "Where Discretion joyns hands, Honesty begets love, and thrifty Temperance makes Constancy, which builds Happiness and Peace for their lives" (p. 170). Her skepticism about romantic love is characteristic of one strain of seventeenth-century women writers.

Sociable Letters, The World's Olio, Nature's Pictures, Orations, and especially the plays explore the real problems of the seventeenth-century conjugal relationship. Occasionally Cavendish came to the momentary conclusion that single life is preferable to an unhappy marriage, another conclusion many women writers of the time draw: "But Marriage is a very Unhappy Life when Sympathy Joyns not the Married Couple, for otherwise it were better to be Barr'd up within the Gates of a Monastery, than to be Bound in the Bonds of Matrimony" (*Sociable Letters,* p. 124). Like her successors Cavendish addresses the ongoing human relationship rather than the abstract institution of the moralists: how to choose a good mate (follow your ears, not your eyes); why marriage kills sexual passion (wives need to act like courtesans); what to do when your husband is unfaithful (be patient); how husbands are angered by unruly wives (wives offend nature); the shallowness of most women's conversation (read better books); the risks of both genders in marriage (both can be unhappy, but men have greater freedom if they are); problems when marriages are unequal in age, social rank, or economic condition (equality of all three greatly enhances chance for happiness), and so on. Cavendish's dowerless marriage to a socially superior man thirty years her senior only gave her confidence in these conventional opinions because she was happy. But the importance of Cavendish's extensive writing about marriage should not be overlooked: she was beginning a social critique that would gradually give women writers what she herself lacked—a set of social terms with which to interpret their predicament as a social group. Calls for reform of the marriage relationship could not develop without a social definition of gender.

That women criticize the institution of marriage in print seems no great surprise to us today, but Cavendish's critique of marriage in the context of the status quo begins a new theme and tradition in women's writing in England. Before Cavendish, writing about marriage was largely the prerogative of men: Erasmus, priests and pastors, moralists, satirists, all wrote about duties within an abstract relationship. Their audience is both genders; their purpose, to enforce conventional social roles, usually with a religious sanction. Cavendish also did not question the status quo; when she wrote an oration about a woman's unhappy marriage, she saw no legal or social remedy for her:

> Yet howsoever were she the Best Wife that could be, and he the Worst Husband, the Law hath no power to Mend him, and Help her, for the Law ought not to intermeddle in their Quarrel, as having no more Power to take away the Prerogative of a Husband, than the Prerogative of Parents and Masters; for whensoever the Law takes the part of a Servant against his Master, a Subject against his Prince, a Child against his Parents, or a Wife against her Husband, the Law doth unjustly Usurp on their Rights and Privileges, which Rights and Privileges their receiv'd from Nature, God and Morality. (*Orations*, p. 124)

Cavendish's thinking was entirely consonant with patriarchal theory of her time and earlier. New is the same spirit that animates her poems about creatures—a deep and warm sympathy for the suffering of others. So, unlike the male theorists, she did not assume that all women must marry, but suggested repeatedly instead that leading apes to hell is preferable to being beaten by a drunken husband and bearing his children. Unwittingly she began a tradition that would yield Chudleigh's challenge to Sprint's wedding sermon and Astell's *Reflections on Marriage*. Cavendish, in fact, had the vocabulary that was used later, but she employed it with her characteristic undoing: "But the Safest Way is to Live a Single Life, for all Wives, if they be not Slaves, yet they are Servants, although to be a Servant to a Worthy Husband, is both Pleasure and Honour" (*Sociable Letters*, p. 427).

It is a small step from such language to Chudleigh's "Wife and Servant are the same."

Indeed, Cavendish may not have been the pattern for later women writers that she aspired to be, but she did anticipate many of their qualities and attitudes. Here Lipking's essay, described in the introduction, is helpful. A woman's poetics, he says, would have to claim first the privilege of writing for women who are traditionally to be silent. (Cavendish's Nature gave woman a silent tongue.) We have already seen how Cavendish defended her privilege of writing; but possibly because she was first, Cavendish was unusual in the degree to which she protested against latent criticism about taking time from housework for writing.

In one of the *Sociable Letters,* she described the criticism of a neighbor that the author's studious life leaves her maids idle. As a result, the author tries spinning only to fail at it. She considers needlework but also lacks that skill. Then she determines to make silk flowers, only to have her servant tell her that tradesmen make them better and cheaper. The author then decides to make preserves, but the servant points out that few people eat sweets because they rot the teeth. The servant finally assures the author that the other servants are happy and that neighbors will always find something to criticize: "Besides, said she, none can want Employment, as long as there are Books to be Read." The author agrees: "Since I am fit for no other Employment but to Scratch Paper, leave me to that Employment, and let my Attending Maids have Books to read" (pp. 313–14). It is a charming picture of the predicament of every studious wife, almost as true now as then. The author's self-mockery here is just another of the many forms of undoing that Cavendish used in virtually every preface, epistle, or dedication. Undoing was, as we shall see, the most popular defense among conservative women writers for most of the seventeenth century. Lipking goes on to summarize the poetics of Aristotle's sister: "Poetry is the expression of a life, personal, incomplete, and proportioned to the self; employing whatever language and conventions one has been allowed to acquire; presented in fragments; and achieving, through sharing the emotions of loneliness and abandonment, a momentary sense of not being alone."[22] Margaret's works conform to this definition, which is largely based on romantic and post-romantic writers, with an uncanny accuracy. Most of Margaret's books are "proportioned to the self." Here is Virginia Woolf:

Nevertheless, though her philosophies are futile, and her plays intolerable, and her verses mainly dull, the vast bulk of the Duchess is leavened by a vein of authentic fire. One cannot help following the lure of her erratic and lovable personality as it meanders and twinkles through page after page. There is something noble and Quixotic and high-spirited, as well as crack-brained and bird-witted about her. Her simplicity is so open; her intelligence is so active; her sympathy with fairies and animals so true and tender.[23]

Even her works of natural philosophy are personal and fragmented. *The World's Olio, The Sociable Letters, and Poems and Fancies* are composed of bits and pieces, with an arbitrary order, joined by the whim or will of the author. The title of *The World's Olio* conveys this quality immediately for an *olio* is a heterogeneous mixture. Fancies come and go. Without an education Cavendish knew few conventions to bind her–or to guide her either. She felt entirely free to create totally unstageable plays and still to muse in print about why they were never acted. They contain, as we have seen, some of her more radical ideas about women. These dramas, written with the aid of Newcastle, an experienced playwright, flouted the most conventional and communal of genres to please their author. Because she was first, her lack of discourse, a coherent set of terms with which to address a subject, makes even her scientific writing confused and discontinuous. Grant comments on her lack of a consistent terminology. Yet as both Bowerbank and Sarasohn demonstrate, there is feminist method in Cavendish's madness:

> Rather than calling for the destruction of social hierarchy and institutions, which she supported for class and personal reasons, she advocated everything that was intellectually subversive within traditional society. She developed a natural philosophy that could not be restrained by either method or authority, repudiating both the old and new system of thought. In her own life, she scandalized social mores with her outlandish dress and eccentric behavior, proclaiming the independence of intellectual women, not from fundamental societal norms, but from cultural conformity.[24]

Her inconsistency may be partly also the result of the novelty of her subjects, as can be shown by comparing her autobiography with her biography of her husband. Cavendish was still a relatively inexperienced writer when she composed her autobiography in Antwerp, and *The True Relation of My Birth, Breeding and Life* shows signs of ineptitude in its scattered character. Yet, as Mary Mason says, *The True Relation* is not so chaotic as some critics have said. Mason shows how the first part describes her birth, breeding, and actions (though not all important actions, to be sure); and the second gives "an interior portrait, including the sitter's temperament and her moral character."[25] The work concludes with Cavendish's defense for writing her own life, including an assertion that she wrote for herself–and for fame, an audience in some distant future, that her name might live. Yet within this basic structure, there lie deep ambivalences, some of which Mary Beth

Rose has identified.[26] She shows how Cavendish has internalized the Renaissance ideal of the chaste, silent, modest woman while compromising that ideal with contradiction and hyperbole. For example, Cavendish made the long journey to recoup Newcastle's lands, but then could not bring herself to plead for them publicly; and then she displaced her rage at this failure on the women petitioners who transgressed the boundaries she respected. Because of her conservatism, Cavendish was unable to fashion a new set of terms to deal with the Renaissance ideal of womanhood. So her autobiography is full of strategies that we have seen her use to undo psychologically her assertiveness, her ambition, the privilege of writing. First, we have an epistle in which she apologized for her writing: "I desire all my readers and acquaintance to believe, though my words run stumbling out of my mouth, and my pen draws roughly on my paper, yet my thoughts move regular in my brain" (p. 154). This statement, she hoped, would mitigate the fact that she was one of the few women who wrote her own life for publication in the seventeenth century and one of even fewer who did not attach it to a biography of her husband. That gesture awaited later editors.

Cavendish's strategy here as elsewhere was to offer the reader other figures (to whom she is inferior) who fit the ideals she flouted. Thus she used the highly relational features of a woman's life to mask the fact that she did not fit the model of womanhood that she accepted. Instead she offered her mother, who was clearly an able and inspiring presence for Margaret, as an idealized portrait of Renaissance womanhood. As an extension of her mother's presence, we have her marvelous family with heroic sons and loving daughters. Cavendish's brothers are part of a series of male portraits that also include, of course, Newcastle and his brother, all of whom were very dear to Cavendish. Yet their large presence in her story effectively allows the reader to forget that it is her story, one written for publication and for immortality, especially as she compared herself as a writer invidiously to Newcastle: "Also he creates himself with his pen, writing what his wit dictates to him, but I pass my time rather with scribbling than writing, with words than wit" (p. 172).

As Mary Beth Rose has said, Cavendish's portrait of herself is filled with contradictions and with constant qualifications of her assertions because she was trying to fit an ideal that she continually exceeded. This leads to the chaotic impression that *A True Relation* makes:

> Also as I am not covetous, so I am not prodigal, but of the two I am inclining to be prodigal, yet I cannot say to a vain prodigality, because I imagine it is to a profitable end; for perceiving the world is given, or apt to honour the outside more than the inside, worshipping show more than substance; and I am so vain (if it be a vanity)

as to endeavour to be worshipped, rather than not to be regarded. Yet I shall never be so prodigal as to impoverish my friends, or go beyond the limits or facility of our estate. (P. 177)

These many forms of defense show a modern reader how deeply conflicted Cavendish's old-fashioned social ideals made her feel about her transgressive gestures.

A decade later, when she came to write *The Life of the thrice Noble, High and Puissant Prince William Cavendish*, Cavendish had a clear purpose and a principle by which to select material. Her purpose was to vindicate Newcastle, to demonstrate that the course of his career was determined not by his defects as man or leader but by the incompetence of inferiors and the betrayal of superiors to whom he was steadfastly loyal. The first section of the narrative about his military career arranged the incidents so that they support the impression about which she generalized toward the end of the section:

> In all these encounters my Lord got not the least hurt, though several were slain about him; and his White Coats showed such an extraordinary valour and courage in that action, that they were killed in rank and file. And here I cannot but mention by the way, that it is remarkable, that in all actions and undertakings where my Lord was in person himself, he was always victorious, and prospered in the execution of his designs; but whatsoever was lost or succeeded ill, happened in his absence, and was caused either by the treachery or negligence and carelessness of his officers.[27]

In later parts of the biography, she effectively balanced his loyalty to Charles II, his suffering and deprivations with the king's neglect of him after the Restoration so that Newcastle becomes a martyr-hero in the reader's eyes. Here Cavendish did for her husband what he never could have done for himself. Because the image of him as totally loyal could not allow Newcastle even to hint a criticism of the king, Cavendish took upon herself anger at her husband's situation after his return to England whereas he was a model of patience:

> After I was safely arrived in London, I found my Lord in lodgings; I cannot call them unhandsome; but yet they were not fit for a person of his rank and quality, nor of the capacity to contain all his family. Neither did I find my Lord's condition such as I expected: wherefore out of some passion I desired him to leave the town, and retire into the country; but my Lord gently reproved me for my rashness and impatience, and soon after removed into Dorset House; which, though it was better than the former, yet not altogether to my satisfaction,

we having but a part of the said house in possession. By this removal
I judged my Lord would not hastily depart from London; but not
long after, he was pleased to tell me, that he has despatched his business, and was now resolved to remove into the country, having already given order for waggons to transport our goods, which was no
unpleasant news to me, who had a great desire for a country life.
(P. 68)

Newcastle's use of denial in his farewell interview with the king shows him
to be a master of the use of defenses equal to Cavendish: "'Sir,' said he to
his Majesty, 'I am not ignorant, that many believe I am discontented; and
'tis probable they'll say, I retire through discontent: but I take God to my
witness, that I am so joyed at your Majesty's happy restoration, that I cannot be sad or troubled for any concern to my own particular; but whatsoever your Majesty is pleased to command me, were it to sacrifice my life,
I shall most obediently perform it; for I have no other will, but your Majesty's pleasure'" (p. 68).

William Cavendish made a public career, and the values to guide the subject and the biographer are clear. Margaret Cavendish wrote a public, political document, and although *The Life* has diverse sections, especially in the
Third Book, the details supply the reader with a fully developed sense of
Newcastle's character and life after the end of his military career, and they
are selected to conduce to one's admiration for all sides of his nature. Even
"Of the Entertainments he made for King Charles the First" makes sense
as one recalls the importance of such events for Stuart noblemen, especially
of Newcastle's generation. But the brief section has another function: it reminds us how close Cavendish was to his royal masters, how much he did
for them and, implicitly, how little they did for him.

One should not exaggerate the differences between the two works, for
The Life, with which Margaret had help from John Rolleston, rattles on in
her characteristic style, and *A True Relation* contains a discernible organization. Yet there is a harmony between Newcastle's life, with all its failures
and suffering, and his ideals that Cavendish could never achieve in her own
life, and her style in *A True Relation* reflects the psychic dissonances. She
was always too much at odds with the ideals of womanhood she accepted,
but which only her mother could be made to represent. So, to return to
Lipking's phrase, "proportioned to the self," we can appreciate both Cavendish's attempts to shape that proportion as well as her struggles to achieve
a self in the first instance.

Cavendish eloquently articulated another important tradition among
women writers: the need for a room of one's own, "the need of women
for a private space and time."[28] She not only led a solitary, contemplative
life, "passing my time with harmless fancies, their company being pleasing,

their conversation innocent";[29] but she chose to spend her life in the country, infrequently creating the sensation recorded by diarists of her time in going abroad in town, dressed in her original, outlandish costumes. As she outlines the reasons for country living in one of her *Sociable Letters,* the country agrees with her solitary humor, it is better for her health, and they have no house in London. Clearly, the years of exile reinforced Cavendish's childhood preference for the country, but the king's indifference to Newcastle after the Restoration fixed the matter for life. As Grant says, "Newcastle was no fool, and when once he had recognized the hopelessness of expecting to play any part at court, he decided that the best course would be to retire to the country and set about restoring his wasted estates."[30] It would be interesting to have watched Cavendish's development if her husband had resumed his public career. As it is, she was the first of a long series of conservative women writers who seek not only private space for work but country life as well. Sometimes they seek what Lipking calls, "a sanctuary where the person can be forgotten and the self remembered" (p. 70). And sometimes they voice a longing for, or celebration of, the austere rural cell ideologically, as Cavendish did when she wrote of a "low Thatcht House" when she was living in Rubens's house in Antwerp. Still, authentic nature and class differences meant too much to Cavendish for her to sympathize with pastoral conventions:

> The *Shepherdesses* which great Flocks doe keep
> Are dabl'd high with dew, following their Sheep;
> Milking their Ewes their hands doe dirty make,
> For, being wet, dirt from their Duggs doe take.
> The Sun doth scorch the skin, it yellow growes;
> Their eyes are red, lips dry with wind that blowes.

Cavendish exhorts her fellow poets not to idealize such repulsive dolts: the rural ideology founders on her sense of what the country is really like and her place in society.[31]

Cavendish seems to have made a great virtue of necessity, whereas her solitary life allowed her two important kinds of power. There she could create alternative worlds to the one that offered her no place or power—a Blazing World in which she or a double could be all powerful. Second, through her writing she could control her relationship to the public world, in which readers meet her on terms that she creates. Those terms could be adjusted to her self instead of to the person the world would make of her. In such a predicament, writing becomes a means of creating a community with the reader so that one is not alone but dealing with another on one's own terms. If one sees her writing from that perspective, Cavendish's elaborate prefaces, epistles, and multiple addresses to the reader begin to make sense. Not only did she need to justify the privilege of writing itself, but she also sought again and again to create a special relationship with the reader, who is simply presented not with a text but with Cavendish in the text, an indelible presence, to which we have seen Woolf's earlier response. Cavendish's writing forms with the reader a community like that of her fancies, "for it is as great a grief to leave their society as a joy to be in their company."[32]

Like her successors as women writers, Cavendish retired to a space where her individuality could develop; she avoided playing cards, paying visits, dancing, reveling, feasting: "I do often fast, out of an opinion that if I should eat much, and exercise little, which I do, only walking a slow pace in my chamber, whilst my thoughts run apace in my brain so that the motions of my mind hinders the active exercises of my body; for should I dance or run, or walk apace, I should dance my thoughts out of measure, run my fancies out of breath, and tread on the feets of my numbers" (p. 173). From her delicious solitude, Cavendish's writing could reach the world according to her terms and rescue her, not from loneliness that held little fear, but from oblivion.

Although Cavendish was too eccentric to have artistic progeny, many of her themes are prophetic for later women writers: the themes form a nexus among her successors, whatever tradition they drew upon. Cavendish's devotion to nature and nature's creatures, for example, is part of an almost continuous strain of nature poetry (in a variety of genres) among many women writers throughout the century, a tradition that culminates in the achievements of Anne Finch, the countess of Winchelsea. Winchilsea and Cavendish have much in common: their noble class, which breeds conservatism; their happy, exemplary, childless marriages to men who encouraged their writing; their scorn of other women's wasted, trivial lives; their old-fashioned ways; and their penchant for melancholy.

Melancholy was another of Cavendish's prophetic themes. Among her better known poems is "A Dialogue *between* Melancholy, *and Mirth*," which has sometimes been compared to Milton's *L'Allegro* and *Il Penseroso*. But unlike Milton, who is relatively evenhanded about the two moods and styles, Cavendish ends her poem with a vindication of melancholy:

> Thus am I *solitary,* and live alone,
> Yet better lov'd, the more that I am knowne.
> And though my *Face* b'ill favoured at first sight,
> After Acquaintance it shall give delight.
> For I am like a *Shade,* who fits in me,
> Shall not come *wet,* nor yet *Sun-birned,* be.

I keep off *blustring Stormes,* from being hurt,
When *Mirth* is often smutch'd with *dust,* and *durt.*
Refuse me not, for I shall constant be,
Maintaine your *Credit,* keep up *Dignity.*

(P. 80)

This sentiment came easily to Cavendish, who describes herself as "more inclining to be melancholy then merry, but not crabbed or peevishly melancholy, but soft, melting, and contemplating melancholy" (*True Relation,* 175). As we shall see, this mood or temperament was shared by a number of women poets of seventeenth-century England.

Cavendish's protests against violence, hunting, war—particularly, of course, civil war—are recorded in her poetry, in *The World's Olio,* and in *Sociable Letters* and *Orations of Divers Sorts.* Her poems of sympathy with the hunted stag and Wat the hare are among her best-known. Although she admired male heroism in battle, her reaction to war was negative, as in "A Dialogue between a Bountifull Knight, and a Castle ruin'd in War," "Of an Island," "The Ruine of the Island," and "A Description of the Battle in Fight" from *Poems and Fancies* and "A Description of Civil-Warrs" from *Nature's Pictures.* The Empress of the Blazing World, hearing that her native country is at war, enlists the aid of Cavendish and returns with submarines and firebombs to save her country and forge a lasting peace in the world. *Orations of Divers Sorts* spell out the misfortunes of civil war in detail, and the following statement from *The World's Olio* is typical of Cavendish's views: "The greatest storm that shipwracks honest education, good laws, and decent customes, is civil-wars, which splits the vessel of a Common-wealth, and buries it in the waves of ruine . . . intermixing the Nobles and Commons, where loyalty is shuffled from the crown, duty from Parents tendernesse from children, fidelity from Masters, continencies from husbands and wives, truth from fiends, from justice innocency, charity from misery; Chance playes, and fortune draws the stakes."[33]

In *Sociable Letters,* however, the author reminds her correspondent that the English Civil War was an affair among men: "But however, Madam, the disturbance in this Country hath made no breach of Friendship betwixt us, for though there hath been a Civil War in the Kingdom, and a general War amongst the Men, yet there hath been none amongst the Women" (p. 28). The reason for this difference is not far to seek: "Though Worthy men go to the Wars with Joy, hoping to gain Honour, yet Women Depart from those Friends with Grief, for fear of their Death, and in their Absence they never enjoy a Minutes Rest or Quiet" (p. 387). Further dissociating women from war, the Sociable Virgins voice a familiar sentiment in *The Unnatural Tragedy:* if women ruled the world, it would be at peace, "for the

60

whole World is together by the Ears, all up in Wars and Blood, which shows there is a general defect in the Rulers and Governors thereof."[34]

Cavendish's concern about peace seems natural enough in view of her experience, but more remarkable and prophetic too was the amount of political writing she did about themes she always acknowledged as out of the sphere of her sex. Although *The Life of William Cavendish* is not overtly a political work, it is clearly an extended defense to an age that had passed them by, not just of the duke's career and life, but also of the royalist values for which he—and she—had sacrificed so much. Dedicated to Charles II, *The Life* was meant to challenge an ungrateful age in which restored monarchy proved only slightly better than the rule of the saints. Cavendish must set the record straight so that present scorn would not give way to lasting oblivion:

> Indeed, my Lord, I matter not the censures of this age, but am rather proud of them; for it shows that my actions are more than ordinary, and according to the old proverb it is better to envied than pitied: for I know well, that it is merely out of spite and malice, whereof this present age is so full, that none can escape them, and they'll make no doubt to stain even your Lordship's loyal, noble, and heroic actions, as well as they do mine, though yours have been of war and fighting, mine of contemplating and writing; yours were performed publicly in the field, mine privately in my closet: yours had many eye-witnesses, mine none but my waiting maids. But the great God, that hath hitherto blessed both your Grace and me, will, I question not, preserve both fames to after ages, for which we shall be bound most humbly to acknowledge His great mercy.[35]

An even more audacious gesture was the composition of *Orations of Divers Sorts*, which I have already discussed. Cavendish's fantasy of public life for a woman is represented by a gentleman's speech about Lady Sanspareille in *Youth's Glory and Death's Banquet:* "This Lady Sanspareille hath a strange spreading wit, for she can plead causes at the Bar, decide causes in the Court of Judicature, make Orations on publick Theaters; act parts, and speak speeches on the Stage, argue in the Schooles, preach in the Pulpits, either in Theology, Philosophy, moral and natural, and also phisick and Metaphysick."[36] Although Cavendish's entire dream of woman's achievements is not yet fully realized, we will discover that her immediate successors wrote a surprising amount of political poetry, drama, and fiction despite the fact that they had no legal status if married and no access in any of the public arenas enjoyed by Lady Sanspareille, except the stage.

Cavendish's delight in friendship among women is another of her prophetic qualities. Because she is so critical of most women and their wasted lives and because she is such a solitary person, her images of women's friendship are impressive and moving. She enjoys elaborate fantasies about platonic love of women's souls in *The Description of a New World*. *The Sociable Letters* represent the author's correspondent as a dear female friend, "your ladyship," to whom the author constantly pledges love, loyalty, and sisterhood. Some of the letters, as we have seen, represent historical facts of Cavendish's life; but most seem addressed to an imaginary, ideal confidante, her artistic support, her equal. In *The Description* the souls of the Empress and the Duchess enjoy a platonic friendship that transcends worlds: "After some time the Empress gave her leave to return to her Husband and Kindred into her Native World, but upon condition, that her Soul should visit her now and then; which she did: and truly their meeting did produce such an intimate friendship between them, that they became *Platonick* Lovers, although they were both Femal."[37]

The souls of the Empress and the Duchess not only visit the theater and the court in England, but they journey to the Duke at Welbeck and take up residence in his body: "The Duke would have been like the *Grand-Signior* in his *Seraglio,* onely it would have been a *Platonick* Seraglio" (p. 110). After much friendly diversion, the Empress must return to her husband and people in the Blazing World. The Empress assures the Duchess of her fondest dream and they part: "You will get a glorious fame in this World, and an Eternal Glory hereafter; and I shall pray for it so long as I live. Upon which Advice, the Empress's Soul embrac'd and kiss'd the Duchess's Soul with an Immaterial Kiss, and shed Immaterial Tears, that she was forced to part from her, finding her not a flattering Parasite, but a true Friend; and in truth, such was their Platonick Friendship, as these two loving Souls did often meet and rejoice in each others Conversation" (p. 123). In the Epilogue to the Reader, Cavendish explains that although she is as ambitious as Caesar or Alexander, she had to create a philosophical world for herself because she could not usurp the government of the Blazing World ruled by the Empress, "my dear Platonick Friend."

Why, we may ask, did Margaret insist on the platonic friendship of souls? Partly because they can move about the universe with ease. Partly because souls do not raise all kinds of sexual innuendos that bodies might. But largely for the same reason that platonic friendship of souls will become important to other women writing in the period: friendship is ideally between equals and souls are equal. As the Lady Speaker of *The Female Academy* says, "It is very difficult to make a right Friendship, for hard it is to match men in agreeable Humours, Appetites, Passions, Capacities, Conversations, Customs, Actions, Natures and Dispositions, all which must be to make a true and lasting Friendship; other wise, two Friends will be like two Horses that draw contrary waies, whereas Souls, Bodies, Education and Lives, must equally agree in Friendship."[38] Because bodies, lives, and education all become loaded with a heavy social freight, it is far easier to imagine an ideal friendship between souls. The Duchess need not be jealous of the Empress's delight in Newcastle's company, and yet they may still shed immaterial tears. The religious notion that souls are equal before God feeds this idea — not for Cavendish, but for some of her successors — and it also feeds the general notion of human equality.

Although Cavendish idealized friendship with other women, she stopped short of sisterhood, of conceptualizing bonds among all women. Although she began to think of women as a sociological group, her thinking about them was almost always negative, as we have seen. Her thinking was constrained by allegiance to nature and to ideals she herself had outgrown. She conceived of women friends as supportive of her fondest dreams, but they, like her, were exceptions to the norm of a group destined by nature to inferiority. Yet when one thinks of how much Cavendish achieved, one can hardly blame her for feeling the exception — she certainly was quite extraordinary, as Bathsua Makin said in the year Cavendish died: "The present Dutchess of New-Castle, by her own Genius, rather than any timely Instruction, over-tops many grave 'Gown-Men.'"[39] And one can also be pleased that in our time she has begun to enjoy the fame she hoped for above all.

Chapter Two

Orinda and Her Daughters

Orinda Herself:
Katherine Philips (1631–64)

Katherine Philips, the Matchless Orinda, was to vie with Aphra Behn for the claim to be the most important woman poet of the seventeenth century. Although she was not as fine a writer as Behn, Orinda became a model for one kind of woman writer throughout the seventeenth and early eighteenth centuries. Her artistic and intellectual progeny are many: Anne Killigrew, Lady Mary Chudleigh, Anne Finch, countess of Winchilsea, Jane Barker, Mary Masters, Mary Barber, Elizabeth Singer Rowe, and Mary Astell. Sarah Fyge Field Egerton also claimed Orinda as part of a combined artistic heritage. Katherine Philips was also a symbol of achievement for other women writers such as Bathsua Makin and Hannah Woolley. Her contributions and the magnitude of her influence are especially impressive because Orinda was almost painfully self-deprecatory. As we have seen, Cavendish made ample use of undoing, but Orinda raised the technique to a higher art. Although she constantly protested that she did not seek fame or publication, she wrote a substantial volume of poems, another of letters, and translated one play and most of another, all before her untimely death at thirty-three.

Orinda's way of dealing with the privilege of writing was to disown any assertion in the process. Her description for Sir Charles Cotterell of her purposes in writing is characteristic: "I am so far from expecting Applause on account of any thing I write, that I can scarce expect a Pardon: And sometimes I think that to make Verses is so much above my Reach, and a Diversion so unfit for the Sex to which I belong, that I am about to resolve against it for ever. . . . The Truth is, I have always had an incorrigible inclination to the Vanity of Rhyming, but intended the Effects of that Humour only for my own Amusement in a retir'd Life."[1] The seesaw of gestures to which Orinda's use of undoing and denial led her is quite apparent in her predicament about dedicating her translation of Corneille's *Pompey* to the duchess of York. Although performance of the play in Dublin and in England made her famous, Orinda would never sign her name to the printed copies of the play. Instead, Cotterell presented a copy of the play to Charles II, but Orinda cautioned Cotterell never to reveal her name in printed copies: "I thank you for presenting *Pompey* to his *Majesty,* and for the favourable Account you give me of his Royal Goodness for that Trifle. I consent to whatever you think fit to do about printing it, but conjure you by all our mutual Friendship, not to put my Name to it, nay, not so much as the least mark or hint whereby the Publick may guess from whence it came" (p. 153).

Later she wrote a poem to the duchess about this incident. She wrote constantly to Cotterell about plans for publication, about her rivalry with a competing translation of *Pompey* by a group of male wits led by Waller, about the pirated publication of her poems, about the many compliments she received on *Pompey,* and yet she firmly maintained that her poems were trifles, written only for herself, that she feared being perceived as a rival to Waller, that the Wits's translation was far superior to hers, that she wrote only because she could not help herself (p. 179). Thus did she tread the ambiguous line between being silent and submissive as a woman and her transparent energy and ambition as a writer.

She achieved similar kinds of balancing acts with regard to her marriage and her retired life. When she returned to Wales and to the side of her husband after her triumph in Dublin, she very much wanted to escape the boring isolation of the country; but she was afraid of how her leaving her husband again might look to society. She had praised the values of a retired life, but understood its bad effects upon her art: "All I desire is, that when you read this Poem, you will not condemn me for a dulness that you will find growing upon me, but consider, that my Absence from all the Conversation that can refine my Wit, the Employments of a Country Life, and the Uneasiness of my Fortune, are able to blunt a much finer Pen than ever I was Mistress of" (p. 202). Her remedy for both the problems was the same: manipulation of men to urge her to do for them what she would not do for herself. In letter after letter to Cotterell, Orinda appealed to him to arrange an excuse for her to go to London. She could not go there unless James Philips insisted, and so she had her nephew, Hector Philips (the Trojan), seek out possible opportunities in London for her to act on James Philips's behalf. She was frantic when no mail from Cotterell arrived, for she hoped he would also inspire requests from Lady Cork to visit in London.

When she finally heard from Cotterell and her plans were aligned, she asked Cotterell to write Philips: "Repeat the Assurances you have formerly given him, of your generous Friendship, and acquaint him that I ought to hasten to Town as soon as possible, in order to solicite for him the Affair the *Trojan* has found out" (p. 223). The coveted journey to London proved the death of her there of smallpox in June 1664. Her death was lamented by many famous male poets, but her life and poetry inspired even more women poets.

Orinda's strategies for getting to vital London from boring Wales were characteristic of her ways of promoting her talent in a hostile world: she let men fight the battles for her, once they had shown interest and she had instructed them. With men her deferential attitude would yield imperatives to act in ways she wished. Orrery insisted, for example, that she translate Corneille's *Pompey* after seeing a scene that mysteriously came to his hands:

> By some Accident or another my Scene of *Pompey* fell into his Hands, and he was pleas'd to like it so well, that he sent me the *French* Original; and the next time I saw him, so earnestly importun'd me to pursue that Translation, that to avoid the Shame of seeing him who had so lately commanded a Kingdom, become a Petitioner to me for such a Trifle, I obey'd him so far as to finish the Act in which the Scene is; so that the whole third Act is now *English*. This I the rather did, hoping to undeceive him in the partial Opinion he had of my Capacity for such an Undertaking; and not doubting but he would have dispens'd with my farther Trouble therein. But he no sooner had it, than (I think to punish me for having done it so ill) he enjoin'd me to go on; and not only so, but brib'd me to be contented with the Pains by sending me an excellent Copy of Verses, which, were I not conscious of my own Unworthiness, would make me rather forget the Subject, than disbelieve the Complements of his Lordship'd Muse. (P. 66)

Once Orinda had composed the translation, Orrery was effusive in his praise, claiming that if Corneille could read her Pompey, "he like us would call / The copy greater than th' Original." He went on to assert "that 'tis Orinda's work, and but his Play." Like Orinda's other male admirers, Orrery denies envy of Orinda's achievements because she is a woman:

> In me it does not the least trouble breed,
> That your fair Sex does Ours in Verse exceed,
> Since every Poet thus great Truth does prove,

Nothing so much inspires a Muse as Love;
Thence has your Sex the best Poetick fires,
For what's inspir'd must yield to what inspires.[2]

Because she pretended never to compete with them and men supported
Orinda's poetic efforts, she could always claim that men had virtually forced
her into actions that she alone might never have risked. Therefore much
of the credit was theirs. And indeed throughout the century after her
death, the adulatory poems of Orrery, of the earl of Roscommon, and of
Abraham Cowley serve as witness to her worth. Roscommon seems to have
encapsulated her delicate balance between assertion and submission, as he
describes the effect of her verse upon the animals:

And when the thirsty Monsters meet,
They'll all pay homage to my feet.

6.

The Magick of ORINDA's Name,
Not only can their fierceness tame,
But, if that mighty word I once reherse,
They seem submissively to roar in Verse.
(Sig. b^{v}2)

Here Orinda replaces Orpheus, who led the beasts and moved rocks with
his song.

Cowley's widely quoted poem "Upon Mrs. K. Philips her Poems" acknowledged a series of stereotypes of women that Orinda modifies, but that
are never finally rejected, except for "*Apollo's* Salick Law," to which Orinda
is not the traditional exception, as we shall see in chapter 3, but which she
cancels with her triumphant wit. Although "Man may be the Head," Cowley said, "Woman's now the Brain." Women, said Cowley, have lived as if
they transmit only their bodies to their posterity, but Orinda's verses are
her "immortal Progeny," which compensate for the "ancient Curse to womankind" because they are borne without pain. The claim for the immortality
of their art was one that few women risked in the seventeenth century, but
here Cowley had made it for Orinda. Cowley especially praised Orinda's virtue, which shines through her verse, in contrast to Sappho, whose fame
is tarnished by "Ill Manners" (sig. C). We will explore the importance of
Orinda's virtue below, but Cowley's emphasis on the quality and its con-

trast to a "looser" tradition is characteristic of Orinda's image from the beginning. For Cowley, Katherine Philips is the poet of honor, of friendship, and above all of civility. Thus by translating *Pompey* and *Horace,* she has not only triumphed over Rome but also over angry and powerful women: "the warlike *Amazonean* Train" and "Boadicia's angry Ghost" are pleased at her success in conquering their ancient enemies through "Wit's mild Empire."

Men liked Orinda. Instead of competing with them, she was consistently deferential, and she knew how to roar submissively in verse and in gesture. Through the careful manipulations and the cautious deportment we see everywhere in the *Letters to Poliarchus,* Orinda was able to enjoy the fame that Cavendish only longed for, but within the conventional roles seventeenth-century English society assigned to women. Because of her more accessible class and more conventional personal style, Orinda was also able to be the model for many women writers to come.

Her avenue into the poetic mainstream was the discourse of the poetry of retirement, the tradition of the *beatus vir,* the happy man of Horace on his Sabine farm. This tradition was a compound of classical themes, which are amply summarized in Maren-Sofie Røstvig's *The Happy Man.* The *beatus vir* renounces accepted authority in active, public life; he seeks self-sufficiency, frequently based in the seventeenth century on concepts of reason from either Cartesian or Neoplatonic sources; he holds firmly to the conviction that a moral life can only be achieved in a rustic setting. To these basic ideas may be added Christian pietism, Stoic independence, or Epicurean contentment in the company of friends and books, depending on the emphasis of the particular poet.[3] In addition, the Horatian tradition is complicated by importations of ideas from the Vergil's Georgics, largely by Cowley, a central figure in retirement poetry.[4] The themes of this tradition were especially attractive to readers of Orinda's generation, which was still deeply conflicted by the civil war, the experience of the Commonwealth, and then the Restoration. Some individuals were forced into retirement because of being non-jurors; but many writers adopted the discourse of retirement ideologically, and Orinda is prominent among this group. James Turner has analyzed the economic, political, and social implications of this ideology in *The Politics of Landscape,* and his book is useful in reading Orinda and others who write in the retirement tradition.

As we have already seen from her letters to Cotterell, Orinda did not enjoy rustication in Wales, and so Turner contrasts her personal situation and the ideological stance of one of her most famous poems, "A Country-Life," which celebrates the retired state:

> How Sacred and how Innocent
> A Country-life appears

How free from Tumult, Discontent,
  From Flattery or Fears!
This was the first and happiest Life,
  When man enjoy'd himself;
Till Pride exchanged Peace for Strife,
  And Happiness for Pelf.

                    (P. 88)

The Golden Age of love, not passion, of honor and of poetry, is best to be reclaimed through retirement, which for the speaker of the poem has been chosen, not forced:

There are below but two things good,
  Friendship and Honesty,
And only those of all I would
  Ask for Felicity.
In this retir'd and humble seat
  Free from both War and Strife,
I am not forc'd to make retreat
But chuse to spend my Life.

                    (Pp. 90–91)

Turner comments bitterly about the contradictions within Orinda's life that are suppressed in the simplicity of the poem:

She is indeed "unconcern'd" with politics, and she does write "secure" within a country dwelling; but of what kind? Katherine Philips was a London merchant's daughter, "who never could be high" in a caste sense. She married James Philips, a parliamentary colonel who distinguished himself both during and after the civil war by ferocious suppressions of local royalist rebellions. The poet is therefore acutely qualified to attest the cruel world's "Fire and Sword," and the freedom of the countryside from tumult and strife. Did not the colonel himself guarantee this happy state, and bravely "civilize the rude"? The lack of Pelf and Thoughts of Gain can also be attributed to James Philips. He personally sequestered at least eleven estates in South Wales.[5]

As further confirmation of the maze of contradictions in Orinda's life and art, Turner might have added that her sentiments throughout the civil war

69

and after were definitely royalist. Turner's comments make transparently clear that Orinda's commitments to country values were to an ideological fiction and not the result of personal experience. Yet for Margaret Cavendish and for Winchilsea, the experience of nature in retirement was real; and for Orinda, Abaraham Cowley's retirement and his poetry of retirement were central to a vision of the tradition, as his poetry was for many writers from the Restoration to the end of the century.[6] Orinda's ode, "Upon Mr. Abraham Cowley's Retirement," typifies him as the Happy Man, self-sufficient and self-governed:

> Nor from my self shouldst me reclaim
> With all the noise and all the pomp of Fame.
> Judiciously I'le these despise;
> Too small the Bargin, and too great the Price,
> For them to cozen twice.
> At length this secret I have learn'd;
> Who will be happy, must be unconcern'd,
> Must all their Comfort in their Bosom wear,
> And seek their treasure and their power there.
> (P. 123)

The ode projects Cowley as triumphant in his crucial gesture and thus an example for others:

> Who do enjoy thee [the world] least and understand thee most.
> For lo, the Man whom all Mankind admir'd,
> (By ev'ry Grace adorn'd, and ev'ry Muse inspir'd)
> Is now triumphantly retir'd.
> (P. 124)

The praise of a retired life allowed Orinda as a poetic persona to achieve a detachment from a highly conflicted society, religiously, economically, and politically. The *beatus vir* tradition gave her position from which to reject a world in which her own place was problematic, but in which she was still the first woman poet to achieve substantial recognition. The retirement tradition was useful for women writers who follow Orinda in that it praises personal virtues, achievable in private life, and rejects arenas in which women have little part. In addition, because the *beatus vir* discourse is largely identified with preserving an old order, which is made to seem natural, its themes were congenial to the conservative politics of Orinda and most of her followers.[7]

Central to Orinda's vision of retired happiness is the theme of friendship, a traditional theme in retirement poetry, but one for which she was especially noted: "In her poetry the motif of solitary retirement was cleverly combined with a half Platonic, half Epicurean concept of friendship."[8] In writing of friendship, Orinda was indebted to Francis Finch, of whom more later. His Platonic *Discourse of Friendship* was written in 1653 and inspired Orinda's poem "To the noble *Palaemon,* on his incomparable Discourse of Friendship," in which she compares his work to the Northern Star, guiding men, like wandering mariners, to their happiness. Finch has rescued friendship from disgrace and obscurity. His work will immortalize him (pp. 14–15).

In "Invitation to the Country," Orinda forges the link between retirement poetry and the theme of friendship. The speaker invites Rosania to share a retirement from the noise of the town. The country life, the speaker says, assists the detached observer to understanding the true values of the world, nature, and the Deity:

> Man unconcern'd without himself may be
> His own both Prospect and Security.
> Kings may be Slaves by their own Passions hurl'd,
> But who commands himself commands the World.
> A Country-life assists this study best,
> Where no distractions do the Soul arrest;
> There Heav'n and Earth lie open to our view,
> There we search Nature and its Author too.
> . . . .
> There (my Rosania) will we, mingling Souls,
> Pity the Folly which the World controuls.
>
> (p. 104)

Unlike sexual or married love, friendship exists between equals and is usually therefore a same-sex bond: it is an affair of souls: "The Soul, which no man's power can reach, a thing / That makes each Woman Man, each Man a King" (p. 112). In "A Friend" Orinda defined the relationship as an abstract of prelapsarian love, "refin'd and purg'd from all its dross. / The next to Angels Love, if not the same, / As strong as passion is, though not so gross" (p. 94). Friendship is nobler than love of family or spouse because it is more free, and women are just as capable of friendship as men. In a rare feminist moment, Orinda asserts,

If Souls no Sexes have, for Man t'exclude
  Women from Friendship's vast capacity,
Is a Design injurious or rude,
  Only maintain'd by partial tyranny.
Love is allow'd to us and Innocence,
And noblest Friendships do proceed from thence.

(P. 95)

Friendship is a relationship of sympathy and trust, "for none can be a Friend that is not good." Because a friend must keep confidences and give counsel, "He cannot be a Friend that is a Fool." Friendship thrives on a free exchange of ideas, without judgment of the other, but with an attempt to help the friend achieve a full potential:

Friends should observe and chide each others Faults,
  To be severe then is most just & kind:
Nothing can 'scape their search who knew the thoughts:
  This they should give and take with equal Mind.
For Friendship, when this Freedom is deny'd,
Is like a Painter when his hands are ty'd.

(P. 97)

The *summum bonum* of friendship is to sacrifice one's self for one's friend, an echo of Christ's act and word. The ideas are traditional, but the connection to the retired life and the emphasis on women's friendships are distinctive.

As some readers may be aware, Orinda attempted to live her ideal in relationships with men and women, intellectually with men and passionately with women. Although as Souers suggests, there is no evidence that her Society of Friendship was more than an elegant fiction, her poems provide a record of her relationships with Mrs. Ann Owen (Lucasia) and Mrs. Mary Aubrey (Rosania), as well as others whose identities are less significant: Reginia, Pastora, Phillis, Celimena.[9] The use of the pastoral pseudonyms accords with Orinda's other balancing acts. She wished to suggest a society, a community with a set of rituals and language evoking the platonic games at court, but she also wished a certain distance that would allow the participants a modest concealment of personal identity and the creation of personae by the poet. Orinda controls the reader's experience of the community through the fiction of the society and its personae.

But living according to the ideals proved difficult: women's capacity for friendship had been challenged by the ancients; marriage might conflict

72

with friendships; friendships might also conflict with Christian charity to all. In her thinking about friendship, she sought support from Jeremy Taylor and inspired his delightful essay on the subject, *The Measures and Offices of Friendship* (1657). Orinda had written Taylor to inquire, "How far a dear and a perfect friendship is authorized by the principles of Christianity."[10] In the course of his essay, Taylor addressed several of the issues Orinda had raised in her poems about friendship. She had, for example, full support from Taylor on women's capacity for friendship; he acknowledged that because she is ignorant of the public world, a woman may not be "so good a counsellor as a wise man, and cannot so well defend my honour, but a woman can love as passionately and converse as pleasantly, and retain a secret as faithfully, and be useful in her proper ministries; and she can die for her friend as well as the bravest Roman Knight" (p. 96). As the reader may see from this quotation, Taylor and Orinda shared a conception of friendship that was far more capacious and generous than that of Bacon or most ancient writers who concentrated on what Bacon called the "fruits" of friendship: what is to be gained instead of what is to be given. Taylor assured Philips that friendship is authorized by Christianity, "as it is warranted to love wisdom and virtue, goodness and beneficence, and all the impresses of God upon the spirits of brave men" (p. 47).

Although Taylor and Orinda agree in general about friendship, the minor differences they have are also instructive. It is clear, for example, that Taylor saw Platonic friendship as trivializing bonds: "But if you call this friendship, you give a sacred name to humour or fancy; for there is Platonic friendship, as well as Platonic love; but they being but the Images of more noble bodies are but like tinsel dressings, which will shew bravely by candle light, and doe excellently in a mask, but are not fit for conversation, and the material intercourses of our life" (p. 43). For Orinda, on the other hand, the Platonic fiction allowed a range of powerful, erotic emotions to be addressed to female friends without moral censure. In many poems she adopts the language of Donne with the compasses, the religion of love, the chemical and political vocabulary, to explore a whole range of powerful emotions involved in any love affair; meeting, the development of passion, the sense of uniqueness, intensity of commitment, conflicts within the relationship, and, sometimes, abandonment.[11] All these emotions are, moreover, attached to women, who are clearly identified as such. Thus what for Cavendish was a whimsical vision of a Platonic friendship with an all-powerful empress became for Orinda a fantasy to mediate eroticized relationships with women. Orinda's friendship poems, as Lillian Federman correctly observes, begin an important tradition in women's writing: female bonding. Yet such intense emotions can be contained for a temperament like Orinda's in the Platonic fiction: "It is impossible to be certain what Katherine Philips's passions meant to her, but we can be fairly sure that they were regarded by those who believed her to be a model of the perfect romantic friendship as an expression of platonism which delighted not in physicality but in the union of souls and in philosophizing and poetizing."[12] Just as Jeremy Taylor viewed them in fact. The relationships are not courtly posturing: they are real and involve tension and irony as they are played out in art and life.

Taylor and Orinda also differ about the relationship of friendship to marriage. Taylor asserts precisely that no friend can be more than husband or wife "because the marriage is the Queen of friendships, in which there is a communication of all that can be communicated by friendship: and it being made sacred by vows and love, by bodies and souls, by interest and custome, by religion and by laws, by common counsels and common fortunes; it is the principal in the kind of friendship, and the measure of all the rest" (p. 80). Orinda measured this conventional idealism by her experience as a woman who believed, as we have seen, that friendship is a nobler relationship than those to spouse or family because it is more free. Friendship is pure, whereas marriage may be corrupted by lust or interest:

> All love is sacred, and the Marriage-tie
> Hath much of Honour and Divinity.
> But Lust, Design, or some unworthy ends
> May mingle there, which are despised by Friends.
>
> (P. 79)

From her earliest juvenalia, Philips had been skeptical about romantic love and the marriage relationship.[13]

But the problem revealed in *Orinda's Letters to Poliarchus* and her poems is that a prior friendship among women seldom survives the marriage of one of them. Rosania seems to have been the first defector from friendship to marriage, and her betrayal is chronicled in "Rosania's Private Marriage" (pp. 52–53), "Injuria Amicitiae" (pp. 53–55), "Philoclea's Parting" (p. 56), and "To Rosania, now Mrs. Montague, being with her" (pp. 56–58), when Orinda writes:

> Divided Rivers lose their name;
> And so our too unequal flame
> Parted, will Passion be in me,
> And an Indifference in Thee.
>
> (P. 57)

Orinda continues to address poems to Mrs. M. A., Rosania, but they are those of a loyal friendship that is not reciprocated. In the meantime, Orinda's relationship to Lucasia is idealized and explored as a contrast to the perfidious Rosania: "Hail Great *Lucasia,* thou shalt doubly shine, / What was *Rosania's* own is now twice thine" (p. 106).

The rest of the personal drama is shadowed for the reader in a poem, "To my dearest friend Mrs. A Owen, upon her greatest loss," a eulogy of Lucasia's husband with whom the poem foresees a reunion on the day of judgment (pp. 137–39). After that there are poems of parting with Lucasia and other poems of mourning and separation from others until the poem that ends the poetry in the volume of 1667: "To my Lord and Lady *Dungannon* in their Marriage 11. May 1662," which commemorates Lucasia's marriage to a person Orinda found entirely unsympathetic. Although she sailed with the pair to Ireland after their wedding, disillusionment with Lucasia's husband and with Lucasia, too, quickly set in, and so she wrote to Poliarchus in the next year: "I find too there are few Friendships in the World Marriage proof; especially when the Person our Friend marries has not a Soul particularly capable of the Tenderness of that Endearment, and solicitous of advancing the noble Instances of it, as Pleasure of their own" (pp. 57–58). If friendship between equals was the nobler relationship, Orinda's experience taught her that it could seldom resist pressures from the interest, vows, and custom that sustained marriage.

Friendship, then, as often faced Orinda with abandonment as would sexual relationships. In fact, friendships allowed Orinda to write about abandonment within the context of a happy marriage to Antenor, whose interests she pursued abroad, but he should not be responsible for her errors while he was at home: "My Love and Life I must confess are thine, / But not my Errours, they are only mine" (p. 47). Thus she managed to have the drama of separation within the wider context of a carefully preserved marriage.

Although Røstvig characterizes Orinda as an innocent Epicurean, there is a dark side to the poet's experience because of a variety of losses: her infant son, her friends, the world radically disrupted by the civil war, and frequently the death of children not her own. Indeed, the deaths of children brought her, like most of us, to the very heart of loss:

> Alas! we were secure of our content;
> But find too late that it was onely lent,
> To be a Mirror wherein we may see
> How frail we are, how spotless we should be.
>
> (P. 41)

She saw that our lives teeter constantly on the brink of loss, a feeling that the civil war greatly intensified in Orinda, and she saw happiness and contentment as a person's decisive commitment to "valuing only what he cannot lose" (p. 118). In that sense her experience of loss would "steel the soul," as Lawrence Lipking has it.[14] Her poems in this mode are more personal than the poems on traditional themes and contain telling details. For example, her epitaph for her son, born after seven years of marriage and dead at six weeks, asks, "What on Earth deserves our trust?" and the question is echoed in the next poem (in the 1667 edition) "On the death of my Lord Rich, only Son to the Earl of Warwick, who dyed of the small Pox, 1664," which ends "For since such expectations brittle prove, / What can we safely either Hope or Love?" (p. 136). Nothing in Orinda's experience led her to trust the world, and so her ideal was a personal integrity that limited investment in others and valued command of the self. The retirement discourse offered a moral vocabulary, and the models that she saw in her world had a telling personal integrity that could sustain disaster with poise and certainty of purpose.

In his elegy for Orinda, Cowley says,

> *Orinda* does our boasting Sex out-do
> Not in wit only, but in virtue too:
> She does above our best examples rise,
> In hate of vice, and scorn of vanities.
>
> (Sig. g)

And indeed, when she thought of her own death, Orinda wanted to have achieved a moral distinction:

> If I be sure my Soul is safe,
> And that my Actions will provide
> My Tomb a nobler Epitaph,
> Then that I only liv'd and dy'd.
>
> (P. 120)

In setting forth moral ideals in her poetry, Orinda proceeds by a favorite seventeenth-century device, the character. She turns elegies, poems of tribute, and occasional verses into opportunities to celebrate qualities she valued in those around her. As Cowley implies, she proceeds by example more than precept.

Orinda had definite ideals that applied to both genders, even if women enjoyed a more restricted sphere in which to act. She develops her model woman in an early elegy "In memory of that excellent person Mrs. *Mary Lloyd* of *Bodidrift* in *Denbigh-shire*, who died Nov. 13. 1656. after she came thither from *Pembroke-shire*." The poem begins by instructing the "brutish" in Mrs. Lloyd's virtues. She fulfilled the conventional roles of woman: she was meek, prudent, obedient. Her family was a well-ordered commonwealth; she was a fine sister and friend and so pious that she scarcely changed company when she died. Her griefs are what give Mary Lloyd's example individuality: she maintained composure while her world collapsed around her; her husband's death was followed rapidly by the loss of all her sons and then litigation to deprive her of her rights. All these sufferings she bore with the equanimity that Philips invariably admires most:

> But she, though sensible, was still the same,
> Of a resigned Soul, untainted Fame,
> Nor were her Virtues coarsely set, for she
> Out-did Example in Civility.
>
> (P. 44)

While the world went to pieces, Mary Lloyd chose to shine in retirement, bringing out the best in others. At the end she went home to die, to be buried with her mate and to be remembered as a saint. The ideals are those of the stoic *beatus vir.*

Orinda's panegyric to Francis Finch, the author of *Discourse on Friendship,* develops similar masculine ideals. He is accomplished but without pride. He has integrity in an uncertain world: "He's his own Happiness and his own Law" (p. 72). His soul is harmonious and peaceful; he makes love turn into friendship and turns honor inward, "free / From Titles and from Popularity." (p. 73) Another meditative poem, "The Resvery," pictures an angry, chaotic, ruined world in which Orinda's ideal of manhood stands out like a jewel in the dark. The model again dares to be good when all around him are fearful and punish virtue as a crime. This is a man who will sacrifice himself for a friend, "who where he gives a Heart bestows it whole." (p. 87) Like Finch, he is above ambition, greed, and prosperity.

> Whose Happiness in ev'ry Fortune lives,
> For that is Fortune either takes or gives;
> Who no unhandsome ways can bribe his Fate,
> Nay, out of prison marches through the Gate;

Who losing all his Titles and his Pelf,
Nay, all the world, can never lose himself.

(P. 88)

Orinda was a better model for other women writers than she was a creative artist, though, as Røstvig suggests, her simplicity was appealing to
readers in the late seventeenth and early eighteenth centuries. Unlike Cavendish she was not eccentric, but found a central place in mainstream
discourse and was therefore very influential. Her poetry was widely read:
her poems were pirated in 1664, edited by Cotterell in 1667, and reprinted
in 1669, 1678, and 1710. She forged a distinctive stance within a discourse to claim for women the ability to build and sustain significant friendships, to voice a healthy skepticism about romantic love and marriage,
to realize identity and integrity in private worlds, and to write about their
personal experience of relationships and of loss. For a woman of middling
background who died at thirty-three in a chaotic age, setting those themes
was no mean achievement.

Angry Voices

Anne Killigrew (1660–85)

Anne Killigrew enjoyed the same kind of acceptance by men that greeted
Orinda. Dryden's ode to her has made her famous to readers who have
never read a word she wrote. Because she also had higher social status—
she was a maid of honor to the duchess of York—and seems to have had
what Ballard calls "the advantage of a polite education," her poetry gave
promise of surpassing Orinda's at the time of her death at twenty-five.[15]
She was apparently more comfortable with the privilege of writing than
was Orinda and so she seldom used undoing with regard to her art. Instead she saw her verse as giving her immortality: "When I am Dead,
few Friends attend my Hearse, / And for a Monument, I leave my VERSE."[16]
Killigrew is the only poet descended from Orinda who made the conventional male claim of gaining immortality through her verse.[17] Distinctive
about her spirit and her verse is a masculine tone, possibly absorbed from
her considerable education.

Dryden links Killigrew to Orinda in his ode because both died early of
smallpox:

O double Sacriledge on things Divine,
To rob the Relique, and deface the Shrine!

But thus Orinda dy'd:
Heav'n, by the same Disease, did both translate,
As equal were their Souls, so equal was their Fate.

(Sig.b')

The connection between Orinda and Killigrew is not original with Dryden;
he was following a linkage forged by Killigrew, who saw herself as Orinda's
heir, though more victimized because an envious age labeled her poetry as
plagarized: "only to Me alone / Will not allow, what I do write my Own"
(p. 47). Yet Orinda, Killigrew observed, was thought even greater than male
rivals because a woman and a poet:

Orinda (Albions and her Sexes Grace)
Ow'd not her Glory to a Beautous Face,
It was her Radiant Soul that shon Within,
Which struk a Lustre through her Outward Skin;
That did her Lips and Cheeks with Roses dy,
Advanc't her Height, and Sparkled in her Eye.
Nor did her Sex at all obstruct her Fame,
But higher 'mong the Stars it fixt her Name;
What she did write, not only all allow'd,
But ev'ry Laurel, to her Laurel, bow'd!

(P. 46)

The bond between the two poets is by no means superficial. Killigrew's
perceptions of the world echo Orinda's. Although Killigrew escaped the
civil war, her sense of the world as a vicious place, hostile to the best that
is in humankind, was more intense, but similar to Orinda's darker moments
of loss. In two long poems, "The Miseries of Man" and "The Discontent,"
Killigrew recounted the evils of the human condition, and provided different reactions to them. "The Miseries" uses pastoral conventions, nymphs
mourning in Arcadia, to question heroic values. The nymphs first review
the poverty and sickness that afflict human kind, but find that men inflict
the worst evils upon one another. Throughout a long middle section, the
poem becomes a diatribe against war:

And yet as if these Evils were too few,
Men their own Kind with hostile Arms pursue;
Not Heavens fierce Wrath, nor yet the Hate of Hell,

Not any Plague that e're the World befel,
Not Inundations, Famines, Fires blind rage,
Did ever Mortals equally engage,
As Man does Man, more skilful to annoy,
Both Mischievous and Witty to destroy.

(Pp. 36–37)

No savage animal is more cruel to its own kind than man. The poem continues with images of thousands lying dead and mutilated on battlefields. A wife saying a fearful farewell to a husband who rides off "born by a brave disdain" may seek him later among the dead: "by rough Encounters broke and tore, / His Face and hair, with Brains all clotted ore, / And Warlike Weeds besmear'd with Dust and Gore" (p. 38). Instead of condemning those who kill as murderers, we give them fame: "Only to fill the future Tromp of Fame, / Though greater Crimes, than Glory it proclaime" (p. 39). The poem ends with the Platonic image of Reason in a chariot, aided by Laws, controlling the sources of conflict: Anger, Fear, and Desire. Killigrew's female vision of war is similar to Cavendish's, but its effect is greatly intensified for the reader by a painter's visual imagination. The poem is highly unusual in presenting antiwar themes with an epic and classical vocabulary. The effect is subversive to the tradition.

In the second poem, "The Discontent," depression about the world drives the speaker into a catatonic state. The scope is larger than "The Miseries," but the poem is made to seem more the result of the speaker's mood than a balanced reaction: "there's nothing Good, / Nought that the World can show, / Nought that it can bestow" (p. 52). The mood of the poem is Hamlet's. Not gold, or power, fame, titles can please, or even friendship because "No happy Two ere felt an Equal Flame." The speaker's reaction to this disillusionment is not Hamlet's hysterical locquacity, but an ego restriction so profound it is akin to death:

All that's past, present and to come I may forget:
  The Lovers sighs, and the Afflicteds Tears,
  What e're may wound my Eyes or Ears,
  The grating Noise of Private Jars.
  The horrid sound of Publick Wars,
  Of babling Fame the Idle Stories,
  The short-liv'd Triumphs Noysy-Glories,
  The Curious Nets the subtile weave,
  The Word, the Look that may deceive.
No Mundane Care shall more affect my Breast,

80

My profound Peace shake or molest:
But *Stupor,* like to Death, my Senses bind,
   That so I may anticipate that Rest,
Which only in my Grave I hope to find.

                (P. 56)

The mood Killigrew portrays here is like Winchilsea's treatment of severe depression in *The Spleen,* but Killigrew is so dramatic a poet that we tend not to identify the mood as her own. She was the Cassandra of her generation.

The moral stances Killigrew assumed in numerous poems are much akin to Orinda's. Her ideal was to ask as little as possible of the world, to resist passion by schooling the emotions, and listen to the world as Ulysses heard the Siren's song (p. 15). For example, she uses the character as Orinda does in "On the Dutchess of Grafton" and praises a self-sufficient beauty that asks nothing from her surroundings:

'Tis Am'rous Beauty Love invites,
A Passion, like it self, excites:
The Paragon, though all admire,
Kindles in none a fond desire:
No more than those the Kings Renown
And State applaud, affect his Crown.

                (P. 80)

There is a fear of being vulnerable to the world that is a definite strain in the Orinda tradition. If one does not heed the world, one will not be hurt by it: the goal is a resolute self-sufficiency, which Killigrew, however, did not attach to retirement themes.

Killigrew treats the vulnerability of maidens in love in three pastoral dialogues. In the simplest of the three, *A Pastoral Dialogue,* she defines the importance of a maiden's choosing carefully in love for she may easily be betrayed: "Tis not enough a Maidens Heart is chast, / It must be Single, and not once mis-plac't" (p. 12). The second dialogue takes place between a wise and virtuous woman, Alinda, and her lover, Amintor. Alinda understands that men are cruel in love, and sometimes the injury women experience kills them. Amintor protests that he loves Alinda for her fine character: her piety, strictness, the fetters on her beauty, her virtue; she replies that if ever she does love, she will love Amintor, but when he begins again to plead, she leaves.

The third dialogue is an even stronger indictment of men in love. Melibaeus, an old man, tells the story of Rodanthe to some nymphs and a pair of lovers. Its upshot is the ruin of Rodanthe:

Hapless Rodanthe, the Fond Rover caught,
To whom, for Love, with usual Arts he sought;
Which she, ah too unwary, did bestow:
'Cause True her self, believ'd that he was so.
But he, alas, more wav'ring than the Wind,
Streight broke the Chain, she thought so fast did bind;
For he no sooner saw her Heart was gain'd,
But he as soon the Victory disdain'd.

(P. 68)

Of the listening couple, the woman is shaken, but the man protests that Melibaeus lacks compassion for youth because of his age. We then learn that the protesting youth has loved and left other nymphs himself. And so we find that Killigrew also was haunted by abandonment and skeptical about romantic love. The "Fond Rover" did not enchant her as he did Aphra Behn and her audiences. The daughters of Orinda and those of Behn saw the same problem: how is a woman to cope with abandonment and the double standard? But their artistic and life solutions to the problem differ widely. Killigrew's poems are cautionary: like all Orinda's daughters she admired those who seek a shelter from the world and maintain their integrity. Because she died so young, we do not know how her thinking might have developed on this crucial question.

Although Killigrew followed Lipking's model in many respects, as we have seen, she did not fashion her poetry to herself. Killigrew was bolder in attitudes and in poetic style than any writer in the Orinda tradition. Possibly this was the result of her classical education, everywhere evident in her poetry. A well-defined role at court may have given her confidence in herself. She was clearly drawn to the active, male genres—the epic and the drama. Her two striking poems about Saint John the Baptist and Herodias, dramatic monologues in which she powerfully evokes Herodias's perception of Saint John, are evidence of this talent. Another is the unfinished "Penelope to Ulysses," which again creates a woman's perspective on the important events of a male world. Dryden seems to have alluded to this capacity for dramatizing a female perspective on famous events when he said:

Art she had none, yet wanted none
For Nature did that Want supply
So rich in Treasures of her Own,
She might our boasted Stores defy:

Such Noble Vigour did her Verse adorn,
That it seem'd borrow'd, where 'twas only born.
(Sig. a3ᵛ)[18]

Here Dryden describes a poet who did not need the male "boasted Stores," but her natural gifts made her poetry seem borrowed from the male tradition; she was a poet who might, as we have seen, use an epic vocabulary to write a poem against war. Had she lived, she might have developed into a significant writer of dramatic monologues or into a fine dramatist. As it is, in a very short lifetime she created a unique voice in seventeenth-century English poetry.

Mary Astell (1668–1731)

Anyone who attempts to situate Mary Astell among the women who raised their voices at the end of the seventeenth century is now fundamentally in debt to Ruth Perry's excellent biography *The Celebrated Mary Astell* (1986), which makes original materials available for the first time and provides a thorough and sensitive account of Astell's life and writing.[19] Viewed from the perspective of the traditions observed in this book, Mary Astell's first work, *A Serious Proposal to the Ladies* (1694), represents a culmination of many of the ideas about women in the school of Orinda, whose name is invoked on an early page: "Remember, I pray you, the famous Women of former Ages, the *Orinda's* of late, and the more Modern *D'acier* and others, and blush to think how much is now, and will hereafter be said of them, when you your selves (as great a Figure as you make) must be buried in silence and forgetfulness?"[20]

Mary Astell may have seen herself as a descendent of Orinda, but she far exceeded her model. Although her proposal has many of the key attributes we have identified in the Orinda tradition, Astell's intellectual scope and rigor push the themes into dimensions far beyond any that Orinda could have envisioned, as we shall see. But first the similarities in their thinking. Astell proposes a school intended for single gentlewomen, a retreat from the temptations of worldly life, in order that the women may develop their minds and set their souls on the hereafter, rather than on frivolous pastimes. Such women would enjoy self-esteem and the integrity Orinda valued:

Let us learn to pride our selves in something more excellent than the invention of a Fashion, and not entertain such a degrading thought of our own *Worth,* as to imagine that our Souls were given us only for the service of our Bodies, and that the best improvement we can

83

make of these, is to attract the Eyes of Men. We value *them* too much, and our *selves* too little, if we place any part of our desert in their Opinion, and don't think our selves capable of nobler Things than the pitiful Conquest of some worthless heart. (Pp. 14–15)

Astell was intellectually more daring than Orinda and most of her followers, but her desire for women to have inner resources that would make them autonomous was very similar to Orinda's belief in loving only what one cannot lose. Astell was, to be sure, far less worldly than Orinda; and in her singleness, men held only intellectual attractions for Astell. So she carried Orinda's ideal of female friendship and praise of country life to a vision of a community of women, bound to one another in friendship and mutual esteem, in a supportive religious retirement, free from interest, lust, or ambition, bent on knowing the truth and achieving salvation. Orinda sought a balance between conventional marriage and strong attachments to women with definite erotic overtones; Astell finally rejected the idea of marriage for a few women like herself and idealized friendship that was spiritualized but existed solely among women:

> Farther yet, besides that holy emulation which a continual view of the brightest and most exemplary lives will excite in us; we shall have opportunity of contracting the purest and noblest Friendship; a Blessing, the purchase of which were richly worth all the world besides! For she who possesses a worthy Person, has certainly obtain'd the richest Treasure! a Blessing that Monarchs may envy, and she who enjoys it happier than she who fills a Throne! (Pp. 133–34)

In sum, the ideas and themes that Orinda and her followers had entertained for individuals or coteries Astell generalized for all women and proposed institutionalizing in a college. Astell saw a justification for women's mental abilities, not just in the example of Orinda, but in the achievements of learned Tudor women, made known by William Wotten's *Reflections upon Ancient and Modern Learning* (1694), and in the models from the French salons.[21]

Despite the generality of her claims for women, however, Astell accepted boundaries within society that were similar to those Orinda accepted. Although the gentlewomen joining the college (they would need to invest five or six hundred pounds to join) would develop their minds and their religious exercises, they were not to prepare for the learned professions or for teaching. They were only to serve as examples to the rest of their sex to lead better and more useful lives, but still within the narrow confines prescribed by society. Like Orinda, Astell was socially conservative. Although she understood, as a good Cartesian, that the conventional arguments about women's natural inferiority were really based on custom, not reason, she accepted as divinely ordained the family structure and social hierarchy of her day. Within these structures Astell saw rather bleak options for women: they could fix their vision on eternity, in which souls were equal, in order to bear better present oppression; they could remain single, daring not to elect a monarch for life, and endure all the problems of support and marginality; they could, through luck and wit, find a mate who was in fact an intellectual and moral equal and therefore make a tolerable marriage. What they could not do was change the power structures within society, even though it was clear to Astell that the Old Testament depictions of women's status were historically based.[22] The continuous questioning of authority during the seventeenth century that inspired some dissenting theorists to question current family structures only frightened royalists like Orinda and Astell, who could not follow out the social consequences of their values and commitments about women. Yet though we acknowledge their conservatism, we must also recognize the deep anger and pessimism of writers like Mary Astell and Lady Mary Chudleigh: they saw marriage as a bleak destiny, so bleak they were willing to counsel against it for some women or to propose structures that would enable some women virtuously to resist it.

Though feminist historians and critics have resisted asking the question, one may wonder why an ascetic, pious single woman, whose main interests were religion and philosophy, would write a pamphlet on marriage—even in a single afternoon.[23] Ostensibly, Astell was inspired by the conflicts of authority that arose in the Mazarin case, which may have interested her in part because the duchess was a neighbor in Chelsea. Still it does seem strange that *Some Reflections upon Marriage* (1700) was inspired by the sordid struggle of Hortense Mazarin and the duke of Meilleraye and Mayenne. It seems likely that Astell's concern for women in general, whose one life choice was marriage, had more to do with Astell's writing the essay, which is quite different in subject and purpose from anything else she wrote. The Mazarin case may simply have kept the issue before her, concerning a neighbor as it did.

By 1700 Astell had a considerable reputation as an advocate: both parts of *A Serious Proposal* and her letters to Norris had established her skills. As a result, a number of essays had been attributed to her. In 1696 *An Essay in Defence of the Female Sex* appeared, with three editions by 1697, as did *Six Familiar Essays upon Marriage*, and *A farther Essay Relating to the Female-Sex*. All of these have been ascribed to Astell because, like her, their authors, male or female, draw upon Cartesian thinking made current in England by the translations of Poulain de La Barre's *De l'égalité des deux sèxes* in 1677 and Jacques du Bosc's *The Excellent Woman* in 1682.[24] Instead of having the views of others attributed to her, Mary Astell decided to speak for herself—in fact, to write the best essay on the subject in the period.

The essays of others she is supposed to have authored, along with Egerton's *The Female Advocate* (1686) and Lady Mary Chudleigh's *The Ladies Defence* (1701), form a context in which to place Astell's important statement.
An Essay in Defence of the Female Sex is a thoughtful and serious work based
on premises that would appeal to Astell. The essay asserts that the cause
of women's inferiority to men is cultural, that women are purposely kept
in ignorance to oppress them:

> This is our Case; for Men being sensible as well of the Abilities of
> Mind in our Sex, as of the strength of Body in their own, began to
> grow Jealous, that we, who in the Infancy of the World were their
> Equals and Partners in Dominion, might in process of Time, by Sub-
> tlety and Strategem, become their Superiours; and therefore began
> in good time to make use of Force (the Origine of Power) to compell
> us to a Subjection, Nature never meant; and made use of Natures Lib-
> erality to them to take the benefit of her kindness from us. From that
> time they have endeavour'd to train us to do to those, they reduce
> by Force, that so they may disarm 'em, both of Courage and Wit; and
> consequently make them tamely give up their Liberty, and abjectly
> submit their Necks to a slavish Yoke.[25]

As Hilda Smith points out, the reasoning of *An Essay* is largely based on
Locke rather than Descartes.[26] The main purpose of the essay is to help
women understand their own oppression and resist it through getting a
sound education and looking to books to build their self-esteem rather
than internalizing the negative male images of them. If women build up
their natural intelligence and their capacities to deal with the world, males—
especially, thoughtful males—may wish to converse and enjoy the company
of women rather than belittling them, to the ultimate detriment of both
genders. About the problem that women are barred from Greek and Latin,
the essay is pragmatic: women should not let such limits discourage them
from the pursuit of learning; there are translations, and one can learn a
great deal from all the books written in English. Skepticism about reasoning
from nature or from the authority of the ancients is characteristic of the
lively thought of the eighties and nineties; and these essays, whatever their
persuasion or method, share those premises. We have observed in analyzing
Cavendish's speculations that skepticism cuts across political and religious
convictions in the seventeenth century. The essay concludes with some satiric characters which demonstrate that men have just as many defects as
women. The effect of the whole is to assert the social construction of gender and lay foundations for insights that interrogate all authority: antique,
biblical, and natural.

Six Familiar Essays upon Marriage was attributed to Mary Astell because it is ironic in tone and was published anonymously. It is an analysis of several kinds of bad marriages that flourish in English society, and is addressed to an unhappily married friend of the author. The friend's husband has deserted her, and the author gives her friend the conventional wisdom of the time: simply bear the wrong; do not quarrel or separate because all conflict is worse for a woman than a bad marriage. Mistresses are identified as the causes of most marital unhappiness, but it is dangerous for a wife to adopt a gallant because of the double standard. The author recognizes the many foibles of husbands—infidelity, drunkenness, gambling—but counsels against revenge; she would entreat injured wives "that they would banish all anger out of their breasts for one year, and then tell me if they have not more content in forgiving than returning a reproach."[27] The imputed reader is given a few examples of why marriages turn bad because of "inequalities" of wealth, age, or social status, and is finally consoled that her husband's desertion is a deliverance from his bad behavior. Although this essay preaches the socially constrained bromides of the day, its comments about marriage are sufficiently acerbic to add to the growing critique of the institution at the turn of the century.

A farther Essay Relating to the Female-Sex is written in a male voice, and contains a good deal of satire about women; but its basic claim is similar to those of the others just described: it would have women control their lives within their social confines and achieve the education to do so. The author of A farther Essay is, however, not always in control of his tone and effect; and so the characters that are satiric about women—the coquette, the opinionated woman, the hypocrite, the litigious woman—give way to such gusto that his serious purpose is sometimes lost and the essay has the same frivolous, self-conscious tone that others which enter the controversy about women only to sell books have throughout the century. Yet beneath this shallow style, there is a discernible theme of women's gaining knowledge so that they may control their passions, especially avarice or stinginess, as well as other excesses that may lead to abuse of their families. Part 2 counsels against self-love, especially in women, who are prone to it because of their lack of education and their social conditioning; but the book ends with a character of the beau who is consumed with self-love. The writer's conclusion is that if women can conquer self-love, "it must be confest that by vanquishing so obdurate a passion, they would gain more Honour, than men by their Fortitude and Valour, have obtain'd by their Renowned Conquests for many Ages."[28] Although the author's tone and perspective waver, the final effect is a plea for women to take charge of their lives.

When one puts Mary Astell's *Reflections* into this context, it seems both less original and more extraordinary. Astell's essay appears conventional in its descriptions of the miseries of enforced marriage, in its cautions not to retaliate against faithless husbands, in its warnings about predatory gallants, in its analyses of the sources of bad marriages (marrying for money, marrying for beauty, male infidelity), and in its conservative attitude toward the institution. All of these points we have seen made by Astell's lesser contemporaries. Extraordinary about her work are her anger, which drives a brilliant, ironic style, and her force of intellect, which leads her to follow logic in her arguments farther than others can and therefore to produce a radical statement. Her description of the realities of the marriage relationship will allow the reader to see her style and her anger:

> Let the Business be carried as prudently as it can be on the Woman's Side, a reasonable Man can't deny that she has by much the Harder Bargain: because she puts herself entirely into her Husband's Power, and if the Matrimonial Yoke be grievous, neither Law not Custom afford her the Redress which a Man obtains. He who has the Sovereign Power does not value the Provocations of a Rebellious Subject; he knows how to subdue him with Ease, and will make himself obey'd: But Patience and Submission are the only Comforts that are left to the poor People, who groan under Tyranny, unless they are Strong enough to break the Yoke, to Depose and Abdicate, which, I doubt, would not be allow'd of here. For whatever may be said against Passive-Obedience in another case, I suppose there's no Man but likes it very well in this; how much soever Arbitrary Power may be dislik'd on a Throne, not *Milton*, not B. H.[oadley], nor any of the Advocates of Resistance, would cry up Liberty to poor *Female Slaves*, or plead for the Lawfulness of Resisting a private Tyranny. (P. 35)

Only Astell understood that the crucial interpretations of marriage in her time hinged on notions of authority, and she made a rueful mockery of thinkers like Milton, who brought down a patriarchal king but would preserve a patriarchal marriage and family. She understood power and how it worked in marriage: "It is the hardest Thing in the World for a Woman to know that A Man is not Mercenary, that he does not act on base or ungenerous Principles, even when he is her Equal, because being absolute Master, she and all the Grants he makes her are in his Power" (p. 42). What is to be done? Women must be as careful as possible to resist male strategems and marry a man with good understanding, a virtuous mind, and as much her equal as may be. The prospect is not heartening, and Astell's representation of men is searing throughout.

The most radical part of *Reflections* was the appendix to the fourth edition (1730), material published in prefaces of previous editions in which Astell analyzes the question of male superiority. Like all Cartesians, Astell believes that custom has put women into subjection, but that does not justify their condition. Nor does biblical authority justify female inferiority because biblical statements are historically contingent: they are limited to the moments and contexts of biblical history (p. 108). If men are born free, why do women live in subjection? If daughters and wives are subject to fathers and husbands, what of unmarried women and widows? To whom do they belong? Her respect for marriage as divinely ordained does not restrain her in her presentation of the subjection of women:

> What though a Husband can't deprive a Wife of Life without being responsibile to the Law, he may, however, do what is much more grievous to the generous Mind, render Life miserable, for which she has no Redress, scarce Pity, which is afforded to every other Complainant, it being thought a Wife's Duty to suffer every thing without Complaint. If *all Men* are born *Free*, how is it that all Women are born Slaves? As they must be, if the being subjected to the *inconstant, uncertain, unknown, arbitrary Will* of Men be the *perfect Condition of Slavery?* (P. 107)

Astell is not optimistic about changes, however: she believes that most women love their chains, and she finds no great comfort in Queen Anne's attitude toward women. Astell's vision was unrelenting, brilliant, and grim. Her ideas inspired Lady Mary Lee Chudleigh in her own time, and they reach us today, as they have in the past when students have had the capacity to listen. Readers who wish to study Astell's work in more detail should consult both Hilda Smith's *Reason's Disciples* and Ruth Perry's *Mary Astell*.

Another feature of *Reflections* that the reader should connect with women's writing covered in chapter 4 is the warning to women about predatory males. As the reader will discover, seventeenth-century amatory fiction, which comes largely but not exclusively from the tradition of Aphra Behn, contains overtly or in many disguises a representation of males as predatory, particularly aristocratic males who hunt innocent country girls of lower social station. It should not be lost upon us that Mary Astell, who scorned fiction as the diversion of frivolous women who lacked education and should have been reading philosophy, saw the same social predicament that the fiction writers defined: women, lacking education and converse with the world, could easily be the victims of predatory males: "It were endless to reckon up the divers Stratagems Men use to catch their Prey, their different Ways in insinuating, which vary with Circumstances, and the Lady's Temper, but how unfairly, how basely soever they proceed, when the Prey is once caught, it passes for lawful Prize, and other Men having the same Hopes and Projects, see nothing to find Fault with, but that it was not their own good Fortune" (p. 73).

Astell views marriage as the goal in her descriptions of male stratagems, but amatory fiction understands that if males can seduce their prey without vows, they will gladly do so; and the woman then most cope with the consequences, which may be immediately far more serious than the long-range consequences of a bad marriage that Astell addresses. The point is that both kinds of writing are addressed to the same female predicament: how to cope with the predatory male, with marriage or just sex on his mind. Mary Astell would probably have been offended by being linked to amatory fiction, which she despised; but the connection demonstrates the breadth of her commitment to women and the extent to which, despite their differing styles, the concerns of women writers in the seventeenth century form a seamless web.

Lady Mary Chudleigh (1656–1710)

Lady Mary Chudleigh is a descendent of Orinda, but, like all the others, she has distinctive qualities that make her unique: her intellectual scope, her anger, and her desire to reform marriage. Chudleigh is among the most overtly feminist of Orinda's artistic progeny, but her commitment to Astell accounts for her combination of conservatism with an angry critique of marriage. Chudleigh differs from Astell in advocating reform of the marriage relationship within a scathing critique of the institution as it existed. Her intensity is usually attributed to Chudleigh's personal history in an unhappy marriage, but there is no historical evidence for this idea.[29] Instead it seems likely that her angry views of marriage are directly linked to Astell's.

Chudleigh used undoing to defend her privilege in writing. When she dedicated *Poems on Several Occasions* (1703) to the queen, she feared the gesture was too assertive, so she sought the Queen's protection: "The Address has too much Confidence; the Ambition is too aspiring; But to whom should a Woman unknown to the World, and who has not Merit enough to defend her from the Censure of Criticks, fly for Protection, but to Your Majesty? The Greatest, the Best, and the Most Illustrious person of your Sex and Age."[30] In *Poems* and the later *Essays upon Several Subjects in Prose and Verse* (1710), Chudleigh was careful to say that she wrote only for women readers: "I am not so vain as to believe any thing of mine deserves the Notice of the *Man*."[31] The poems, she insisted, were written for herself: "They were the Employment of my leisure Hours, the innocent Amusement of a solitary Life: In them they'll find a Picture of my Mind, my Sentiments all lead open to their View" (Sig. A4).

When Bernard Lintott added *The Ladies Defence* (1701) to the second edition of Chudleigh's *Poems* without her consent or her preface, she was deeply offended, as she says in *Essays upon Several Subjects*, because *Defence* was written to divert some of her friends and meant only to satirize the views of Sprint; it was, she says, "a satyr on Vice, and not, as some have maliciously reported, an Invective on Marriage" (Sig. A4ᵛ). However readers took her writings, Chudleigh always insisted that she wrote to persuade women to follow the commands of virtue and rational pleasure, and to contribute to the regular conduct of their lives. She consistently denied that she wanted to make women radical: "My whole Design is to recommend Virtue, to persuade my Sex to improve their Understandings, to prefer Wisdom before Beauty, good Sense before Wealth, and the Sovereignty of their Passions before the Empire of the World" (Sig. A4ᵛ). What woman of 1710, besides Queen Anne, might aspire to Empire of the World is a question Chudleigh never raised, but her formulation of her purposes is distinctly within the tradition of Orinda through Astell.

Because Chudleigh hoped that women would make their passions submit to reason, she wanted better education for women and also that women would adopt a model of behavior like that advocated by Orinda and Killigrew, a stoic integrity:

> The way to be truly easie, to be always serene, to have our Passions under a due Government, to be wholly our own, and not to have it in the power of Accidents of things foreign to us to ruffle and disturb our Thoughts, is to retire into our selves, to live upon our own Stock, to accustom our selves to our own Conversation, to be pleas'd with nothing but what strictly and properly speaking, we may justly pretend a Right to; of which kind, such things can never be said to be, of which 'tis in the Power of Fortune to deprive us. (*Poems,* Sig A4)

According to the discourse of the retirement tradition, Chudleigh sought a repose in which one was not vulnerable, and a private life led according to reason and not the senses, which could keep one from being easily hurt:

> Those few who dare be good, must live alone
> To all mankind, except themselves, unknown:
> From a mad World, to some obscure Recess,
> They must retire, to purchase Happiness.
> (P. 31)

In addition, the innocent Epicurean linkage of retirement with the enjoyment of books makes the connection between women's education and their cultivation of the retired life.[32] Thus Chudleigh urged women readers to become as well educated as possible, to eschew a love of wealth, to read history. Women should, said Chudleigh, retire into themselves to be happy and poised: "'Tis impossible to be happy without making Reason the Standard of all our Thoughts, Words and Actions, and firmly resolving to yield a constant, ready, and cheerful Obedience to its Dictates. Those who are govern'd by Opinion, inslav'd to Custom, and Vassals to their Humours, are Objects of Pity" (Sig. A4).

Chudleigh believed in retirement into a private world similar to that idealized by Orinda, and she believed just as ardently in friendship. In "The Wish," for example, the speaker expresses a longing for just one kind and faithful friend because then she would not envy anyone; friendship, the poem says, "is a bliss divine" (p. 35). Like other descendants of Orinda, Chudleigh was skeptical about sexual love: "A Dialogue between Alexis and Astra" reveals that the true affection is that removed from sense. Chudleigh's pseudonym was Marissa, and in that persona she addressed many poems to female friends. Unlike sexual love, friendship is constant and is a commitment to virtue:

> My Love to Virtue, Love to you,
> Was ever strong, and ever true;
> And still the same shall ever prove;
> Nothing my fixt Resolves shall move.
> (P. 114)

Chudleigh's vision of friendship was less an exploration of personal emotions in a safe relationship, as it was for Orinda, than a fixed moral commitment in an unkind world. Despite her sense of the uncertainty and vanity of the world, Orinda's happy relationships with many men and women contrast with Chudleigh's argumentive and solitary spirit. Orinda could manipulate the social system; Chudleigh wanted to change the relationships of men and women. The vision of female friendship became a reassuring anchor in her struggle with a hostile male world:

> To your loved bosom pleased Marissa flies;
> That place where sacred friendship gives a right,
> And where ten thousand charms invite,
> Let others power and awful greatness prize.
> (*WD*, 274)

Chudleigh's long dialogue poem *The Ladies Defence* ends with a vision of the reward women will experience from pursuing virtue in spite of misogyny:

> Thus will we live, regardless of your Hate,
> 'Till re-admitted to our former State;

92

> Where, free from the Confinement of our Clay,
> In glorious Bodies we shall bask in Day,
> And with enlightened Minds new Scenes survey . . .
>
> We shall, well-pleas'd, eternally converse,
> And all the Sweets of sacred Love possess:
> Love, freed from all the gross Allays of Sense,
> So pure, so strong, so constant, so intense,
> That it shall all our Faculties employ,
> And leave no Room for any Thing but Joy.
>
> (Pp. 268–69)

The idea of the equality of souls before God is mirrored in pure female friendship, which will be continued in an even better state after death. The notion is empowering and also consolatory for women's earthly predicament.

In the meantime, Chudleigh idealized the retreat from the world dear to Orinda and Mary Astell. The retreat is a place where she can be free to be herself—intellectual, self-sufficient, contemplative:

> When all alone in some belov'd retreat,
> Remote from noise, from business, and from strife,
> Those constant cursed attendants of the great;
> I freely can with my own thoughts converse,
> And clothe them in ignoble verse,
> 'Tis then I taste the most delicious feast of life:
> There, uncontrolled I can my self survey,
> And from observers free,
> My intellectual powers display.
>
> (*WD*, 274)

Chudleigh's intellectual powers, like those of Mary Astell, were considerable, and she made significant contributions to the poetry of retirement. She combines John Norris's Platonic vision of retired happiness in the pleasures of the mind and the contemplation of the beauties flowing from the Almighty Creator.[33] For Chudleigh the retired life is one of study, for which only a select few are suited. Less religious than her predecessors, she finds satisfaction in a vision of the soul soaring above the earth to achieve greater understanding and knowledge of reality, rather than a mystic union with the Creator.

Chudleigh follows the tradition of Orinda in writing much occasional verse upon personal events: she shapes her poetry to herself. Reading through *Poems on Several Occasions*, we learn of her grief at the death of her daughter and of her mother, of her gratitude to the physician who saved another child's life, of her reading in religious writers, philosophers, history, and antique poetry. But far more important than her conformity to the model of Orinda is Chudleigh's deviance: the intensity of her anger at women's predicament and her forging that anger into one of the first clear definitions of the social terms of their condition.

Chudleigh, inspired by Mary Astell's example as a serious scholar and as an analyst of marriage, was among the first English women to view women as a social group with a unique set of problems.[34] Yet Chudleigh's moment arose in the characteristic turmoil of the century: controversy over wifely obedience. If John Sprint had not existed and written his now-famous sermon *The Bride-Womans Counsellor* (1699), Chudleigh would have had to invent him. His sermon provided her with a perfect occasion to develop ideas that she summarizes in the feminist poem that appeared in the first edition of *Poems* (1703): "To the Ladies." In that virtually unique statement, Chudleigh warns other women of the tyranny of men in marriage and the corresponding lack of status married women have:

> Wife and servant are the same,
> But only differ in name.
> For when that fatal knot is ty'd,
> Which nothing, nothing can divide:
> When she the word *obey* has said,
> And man by law supreme has made,
> Then all that's kind is laid aside,
> And nothing left but state and pride.
>   (*FF*, 237)

The poem characteristically develops memorable definitions of the marriage relationship without any hope for change:

> Him still must serve, him still obey,
> And nothing act, and nothing say.
> But what her haughty Lord thinks fit,
> Who with the power, has all the wit.

Although it is bleak about changes in the marital relationship, the poem is not unresolved. It urges women to shun marriage and to "value yourselves, and men despise, / You must be proud, if you'll be wise." This is a conclusion similar to that expressed a few years later by Defoe in *Good Advice to the Ladies; that as the World goes & is Like to Go, the best Way for them is to remain Unmarried* (1702). As we learn in reading *The Ladies Defence*, Chudleigh was convinced that men would not change their treatment of women because the difference in status was in men's interests, and so she felt that if changes were to take place, they would have to be in women's attitudes toward themselves and in the personal resources they brought to their condition. The greatest danger, Chudleigh perceptively saw, was that women would internalize the misogynistic images of them and accept the slavery of a marriage forced upon them by the interests of their fathers: "Men believe they have a right to dispose of their Children as they please" (*FF*, 218). Furthermore, in her *Essays upon Several Subjects*, Chudleigh was concerned that by overvaluing riches women might be "under the Temptation of selling their Liberty." Instead, for their own good, "they would, in their Marriages, prefer Virtue before a Title, good Sense before an Estate, and choose a Man of Honour in Rags, rather than a Vicious Prince, though he were Master of the World" (pp. 69–70). Chudleigh warns women against the twin evils of amatory fiction: interest and ambition; but her motive is to change the attitudes of women, not simply warn them about men.

Chudleigh's *Defence* was, like Mary Astell's *Some Reflections on Marriage*, a critical analysis of marriage from a woman's perspective, and the representation is depressing despite the liberating conclusion we have already acknowledged. In this dialogue Melissa, the only woman, takes on Sir John Brute, the Parson, and Sir William Loveall. As Chudleigh said, John Brute "has all the extraordinary Qualifications of an accomplish'd Husband; and to render his Character compleat, I have given him the Religion of a Wit, and the good Humour of a Critick." In her "Preface to the Reader," Chudleigh revealed one of the foremost points of her argument: "That we are generally less knowing, and less Rational than the Men, I cannot but acknowledge; but I think 'tis oftener owing to the illness of our Education, than the weakness of our Capacities" (*FF*, 217). With regard to a male audience, Chudleigh reveals three purposes: first, she would have them value virtue, good sense, and agreeable humor above beauty, wealth, or rank in their marriage choices. Second, she would have men treat their wives with affection; third, she would have men treat their wives as friends.

The dialogue itself begins with an acknowledgment that Sprint's sermon was the result of mutual anger. Sir John Brute says that the Parson writes as he does because "Resentment sparkles in each poignant line." Clearly the Parson has suffered at the hands of a wife, treatment spared Sir William, who remarks drily that "I've had Mistresses a numerous Store," but that he is unmarried by fate, not choice. The Parson then reveals that he has simply told women their duty to obey and please their husbands but all in the kindliest terms. Melissa responds that the terms of the doctrine of passive obedience are outmoded, an argument we recall from Mary Astell; Melissa observes that males who have discarded passive obedience for themselves still apply the doctine to women in marriage:

> Must we pay all, and look for none from you?
> Why are not Husbands taught, as well as we;
> Must they from all Restraints, all Laws be free?
> Passive Obedience you've to us transferr'd,
> And we must drudge in Paths where you have err'd:
> That antiquated Doctrine you disown;
> 'Tis now your Scorn, and fit for us alone.
>
> (*FF*, 220)

The Parson acknowledges that wives may earn respect and love through their obedient submission, but those relationships are not their rights. Sir John insists on the male prerogative "of being wise." Melissa chides him for not having spoken in such a fashion when he courted Lenera, but he retorts that he can't be kind to her now that he owns her.

In a long speech, Melissa then describes the plight of many women in marriage:

> Unhappy they, who by their Duty led,
> Are made the Partners of a hated Bed;
> And by their Fathers Avarice or Pride,
> To Empty Fops, or nauseous Clowns are ty'd . . .
> They are like Victims the the Altar led,
> Born to Destruction, and for Ruin bred;
> Forc'd to sigh out each long revolving Year,
> And see their Lives all spent in Toil and Care.
>
> (*FF*, 221–22)

The Parson is astonished: "Why all this Rage? We merit not your Hate; / 'Tis you alone disturb the Marriage State." And the reverend concludes that women "need all the Aid that I can give, / To make you unrepining Vassals live" (*FF*, 223). Sir John adds that wives are a nuisance and that men must roam, like Jove. Melissa protests that genuine lovers center their affection on one person, and that roving will produce anger in a mate. Sir William supports her observation: "Your barbarous Usage does Revenge produce."

The Parson replies that men will behave when women obey. In a long speech, he sees not only woman's subordination in Eve's sin but also male ill humor and haughtiness. As a result, a husband expects his humor to be matched and his moods to be manipulated. Sir John protests that women will cross men at every opportunity. The Parson reproaches Melissa for the interruption and continues his counsel that wives must adjust to their husbands: "They must Submit and flatter all their lives."

Melissa's reply is the heart of Chudleigh's thinking. She says that women are despised by those who are no better than the women they deride, but most women cannot defend themselves because they are uneducated fools:

> Who think us Creatures for Derision made,
> And the Creator with his Works upbraid;
> What he call'd Good, they proudly think not so,
> And with their Malice, their Prophaneness show.
> Yet kept from knowing what wou'd make us priz'd:
> Debarr'd from Knowledge, banish'd from the Schools,
> And with utmost Industry bred Fools.
>
> (*FF*, 229)

Melissa goes on to say that many women reinforce the misogyny of men by deriding their sex in the hope of gaining credit with men. These women are also content with being able to write, to dance and dress, and like puppets "to divert Mankind." Melissa ends by wishing that women had the necessary learning in history and the ancients to discipline their reason and earn respect. Sir William interjects that women's learning is against men's interest:

> Then blame us not if we our Int'rest mind,
> And would have Knowledge to our selves confin'd,
> Since that alone Pre-eminence does give,
> And robb'd of it we should unvalu'd live.
> While You are ignorant, we are secure,
> A little Pain will your Esteem procure.
>
> (*FF*, 231)

Sir John finds the fault in books and the Parson in women, but both believe that women should not "our Prerogative invade." Sir William pleads with Melissa that women should be content with being beautiful, a quality unique to women. Melissa replies that she values beauty slightly and that women wish only to rule their own minds.

You shall be Chief, and still your selves admire:
The Tyrant Man may still possess the Throne;
'Tis in our Minds that we wou'd Rule alone:
Those unseen Empires give us leave to sway,
And to our Reason private Homage pay:
Our struggling Passions within Bounds confine,
And to our Thoughts their proper Tasks assign.
This is the Use we wou'd of knowledge make;
You quickly wou'd the good Effects partake.

(*FF*, 233)

The idea that women must have enough education to control their own thinking about themselves is a powerful one in the period, one that is repeated in feminist discourse. Knowledge would also make women better conversationalists, better friends, neighbors, wives. Melissa gives examples of excellent learned and virtuous women. If women are better educated, Melissa speculates, the stereotypic men may not be so much tolerated by society: the military, the lawyers, courtiers, scholars, preachers, justices, knights, gentlemen, physicians, tradesmen. She says that women would be models of morality and wifely submission:

Honour and Love we'll to our Husbands give,
And ever Constant and Obedient live:
If they are ill, we'll try by gentle Ways
To lay those Tempests which their Passions raise:
But if our soft Submissions are in vain,
We'll bear our Fate, and never once complain.

(*FF*, 236)

The poem ends, as we have seen, with a vision of a female community in heaven. "To the Ladies" is more fierce than *The Ladies Defence*: the shorter poem follows out the consequences of male tyranny: only a fool would marry, given male attitudes and the conditions of the relationship. *The Defence* assumes the desire of women to conform in marrying, and so its attempt is to reform the institution through education for women and attitudinal changes.

Throughout the dialogue Chudleigh maintains that the restrictions on women's activities and education are socially grounded. Although the Parson bases women's submission on Eve's sin, he quickly moves to male habits to which women should respond. The effect of the entire poem, then, is to make women's subordination socially based. Even though Chudleigh herself never suggested or hinted that such a custom might be changed, the potential for social change is there, once female subordination is loosened from its basis in nature, reinforced by religion.

Another significant feature of the *Defence* is its resolution to effect a change not in the attitudes of men but in those of women:

> But spite of you, we'll to our selves be kind;
> Your Censures slight, your little Tricks despite,
> And make it our whole Business to be wise:
> The mean low trivial Cares of Life disdain,
> And read and think, and think and read again.
> And on our Minds bestow the utmost Pain.
> Our Souls with strictest Morals we'll adorn,
> And all your little Arts of wheedling Scorn;
> Be humble, mild, forgiving, just and true,
> Sincere to all, respectful unto you.
>
> (*FF,* 236)

The sense that through education women could change the way in which they would cope with their own predicament is both wise and powerful. It was an agenda for a woman who expected very little from men on the basis of her observation and experience, and who was also politically and socially conservative.

Chudleigh's insistence, largely through her vocabulary, that the personal is political, is among the strikingly modern features of her feminist thought. Although Astell and Egerton also understand and use the argument, Chudleigh is the most emphatic about the question, especially in *The Ladies Defence.* Chudleigh's negative view of men is by no means unique in her time. We will encounter varieties of this representation to other writers both of the Orinda and the Aphra tradition. Although the attitude produced anxiety in all the men in Chudleigh's *Defence,* the anger is more important than first it seems, for it assumes that the oppression of women is a matter of social custom and human assumption. What is customary and assumed can be changed. The shift from Cavendish's thinking about women's predicament to Chudleigh's is profound, even though both are socially and religiously conservative. Chudleigh's new assumptions are crucial to the development of genuine feminism in the seventeenth century.

We must not leave Lady Mary Chudleigh without paying tribute to her anger and her intelligence, both of which she turned into inspiring ideas for women. She seems to have been aware that her anger would frighten readers, yet she confessed about Sprint's sermon:

> Besides it vex'd me to think he should have the Satisfaction of believing, that what by Malice of some, the Neutrality of others, and the Sacredness of his Character, he was secur'd from all Opposition, and might triumph over you at his Pleasure: it also troubl'd me to find that but one of our own Sex had the Courage to enter the Lists with him [Chudleigh is referring to Eugenia, author of *The Female Advocate*, another reply to Sprint]: I know there are several other Ladies, who, if they wou'd be so kind to themselves, and you, as to undertake the Quarrel, wou'd manage it with more Learning, Eloquence and address, than I dare pretend to, as being infinitely my Superiours in all the Indowments of the Mind; but since they think it fit to decline it, I hope they will permit me to enter the Field, and try my Fortune with our mighty Antagonist. (*FF,* 214)

Her concern for all women should never be forgotten. Although she began as a writer with the apologies of a daughter of Orinda, Chudleigh's anger carried her far beyond self-deprecation. She is among the first women writers in English to address women as a group consistently.[35] Cavendish, Orinda, and Anne Killigrew assumed that they and women like them were exceptional. Mary Astell conceived her college for a few women who would serve as examples to their sex of what women could achieve. Chudleigh also began with the notion of a retired few friends who were capable of education and a virtuous life. But her anger at Sprint carried her to advocacy for all thinking women who might marry, and so, like Astell, she breaks out of the model of Orinda with which she started. Did Chudleigh understand her own anger? I believe so. In her *Essays,* addressed, as we recall, to women, she writes about anger and observes that it arises when one is powerless to prevent a harm. Then she addresses women directly: "Again, remember, that when any Man reviles or strikes you, 'tis not the Tongue that gives you the opprobrious Language, or the Hand that deals the Blow, that injures or affronts you; but 'tis your own Resentment of it that makes it such to you; When therefore you are provok'd, 'tis owing entirely to your Apprehensions of Things; therefore you ought to be very careful that you are not transported with Rage" (pp. 125–26). Lady Mary Chudleigh has the distinction of defining a major problem in women's psychological history: their tendency to internalize society's negative treatment of them to their own detriment and then to turn their anger against themselves, frequently transforming it into depression. Her insights were clear and powerful.

Another answer to Sprint's sermon was Eugenia's *Female Advocate; or a*

Plea for the just Liberty of the Tender Sex, and particularly of Married Women (1700). Chudleigh was aware that Eugenia was one of the few defenders of her sex against Sprint, and there is a good deal of common ground in Eugenia's and Chudleigh's arguments. Eugenia sets up her argument by admitting that she never had a husband, that she doesn't know Latin or Greek, but that, because she has traveled, she knows that other societies do not keep women in "a Slavery so abject as this Author would fain persuade us to."[36]

Mary Astell is for Eugenia an example of the accomplishments women are capable of, and Eugenia's purpose in writing is to encourage women to choose for their mates men who are "the Great, the Generous, the Brave and Deserving Souls, Men who will as much hate to see us uneasy as this Gentleman is afraid of coming under the Discipline of the Apron" (pp. vii–viii). She closely resembles Chudleigh and Astell in wanting women to make the wisest possible marriage choices.

Eugenia accuses Sprint of writing his sermon to gain attention and possible parishioners. She sees Sprint's doctrine as working because it blames victims for their own oppression, that he puts full responsibility for the marriage relationship on the wife, and that Sprint and his ilk find encouragement in the acquiescence of women to male dominance. She replies that good husbands do not make their wives their servants, that true companions will please men and make them happier longer than slaves, and that women should not accept their own oppression: "I think he goes a little too far when he makes it a Woman's duty to lie like a Spaniel at her Husband's feet, and suffer her self very civilly to be trampled on" (p. 40). Like Mary Astell and Chudleigh, Eugenia reproaches men for expecting women to adopt passive obedience, a doctrine men reject for themselves in relation to their governors: "So, because the Ladies can't bear so harsh and imperious a Doctrine as his is, therefore it shall be a Justification of his Doctrine that they cannot, and prov'd to be reasonable because 'tis intolerable" (p. 6).

Finally, Eugenia argues that men know very well what they expect from marriage, and they should not betray their future wives by being all flattery and tenderness beforehand and tyranny and command afterward:

> I am sure (whatever a Woman is antecedently obliged to) that when the Men shall promise and vow, when they shall protest by the most sacred things, that such shall be their Indulgence and Tenderness, as shall never give the least cause of Repentence; when they shall declare and swear to be their Servants; they hereby oblige themselves beforehand to consider the Complaints that shall be made to them, if they are severe. So that in this sort of Tyranny, a Man not only violates common Justice, but his own Vows and Obligations. This Gentleman

knows the vast difference between [Bright and Transcendental Madam!] and the *Persian* Shoo; between [Yours to the Center of the Earth, and your Servant to the Antipodes] and know your Lord and Master. (P. 54)

Eugenia would have men abandon some of the courtship conventions both genders have learned from their reading, but her polemic, like a great deal of the literature covered in this study, is monitory to women about men so that the woman reader can deal as realistically and effectively as possible with her predicament. Her argument is based on the distinctively feminist assumption that the personal is political. The political and constitutional turmoil of the seventeenth century thus had fundamental consequences for women's thinking about themselves.

Temperate Voices

Jane Barker (1652–1727?)

Jane Barker was one of the most self-conscious daughters of Orinda, and her career began in a way that would have made the identification logical. Early in her career, Barker enjoyed the encouragement of men: *Poetical Recreations: Consisting of Original Poems, Songs, Odes* (1688) was jointly created by Barker with "several gentlemen of the universities," who, we learn from the book, were friends of Barker's brother, a physician who shared his learning with her.[37] She was also apparently educated by a clergyman in Lincolnshire after her father had lost his court position and the family lived on his pension from the king after 1675.[38] We learn from the volume that, although her mother had reservations about educating her, Barker seems to have learned a good deal from her brother and his friends at Cambridge. Yet the approach her publisher took to her share of *Poetical Recreations* also used the familiar technique of undoing as he compared her poetry to that of men:

> The *First Part* of the *Miscellanies* are the effects of a Ladies Wit, and I hope all the Courtly will (though out of a complement) allow them for valuable: But however, not to say much more of her Verses, I doubt not but they will commend themselves for better than I can pretend to; for all good things carry with them a certain irresistable Authority, not to be oppos'd.
>
> The *Second Part* flows from the *Pens* of those whose Educations gave them the opportunity of improving their natural Endowments at the *Universities,* and some others who wanted those advantages; and by

reading you may find the difference of Parts improv'd, and Parts as barely natural. (Sigs. A3ᵛ–A4)

The male authors of the dedicatory poems in *Poetical Recreations* represent men as monopolizing wit, as triumphant after Orinda's death until Barker's appearance:

> But, lo, the Heiress of that Ladies *Muse,*
> Rivals their Merits [male poets] and their Sence out-do's;
> With swifter flights of fancy wings her *Verse,*
> And nobler Greatness valient acts reherse.
>
> (Sig. A4)

Another poem repeats the idea that since Adam named the beasts, men have exclusively claimed power over words, but "How grossly we mistook, *Orinda* knew, / We are convinc'd too by your *Verse* and *You*" (Sig. a). Although a poem in part 2 praising Barker's romance *Scripina* also alludes to Behn ("Thy *Lines* may pass severest *Virtue's Test,* / More than Astrea's soft, more than Orinda's chast" [11, 32], the primary identification Barker's circle made was with Orinda, one that Barker assiduously cultivated in her fiction and her poetry. Barker is one of the creators of the Orinda tradition. Barker's art is a complex mixture of autobiography, fictional self-representation, and fantasy, much of it dedicated to the development of the image of a woman writer, Galesia, who has much in common with Barker and who dreams of Orinda's apotheosis in one of her latest novels *The Lining of the Patch-work Screen* (1726). Barker's fiction is covered in chapter 4, below, but its autobiographical details are helpful in dealing with her poetry here.

Barker's poetry records that her brother's death was a blow to her, but it seems not to have crippled her life in the way Elizabeth Elstob's brother's death transformed hers. Barker and her mother seem to have moved to London after the death of her father around 1675, and her mother died in London in 1685. There is evidence that after James II fled England in 1688, the year of *Poetical Recreations,* Barker fled to France, where she became an ardent Roman Catholic and retired to the court of Saint Germain. She returned to Lincolnshire by 1715, where she lived on her father's royal grant. These transitions may account the division in her career between 1688 and 1713, with her published poetry identified with the earlier era and her fiction published after her return to England.[39] A Magdalen College manuscript reveals that Barker was revising her poems at the end of the century, and her fiction contains a number of poems, several from *Poetical Recreations.*

Although in later life Barker represents her persona as ambivalent about women's learning, in *Poetical Recreations* she is deeply envious of her friends at Cambridge, a place that should be Paradise, but only certain people – males – are allowed to eat of the tree of knowledge. Women are excluded by their original transgression:

> For in our maker's Laws we've made a breach,
> And gather'd all that was within our reach,
> Which since we ne're could touch; Altho' our Eyes
> Do serve our longing Souls to tantalize
> Whilst kinder fate for you do's constitute
> Luxurious Banquets of this dainty Fruit.
>
> (P. 4)

Barker therefore invites her Cambridge friends to join her in a retreat where in solitude one can maintain innocence and avoid pride, avarice, ambition, luxury, and wantonness – all the temptations of the world.

In a fascinating poem about a minor incident – an apothecary putting *her* recipes for cures under the name of her physician brother – she fantasizes about women's being educated enough to find cures for men's ills, which are, of course, not imaginary as women's are. (She confesses that if Strephon had not jilted her, she would never have learned medical arts.) At the end of the poem, she resolves to write all her cures in verse ("The Gout and Rickets too shall run on feet"): "For since the Learn'd exalt and own our Fame. / It is no Arrogance to do the same, / But due respects and complaisance to them" (p. 34). Barker's irony ill conceals her envy of male learning and status or even her bitterness at conventional female roles that preclude women's education. Yet the irony and the shifts in tone also suggest Barker's continuous ambivalence about her own goals and her place in society. This poem is one included in *A Patch-work Screen for the Ladies* (1723). Characteristically, she excused her writing poetry because she was compelled to do it by "necessity of fate." She has forsaken, she says, honors, pleasure, riches,

> All for the *Muses* Melancholy Tree,
> E're I knew ought of its great Mystery.
> Ah gentle Fate, since thou wilt have it so,
> Let thy kind hand exalt it to my brow.
>
> (P. 40)

Making fate responsible absolved Barker from any violation of social norms in the privilege of writing.

Like others of Orinda's daughters, Barker idealized a retreat from the world, which she viewed as having become hopelessly corrupt. In fact, she was one of the poets who genuinely enjoyed the country, and lived in her later years as a spinster on her father's tenancy. In these early poems, she urged others to escape in order to preserve virtue and integrity:

> 'Tis hard we must (the World's so wicked grown)
> Be complaisant in Sin, or live alone:
> For those who now with Verture are endu'd,
> Do live alone, though in a multitude.
>
> . . . .
>
> 'Tis not ignoble an escape to make:
> But where no Conquest can be hop'd by fight,
> 'Tis honourable, sure, to 'scape by flight.
>
> (P. 22)

Retreat, then, is as much a moral decision about contemporary society as an attraction to country life. Barker's grim feelings about the state of things were no doubt intensified by her royalist and Roman Catholic perspective on the events leading to the Glorious Revolution. She left for France in 1688.

Barker's Roman Catholicism also gave a distinctive cast to her formulations of the personal integrity so much valued in the Orinda tradition. For Barker the celibate life of single blessedness was a realistic alternative for women. In one of her best-known poems, which repeats Orinda's in the title, "A Virgin Life," the speaker prays that she will be able to withstand "Men's almost Omnipotent Amours," even as the dreadful age of twenty-five approaches with the prospect of scornfully being called an old maid. A virgin has equanimity: she is a true friend, a charitable neighbor, an obedient subject. Alone, she enjoys the society of God: "She drives her whole Life's business to these ends, / To serve her God, enjoy her Books and Friends" (p. 13; *WD*, 227).

In a song from the romance *Scipina,* Barker went even further in presenting Anchorites as the essence of personal integrity:

> Ah, happy are we Anchorites that know
> Not Women's Ebbs, nor when their love will Flow
> We know no storms that rage in women's Breasts,
> But here in quiet build our Halcyon Nests;
> Where we deceitfull Calm our Faith beguiles,

No cruel frowns, nor yet more cruel smiles;
No rising Wave of Fate our hopes advance;
Nor fear we fathomless despair of Chance;
But our strong Minds, like rocks, their Firmness prove,
Defying both the Storms of Fate and Love.

(P. 91; FF, 173)

Here we see that Barker was not, like Chudleigh, rejecting marriage because it was demeaning and oppressive for women, but celebrating a version of the ideal female integrity that many of Orinda's followers extolled. For Barker the ideal extended to virginity and monastic peace because her faith still supported that vision.

Paradoxically, however, Barker was one of the few of Orinda's progeny who wrote of sexual love; and this, I believe, is a function of time and temperament. Her sensibility was formed after the Restoration and its freer mores took hold, and her temperament as an artist positively relished irony and ambivalence. So, although she wrote about Strephon, Exillius, and other lovers, Barker's speakers do not trust men, who invariably represent "interest" in relationships, abandon women, or seek only their fortunes. In "To Dr. R. S. my indifferent Lover, who complain'd of my Indifferency," the speaker tells R. S. that he has little reason to complain of her "since I by many a circumstance can prove, / That int'rest was the motive of your love." Such courtship may be suitable for cunning baggages in town, but not for honest country maids. The speaker was saved by her temperament—her ill nature—from taking Dr. R. S. seriously, but she hates to think what might have happened to another woman because "Your Flames and Sighs only for Money were. / As Beggars for their gain turn Blind and Lame." This experience has taught the speaker "ne'er to be *Mistress* more" (pp. 16–17). In another poem, "To my Unkind Strephon," the speaker speculates about how to react to Strephon's withdrawal of love; she decides that "like good old Romans, although banish'd I / Shall still retain my first integrity" (p. 35). As she explores the probable causes for his waning feeling, the speaker concludes that Strephon, like Dr. R. S., is driven by interest: "But now, alas, Love's Powers are all deprest, / By th' pow'rfull Anarchy of Interest" (p. 36).

On her side a woman must have the favor of fortune if she is to be loved by most men, as in "A Song of Scipina":

In Vain do's *Nature* her free gifts bestow,
   To make us wise or fair;
If *Fortune* don't her Favours show,

Scorn'd or neglected we may go,
Not worth a Look, much less a Lover's care.
(P. 79)

This cynical thinking becomes an assumption of Barker's thought as in these lines about why she is forsaking poetry, written presumably in her own voice: "No more than Beauty, without Wealth, can move / A Gallant's heart to strokes of Love / . . . No more can verse in London grow" (p. 108).

The representation of men that emerges here is the one we find in seventeenth-century fiction written by Aphra Behn and her followers: males are predatory and motivated by the worst values of a commercial economy that will destroy women if they do not learn how to cope with it. In another context Barker meditates about the mistakes made by classical ladies in "To Ovid's Heroines in his Epistles" (pp. 28–29). Women, Barker's poems suggest, have in their capacity to control their lives if they are willing to accept the consequences of independence and possibly live out their destinies unconventionally on the margins of society. Her religion, moreover, did not lead her to balk at such alternatives.

Although she helped create and perpetuate the tradition of Orinda, Barker is full of ironic complexity, more of which will be apparent in analysis of her fiction in chapter 4. She continued the identification of her self-representation (Galesia) with Orinda in the later fiction, although it represents the artist not in rural retirement but coping with the oppression of women in London. She was constantly ambivalent about the value of learning for women. She was a committed celibate who wrote eloquently of women's problems in courtship and marriage. She was an ardent Jacobite, whose sympathy for the suffering of marginal people of London is palpable in her fiction. She was the most complex of Orinda's daughters, much resembling Margaret Cavendish in her swings of attitude, but she is an almost perfect example of Lipking's paradigm: "Poetry is the expression of a life, personal and incomplete, and proportioned to the self; employing whatever language and conventions one has been allowed to acquire; presented in fragments; and achieving, through sharing the emotions of loneliness and abandonment, a momentary sense of not being alone."[40]

Elizabeth Singer Rowe (1674–1737)

The career of Elizabeth Singer Rowe, who was known as Philomela, bears uncanny resemblance to Barker's in that both published an early volume of poetry and then, after retiring to the country, both wrote fiction that enjoyed a wide audience. Both also had the encouragement of a sympathetic circle of admirers. In her youth Rowe moved "in pious but elegant dissenting circles."[41] The connections among Orinda's daughters are many, despite the fact that several of them retreated to the country. Rowe, for example, was a close friend of Frances Thynne, countess of Hertford and later duchess of Somerset. Thynne was also a friend of Winchilsea, and a poem in the Wellesley manuscript testifies to Winchilsea's literary connections with Rowe as Philomela and with Thynne as Cleone, who is also frequently alluded to in Winchilsea's published poems.[42] Although they admired one another as artists, their politics could have separated the Jacobite Winchilsea from the Williamite Rowe. Matthew Prior was friendly with both poets, and is said to have proposed to Elizabeth, who later married a classical scholar, Thomas Rowe.[43] Mary Chandler, author of *A Description of Bath* (1733), was friendly with both Rowe and Mary Barber, as was the earl of Orrery.[44]

Although Rowe seems to have had little formal education, her father, a Nonconformist minister, gave her a religious education and hired masters to teach her music, drawing, and poetry. She was also tutored in the household of Henry Thynne, at Longleat, Somerset. She began writing poetry early, and at seventeen was published in several journals produced by John Dunton for the Athenian Society. This organization had two purposes: "teaching Christian tenets and good working habits to the poor and expanding the knowledge of those unable to attend grammar schools or universities."[45] Two issues of the *Athenian Mercury* (1694–95) were devoted to Rowe's verse, and she became the Pindarick Lady. Her poems were gathered into a collection published in 1696: *Poems on Several Occasions Written by Philomela*. Rowe's relationship to the quirky Dunton was strange: he encouraged her writing, but then began a platonic correspondence with her when his wife died in 1697. He gives an account of the correspondence and the fact that her father brought it to an end, as well as a flattering character of Madam Singer as a primitive Christian in *Athenianism: or, the New Projects of John Dunton* (1710).[46] Like Orinda, Rowe was attractive to men, enjoyed their support all her life, and warmly returned their admiration.

Although Rowe published under a classical pseudonym, reflecting the studied modesty that makes her a descendant of Orinda, Elizabeth Johnson's Preface to the Reader is distinctly assertive in its tone, for she presents Rowe's achievements as ample evidence that men cannot monopolize sense and learning, becoming tyrants that "will not let us say our souls are our own."[47] We should recall that Barker's male sponsors made the same accusation that men were monopolizing wit and learning. Such terms are part of the debate about the Salic Law of Wit, which is developed in chapter 3. Such assertations of a male monopoly of wit Johnson sees as "a plain and open design to render us mere slaves, perfect Turkish wives, without properties, or sense, or souls; and [women] are forced to protest against it, and appeal to all the world, whether these are not notorious violations on the liberties of freeborn Englishwomen?" (Sig. A3; *WD*, 290).

In what amounts to a brief defense of women, Johnson cites "not only Bonducas and Zenobias; but Sapphos and Daciers; Schurmans, Orindas and Behns, who have humbled the most haughty of our antagonists, and made them do homage to our wit, as well as to our beauty" (Sig. A3ᵛ). Rowe's work silences the enemies of women, for they will find there a vivacity of thought, purity of language, softness and delicacy in love poetry, strength and majesty in heroical themes, piety and devotion in religious poems, all qualities "they will hardly find exceeded in the best authors of those different kinds of writing, much less equalled by any single writer" (Sig. A4; *WD*, 291). This effusive praise is followed by a dedicatory poem that compares Rowe favorably to Waller, Cowley, and Dryden:

> What age can equal, what historian find
> Such tenderness, with so much duty joined?
> Sappho and Behn reformed, in thee revive,
> In thee we see the chaste Orinda live.
>
> . . . .
> Prepare then for that fame which you depise!
> (P. 3)

With such enthusiastic friends, Rowe could easily adopt the familiar self-deprecating attitude of Orinda's followers, and she was one in whom reclusiveness and genuine piety seem wholly natural. Although it may be difficult for the modern reader to accept this high praise of Rowe, we should remember that she remained the "celebrated Mrs. Rowe" throughout the eighteenth century and that Pope included her elegy for her husband in the 1720 edition of "Eloisa to Abelard."[48] If women's history had not been neglected, their contemporary fame might be more credible for us.

Rowe employed the Orinda themes—friendship, platonic love, for example—but there are many political, religious, and love poems in the volume as well. Like Barker, Rowe was less reserved in writing about heterosexual love than were poets who held closer to their model. We notice, for example, that a poem praising platonic love is answered by one of a "Country Gentleman," who asserts, "I love the body" (p. 6), and alludes to the biblical injunction to increase and multiply.

Rowe's approach to love poetry is interesting. In poems addressed to men or in those about heterosexual love, she identifies males with the pursuit of interest, the hazard of desertion, or the chains of slavery to the male prerogative. The atmosphere of Rowe's poetry seems so unassuming that one overlooks the occasional poem addressed to a male. Yet all of them use the language of tyranny and slavery, identifying men with interest and ambition. "The Female Passion" testifies to the speaker's desire to rid herself of the relationship that has all but destroyed her honor and pride:

> One dart from his *insulting eyes,*
> Eyes I'm undone to meet,
> Throws all my boasting faculties
> At the lov'd Tyrant's feet.
>
> (P. 30)

At the end the speaker likens her destiny in coping with this coercive relationship to that of Sysiphus dealing "with his Eternal Doom." The associations with passion are not attractive. The next poem, "To Strephon," identifies the male with interest and ambition, values foreign to a woman's breast:

> To me his sighs, to me are all his vows,
> But there's my hell, the depth of all my woes,
> We burn alike, but oh the distant bliss,
> A view of that my greatest torment is;
> Accurst ambition, groveling interest,
> Such heated crimes as yet did never rest
> Within my soul, must now unjustly keep
> Me from my Heaven would they may sink as deep,
> As that black Chaos whence they sprung, and leave
> Those mortals wretched which they now deceive.
>
> (Pp. 31–32)

The destructive twins of amatory fiction, interest and ambition, here frustrate authentic love.

Among the final poems in the book are two that again reject a man's love as tyranny. The speaker of "The Reply to Mr.—" remains unmoved by tender thoughts, words, gallantries, enticing eyes,

> All the Genuine *charms* and Courtly *Arts,*
> By which your Treacherous *Sex* invade our *Hearts:*

No more those excellent Things contract my *breast*
By a Diviner Excellence possesst.

(Pp. 59–60)

The speaker, liberated from bondage, will not be tempted by another relationship: "Nor would I even for my late splendid Chum / Forgo this Charming *Liberty* again" (p. 61). Similarly the last poem in the volume rejects love:

And therefore flattering hopes, and wishes too,
With all loves soft Concomitants, adieu:
No more to its Imperious Yoke I'll bow;
Pride and Resentment fortify me now.
My inclinations are reverst; nor can
I but abhor the Slavery of Man,
How e'er the *empty Lords of Nature* boast
O're me, their fond Prerogative is lost.

(P. 66)

Rowe was similar to Barker, then, in writing a good deal about sexual love, while at the same time rejecting it because of male dominance or treachery. The difference is that although Barker's life was close to that of her poetic persona, Rowe's life contradicted hers.

About friendship with women, on the other hand, Rowe composed with a distinctive hand, for many of her poems addressed to women friends employ a vocabulary of sexual love. A simple praise poem addressed to "Mrs. Mary Friend; Knowing her but by Report" avers that Mary's charms and bright form are equal to those of saints, and that Mary has made a true conquest:

Charming, and Gay, your *Fair Idea* seems
As Gay, as if compos'd of Love and Beams;
Such Heavenly Rays adorn your Lovely Eyes,
That, by *Imagination,* they surprise,
And at your feet, a Female Victim lies.

(P. 7)

Rowe seems to have been comfortable with a conventional sexual vocabulary for a variety of social situations involving other women. Relationships with women, moreover, become alternatives to those with men, as in the precious and effusive poem, "To Celinda":

> *Celestial* flames are scarce more bright,
>   Than those your worth inspires,
>   So Angels love and so they burn
>   In just such *holy fires*.

> V.

> Then let's my dear *Celinda* thus
>   Blest in our selves contemn
> The treacherous and deluding Arts,
>   Of those *base things call'd men*.
>   (P. 28)

"On Mrs. Rebecka" again uses a sexual vocabulary to develop the theme of female friendship. In a similar vein, a pastoral, "To Madam S—— at the Court," uses the escape conventions of the anti-court theme: "Come prithee leave the Courts / And range the Fields with me" (p. 46). Although the poem refers only to innocence, conversation, and the mind—never straying to Marlovian pleasures—all of the conventions of a love affair are expressed:

> And like those happy Lovers we,
>   As careless and as blest;
> Shall in each others converse be
>   Of the whole world possest.
>   (P. 47)

Rowe's love poetry addressed to women presents a positive, happy alternative to relationships with men, which are associated with oppressive worldly values. These features of Rowe's poems decidedly complicate her pious image, derived largely from her later fiction. Ironically, these attitudes are also characteristic of the tradition of amatory fiction in which she also wrote, as well as the tradition of writers who descend from Aphra Behn. By the end of her career, Rowe will have turned the amatory vocabulary of the poetic and fictional discourse within which she wrote to the purposes of domestic piety. The route she navigated to that end is complex and instructive for how these writers put to distinctive use the conventions of literary genres.

Anne Finch, Countess of Winchilsea (1661–1720)

Anne Finch, countess of Winchilsea, took measures more serious than undoing to cope with having assumed the privilege of writing: she not only resisted publication of most of her poetry until 1713 but also suppressed many of her poems in manuscript throughout her life. The decisions that she made about poems to publish and those to withhold in carefully copied, beautifully bound volumes are as instructive as her comments about being a woman writer.[49] No writer included in this study wrote or thought more about being a she-author than did Winchilsea.

She was resolutely ladylike and therefore a natural daughter of Orinda, and so she is consistently defensive about her writing. In "Mercury and the Elephant," which began her *Miscellany Poems, on Several Occasions, Written by a Lady,* she uses a fable to represent the predicament of the woman writer.[50] Just as the god Mercury cannot be bothered with the quarrels of an elephant and a wild boar, so men can hardly be troubled with what women write:

> What Men are not concern'd to know:
> For still untouch'd how we succeed,
> 'Tis for themselves, not us they *Read;*
> Whilst that proceeding to requite,
> We own (who in the Muse delight)
> 'Tis for our Selves, not them, we *Write.*
>
> (P. 4)

The tone is light and self-deprecating but also ironic about godlike males; the defense of writing for each other leaves women relatively invulnerable to male criticism, but also incapable of affecting the male audience.

More touching are two suppressed works: "The Introduction" and the preface to the manuscript folio. "The Introduction" describes women's past achievements. Presenting an amalgam of biblical incidents, it praises women who sang to celebrate the bringing of the Ark into Jerusalem, the women greeting the victorious David with songs, and, most of all, Deborah:

> A Woman here, leads fainting Isreal on,
> She fights, she wins, she tryumphs with a song,
> Devout, Majestick, for the subject fitt,
> And far above her arms, exalts her witt,
> Then, to the peacefull, shady Palm withdraws,
> And rules the rescu'd Nation, with her Laws.
>
> (P. 6)

113

Winchilsea saw her contemporaries as greatly diminished from that heroic tradition because, like Cavendish, she despaired at women's lack of education:

> How are we fal'n, fal'n by mistaken rules?
> And Education's more then Nature's fools,
> Debarr'd from all improve-ments of the mind,
> And to be dull, expected and dessigned;
> And if some one, wou'd Soar above the rest,
> With warmer fancy, and ambition press't,
> So strong, th'opposing faction still appears,
> The hopes to thrive, can ne're outweigh the fears.
>
> (P. 6)

Her resolve, therefore, was to keep her muse retired: during her lifetime she achieved her status as an heir to Orinda by keeping her most transgressive poetry for private circulation.

The preface to the folio shows how self-conscious Winchilsea was about Orinda's model, how she used many of the same psychological strategies, even in a manuscript volume, and therefore how deeply ingrained those habits of mind were. First, she explained that she did not expect her scattered efforts at poetry to be attended to, but that through circulation in manuscript, they had "grown by the partiality of some of my friends, to the formidable appearance of a Volume" (p. 7). She never expected, she said, to "reatch Orinda's prayse"; she never wrote any of her poems for publication; indeed, she had almost stopped writing when she and Finch moved to Eastwell, but his nephew, their host, and the beauty of the place inspired her muse: "But now, having pleaded an irresistable impulse, as my excuse for writing, which was the cheif design of this Preface, I must also expresse my hopes of excaping all suspition of vanity, or affectation of applause from itt" (p. 9). She was sensible to the laws of poetry defined by Aristotle, Horace, Rapin, Despreaux, Roscommon, Dryden, and how imperfect her poetry appeared in light of literary theory. Yet she hoped her poetic subjects were inoffensive. She wrote, she said, little of love, using Orinda as a model: "Tho' I must confesse, the great reservednesse of Mrs. Philips in this particular, and the prayses I have heard given her upon that account, together with my desire not to give scandal to the most severe, has often discourag'd me from making use of it" (p. 10). In writing plays too she followed Orinda: "and mine, tho' orginals, I hope are not lesse reserv'd" (p. 11). Finally, in a moving passage, she told how she used poetry as a stay against melancholy and isolation, "achieving, through sharing the emotions of loneliness and abandonment, a momentary sense of not being alone."[51]

And indeed, an absolute solitude (which often was my lott) under such dejection of mind, cou'd not have been supported, had I indulg'd myself (as was too natural to me) only in the contemplation of present and real afflictions, which I hope will plead my excuse, for turning them for releif, upon such as were immaginary, & relating to Persons no more in being. I had my end in the writing, and if they please not those who will take the pains to peruse them, itt will be a just accusation to my weaknesse, for letting them escape out of their concealment; but if attended with a better successe, the satisfaction any freind of mine, may take in them, will make me think my time past, not so unprofitably bestowed, as otherwise I might. (P. 12)

Although she frequently asserted poetry's private uses for her, Winchilsea was more ambitious (in the manuscript poems) for women poets and for herself than first appears. She modestly insisted upon the limitations of her own talent in *The Appology;* "Each Woman has her weakness; mine indeed / Is still to write tho' hopelesse to succeed," but in an early verse she saw the poetry of a friend as reviving the strain of Sappho and surpassing Orinda:

> Since our own Age is happily possesst
> Of such a genius, in a Female Breast,
> As gives us Faith for all those wonders told,
> Producing New, to justify the old.
> Then we'll no more submitt, but (in your name)
> To Poetry renew our Ancient Claime;
> Through itts retirement, we'll your worth persue,
> And lead itt into Public Rule and View.
>
> . . . .
>
> And whilst Orinda's part you far transcend,
> I proudly bear that of her glorious Friend,
> Who though not equaling her lofty Witt,
> Th' occasion was, of what so well writt.
>
> (Pp. 95–96)

The friend, Mrs. Randolph, had represented Winchilsea bearing the mantle of Cowley. The compliments are exaggerations, but supportive nonetheless.[52]

"The Circuit of Appollo" belongs to the genre of "sessions" of the poets and offers judgments about Winchilsea herself and several contemporaries. The poem is based on the terms of the Salic Law of Wit, which generally excludes women from writing, just as they are excluded from the French throne. Only Apollo may make exceptions to the law for truly extraordinary talent, and he usually makes one exception at a time. (See chapter 3 for a discussion of the Salic Law in the period.) Here Apollo judges Aphra Behn for her morals, a general attitude toward the end of the century, and yet her art is praised:

> He [Apollo] lamented for Behn o're that place of her birth,
> And said amongst Femens was not on earth
> Her superiour in fancy, in language, or witt
> Yet own'd that a little too loosly she writt.
> (P. 92)

The other poets, Alinda, Laura, Valeria, and Winchilsea herself as Ardelia, are all judged as worth the bays. But Apollo, noting the outcome of the Judgment of Paris, decides to divide the laurels among all four. The poem is wittily cynical about Apollo's judgment and about women at the end, but it also refuses the dictate of the Salic Law of Wit that there could be only one approved woman poet at a time. The effect of the poem is a witty spoof of the entire idea of the Salic Law of Wit. Winchilsea's description of herself is characteristically self-effacing:

> Ardelia, came last as expecting least praise,
> Who writt for her pleasure and not for the bays,
> But yett, as occasion, or fancy should sway,
> Wou'd sometimes endeavour to passe a dull day,
> In composing a song, or a Scene of a Play
> Not seeking for Fame, which so little does last,
> That e're we can taste itt, the Pleasure is Past.
> But Appollo reply'd, tho' so careless she seemd,
> Yett the Bays, if her share, wou'd be highly esteem'd.
> (Pp. 93–94)

Apollo's attitude admits, on behalf of Winchilsea, that she truly enjoyed the recognition of her achievements, despite her lifelong concealment of her poetry. This exaggerated modesty seems to be a form of undoing because Winchilsea was very much aware, when she wrote about Pope, of how any poet seeks fame:

> For none have writ (whatever they pretend)
> Singly to raise a patron or a friend;

But whatsoe'er the theme or object be,
Some commendation to themselves foresee.

                                                        (P. 104)

Occasionally Winchilsea's religious fervor made her ambitious. She did not publish her most devout religious poetry, probably because it would have seemed enthusiastic. Here, in a poem from the Wellesley Manuscript, she would better Dryden because of divine inspiration:

> My temper frail and subject to dismay
> Be steadfast there spiritualiz'd and gay
> My low Poetick tendency be rais'd
> Till the bestower worthily is prais'd
> Till Dryden's numbers for Cecilia's feats
> Which sooth depress inflame and shake the breast
> Vary the passions with each varying line
> Allow'd below all others to outshine
> Shall yeild to those above shall yeild to mine
> In sound in sense in emphasis Divine.
>
>   (*WM*, pp. 108–9)

Because she herself went to such lengths to tread a narrow line between asserting herself as a poet and being modest as a woman, Winchilsea blamed women poets for the social scorn they earned because they were too public, wrote spiteful verse, or otherwise made social spectacles of themselves. Here she depicts Ardelia's conversation with a fashionable lady:

> They say she writes, and 'tis a common jest.
> Then sure sh' has publickly the skill professt,
> I soon reply, and makes that gift her pride,
> And all the world, but scribblers, does deride;
> Setts out Lampoons, where only spite is seen,
> Not fill'd with female witt, but female spleen.
> Her florish'd name, does o're a song expose,
> Which through all ranks, down to the Carman, goes.
> Or poetry is on her Picture found,
> In which she sits, with pained lawrel crown'd.
> If no such flyes, no vanity defile,
> The Helyconian balm, the sacred oyl,

Why shou'd we from that pleasing art be ty'd,
Or like State Pris'ners, Pen and Ink deny'd?
(Pp. 44–45)

There is possible irony in the mention of *spleen* because her poem by that
name made Winchilsea famous as "the Author of *The Spleen*." Still, women
who kept proper limits, as Winchilsea herself did, should not be criticized
for writing. If the character Phoebe Clinket in *Three Hours After Marriage*
is modeled on Winchilsea, that is a true irony of literary history, for one
of Phoebe's main concerns is getting her work published. The character is
probably a composite of many women writers, with a good deal of Cavendish in her, and the satiric concentration on ambition shows the accuracy
of Winchilsea's judgment about her world.

Even if her modesty did keep her from publishing much of her verse that is
most interesting today, some of Winchilsea's protests about fame seem
psychological strategies. *The Spleen* had been published in 1701, and was a
great success; and after that she could publish as its author. Although she may
have vainly longed for Pope's praise of her *Miscellany* in 1713, she enjoyed the
esteem of many important contemporaries. But, as Ann Messenger has said,
her defenses of the privilege of writing are complex and, I would add, quite
like Orinda's.[53] Winchilsea undoes her deviancy by acknowledging it and
satirizes women's activities as Cavendish did in *Sociable Letters:*

> My Lines decry'd, and my Employment thought
> An useless Folly, or presumptuous Fault:
>   Whilst in the *Muses* Paths I stray
> Whilst in their Groves, and by their secret Springs
> My Hand delights to trace unusual Things,
> And deviates from the known, and common way;
>   Nor will in fading Silks compose
>   Faintly th'inimitable *Rose,*
> Fill up an ill-drawn *Bird,* or paint on Glass
> The *Sov'reign's* blurr'd and undistinguish'd Face,
> The threatening *Angel,* and the Speaking *Ass.*
> (P. 250)

We will return later to her satire on fashionable, contemporary women.

The very selection of poems to be published in *Miscellany* and those to
be preserved in manuscript is a defense strategy in itself. For, if one studies,
as Ann Messenger has, the kinds of poems Winchilsea published and those

118

she suppressed, one sees that many of the poems that fit Lipking's definition of a female poetic remain in manuscript: virtually all the poems that are shaped to the self, are about her life, are about other women or being a woman, are suppressed. This is especially true for the Wellesley manuscript, which is full of personal occasional verse. Published are many fables, thirty-four of eighty-six poems in the volume. The fable, a popular genre of the period, afforded opportunities to translate or imitate famous male writers and was "an appropriately humble form for a women to use."[54] The fable also provided protection for the author: it has inherent distancing that allows its author a range of comments and tones. As Messenger suggests, an insight into how Winchilsea used fables lies in "The Critick and the Writer of Fables." The poet has tired of Pindarics and would use fables to teach and to delight: some will be translated, but the fables will be simple and pleasant. The critic dislikes fables, and so the poet offers epic verse, which the critic also scorns. The critic also rejects the pastoral, but endorses satires. The poet tries to get the critic to accept a pluralistic muse, but the critic is scornful of those diverted with ease. Just as scornful of the critic was Winchilsea (pp. 153–55).

Other genres represented in volume of 1713 are songs, biblical translations, pastorals, Pindarics, a parody of Milton, *The Spleen* (already published), and *The Hurricane,* based on a storm of November 1703. The other long poem is "Nocturnal Reverie," which will be dealt with in chapter 6. There are also a very few love poems addressed to Winchilsea's husband. The generalization that applies to most of these poems is that they offend practically no reader within Winchilsea's society. Her political convictions, her deviant views about women, her many poems about personal relationships and about herself, even some of her poems of married love, all waited in manuscript three centuries for readers.

The themes that mark Winchilsea as a descendent of Orinda can be easily discerned in the published volume, however. Although she suppressed several more personal poems addressed to women friends, several were published in 1713. Winchilsea was especially fond of the theme of inexpressible love, which resolves her most familiar friendship poem:

> *Eph.* This indeed, tho' carry'd high,
> This, tho' more than e'er was done
> Underneath the rolling Sun,
> This has all been said before.
> Can *Ardelia* say no more?
> *Ard.* Words indeed no more can shew:
> *But 'tis to love, as I love you.*
>
> (P. 46)

"To the Painter of an Ill-Drawn Picture of Cleone, the Honorable Mrs. Thynne" is really a friendship poem in which Winchilsea criticizes the painting of Cleone in order to define an ideal of womanhood. The painter has made Cleone look too aggressive: the picture resembles a virago or an Amazon, who would never have captured Theanor's heart. The poem resolves as did the previous one to Ephelia: neither the painter nor the poet could capture "what Nature in Cleone's Face has writ" (p. 60).

In one of her better known and most interesting poems, "The Petition for an Absolute Retreat," Winchilsea blends the favorite themes of retreat from the world, friendship, married love, and politics. The poem is inscribed to "Catherine Countess of Thanet," who seems to have given the Finches refuge during the difficult period after the flight of James II in 1688. The poem fairly bursts with the emotions Winchilsea must have experienced in that moment, but its conventions also lie squarely in the retirement tradition.[55] It begins with the desire for an absolute retreat in which the speaker's existence would be very like that of the Golden Age: all would be simple, old, and natural, expressing "unaffected Carelessness." As heaven has shown the way, the speaker asks for a partner who will also abandon wealth and pride. But these pleasures are those of youth. By means of the figure of an old oak, the poem modulates to the plight of the poet when blasted by a storm over "all the *British* State." In this peril Winchilsea had the comfort of Arminda, a wonderful friend:

> To Woman ne'er allow'd before,
> What Nature, or refining Art,
> All that Fortune cou'd impart,
> Heaven did to *Arminda* send;
> Then gave her for *Ardelia's* Friend:
> To her Cares to Cordial drop,
> Which else had overflow'd the Cup.
> (P. 74)

As friendship is the support of humankind, the speaker hopes for a friend in the retreat also. The poem shows that if Crassus and Sertorius had been content to remain in retreat, Crassus in his cave and Sertorius in the Fortunate Isles, both would have found peace and rest. It ends in a vision of the soul finding the joy of paradise. Winchilsea's retirement because of politics echoes that of Cavendish, and indeed they have other common qualities.

Winchilsea combined political and personal themes with her celebration of rural England and its aristocracy in a poem addressed to Arminda's daughter, "A Poem for the Birth-day of the Right Hon[BLE] the Lady Catherine

Tufton." Here Serena is celebrated, first for her family "In whom our Britain lets us see / What once they were, and still should be"; then for her personal attributes: honor, wit, goodness, and grace. The poem concludes with a vision of Serena as a bride, bestowed by Hothfield, the Thanet country house, and continuing the aristocracy of England:

> Of Fathers, the long-fram'd Design,
> To add such Splendour to their Line,
> Whilst all shall strive for such a Bride
> So Educated, and Ally'd.
>
> (P. 81)

In chapter 5 we will deal again with Winchilsea's politics in relation to the country-house tradition. Winchilsea's emphasis on education is probably unusual in this kind of poetry, but her second adjective about alliance is surely mainstream. Because of her conservatism and her attitudes as a woman, the social implication of her poetry is extremely complex, especially because she circulated her poems privately.

Part of her cluster of individual attitudes was Winchilsea's celebration of domestic happiness. She is more satiric than Cavendish, but like her in making her own marriage an ideal to which others should strive. Two poems in *Miscellany* idealize the relationship of married love. The first, "To Mr. F. Now Earl of W.," satirizes the contemporary world for denigrating married love. When Winchilsea appeals to the Muses for inspiration, they are dismayed to discover her subject:

> The hasty Summons was allow'd;
> And being well bred, they rose and bow'd,
>   And said, they'd poste away;
> That well they did *Ardelia* know,
> And that no Female's Voice below
>   They sooner wou'd obey.
>
> (P. 21)

Only Urania counsels the poet that she need but look in her heart and write. Winchilsea concludes that Flavis alone should hear her love, for if the world so despises married love, it should remain a mystery. The second poem, "A Letter to the Same Person," reverts to Winchilsea's favorite assertion of the inexpressibility of love; yet in passing it pays tribute to the importance of poetry in the life of love:

Love without Poetry's refining Aid
Is a dull Bargain, and but coarsely made;
Nor e'er cou'd Poetry successful prove,
Or touch the Soul, but when the Sense was Love.

(P. 24)

Other and more moving tributes Winchilsea kept in manuscript.

If she conformed to many of the attitudes of the Orinda tradition and her society, Winchilsea was like all of Orinda's daughters in raising a highly distinctive voice. Her special subject was the spleen and the use of poetry to deal with it. *The Spleen* was much admired in its time, and has frequently been reprinted since then. The poem is a fascinating mixture of psychological and physical analysis, personal confession, and social satire. The poem is remarkable in taking the affliction seriously and renders its symptoms graphically, including the affected senses as the victim is made nauseous by certain odors. In addition, the work acknowledges the social dimension of disease, how it may spread by imitation. This kind of fashion can turn its trivial side to domestic quarrels or the fop, but it may be serious as religious despair. The two central sections are structured similarly in moving from domestic scenes to affectations and then to serious artistic and religious depression. These sections are flanked by an introduction that deals with symptoms and a conclusion that dismisses cures. It is an impressive performance, and the confession embedded at its center only establishes the speaker's authority.

Winchilsea did not publish another moving poem she wrote about the same affliction, probably because it was too personal: "Ardelia to Melancholy" (pp. 15–16). The speaker calls melancholy her "old inverterate foe," and the poem is almost a personal continuation of the end of *The Spleen* because one remedy for melancholy after another is rejected as ineffective. The poet has tried music and distracting arts, only to experience more intense pain. (The Wellesley manuscript contains a fascinating account of what we would call the use of music therapy for depression.) Friendship is no remedy, either, and the breaking of friendship only causes greater pain:

Freindship, I to my heart have laid,
Freindship, th' applauded sov'rain aid,
And though that charm so strong wou'd prove,
As to compell thee, to remove;
And to myself, I boasting said,
Now I a conqu'rer sure shall be,

> The end of all my conflicts, see,
> And noble tryumph, wait on me;
> My dusky, sullen foe, will sure
> N'er this united charge endure.
> But leaning on this reed, ev'n whilst I spoke
> It pierc'd my hand, and into pieces broke.
> Still, some new object, or new int'rest came
> And loos'd the bonds, and quite disolv'd the claim.
>
> (Pp. 15–16)

Even poetry, the last resort, is no equal to depression, "and heav'n, alone, can sett me free." It seems very likely that, with the extent of Winchilsea's conformity and conflicting need to use her talent, the anger that occasionally surfaced in her work and that Mary Chudleigh understood and analyzed, turned into Winchilsea's melancholy. If anger and depression are identified as significant women's problems today, we may see that in Chudleigh, Winchilsea, and others studied here, they have been women's problems for hundreds of years; and women have raised their voices about the predicaments that spawn the conditions for centuries without being heard, but they have raised their voices nonetheless.

Many of the other poems that Winchilsea left in manuscript are also those that are the personal expression of her life. There are several love poems addressed to her husband, such as "A Letter to Dafnis April: 2nd 1685." In this poem she draws a magic circle in which he is her only audience: "You know who writes; and I who 'tis that reads." She was not, therefore, flaunting her inexpressible love for him publicly, as other women might. She could express at once her love and the boundary dividing the private and the public.

In addition to frank comments on the difficulties of being a woman writer that we have already seen, Winchilsea wrote many unpublished poems about women. There are sixteen poems in the Wellesley manuscript alone either addressed to women, or about them, or both. There are more poems of friendship, but there are also poems that are critical of female contemporaries. In "On Myselfe" Winchilsea contrasted herself with other women whose lives are consumed with trifles:

> Good Heav'n, I thank thee, since it was design'd
> I shou'd be fram'd, but of the weaker kinde,
> That yet, my Soul, is rescued from the Love
> Of all those trifles, which their Passions move.
> Pleasures, and Praise, and Plenty haue with me

But their just value. If allow'd they be,
Freely, and thankfully as much I tast,
As will not reason, or Religion wast.
If they're deny'd, I on my selfe can Live,
And slight those aids, unequal chance does give.
When in the Sun, my wings can be display'd,
And in retirement, I can bless the shade.

(Pp. 14–15)

The spirit is very much that of Orinda and the retirement discourse: a stoic determination to survive a possibly hostile world through a conscious self-sufficiency, a stubborn unwillingness to depend on what the world offers. Like Cavendish, Winchilsea held no brief for most women's lives, not did she believe that most of them had the slightest sympathy for her purposes. The set piece for these views is "Ardelia's Answer to Ephelia," in which the speaker is a bookish, old-fashioned woman from the country and satirizes her friend Almeria. The latter is fashionable, full of affectations in dress and in taste of all kinds, including fancy china and tea. She envies other women's beauty and is insensitive to the virtues and accomplishments of Piso, "who from the Latin, Virgil frees." Almeria betrays the confidences of friends and makes fun of a woman poet. Ardelia cannot wait to bid her good-bye and head for the country:

We parted thus, the night in peace I spent,
And the next day, with haste and pleasure went
To the best seat of fam'd and fertile Kent.
Where lett me live from all detraction free
Till freind, and Foe, I treat with such dispite
May I no scorn, the worst of ills, excite.

(P. 46)

It is difficult to escape the conclusion that even if their political fortunes had not forced them into the country, both Cavendish and Winchilsea were too strong-minded and independent to tolerate life in London.

Although she was as critical of superficial women as was Cavendish, Winchilsea had a social approach to their predicament that Cavendish lacked. For Winchilsea women were "Education's more then Nature's fools." Winchilsea had a social vocabulary in which to view women's problems that Cavendish never developed because of her allegience to Nature. So despite Winchilsea's own happy marriage, she understood that the institution was man-made as an unequal relationship:

Free as Nature's first intention
Was to make us, I'll be found
Nor by subtle Man's invention
Yeild to be in Fetters bound.
By one that walks a freer round.

Mariage does but slightly tye Men
Whil'st close Pris'ners we remain
They the larger Slaves of Hymen
Still are begging Love again
At the full length of all their chain.

(P. 151)

Winchilsea frequently satirized both surly husbands and shrewish wives, as in "Reformation" or *The Spleen*, where she was quite evenhanded. An interesting example of her attitude toward marriage is "A Tale" from the Wellesley manuscript. There on a wager a man will give an apple to dominant wives and a horse to submissive ones. The bet is that he will return with four horses and no apples. He finds mostly shrews until he comes upon a woman who appears to be bullied by her mate. The gambler is about to award the horse when the wife begins to berate her husband about which horse to choose! They are promptly awarded an apple. At the end Winchilsea apologizes for the story, but counsels women to serve their desires by being loving to their mates. Then in closing she also sees clearly that some women may suffer without remedy in marriage:

But if we meet some manly brute
Whose power is all his pride
Nor love nor tears nor mild dispute
Can stem the boysterous tide.

Silently suffering to the Grave
Must be our wretched fate
Eve when she made herself a slave
Determin'd all our fate.

(Hampsten, 13–14)

When her work is taken as a whole, Winchilsea fits consistently into the Orinda tradition and into Lipking's definition of a woman's poetic. How accurate his definition is may be shown by how many of the poems that were shaped by her life and self Winchilsea believed she could never publish. It is also clear why modern critics have found Winchilsea to be a typical Augustan, even if her nature poetry attracted Wordsworth.[56] She was acutely attuned to the taste and attitudes of her age, and, despite her individual perspectives, tried to hew as carefully as possible to what she thought would be socially and artistically acceptable. That we are beginning to understand how far her vision exceeded the bounds she herself accepted is a tribute to the legacy she left unpublished and unacknowledged for hundreds of years.

Winchilsea's many personal poems, contained in the manuscripts from which Reynolds's edition was created and the Wellesley manuscript, suggest a distinctive use of poetry by women: the circulation of poems to private hands was not like that of men, with patrons and clients, because the motive could seldom be ambition. And the publication of poems did not create a large, public community of readership. Even if women were ambitious, they were seldom permitted to express the motive. Instead, women used poetry on behalf of others or to create a relatively small community for at least two purposes: to cultivate an audience, who would help the poet feel more connected with a number of friends despite her retreat to the country; or, as with Mary Masters (fl. 1733) and Mary Barber (1690–1757), to present social ideals and, more important, to inspire specific political actions that readers are expected to take. Both Masters and Barber published by subscription, a practice that in itself creates a community of readers and supporters. The poetry inhabits a liminal space between the private and the public. Women may act for others in ways they are not permitted to act for themselves.

Mary Masters (fl. 1733) and Mary Barber (1690–1757)

Both Masters and Barber are clearly daughters of Orinda: they used undoing; they wrote extensively of female friendship and little of male-female love; both praised the marriage relationship as ideal for women; both enjoyed the prospect of retreat to the country; neither wrote to raise the sights of women, even though Masters acknowledged her anger about specific social conditions and Barber cared deeply about Ireland's problems. Mary Masters's primary sanction for publishing her poems was the patronage of Lord Burlington. The preface to her single volume, *Poems on Several Occasions* (1733), informs us that because her education was limited and her parents discouraged her writing poetry, her work was edited by a friend.[57] Masters begs the reader's indulgence of the defect in her poetry. The dedication to Lord Burlington contrasts his greatness to Masters's lowliness:

> . . . when a British Peer has deign'd to shed
> His gen'rous Favours on my worthless Head;

Silent shall I receive the welcome Boon?
No; 'tis a Crime to take and not to own.

. . . .

The Honour yet above the Gift I place,
When such high Names my humble Volume grace,
So much distinguish'd by the Voice of Fame,
That ev'ry Author would the sanction claim.

(P. 7)

In "The Female Triumph," Masters praises another woman (Calista, and possibly, therefore, Catherine Trotter, so named in *The Female Wits*) whom she sets up as an answer to male vanity and boasting: "Her Thoughts are beautiful, refin'd and new, / Polish'd her Language, and her Judgment true" (p. 8). Masters wishes for Prior's gifts to praise her friend, but her choice of subject vindicates her poetry anyway:

My Thoughts, in rough and artless Terms exprest,
Are incorrect and negligently dresst.
Yet sure my just Ambition all must own
The well-chose Subject has my Judgment shown
And in the weak Attempt my great Design is known.

(P. 10)

Masters's friendship poems consistently present her friends as models, greatly superior to the poet, who is always humble: "All I can boast, is this one single Grant, / Just Sense enough to know how much I want" (p. 12). With such a self-deprecating voice, Masters uses her anger at a particular situation to justify her privilege of writing. Mary Masters is the most angry of this temperate group of Orinda's daughters. From "The Defense of my Self," we learn that the poet came to the defense of a lady who had been maligned in a lawsuit and wrote a satire on the lady's adversaries. The poem replies to "Essay on Satyr," written by a gentleman who criticizes the anger that drives the satire. Masters defended her anger while excusing its object:

Yet let me palliate an erroneous Song,
Assert the Rage, but own th' Expression Wrong.
When Indignation rises in my Breast,
It is the Sin, not Sinner I detest.

(P. 28)

127

The poem then turns the argument on its opponent by asserting that he, like the speaker, cleanse the decadent age, that mild measure will not do for perjury:

> The perjur'd Man's deliberately Ill,
> 'Tis not an inconsiderate, sudden Start,
> He meditates the Mischief in his Heart:
> 'Tis all injurious, wicked, full of Spite,
> And not one Sense regal'd with soft Delight.
>
> (Pp. 29–30)

The occasion, then, and not the poet's gifts or status, justified her taking pen in hand. Later in the volume, we learn that Masters had the familiar woman writer's experience of being accused of having plagiarized a translation of a psalm, and she replied with a witty play on the nature-art debate:

> Poets are only *Born* and never *Made*.
> Where Nature does her friendly Warmth exert,
> A Genius may supply the Pendant's Art.
> Hence 'tis, that I, unletter'd Maid, pretend
> To paraphrase a Psalm, or praise a Friend.
> Wholly unpractis'd in the learned Rules,
> And arduous Precepts of the noisy Schools.
> . . . .
> Whate'er I write, whate'er I impart,
> Is simple Nature unimprov'd by Art.
> Search but those Strains.
> . . . .
> You'll plainly see, in almost ev'ry Line,
> Distinguishing defects to prove them Mine.
>
> (P. 4)

Although Masters first published at eighteen under the guise of a "young Gentleman," in this volume she came to the defense of her male friend Myrtillo, impelled again by her rage. What is a poor half-literate maid doing, taking on critics "that durst their learn'd Authority invade?" Again the justification for her gesture is anger, and she sardonically calls on critics to remove any defects they find from her poem.

Masters's frequent occasional poems and reply poems echo Winchilsea's practices, but Masters's ideals for women were less farsighted. Masters's poems about Marinda and Clemene are scattered throughout *Poems,* and the ideal they celebrate balances the image of the author: they are wives and mothers, reserved, chaste, tender, soft-spoken. Marriage divides Clemene from the poet, who finds restoration in the country, but who does not protest the separation. Despite her conservative vision of women, Masters idealized a companionate marriage of equal passion, if not status:

> When the fond Pair with equal Passion burn,
> And mutually the gentle Flame return.
>
> . . . .
>
> From mutual Cares a mutual Blessing flows,
> And the firm Union more cemented grows.
>
> (P. 151)

After the volume from which I have been quoting, Masters seems to have abandoned poetry, a decision we find recorded by a pair of poems in the book. Mr. J. W. announces that Masters's silence makes all nature fade in "To Mrs. Masters, occasion'd by her Resolution to write no more" (pp. 97–99). The poet replies that she will draw inspiration from his praise, but there is no assurance from succeeding volumes that she did. Instead, the end of *Poems* seems to have been written by the male poet whom Masters called Myrtillo and defended against the critics. Evidence for this conclusion is that the final poems not only are written in a different voice but contain a poem on the coronation of George and Caroline, a poem Masters had requested of Myrtillo. Masters seems to have justified the privilege of writing through advocacy of others or occasions when powerful feeling, especially on others' behalf, exceeded her inhibitions. At least, such is the rhetorical strategy of the poems.

Mary Barber, author of *Poems on Several Occasions* (1734; 1735), was not only better known than Masters, then and now, but also had far more famous patrons: Jonathan Swift and the earl of Orrery, whose ancestor had sponsored Orinda in Ireland.[58] Barber resembled Masters in her use of poetry on behalf of others; an example is a verse petition to Lady Carteret on behalf of a distressed widow. The preface to *Poems* also describes numerous other charitable acts by great families of Ireland that Barber inspired. In addition, the preface excuses Barber for writing poetry because she was frequently sick in bed (p. xviii). Barber herself confessed, "I am sensible that a Woman steps out of her Province, whenever she presumes to write for the Press, and therefore think it necessary to inform my Readers, that my Verses were written with a very different View from any of those which other Attempters in Poetry have proposed to themselves: My Aim being chiefly to form the Minds of my Children" (p. xvii).

But the most distinctive part of Barber's volume is Swift's dedication to Orrery, which is worth quoting at length:

> I have read most of her Poems; and believe your Lordship will ob-
> serve, that they generally contain something new and useful, tending
> to the Reproof of some Vice or Folly, or recommending some Virtue.
> She never writes on a Subject with general unconnected Topicks, but
> always with a Scheme and Method drawing to some particular End;
> wherein many Writers in Verse, and of some Distinction, are so often
> known to fail. In short, she seemeth to have a true poetical Genius,
> better cultivated then could well be expected, either from her Sex,
> or the Scene she hath acted in, as the Wife of a Citizen. (P. vi–vii)

Although his lines drip with condescension to Mary Barber and most of the letter is ironic praise of Orrery, Swift does seem to have been a good friend to Barber: "He invited her to the Deanery, where she acquired the name "Sapphira" and her poems were read and corrected; he introduced her to his friends in England and Ireland and helped her get subscriptions for her *Poems;* when she fell into poverty, he gave her the manuscript of his *Polite Conversation* to sell for her own benefit. She, in turn, conveyed some of his dangerous writings to English publishers, for which she was on one occasion imprisoned."[59] Barber's audacity on Swift's behalf is not so surprising after one senses from her poetry her devotion to the Irish cause. Like Masters, Barber may have been deferential to conventional social ideals of her time, but she found ample sanction to write and act for the good of others.

Barber's friendship with Constantia Grierson (1706–33) offered each writer a mirroring of the other's virtues. In the preface to *Poems,* Barber presents Grierson as an ideal woman writer, and their friendship "will, I think, be allow'd to do Honour to the Female Sex in general, as they are a strong Proof that Women may have so much Virtue, as, instead of depreci-ating, to endeavour to raise the Character of each other" (p. xxv). For her part, Grierson celebrates Barber in the name of Sapphira:

> Oh! cou'd my conscious Muse but fully trace
> The silent Virtues which Sapphira grace;
> How much her Heart, from low Desires refin'd;
> How much her Works, the Transcript of her Mind;
> Her tender Care, and Grief for the Distrest;
> Her Joy unfeign'd, to see true Merit blest;

Her Soul so form'd for every social Care;
A Friend so gen'rous, ardent, and sincere.

(Pp. lxiii–iv)

For all these high moral ideals and the many hortatory poems Barber wrote
for her son and her friends, she had a strong satiric vein in her art as well,
which she expressed in a fascinating poem about getting subscriptions for
her book of poems. The main target for criticism is women who, unlike
Grierson and Barber, deprecate one another. One character, Fulvia, snipes:

Verses are only writ by Men;
I know a woman cannot write;
I do not say this out of Spite;
Nor shall be thought, by those who know me,
To envy one so much below me.

(P. 284)

In general, Orinda's daughters represent most women as critical of she-
authors; but, as the seventeenth flows into the eighteenth century, wom-
en's expectations change. Barber and Winchilsea hope that women as a
group, not just a few exceptional friends, will support women writers;
and when they fail to do so, they are targets of satire. Just as the Female Wits banded together in the face of the hostile world of the theater, so we will see how Winchilsea praised her fellow poets in "The Circuit of Appolo," and Elizabeth Singer Rowe (Philomela), in "A Letter
to Mrs Arrabella Marow," from the Wellesley manuscript. We must recognize, of course, that before Orinda and immediately after her, there were
few women writers for others to praise, but the increasing sense that
women were a social group and audience for one another is perceptible
during the century.

This is not to say that social ideals for women altered greatly. Barber's example of perfect womanhood still lives for others in a pattern where a woman
makes but one decision: whom she marries. After that her life is set in a
defined relational model:

Know Woman's Glory, and her proper End;
Live to her Husband, Family, and Friend:
Thro' varying Life her various Virtues prove,
Honour her Portion here, and Bliss above.

(Pp. 214–15)

131

Barber was aware that she herself exceeded this model, and she wrote an interesting poem that begins with satire on herself as poet-wife: "Her Husband has surely a terrible Life; / There's noting I dread, like a verse-writing Wife" (p. 58). The poem ends, however, on a note Masters had sounded, but one we have heard little before this time: the ideal of the equal marriage. Here Barber advises a husband how to achieve the relationship:

> A Husband's first Praise, is a Friend and Protector:
> Then change not these titles, for Tyrant and Hector.
> Let your Person be neat, unaffectedly clean,
> Tho' alone with your Wife the whole Day you remain,
> Chuse Books for her Study, to fashion her Mind,
> To emulate those who excell'd of her Kind.
> Be Religion the principal Care of your Life,
> As you hope to be blest in your Children and Wife:
> So you, in your Marriage, shall gain its true End;
> And find, in your Wife, a *Companion* and *Friend*.
>
> (P. 62)

Here Barber's ideal of an egalitarian marriage, which is almost identical to Masters's, contrasts with the bleaker vision of the relationship, represented earlier by Egerton, Astell, and Chudleigh. As the more stable eighteenth century followed the turbulent seventeenth, women writers could more assuredly assert equality in the marriage relationship, while at the same time confining the claims to the domestic scene.[60]

We should not leave Mary Barber without a sense of how deeply she felt about the social problems that surrounded her in Ireland and the meaning that poetry had in her life. Many of the defensive strategies she used for taking the privilege of writing are by now familiar. Distinctive about Mary Barber are her care for the Irish and the remedy she found for that care in her poetry:

> Endless Anxiety, I find,
> Hath dire Effects upon the Mind:
> A Life of unsuccessful Care
> Too often sinks us to Despair,
> From such a Life as this, I chuse
> To snatch some Moments for the Muse;
> To slight Mortality, and soar
> To Worlds where Anguish is no more;

Tho' doomed to share her cruel Fate;
Destin'd to pass my joyless Days,
Where Poverty, relentless, preys;
And form'd; unhappily, to grieve
For Miseries I can't relieve.

(P. 33)

She concludes the poem with a regret that she cannot give wealth to the sufferers, but she can "help a Wretch by what I write." The use of poetry for social gestures such as those of Masters and Barber presumes an audience larger than a coterie. In writing for publication volumes supported by subscription, these eighteenth-century writers' practices make an advance on their predecessors. Although most of their defenses and their social ideals are familiar, their notions about equal marriage and their relation to their audience, especially women as an audience, show a definite change that distinguishes the eighteenth from the seventeenth century.

Chapter Three

Behn and Her Daughters

In order to understand the work of Aphra Behn, her literary descendents, and their differences from Orinda and her followers, we should remind ourselves of the varieties of sexual ideologies that coexisted and succeeded one another in seventeenth-century England. The reader must also recognize that the ideologies are not internally consistent, and sometimes their paradoxes lead to change. Here when I speak of a particular ideology, I do not imply that it may be found in all works of a given decade or that it is accepted evenly throughout the society: class, hereditary privileges, and other factors in a traditional society all modulate sexual ideologies, which we now understand as social artifacts. Cavalier skepticism, Puritan patriarchalism, royalist patriarchalism, conservative and radical feminism, and ideas about marriage reform, all exist simultaneously. Another caveat should be added. In dealing with works of art in their historical context, it is easy, even for the experienced literary critic, to neglect the effect of conventions in art. For example, marriage is a conventional ending for a comedy: a playwright's use of the convention does not therefore imply endorsement of the institution in a period of debate about it.

Orinda and her progeny were socially as well as politically conservative, and therefore they tended to accept the sexual roles of the dominant ideology, wishing not to destroy institutions but to reform woman's place in marriage and her educational opportunities. They hoped for attitudinal changes within individuals in coping with the status quo, rather than a changed social structure. They sought not sexual freedom but more nearly equal intellectual and moral status with men. For the most part, these women led settled lives of privilege often within childless marriages, and their perspective on woman's place in society and on male-female sexuality was conditioned by that experience. Aphra Behn and her colleagues, on the other hand, contributed to the changing modes of thought created by philosophical skepticism, the exile of Charles and his followers in France, the monarch's temperament, and the reaction to the Puritan regimes that collapsed in 1660. Changes in poetry, plays, and fiction written by Behn and her followers demonstrate that their work did not simply reflect the ideologies explained here but helped create them. That is, women as playwrights and audiences had as much to contribute to the reform movement of the nineties as Jeremy Collier's *A Short View of the Immorality and Profaneness of the English Stage* (1698). Still, it must be acknowledged that often changes were conservative after the Restoration and that social, political, and sexual ideologies were often contradictory and mixed within any class or social sector. Cavaliers might be politically conservative and sexually radical, and dissenters might be politically Williamite and sexually conservative. And there were variations along a wide spectrum.

Restoration poetry and drama announce a major change in cultural ethos. That part of the change which directly relates to women writers is the cavalier ideology brought to England from exile. The cavalier way of thinking, hatched from many sources beyond our scope, assumed that sexuality is natural and overwhelming, and so beyond the control of institutions, such as religion.[1] According to the cavalier mentality, sexuality must be free from social constraints such as marriage or even constancy. The perpetual conquests of the rakes, with their assertion of radical autonomy, represent the extreme behavior according to this mode of thought.[2] It should be recognized, however, that rakes almost always represent a more radical sexuality than other characters in the same plays, characters who fall in love and mate in more conventional ways. In life the cavaliers were sexually radical and politically conservative. They were, of course, loyal to Charles II, and many remained loyal to James II. They disdained those with fewer social privileges, and they enjoyed all the social markers, manners and wit, that distinguished them from their inferiors.[3] They convey the desperate attempt to continue social distinctions in a society where the authority for the structures and their economic base were vanishing. The verbal wit of the slanging matches and the rake's intellectual control of the dramatic intrigue represents these values in the plays.[4] Libertine ideas appealed to a small group within a larger audience and always coexisted with many other notions about sexual politics from Puritan convictions of the preachers to the continuous debate about parental authority in regard to children's marriage choices, as discussed in the Introduction.

Although they were preoccupied with sexual conquest, the rakes never valued women as individuals. In fact, part of the code was that the rake must tire of his conquest and move on. If a pursued woman seemed too willing, in fact, the rake might become impotent.[5] Behn's poem *The Disappointment* may be a female reaction to this psychology. The center of the ideology, then, is unfettered male self-assertion, which is represented in tragedy through the heroic drama and through the rakes in the sex comedies. The central figure of the heroic play experiences an overwhelming passion that conflicts with his honor, demanded by an institution, and so he is destroyed. We understand he could not behave otherwise. The comedies represent the rake's need for endless self-assertion that confronts all social constraints: it frequently has less to do with sexual pleasure than with power, as male reaction to women's willingness reveals. In fact, the assertion of male will largely depends on the social construction of obstacles to that will.[6]

Such men, and they are by no means the only men represented in Restoration plays, are frequently cruel to women: some are rapists; some are overt misogynists. The ideology puts women in a double bind, based on the double standard. If they reject rakes, they are prudes; if they yield, they are ruined. The ideology's negative construction of women reveals how much it is about power of self-assertion and how little about sex. Bereft of most authority within social structures that were crumbling or being radically transformed, aristocrats, and those who would ape their manners, sought an expression of power in sexuality, power over those who were traditionally powerless—women. The men and the ideology assume that men will abandon the women who have yielded for several reasons: their social status is permanently altered by their having been ruined; once the pair have known one another sexually, the relationship becomes boring; the man no longer feels the thrill of conquest. The mode of thinking simply assumes the predatory male and the abandoned female.

Marriage is abhorrent to such thinking not only because it is the product of property and interest but also because as a long-standing relationship it does not offer the variety necessary to the rake or the lively wife, for that matter. To this way of thinking, the ideal relationship is the extramarital liaison. In such an affair, love is not contingent on property or ambition. It is free, and the relationship need only last as long as desire lasts. This idealization of freedom in love had paradoxical implications for both men and women. Men, who are frequently represented as motivated to marry for ambition or greed, are freed from these imputations.[7] Women could yield to their own desire because not trapped by parental will. But the ideology is largely, though not exclusively, a male fantasy in an era before reliable birth control, when women are left to cope with any resulting pregnancies.

Another important outcome for women of the cavalier ideology was the frequent projection on women of the rake's tendency to roam, so that in some structures women are represented as sexually insatiable, or, in Pope's words, "every woman is at heart a rake."[8] Insatiability is the single means of representing the desire to roam in a confined creature, whereas Pope's generalization betrays the projection of the fantasy of behavior permitted in one gender upon another where it is socially forbidden.

Yet when all these negative consequences of the rake's attitudes are taken into account, an astonishing number of the rakes finally convert to marriage at the end of the play. But these conversions, which become more frequent as the century wears on, are partially the convention of comedy and partially presented as hypocritical or unstable. Yet the slanging matches frequently show the women verbally equal to the men; the frequent marriage proviso scenes are also indicative of some female assertiveness. Until the nineties unhappy young wives still cuckolded their rapacious old husbands. The women identify their interests not with marriage but with exercise of what power social structures and comedic genres allow the powerless: verbal power and the cunning of the trickster. That is why the structures match the trickster rake with a witty woman: both are at odds with social institutions.[9]

The critique of marriage in the drama from 1660 to 1714 is both wider and deeper than the simple conflict with the freedom of the gay couple. The plays of the second half of the seventeenth century were part of a continuing debate about the marriage relationship. Mary Astell's *Reflections on Marriage* and Mary Chudleigh's poems are simply one side of a gradual change in thinking about marriage in the century. Attacks on the authority of king as patriarch easily led to the conclusion that marriage was a secular contractual relationship "of common interest and property." And, as Bishop Fleetwood held, the contract had mutual obligations and rights. These were debated in popular literature, sermons, plays, and courtesy books; and although the old female obligations to submit died hard, there was enough ferment to provoke change in interpretation of the relationship.[10]

Marriage could be perceived as a source of emotional, sexual, and intellectual satisfaction for both mates, and this standard is sometimes the basis for mating in the plays. Above all, the plays protest the marriage that is no longer tolerable: "Plays protest not marriage, but marriage of economic convenience."[11] Even women's greater control over their property may be sometimes represented, especially late in the century, in demonstrating how widows control their lives because they control their property.

The plays treat troubled marriages in a variety of ways. Some attribute trouble to literary ideals, such as a lack of romantic love or a lack of "equality," as the advice books have it—equality of age, or brains, or social class. The plays by women in the century show two major developments in their representations of marriage. One is the realistic problem play, which exposes marital unhappiness in an uncompromising way. The other is the gradual disappearance of the cuckold. By the end of the century, the old and oppressive husband is no longer fair game for infidelity. The increasingly bourgeois audiences of the early eighteenth century required different solutions, among them, divorce.[12]

Both Aphra Behn and Delariviere Manley use cavalier assumptions about women to declare honestly women's equal sexuality. In poems, plays, and fiction, Behn celebrates female desire; and in her fictional autobiography, Manley describes herself as a mistress of the art of love. Behn's plays represent assertive women pursuing men to achieve "free" sexual relationships, sometimes within marriage and as often outside. Manley represents marriage as inimical to love. Her plays also show one strong woman saving oppressive man from his neurotic sexual brutality, whereas another strong woman is destroyed by being confined. Both writers show that male sexual assertion may be brutal and destructive, but that love should be free of institutional constraints or personal interest.

Yet, we must remember, the "boom in sex comedy" did not last. After 1678 "the plays of the next four years show a definite drawing back from the libertine formulas which had flourished briefly in the three years after *The Country Wife* (January 1675)."[13] Wycherley's play brought protests that seem to be identified with objections from women in audiences, who boycotted *The Country Wife*.[14] Ladies in audiences began to protest bawdy plays from this time on, although we do not know on what features of the plays their protests were based. Ironically, Aphra Behn's *Sir Patient Fancy* was an object of protest, and her claim that women have equal rights to be bawdy still confronted her plays' "loss of fame with the Ladies."[15] The same objections to *The Lucky Chance* eight years later revealed that "what the audience was evidently willing to tolerate in stock comedies, it would not as willingly accept in new productions."[16]

By the end of the century, writers were calling for reform of manners and the stage. Under William and Mary, the Society for the Reformation of Manners was organized; and in 1698 Jeremy Collier wrote a famous protest, *A Short View of the Immorality and Profaneness of the English Stage,* which was one of many such that revived some of the Puritan objections to the theater. Catherine Trotter and Mary Pix consciously responded to these calls for reform in their plays.[17] Both create plays that involve intrigues, to be sure, but they are arranged so that the participants are guiltless. Strong women are frequent in their plays; but a desiring woman is usually the agent of evil, whereas good women are frequently agents of reform in their lovers. Trotter and Pix use the old Caroline vocabulary in the new humane drama.

All the plays by Behn and her followers represent the world of money and power as hostile to desire, and they also portray men as agents of that world. In the fiction written by another set of Behn's artistic progeny, men

become genuinely predatory and routinely abandon the women they seduce. Both the drama and the fiction assume that sexuality is a natural, secular, overwhelming force that cannot be regulated by institutions.[18] This
is a major change from the fantasies of Elizabethan and Jacobean comedy
and fiction, which join desire and socioeconomic interest. In the early
period, dramatic structures make their socieconomic structures serve desire.
In *As You Like It*, for example, Orlando unwittingly solves his problem of
being a younger son by loving Rosalind, the daughter of the ruler. The play
denies self-interest in the relationship and changes the duke's status to effect
the outcome. In Restoration fiction and drama, with the confused legacies
of Puritan and cavalier sexual ideologies, social and economic structures
are largely the enemies of desire, probably because the drama accepts the
old social hierarchies that are being challenged by burgeoning commercial
interests.

Behn Herself: Aphra Behn (ca.1640–89)

The voice of Aphra Behn was different from Orinda's, though, as we have
seen, they were frequently identified or compared. Behn assertively com-
peted with men on the stage, in verse, and in fiction. She declared that
women could write as well as men, even if they were not as well educated.
Like Cavendish she was open about her desire for fame: "I value fame as
much as if I had been born a hero," and she vigorously defended her privilege of using the bawdy discourse of her time.[19] She exalted in autonomy
and wrote for money all her audacious life. She was strong enough to be
vulnerable in expressing female sexuality without the protection of social
structures. She vied with Orinda as an alternative model for a woman writer,
but the abuse she endured may demonstrate that, for the less sturdy, the
protective strategies of Orinda were clearly very useful for future writers.
Behn's independence allowed her to adopt the male code of honor, to "seek
physical pleasure and write about it while retaining both a sense of personal
integrity and of loyalty to the larger social order."[20] Clearly Behn was male-
identified, and this psychology explains many of her values and her artistic
strategies; but her identity as a woman also modified significantly what she
selects from, and does with the male discourses of her time. Behn's model
leads her followers to employ the libertine discourse, but to ring individual
variations upon that discourse.

If Behn's honesty may be appealing to the modern feminist, one must
understand that Behn's style required exceptional strength, which was implied in her choice of classical pseudonym: Astrea, the goddess of justice,

the last deity to abandon degenerate humankind, whose return to earth Dryden identified with the Stuart Restoration. Although she was constantly judged morally by her contemporaries, Behn stood for a coherent set of values, defined and defended by her anonymous biographer in 1696:

> She was of a generous and open Temper, something passionate, very serviceable to her Friends in all that was in her Power; and cou'd sooner forgive an Injury, than do one. She had Wit, Honour, good Humour and Judgment. She was Mistress of all the pleasing Arts of Conversation, but us'd em not to any but those who lov'd Plain-dealing. She was a Woman of Sense, and by Consequence a lover of Pleasure, as indeed all, both Men and Women, are; but only some wou'd be thought to be above the Conditions of Humanity, and place their chief Pleasure in a proud, vain Hypocrisie: For my part, I knew her intimately, and never saw ought unbecoming the just Modesty of our Sex, tho' more gay and free than the Folly of the Precise will allow. She was, I'm satisfy'd, a greater Honour to our Sex than all the canting Tribe of Dissemblers, that die with the false Reputation of Saints. This I may venture to say, because I'm unknown, and the revengeful Censures of my Sex will not reach me, since they will never be able to draw the Veil, and discover the Speaker of these bold Truths. If I have done my dead Friend any manner of Justice, I am satisfy'd, having obtain'd my End: If not, the Reader must remember that there are few Astrea's arise in our Age; and till such a One does appear, all our Endeavours in Encomiums on the last, must be vain and impotent.[21]

If we may grant with Behn's biographer that such heroines are extremely rare, she nonetheless inspired a company of successors, most of whom wrote drama and fiction: Ephelia (fl. 1679), Sarah Fyge Field Egerton (1669–1723), Delariviere Manley (1663–1724), Catherine Trotter Cockburn (1679–1749), Mary Pix (1666–1720), Mary Hearne (fl. 1718–19), and Susanna Centlivre (1669–1723). Another descendent, Eliza Haywood (1693–1756), is included in chapter 4. These writers followed Behn in usually writing for money, competing directly with men, and using a variety of genres and contemporary discourses. They envisioned both men and women as an audience, and they were frankly eager for public recognition. Their lives were sometimes unconventional and unsettled, and in their writing they were generally more open about sexuality than were Orinda's daughters. Their drama and fiction represented property as the possible enemy of desire and males as predatory, according to the basic terms of the cavalier ideology.[22] Behn and Manley exalted love, but usually in protest of conventional social structures, free from interest or ambition. Because men are frequently driven by ambition or interest, or both—or simply love conquest—men frequently betray women in these fantasies; and the fiction, as we shall see, explores women's strategies for survival of abandonment. Behn's drama frequently deals with enforced marriages and feisty heroines, whereas her poetry ideal-izes love and sexual pleasure immune from coercive, wordly concerns. The later drama of the Female Wits and Centlivre tames these fantasies into more conventional representations of love and marriage, as well as more sympathetic middle-class characters or London "cits."

Because Behn's followers wrote mostly drama and fiction, we will con-sider her poetry first and then that of Ephelia and Sarah Fyge Field Egerton. After that discussion, we will deal with the Female Wits and the Salic Law of Wit. Then we will return to Behn's drama and explore her plays and those of her successors, Manley, Trotter, Pix, and Centlivre.

Behn on the Privilege of Writing

Anyone who now studies the work of Aphra Behn must be in debt to Mary Ann O'Donnell's excellent annotated bibliography, *Aphra Behn* (1986). I have tried to make all my assertions about Behn conform to her careful scholarship.[23] All of Behn's ideas about the privilege of writing turned on two basic assumptions: that women could write as well as men and that the poet in a male or a female is masculine. She believed that, even if women were not as well educated as men and few had accomplished much as writ-ers, there was no reason "why women should not write as well as men." In the epilogue to *Sir Patient Fancy* (1686), spoken by Nell Gwyn, from which this line comes, Behn argued that the subordination of women was new: "We once were famed in story, and could write / Equal to men; could govern, nay, could fight" (4:115). She continued to explain that the kind of play-writing then in fashion was easy for women: "By how much more we're sensible of love; / Quickest in finding all the subtlest ways / To make your joys, why not to make you plays?" Men's practices of going by the three unities "must all give way to the unlaboured farce." And so, by Behn's logic, if women could manage the discourses of the time, they had as good a claim as men upon the attention of an audience. We should understand, however, that this epilogue was a defense: her own experience proved other-wise, but her argument is as basic to Behn's notion about writing women as undoing was for Orinda. We should notice, moreover, that Behn's politi-cal and economic conservatism is brought into line with her feminism by appeals to history as authority for women's equality. Her ideas are not al-ways so consistent, as we shall see.

Others of Behn's ideas about the privilege of writing came from her second premise that the poet in a male or a female is masculine. "All I ask," she said, "is the Privilege for my Masculine Part, the Poet in me, (if any such you will allow me) to tread in these successful Paths my Predecessors have so long thriv'd in, to take those Measures that both the Ancient and Modern Writers have set me, and by which they have pleased the World so well: If I must not, because of my Sex, have this Freedom, but that you will usurp all to yourselves; I lay down my Quill" (3:187). Having no female tradition on which to build, Behn was unabashedly male-identified, for she would not be excluded from writing by her gender. Occasionally, to be sure, she hoped for immortality with Sappho and Orinda:

> Among that number, do not me disdain,
> Me, the most humble of that glorious train,
> I by a double right thy bounties claim,
> Both from my sex, and in Apollo's name:
> Let me with Sappho and Orinda be
> O ever, sacred nymph, adorned by thee;
> And give my verses immortality.[24]

But most frequently she looked to male models—Rochester, Waller—and delighted in late praise from Bishop Burnet, who had earlier defamed her. Three poems illustrate Behn's attitudes toward her models and her audience. In her elegy for Edmund Waller, Behn describes the development of her powers as she was tutored by reading Waller's poetry:

> Hail, wondrous *Bard*, whose Heav'n-born *Genius* first
> My Infant *Muse*, and Blooming *Fancy* Nurst.
> With thy soft *Food* of *Love* I first began,
> Then fed a nobler *Panegyrick* Strain,
> Numbers *Seraphic!* and at every View,
> My Soul extended, and much larger grew.
>
> (6: 406)

Waller becomes a god for Behn as soon as he becomes a model for her poetry. She also envisioned Waller's practice as a model for the entire Restoration, especially in liberating the age from the Puritan repression of sexuality.

Another poem about poetry was addressed to Anne Wharton, "To Mrs. W. On her Excellent Verses (Writ in Praise of some I had made on the Earl of *Rochester*) Written in a Fit of Sickness." It has an interesting history. In 1680 Rochester died at thirty-three, and Behn wrote a long elegy for her hero. Rochester's cousin, Anne Wharton, an aspiring poet herself, wrote Behn praising the elegy and offering gratuitous advice. Astrea is an inspiration whose fame should exceed Sappho's:

> May you have all her wit, without her shame:
> 'Tho she to honour gave a fatal wound,
> Employ your hand to raise it from the ground . . .
> Scorn meaner themes, declining low desire,
> And bid your Muse maintain a Vestal fire.
> If you do this, what glory will insue,
> To all our sex, to poesie, and you?[25]

Although Angeline Goreau rightly scorns Wharton's condescension in advising a writer of ten years professional experience, the issue here seems moral rather than literary. A woman's questionable morality always allows others to take liberties with her. Behn did not, however, take umbrage. Instead, she replied in a poem focused on the meaning Rochester had for her poetry. His ghost appears to the speaker in a dream, and because of its condescension, she knows it to be Rochester:

> It did advance, and with a Generous Look,
> To me Addrest, to worthless me it spoke:
> With the same wonted Grace my Muse it prais'd,
> With the same Goodness did my Faults Correct;
> And careful of the Fame himself first rais'd,
> Obligingly it School'd my loose Neglect.
> The soft, the moving Accents soon I knew
> The gentle Voice made up of Harmony;
> Through the Known Paths of my glad Soul it flew;
> I knew it straight, it could no others be,
> 'Twas not Alied but very very he.
>
> (6:172)

The rest of the poem compares Rochester to a god descending to be among shepherds and the poet to a rustic swain: "Whilst the transported Swain the Honour pays / With humble Adoration, humble Praise" (6:173). Even if one allows for the exaggerated gestures of the time, the poem is florid, yet the lines about instruction are clear: Rochester was one of the models to whose ways Behn schooled her verse. Her response to Wharton's moralistic counsel was, moreover, characteristic: she simply concentrated the reader's attention and her own on poetic art. Such emphasis did not keep others from disapproving her morality. Gilbert Burnet, of whom more later, wrote to Mrs. Wharton, "Some of Mrs. Behn's songs are very tender; but she is so abominably vile a woman, and rallies not only all religion but all virtue in so odious and obscene a manner, that I am heartily sorry she has writ anything in your commendation."[26] In the complex world of Restoration politics, Burnet's disdain for Behn's morals did not prevent him from soliciting a poem from her in 1688.

As her response to Wharton shows, Behn may have been independent and committed to her art, but she seems to have been inordinately grateful for praise. At the end of her life, Behn addressed a Pindaric to the same Bishop Burnet who scorned her morality earlier. The occasion of the poem was the Whig divine's invitation to write a eulogy to William III. Behn could not abandon her political principles, which Burnet apparently assumed were as easy as her sexual morals seemed to him. In "A PINDARIC POEM *to the Reverend Doctor Burnet, on the Honour he did me of Enquiring after me and my* MUSE," she gracefully explained why she declined the honor. She could not abandon her loyalty to the Stuarts, and she cleverly used the occasion to turn political tables on Burnet. Behn acknowledges the power of Burnet's pen, which almost persuades her of his position, in spite of herself. She also acknowledges that Burnet's praise makes recompense for previous wounds, but then she indulges in an ironic fiction, pretending that she, one of the most prolific political writers of her time, had only written pastorals until praised by Burnet:

> Till now, my careless Muse no higher strove
> T'inlarge her Glory, and extend her Wings;
>   Than underneath *Parnassus* Grove,
> To Sing of Shepherds, and their humble Love;
> But never durst, like *Cowly,* tune her Strings,
>   To sing of Heroes and of Kings.
>
> (6:408)

The pretense, of which practically any reader would be aware, then as now, depends on the idea that public poetry exists only when recognized by authority: "Since by an Authority Divine, / She is allow'd a more exalted Thought; / She will be valu'd now as Current Coyn" (6:409). Although Burnet's praise delights Behn, she cannot bend her stubborn Muse to praise

William: "But Loyalty Commands with Pious Force, / That stops me in the thriving Course." She confesses that although she may deplore the "Wond'rous Change," she adores the "great Design," the fact that England has a stable government. But even her poverty and illness cannot bring her to praise "this Unpresidented Enterprise." She therefore reverses the gesture with which the poem began and invites Burnet to praise William: "Your Pen shall more Immortalize his Name, / That even his Own Renown'd and Celebrated Fame" (6:410). The length and elaborateness of the poem confirm the importance of Behn of being artistically equal to Bishop Burnet, as the reversal of the gesture implies. Even if one excludes her love poems, most of Behn's occasional verse is addressed to men, many of whom are implicated in her art. They were for her a crucial audience. She was a strong person and a gifted writer, yet the tone she invariably adopts in relation to her male counterparts is so vulnerable that one suspects it is a strategy to undo her strength and balance her claims of equality.

Although she was not above exploiting the supposed gallantry of a largely male audience, Behn used the vocabulary of wit and beauty to convey the principle of sexual equality. We see this in the prologue and epilogue to her first play, *The Forc'd Marriage*. In the prologue a male actor begins by warning the audience that the fair sex are trying to conquer men with both wit *and* beauty, but that the play is the author's first venture: "Discourage but this first attempt, and then / They'll hardly dare to sally out again." The actor is interrupted by an actress who asks, "Who is't that to their Beauty would submit, / And yet refuse the Fetters of their Wit?" Women, she declares,

> . . . shall obliging prove
> Imposing Nought but Constancy in Love:
> That's all our Aim, and when we have it too,
> We'll sacrifice it all to pleasure you.
>
> (3:285)

Having set up the wit-beauty dichotomy in the prologue, Aphra continues it in the epilogue, spoken by a woman, which ends, "But we are upon equal treatment yet, / For neither conquer, since we both submit; / You to our Beauty bow, we to your Wit" (3:381). We notice that the female speaker represents with her wit not the author but women generally, for whom beauty only is power: "Tis Beauty only can our Power maintain." Behn gracefully asserts the principle of equality, but the terms of gallantry trivialize the idea.

In the epistles and prefaces to other plays, Behn dealt with more serious issues surrounding her notion of women writing as well as men. In the epistle to the reader of *The Dutch Lover,* for example, she copes with the limited education of women if they aspire to be playwrights. She ridicules a fop who tells the audience in the pit "that they were to expect a woful Play, God damn him, for it was a womans" (1:224). In the long and angry diatribe, Behn addresses the issue of women's ignorance of the ancient languages when she says, "For waiving the examination, why women having equal education with men, were not as capable of knowledge, of whatever sort as well as they: I'l only say as I have touch'd before, that Plays have no great room for that which is men's great advantage over women, that is learning" (1:224). Proof of this assertion is that Shakespeare's plays please more than the learned Jonson's, although even Jonson was not as learned as reputed. Moreover, she avers that, except for the laureate, no modern playwrights compose so well, "but that a woman may well hope to reach their greatest heights." If women are ignorant of the three unities, they do not serve well at the present time anyway. In short, a woman can compete if she learns the craft and the taste of the time. There is also more than a hint that women really are capable of learning anything men learn, but that issue is set aside.

In another address to the reader, the preface to *Sir Patient Fancy,* Behn asserted the equal privilege of women to be bawdy in their plays. The epilogue, as we have already seen, asserted equality in literary potential. The prologue ironically ridicules the audience by saying that poets of that time are inferior to the ancients as well as to the previous generation: small wits may now claim attention, "Nay even Women now pretend to reign; / Defend us from a Poet *Joan* again!" (4:8). The self-deprecation is a strategy that smacks a bit of Orinda, but the preface defends the right of a woman writer to be as bawdy as a man; such a claim follows from her assumptions that the poet in a woman is masculine and that women writers should follow the discourse of their time.

She would be "vindicated from the most unjust and silly aspersion, women could invent to cast on women; and which only my being a woman had procured me; *That it was Bawdy,* the least and most excusable Fault in the men writers, to whose plays they all crowd, as if they came to no other end than to hear what they condemn in this: *but from a woman it was unnatural.*" Behn continued a similar defense of her right to be as bawdy as her age in the preface to *The Lucky Chance* (1687), where she recites the names of many favorite plays of the age and reminds the reader of their use of bawdry: "All these I Name as some of the best Plays I know; If I should repeat the Words exprest in these Scenes I mention, I might justly be charg'd with course ill Manners, and very little Modesty, and yet they so naturally fall into the places they are designed for, and so are proper for the Business, that there is not the least Fault to be found with them; though I say those things in any of mine wou'd damn the whole Piece, and alarm the Town" (3:186). Although, as Goreau emphasizes, Behn goes on contradictorily to argue that her play is not indecent and that she would be a fool to make it so, we may forgive her confusion of logic because, like Cavendish, she was working ideas through for the first time and was greatly on the defensive.[27] She simply cannot think her way through her anger at a stubborn ideology that judges a woman writer primarily as a woman, held to certain restricted social codes, and secondarily as a writer with an audience to please.

Like all writers of whatever time, Behn lamented the degenerate taste of her age, but she always understood the need to write plays within the fashion of the day. In the epilogue to *The Feign'd Curtezans* (1679), she reminds the audience that if they do not support the theater, the poets will write lampoons and libels instead of plays. Then follows a fine piece of social satire, revealing how secure was Behn's grasp of comedic stereotypes and behavior codes in contemporary drama:

> The precise whoring Husband's haunts betray,
> Which the demurer Lady to repay,
> In his own coin does the just debt defray.
> The brash young Beauty link'd to Lands and Age,
> Shuns the dull Property and strokes the youthful Page;
> And if the Stripling apprehend not soon,
> Turns him aside, and takes the brawny Groom;
> Whilst the kind Man so true a Husband proves,
> To think all's done by the things he loves,
> Knows he's a Cuckhold, yet content to bear
> Whate'er Heaven sends, or Horns, or lusty Heir.
>
> (2:411)

Whatever she may say about the taste of her age, Behn's joy in the dramatic practice of her time is palpable.

Yet her contemporaries were also conscious that whatever her gifts as a dramatist, Behn's distinction lay in her poetry about love. So we come to understand that to write poetry about passionate love as she wished, Behn sacrificed the value of modesty, as she had in creating plays according to the taste of the age. Behn seems to have expected her superior gifts as an artist to balance the social sacrifice Orinda found ways not to make. The poems of tribute to Behn's volumes of poetry demonstrate these patterns. In a poem praising *The Lover's Watch,* Charles Cotton wrote, for example,

Of Buskin, and of Sock, you know the Pace;
And tread in both, with equal Skill and Grace,
But when you write of Love, Astrea, then
Love dips his Arrows, where you wet your pen.
Such charming Lines did never Paper grace;
Soft, as your Sex; and smooth, as Beauty's Face.
And 'tis your Province, that belongs to you.

(6:6)

Nahum Tate identified Behn with Orinda: "The Pride of Greece we now out-rival'd see: / Greece boasts one Sappho; two Orinda's we" (6:7). As we have seen, the identification was often made; but other male admirers made sharper distinctions between the two poets. In a tribute to *Lycidus: Or the Lover in Fashion*, Kendrick compared the art of Behn favorably to that of Orinda, Sappho, and even Ovid in dealing with the theme of love:

The female Laurels were obscure'd till now,
And they deserv'd the Shades in which they grew:
But *Daphne* at your call return's her flight,
Looks boldly up and dares the God of Light.
If we *Orinda* to your works compare,
They uncouth, like her countreys soyle, appear,
Mein as its peasants, as its Mountains bare;
Sappho tasts strongly of the sex, is weak and poor,
At second hand she russet Laurels wore,
Yours are your own, a rich and verdant store.
If Loves the theme, you outdo *Ovids* Art,
Softer than's plumes, more piercing than his Dart.

(6:297)

If Orinda is gradually praised for her chaste life, no contemporary denies Behn is the better artist. Behn's artistic situation and reputation are paradoxical. Because she identified with male writers and used male discourse, she sought an equality for her art that she never achieved, and she was constantly vilified for her personal life or condescended to as a woman. Yet her complex attitudes led to her writing of love as no woman ever had and few have since. Her identification with men earned her abuse, but also led her to achievements other women writers could hardly imagine. It is to her distinctive writing poetry about love that we now turn.

Behn's Poetry

Judith Gardiner is certainly right in saying of Behn: "Her single dominant theme in plays, novels, and poetry is human sexuality, its powers and problems."[28] Gardiner further suggests that Behn's male identification led to her devotion to the Stuarts and to the cavalier ideal that love should be free. Behn simply transferred to women the autonomous male stance in which the code of honor accompanied a frank sexuality outside social structures. The ideal relationship is one in which both lovers are free and outside marriage, property, and other worldly values. Behn did not scorn her gender, as did Wycherley or Rochester; she simply allowed women the privileges of men. She saw cavalier love poetry as liberating her age from Puritan oppression. She said of Waller:

> Darkness was o're the *Muses* Land displaid,
> And even the *Chosen Tribe* unguided staid.
> 'Till, by thee rescu'd from th' *Egyptian* Night,
> They now look up, and view the God of Light,
> That taught them how to *Love,* and how to Write.
>   (6:407)

Behn tends to use a traditionally male vocabulary to convey women's emotions. In "The Willing Mistress," for example, Amyntas's eyes are singled out, as would be those of a Petrarchan lady, only to be surpassed his mistress's passion: "His Charming Eyes no Aid requir'd / To tell their softning Tale; / On her that was already fir'd, 'Twas Easy to prevaile" (6:163). The frankness of the woman's sexuality changes entirely the power relationship of conquest and surrender. Instead, the wit of the poem is that the mistress wills what takes place as much as the lover. "Bright Eyes" are again a figure in Behn's most famous lyric, "Love Arm'd," from the tragedy *Abdelazar,* where the dramatic context specifies a woman wooing a man. The man has all the pride and cruelty of the Petrarchan mistress. But the most extensive use of eye imagery for the male lover is "On a *Pin* that hurt *AMINTAS' Eye.*" The speaker addressing the pin is clearly female and sees the pin as a rival from the beginning: "Base Instrument, so ill thou'st play'd thy part, / Wounding his Eye, thou'st wounded my poor Heart (6:392). The pin is accused of ambition, but finally the speaker is convinced that the pin's power was a single occurrence: "Hence from my Sight, and mayst thou ever lie / A Crooked Object to each scornful Eye" (6:393). Behn's gender provided a fresh approach to long-standing poetic conventions.

The Pindaric "On Desire," which again associates eye imagery with the male, is one of her most interesting poems. For men and women, desire is equal:

> Tell me, thou nimble fire, that dost dilate
>   Thy might force thro every part,
> What God, or Human power did thee create
>   In my, till now, unfacil heart?
> Art thou some welcome plague sent from above
>   In this dear form, this kind disguise?
>   Or the false offspring of mistaken love,
>   Begot by some soft thought that faintly strove
> With the bright piercing Beautys of *Lysanders* Eyes.
>   (6:358)

Desire haunts the speaker's hours; its enemies are clearly marked: honor, interest, ambition. One does not find desire by searching for it in either the country or the court, but instead comes upon it by accident in Lysander's eyes:

> When the dear Shepherd do's appear,
> I faint, I dye with pleasing pain,
> My words intruding sighing break
> When e're I touch the charming swain
> When e're I gaze, when e're I speak.
>   (6:358–59)

Women who pretend to virtue really lack desire "to thaw the Virgin Ice." So the speaker questions the real desire of women who would preserve chastity with adorers at their feet:

> Deceive the foolish World—deceive it on,
> And veil your passions in your pride;
> But now I've found your feebles by my own,
> From me the needful fraud you cannot hide.
>   (6:359–60)

As Judith Gardiner says, "Both men and women desire blindly in her work; both are fickle; both pine for what they cannot have; both wish to domineer; the innate psychology of both sexes is identical."[29]

This attitude allowed Behn to parody the imperfect enjoyment poem from a woman's perspective in *The Disappointment* (6:178–82). It also allowed her to imagine a pan-sexuality in which both sexes are objects of desire of either one. A lesbian poem, "To the fair Clarinda, who made Love to me, imagin'd more than Woman," stresses Clarinda's androgynous attractions. Like Behn herself, Clarinda has a manly part that tempts the poet, "With thy deluding Form thou giv'st us pain, / While the bright Nymph betrays us to the Swain." The poem ends with a tribute to the virtues of both sexes combined in Clarinda:

> Thou beauteous Wonder of a different Kind,
> Soft *Cloris* with the dear *Alexis* join'd;
> When e'er the Manly part of thee, wou'd plead
> Thou tempts us with the Image of the Maid,
> While we the noblest Passions do extend
> The Love to Hermes, Aphrodite the Friend.
>
> (6:363)

Bisexuality is also clear in "To Amintas Upon reading the Lives of some of the Romans." Here the poet announces that if ancient figures had been as beautiful as Amintas, the course of history would certainly have been changed:

> Had'st thou, Amintas, liv'd in that great age,
> When hardly Beauty was to nature known,
> What numbers to thy side might'st thou engage
> And conquer'd Kingdoms by thy looks alone.
>
> (6:360)

The examples of possible conquests are both male and female: Scipio, Sophonisbe, Massanissa; Caesar, Cleopatra; Tarquin, Lucrece; Pompey, the king of Egypt. Amintas is universally attractive: "neither sex can thy fetters shun." A pastoral sequence, "Our Cabal," shows homosexual relationships rivaling the heterosexual. Philander loves Lycidas, "softer Youth was never seen, / His beauty Maid; but Man, his Mein," and the speaker urges Cloris to "try thy power with *Lycidas*" (6:162) As Gardiner suggests, many of

Behn's songs remain sexually ambiguous because the reader is uncertain of the speaker's gender.

If the gender of lovers is relatively unimportant to Behn, the process of loving—its vagaries, pains, and pleasures—are dominant themes of both her original verse and the several works she was drawn to translate: Bonne-corse's *Le Montre,* Tallamant's *Le Voyage de l'Isle d'Amour,* and *Lycidas: or The Love in Fashion.* These are translations of allegorical works that represent the psychological states and changes in the experience of love: rivals, absence, jealousy, resentment, ecstasy, memory, coquetry, constancy, indifference, and so on. Much of the sentiment is commonplace and perfunctory, but such structures relate to Behn's fiction and seem, like the many novellas she wrote, intended to educate the reader in experiencing emotions that are socially constructed but represented as both natural and inevitable.

The freedom, independence, and autonomy Behn idealized in love had very different social consequences for the genders, however: "Women may be ruined for what men take as pleasure, and women thus fear being 'conquered' only to be abandoned."[30] Although Behn sought the same freedom for women to rove as men enjoyed, in poem after poem she acknowledged that men deserted women as the need for new conquests drove them from one woman to another. In "The Reflection: A Song," Serena describes how a cruel swain charmed her with eloquence, flattery, arts, gifts, and letters:

> Till by such Obligations Prest,
> By such dear Perjuries won:
> I heedlessly Resign'd the rest,
> And quickly was undone.
> For as my Kindling Flames increase,
> Yours glimeringly decay:
> The Rifled Joys no more can Please,
> That once oblig'd your Stay.
> (6:187–88)

"An Ode to Love" declares that Lysander has all the characteristics of Cupid, as Lysander lays siege to each fair:

> Thy bow, thy Quiver, and thy Darts:
> Even of thy Painted Wing has [he] rifled thee,
> To bear him from his Conquer'd broken Hearts,
> To the next Fair and Yielding She.
> (6:209)

Although she believed in equality of love, Behn wrote in a tradition and at a time when men were simply assumed to be predatory and faithless, and women always vulnerable to abandonment. Insofar as she represented the ideal of honest equality, her love poetry is distinctive, but the social realities and poetic conventions of Restoration England found their way into her poems too:

> They fly if Honour take our part,
> Our Virtue drives 'em o're the field.
> We lose 'em by too much desert,
> And Oh! they fly us if we yield.
> Ye Gods! is there no charm in all the fair
> To fix this wild, this faithless, wanderer?
>
> Man! our great business and our aim,
> For whom we spread our fruitless snares,
> No sooner kindles the designing flame,
> But to the next bright object bears
> The Trophies of his conquest and our shame:
> Inconstancy's the good Supream
> The rest is airy Notion, empty Dream.
>
> (6:349)

Occasionally Behn's poetry anticipated her fiction in showing women bonding with one another to cope with male unfaithfulness. Selinda, whom Alexis now woos, meets Cloris, whom Alexis has betrayed. Selinda is persuaded by Cloris's story to give Alexis up, and the two women swear loyalty to one another (6:377–78). Twice Behn addressed roughly the same poem to contemporaries, Mrs. Harsenet (6:393–94) and Lady Morland (6:175–77), in which the speaker concedes the greater beauty of her rival and finds it justifies Amintas's desertion of her: "But now I find 'tis Just he should Adore. / Not to love you, a wonder sure would be, / Greater than all his Perjuries to me." Yet, at the end of the poem, the speaker asserts that Cloris deserves a better love than the perjured Amintas: "A Heart that nothing but your Force can fear, / And own a Soul as Great as you are Fair" (6:177). The poems are interesting for two qualities. First, the poet's refusal to blame the rival for the lover's defection, which means that she can praise the rival and value her more than the lover. Second, the repetition of the poems, with only minor changes in wording, using the same lover's name, suggests that Amintas was habitually unfaithful and that the poet took her revenge through praising her rival. When one considers the strong pressures men

153

have always brought on women to blame one another for a lover's desertion, the poems testify to the fact that Behn did not accept the rivalry game any more than any other. Despite the social conventions of her age, Behn found ways, using the ideology of cavalier discourse, to create two realms in which love could exist as she envisioned it: the golden age of the pastoral and in some fantasies of her drama, as we shall see below.

Poets: Ephelia (fl. 1679)
and Sarah Fyge Field Egerton (1669–1723)

Both of the poets who write in the Behn tradition also have certain characteristics they share with Orinda, and it is well to note these at the outset. Ephelia published with a female pseudonym, and so her identity is a mystery to this day.[31] In fact, Ephelia is reputed to have been Orinda's daughter, Joan Philips. Yet because a vivid series of love poems is the center of her single volume, and by her own identification, Ephelia seems to have more in common with Behn than with Philips. Sarah Fyge Field Egerton also identifies herself with both writers, but, like Ephelia, she follows Behn in her poetic practice of developing a female identity in the context of powerful love affairs.

Ephelia, the author of a single volume of poetry, *Female Poems on Several Occasions* (1679), continues the development of female subjectivity explored by Aphra Behn. As we have said, Ephelia combines the models of Behn and Orinda. Ephelia is known as Joan Philips, but because little or nothing is known of Philips and Ephelia's poetry seems purposely autobiographical, the reader is in a double bind, frustrated by lack of knowledge to which the poet clearly alludes.[32] Still the poems continue many of the themes and much of the spirit of Aphra Behn, who represents a model for Ephelia, one she combined with that of Orinda. In a poem of tribute, "To Madam Bhen," Ephelia marvels at Behn's poetry, which inspires her own:

> Madam! permit a Muse, that has been long
> Silent with wonder, now to find a tongue:
> Forgive that zeal can no longer hide,
> And pardon a necessitated pride.
> When first your strenuous polite lines I read,
> At once it wonder and amazement bred,
> To see such things flow from a woman's pen,
> As might be envied by the wittiest men.
> . . . .

154

As in your self, so in your verses meet,
A rare connection of strong and sweet;
This I admired at, and my pride to show,
Have took the vanity to tell you so.[33]

Ephelia's admiration for Behn combined with her humble tone conveys a distinctive blend that she makes of Behn's assertiveness and willingness to deal with sexual love as a theme with Orinda's modesty about her art. The dedication of *Female Poems* to Princess Mary asks for her protection in an Orinda-like way, and a prologue to a lost play, *The Pair-Royal of Coxcombs,* makes a gesture of undoing after taking an assertive tone:

Gallants,
If, as you say, you love variety,
We have hopes that you so kind will be
To the poor play, to give it your applause,
Though not for wit, nor worth, but yet because
A woman wrote it; though it be not rare,
It is not common.
. . . .
She hopes too, the great wits, who crowd the age,
. . . .
Won't undervalue so their mighty wit,
To criticize on what a woman writ:
Yet if you'll have it so, it shall be naught,
They that dislike, are welcome to find fault;
For she protests, she had no other ends
In writing this, than to divert her friends.

(Pp. 16–18; *WD,* 223–24)

After two poems about public life, Ephelia finds her stride in *Female Poems* and offers a series of poems that trace the process of an unhappy love affair from its irresistible inception in "Love's first Approach" (p. 7) through Ephelia's growing sense that she cannot stop loving the disdainful Strephon (Mr. J. G.), who leaves her for Africa without saying farewell and, when he returns, resides in London six days before coming to see her. The poems analyze Ephelia's passion and anger at his treatment of her: "I wou'd not love, and yet I cannot hate" (p. 12). Strephon's behavior, his abandonment of Ephelia because of business interest, is very like the pattern of the males in the amatory fiction studied in chapter 4, below. Her tortures are similar to those of the abandoned heroines of the fiction as well:

My Days no Pleasure know, no Sleep my Nights:
With wand'ring thoughts each Pray'r thou dost prophane,
(I offer to my God) and mak'st them vain.
Sometimes with Books I wou'd divert my mind,
But nothing there but J's and G's I find:
Sometimes to ease my Grief, my Pen I take,
But it no Letters but JG will make.

(P. 29)

Characteristic of Ephelia's art is her pun in "I offer to my God," which is like the one on "common," which we may observe in the prologue to *Coxcombs*. For all her victimization by Strephon, Ephelia maintains her self-respect through expression of anger, which she sometimes displaces on another lover, Clovis, but which she understands Strephon really deserves. After Strephon marries in Africa in a total and devastating betrayal, Ephelia understands that she has created Strephon and could destroy him if she wished:

'Twas I that rais'd him to this Glorious State,
And can as easily Annihilate:
But let him live, Branded with Guilt, and Shame,
And Shrink into the Shade from whence he came.

(P. 37)

Yet because of the sexuality she accepts—one very like that of Behn, who wrote about her tortured love for John Hoyle—Ephelia thinks of herself as fated to love J. G. in spite of herself:

. . . he's twice my Age and more;
And yet I love this false, this worthless Man,
With all the Passion that a Woman can;
Doat on his Imperfections, though I spy
Nothing to love; I Love, and know not why.
Sure 'tis Decreed in the dark Book of Fate,
That I shou'd Love, and he shou'd be ingrate.

(P. 59)

Ephelia's passion for Strephon blights, but does not preclude, other loves. Celadon tries unsuccessfully to persuade her that she should abandon her relationship with Strephon, but she confesses it is hopeless (pp. 71–72). She

156

also pledges only friendship to her bashful lover Clovis, but after Strephon marries and Clovis falls in love with Marina, she acknowledges a new feeling for him in "Passion discovered" (p. 91). Throughout the volume Ephelia shows a keen awareness of imitation in love relationships, for, as René Girard has taught us, nothing stimulates desire like a rival. At times Ephelia is like Aphra Behn in imagining herself as masculine, as when she invites Phylocles to friendship:

> We will forget the Difference of Sex,
> Nor shall the World's rude Censure us Perplex:
> Think Me all Man: my Soul is Masculine,
> And Capable of as great Things as Thine.
>
> (Pp. 85–86)

This spirit, which echoes Behn's, also allows Ephelia a similar sexuality in its liberation from convention, as in her "Poem on Maidenhead, Written at the Request of a Friend," which is full of the kind of punning we observed earlier:

> Thou short liv'd Tyrant, that Usurp'st a Sway
> O're Woman-kind, though none thy pow'r obey,
> Except th' Ill-natur'd, Ugly, Peevish, Proud,
> But what's the Reason they Obey so well?
> Because they want the Power to Rebell:
> But I forget, or have my Subject lost:
> Alas! thy Being's Fancy at the most:
> Though much desired, 'tis but seldom Men
> Court the vain Blessing from a Woman's Pen.
>
> (Pp. 40–41)

As a consequence of her male-female perspective on sexuality, Ephelia's friendship with a woman is very different from those of the Orinda tradition. She sees Eugenia as needing more flattery than her poetic powers can summon: "were I Orinda," she wryly observes, she could not do Eugenia justice (p. 87). A seduction poem gives an insight into the spirit with which Ephelia endows women, however: she sees them not as passive victims but as those who long to possess anger and aggression:

> Let me not live in dull Indiff'rency,
> But give me Rage enough to make me die:

157

For if from you I needs must meet my Fate,
Before your Pity, I wou'd choose your *Hate*.

(P. 106)

The volume ends with a poem addressed "To Madam G," who, one guesses, is Strephon's wife and therefore what may first appear as a resolution of sorts is a work drenched with irony. The fulsome praise for her rival raises more questions than it answers about Madam G., especially because a poem earlier in the volume, "My Fate," reveals that Strephon is now unhappy in his African marriage (pp. 95–98). Ephelia summons the conventions of the praise poem to raise doubts about the G.s' relationship because of the poem's contrast with what we have learned in the rest of the volume. The husband is hardly a prince, and the poet herself has been Mrs. G.'s major rival:

So Bright your Beauty, so Sublime your Wit,
None but a Prince to wear your Chains is fit.
. . . .
. . . I wish you a Perpetual Spring
Of Youth and Blooming Beauties: such as may
Make all your Envious Rivals pine away.

(Pp. 111–12)

Ephelia's single volume conforms to Lipking's construction of the woman's poetic, especially as it is fashioned to the self and deals with abandonment. It is certainly one of the major premises of feminist criticism that women's art is autobiographical. Yet as we read *Female Poems* without exact knowledge of Ephelia's "real" life, we understand the sense in which the autobiographical mode in women's writing is an artistic construct like any other and, unlike Ephelia's passion for Strephon, not inevitable because she was a woman writing. We also may be struck by the similarity in the unkindness of Strephon to that of Behn's fictional and real-life lovers. Here we may recall Goreau's observation about John Hoyle's treatment of Behn: "In choosing John Hoyle, she could give herself entirely to her passion without bearing the usual consequences, maintain her ideal of love without living it out in social convention."[34] Loving a man who will abandon her may be a requirement for the woman artist of the seventeenth century, for it allows her the experience and the freedom to write about it afterward.

Of all the writers in this study, Sarah Fyge Field Egerton (1669–1723) made the most serious attempt to blend the heritages of Orinda and Aphra

Behn. Her writing career was enmeshed in controversy about women, and her views of men and marriage were grim. Yet she wrote extensively about sexual love, and the expression of emotions attached to a series of sexual relationships ties her poetry to the tradition of Behn. There is, in fact, evidence that Egerton had friendships—and quarrels—with a number of Behn's followers: Manley, Pix, Trotter, and possibly Centlivre.[35] Yet Egerton was always careful to claim Orinda as a co-progenitor with Behn, possibly because of contemporary attitudes like those of Robert Gould. As we have seen in the Introduction, Gould vilified Behn at Orinda's expense; and one of Egerton's first poems answers him: she will not despise either strain. A dedicatory poem to Egerton's *Poems on Several Occasions* (1703) admirably describes, in terms of the two traditions, the combination of qualities we find in her poems: "In thy harmonious Strains at once admire, / *Orinda's* Judgment and *Astrea's* Fire."[36] Many of Orinda's gestures endure in Egerton, and Astrea's fire expresses both her sexual passion and feminist anger.

Egerton used undoing frequently, possibly because she began her career in controversy at fourteen. In the preface to *The Female Advocate* (1686), she argues the question of publication, always a vexed issue for Orinda's tradition. She reveals how knowing she is, even at this early age, about rhetorical strategies:

> I might, if I pleas'd, make an excuse for the Publication of my Book, as many others do; but then, perhaps, the World might think 'twas only a feign'd Unwillingness: But when I found I could not hinder the Publication, I set a resolution to bear patiently the Censures of the World, for I expected its Severity, the first Copy being so ill writ, and so much blotted, that it could scarce be read; and they that had the Charge of it, in the room of the blots, writ what they pleas'd, and much different from my Intention. I find the main Objection is, That I should Answer so rude a Book, when, if it had not been against our Sex, I should not have Read it, much less have Answer'd it; but I think its being so, required the sharper Answer, and severer Contradictions. (*FF,* 154–55)

Although Egerton was aggressive about her answer to Gould, she was far less assertive about her later *Poems on Several Occasions,* which, after all, had no special moment that called it forth. She calls her poems trifles: "Most of the Copies being writ, 'ere I could write Seventeen; long they lay in neglected Silence, and ne'er design'd to disturb the World; but an unlucky Accident forc'd them to the Press, not giving time for that Examination and Correction, which might have made them, (tho' a smaller) yet more worthy Offering." (Sig. A2ᵛ)

Later in the same dedication to Lord Halifax, Egerton said her poems were "just snacht from their Recluse in their native Rudeness. . . . They never were abroad before, nor e'er seen but by my own Sex, some of which have favour'd me with their Complements, and I was too much a Woman to refuse them" (Sig. A4). The self-deprecation and exaggerated modesty are echoes of Orinda's manner, although some of the modesty may be in order because of Egerton's youth. Yet her comments to Halifax about women's sphere seem so unlike her usual voice that she might be imitating Orinda's appeals to male sponsors: "I hope your Lordship is of my Opinion, that where the Circumstances do not make Love a Crime, the confessing it can be none. Besides, our Sex is confin'd to so narrow a Sphere of Action, that things of greater Consequences seldom fall within our Notices; so that Love seems the only proper Theme (if any may be so) for a Woman's Pen, especially at the Age they were writ in" (Sig. A3). Here Egerton moves toward Behn, for, although appeal to a powerful male is like Orinda, writing about love is not because Philips had that great "reservedness" on the theme that Winchilsea noticed. All the more need, one might guess, for a dedication that tried to undo as much as possible the transgressive stance about women's writing in "The Liberty," about women's lot in "The Emulation," about the Salic Law in a poem addressed to the queen, and many poems about love. According to Medoff, Egerton's strategy seems to have worked, for she reported to a friend that she had "my Lord H——x's repeated thanks, and he made me a noble present."[37] Certainly, Egerton had more to apologize for and undo than most of Orinda's daughters!

Her poem on the privilege of writing is "The Liberty," and it not only asserts her intention to write but also attacks socially prescribed female behaviors:

> Mysteries must not be, with my search Prophan'd,
> My Closet not with Books, but Sweet-meats cramm'd
> A little *China,* to advance the Show,
> My *Prayer Book,* and seven *Champions,* or so.
> My Pen if ever us'd imploy'd must be,
> In lofty Themes of useful Housewifery,
> Transcribing old Receipts of Cookery:
> And what is necessary 'mongst the rest,
> Good Cures for Agues, and a cancer'd Breast.
> (*FF,* 168–69)

Instead Egerton was compelled to write, and, like Ephelia, she used images of slavery to describe her feelings about the restrictions on her activities:

Some boast their Fetters, of Formality,
Fancy they ornamental Bracelets be,
I'm sure their Gyves, and Manacles to me.
To their dull fulsome Rules, I'd not be ty'd,
For all the Flattery that exalt their Pride:
My Sex forbids, I should my Silence break,
I lose my Jest, cause Women must not speak . . .
My daring Pen, will bolder Sallies make,
And like my self, an uncheck'd freedom take;
Not chain'd to the nice Order of my Sex,
And with restraints my wishing Soul perplex . . .
(*FF,* 168–69)

She would avoid sin and secure her virtue, but she cared little for maintaining her "precarious Fame." In this attitude Egerton again moved closer to Aphra than did most followers of Orinda, who were generally more respectful of social proprieties.

Egerton paid a heavy personal price for her assertion. Her *Female Advocate* cost her a father's love, and her autobiographical poem "On my leaving *London,* June the 29" explains that she was banished from London, probably to Windsor, at her father's command: "I had not fled, but strongly forc'd by you, / In haste bid Mother, Sisters sad adieu" (p. 23). Egerton resembles Orinda in having retreated from town to country, but her retirement was, like that of Cavendish and Winchilsea, more thrust upon her than a choice. Just as some of Egerton's poems exalt friendship of gentle and civil natures over public greatness or vulgar business activity, so others picture her removed from the gaudy sphere of the town in the shades of a silent village: "I'll lie serene in safe obscurity" (p. 31). Despite expression of these conventional retirement themes, Egerton's nature was too turbulent for such detachment.

Instead we learn from several other autobiographical poems that the poet, married to a man for whom she had little feeling, fell in love with another man, but decided against an extramarital affair. Egerton's poems about Alcander—and other loves—are frank, pragmatic, and written from a woman's perspective.

I thought my self secure, within these Shades,
But your rude Love, my Privacy invades,
Affronts my Virtue, hazards my just Fame,
Why should I suffer, for your lawlesse Flame?

For oft 'tis known, through Vanity and Pride,
Men boast those Favours which they are deny'd:
Or others Malice, which can soon discern;
Perhaps may see in you some kind concern.
So scatter false Suggestions of their own,
That I love too: Oh! Stain to my Renown;
No, I'le be Wise, avoid your Sight in time,
And shun at once the Censure and the Crime.

(P. 27)

Another series of poems plays out the drama of Egerton's first marriage to a man whom she only learned to love as he died (pp. 68–70). In "The Gratitude" she viewed Field as an injured lover to whose dust she would pay the passion she owed him in life. Although, as Medoff suggests, Egerton was always the center of her own imagination ("One moment's Grief of mine is of more Cost, / Than a Majestick thirty Days can boast."), her depiction of the anguished grief that comes from guilt accounts for some of the poem's hyperbole.[38] It concludes with lines that echo Orinda's "Wiston Vault": "My bleeding Heart shall this inscription give, / Not here you lie, but here for ever live." A second poem about the marriage, "On my wedding Day," describes similar feelings: the poet married out of duty and only learned to love "when 'twas almost too late," and so the grieving soul blots the wedding day from the calendar in a blend of guilt and mourning. The poems are stylistically crude, but they render a woman's predicament vividly. On his deathbed Egerton's first husband seems to have designated a protector for her, Alexis, with whom she was fated to fall in love. The poems associated with Alexis and Exalis (the letters of the name self-consciously permuted) suggest that the poet's passion was never requited. They are poems of longing in which constancy is a curse, and in which not to love is vain: "Now I'm a double Slave to Love and Vows" (p. 42). There is also in some poems a cynical sense that passion for Alexis is better as a fiction: "Was my Passion approv'd, / It would quickly be gone" (p. 51).

Marriage was not kind to Egerton, who, as a young, well-to-do widow, was soon married again, possibly by her parents, to Thomas Egerton, a rector old enough to be her father. The union was stormy, filled with quarrels and litigation. Their relationship seems to have inspired one of the most outspoken poems about women's condition in the seventeenth century, "The Emulation." Here Egerton's bitterness makes Chudleigh's seem mild, and the anger is cosmic. Throughout her life a woman is a slave:

Say Tyrant Custom, why must we obey,
The impositions of thy haughty Sway;

From the first dawn of Life, unto the Grave,
Poor Womankind's in every State, a Slave.
The Nurse, the Mistress, Parent and the Swain,
For Love she must, there's none escape that Pain;
Then comes the last the fatal Slavery,
The Husband with insulting Tyranny
Can have ill Manners justify'd by Law;
For men all join to keep the Wife in awe.

(*FF,* 169)

Like Chudleigh, Egerton saw women as a group and men in much the same way. The poem attributes women's thralldom to their lack of education, which men pretend is designed for them alone, like the priests of old in excluding the vulgar from knowledge of religious mysteries. The poem ends with a call for women to emulate the heavens where ten celestial females and but two gods govern wit. Several characteristics of Egerton's thinking mark changes in women's ideas about their predicament. First, the poem clearly identifies social custom and not nature or religious authority as the source of women's oppression. Oppression is called by its name, and it is a social construct that could be altered. Second, the poem urges women to improve their minds in order to escape slavery: knowledge will empower them. And, third, the poem contains a not too veiled threat that if women were given true freedom to learn all they wished, they might surpass men intellectually: "They fear we should excel their sluggish Parts, / Should we attempt the Sciences and Arts." The solution to women's plight is not a private sanctuary in which to maintain a stoic integrity and relationships with other female kindred spirits but a competition with men for "Wit's Empire." One senses that *emulation* has a second meaning in the poem, that women are covertly urged to imitate men as well as the muses. In her combativeness, her direct competition with men, as well as her willingness to write openly about sexual love and her serial relationships with men, Egerton possesses Astrea's fire.

These features of her work may arise from her having begun writing as a controversialist. *The Female Advocate,* composed when Egerton was fourteen, answers, as we have said, Robert Gould's *A Late Satyr Against Pride, Lust, and Inconstancy* (1680), which was written as one of a number of satires, among them one on men and another on theatergoers. Although Gould's work drew on the more-or-less continuous controversy about women, his style is such that his criticisms are no more to be taken seriously than his satire is intended to reform manners and morals.[39] The speaker of the satire is a rejected lover, whose bias against his subject is constantly made apparent to the reader. Gould wrote to amuse and to sell books. It is characteristic of the attacks upon, and defenses of, women that men engage in these lightly; but for women, especially young women like Egerton, the subject is deadly serious. Although *The Female Advocate* is overlong, another evidence of Egerton's extraordinary assertiveness, and its examples of Eve's creation, Lucretia, the immolation of Indian women, the constancy of the wives of Vensburg among women and treachery of Ptolomey and Brutus among the men, are familiar, the premises of the poem are important to notice. Egerton used the conventional method of argument by example, but she kept the reader's attention focused on male attitudes as sources for Gould's conclusions, and she understood the projection of male feelings upon women:

> All Pride and Lust too to our charge they lay,
> As if in sin we all were so sublime
> As to monopolize each hainous crime;
> Nay, Woman now is made the Scape-goat, and
> 'Tis she must bear the sins of all the land.
>
> (*FF,* 166)

Egerton began her career, then, with the assumption that the predicament of women was a social construct, largely in the control of men. This is a crucial assumption because it suggests, as did Chudleigh's similar thinking, that alternative attitudes and customs are possible. She continued to make this assumption throughout her life, and this may be one of the reasons that, despite her Orinda-like prefaces and dedications, she seems never to have lost her anger, which she identified as a source of anguish in writing poetry: "Here all the Spite and Rage of Womankind, / Cannot enough advance my threatning Mind" (p. 14). The belief that, if they only would, men could change the oppression of women, combined with bitter personal experience and a turbulent spirit, was enough to inspire Delariviere Manley to describe Egerton as sitting for a picture of a collection of Furies. In an poem to the queen, Egerton evokes a martial spirit that epitomizes her remarkable feminism:

> Revenge on your proud Foes, their *Salick* Law,
> With your fair Hand, their boasted Greatness awe.
> Why are we barr'd, or why I Woman made,
> Whose Sex forbids to Fight, and to Invade,
> Or give my Queen, more than my wish for Aid?
> I shall not tremble, at the Launce, or Sword
> Will strait turn *Amazon,* but speak the Word;

Scarce can I curb, my eager loyal Soul,
For you I'd fight, Mankind from Pole to Pole,
Till all the Kingdoms, in one Empire meet,
Then lay the Crown at your Imperial feet.

(Pp. 17–18)

This feisty poem is one of many examples of how much Queen Anne's reign symbolized for women writers. Even though the queen herself was pliant and conventional, her mere presence on the throne was liberating.

Although her poetry is sometimes artistically crude (we must remember that she began writing in her teens), Egerton made another remarkable contribution to women's poetry. She used a volume of occasional poems as a semifictional autobiography. The pastoral names and the adjustment of details from life should not trouble a reader who understands that all autobiography is a fiction about a fiction: a story about a self, both of which are created by the author.[40] Insofar as one may reconstruct Egerton's historical life, the poems may be read as they have been presented here. But there is another way of reading them, just as valid. They present a brief poetic autobiography of a seventeenth-century woman, "the expression of a life, personal, incomplete, and proportioned to the self."[41] Cavendish's autobiography is a public document meant to vindicate herself and those she loved. Egerton represented her hopes, her defeats, her pains and guilt in love, her dreams of learning and of what women might accomplish, her anger at men and her insights into their behavior. Jeslyn Medoff, who knows more about Egerton than anyone else, says, "The question of exactly who Sarah Fyge Field Egerton was is still, in a sense, unanswered." For Medoff, Egerton is most valuable when she rises above the personal, "insisting on the rights of women to education, self-expression, self-government."[42] I would add, with Lipking, that her poetry—complex, contradictory, incomplete, unpolished—is just as important as a narrative of the self. We witness in Egerton's poetry the development of woman as subject, in the terms used by Catherine Belsey in the final chapter of *The Subject of Tragedy*. Egerton should be remembered for two accomplishments: her advocacy for women as a group and her fashioning of herself as a subject.

The Female Wits and the Salic Law of Wit: Delariviere Manley (1672–1724), Catherine Trotter Cockburn (1679–1749), Mary Pix (1666–1709)

As we have seen, Aphra Behn asserted women's privilege of writing as equal to that of men. She claimed for women wit as well as beauty. Moreover, a poem of the time that supported women's achievement and education was entitled *Triumphs of Female Wit* (1683). It seems quite natural, then, that Aphra's followers in drama – Delariviere Manley, Catherine Trotter Cockburn, and Mary Pix – would be called the Female Wits. They were, accordingly, parodied in a play entitled *The Female Wits or the Triumvirate of Poets at Rehearsal* (1697). What the heirs of Behn faced as they assumed the privilege of writing was known as the Salic Law of Wit, which has been fully described by Nancy Cotton.[43] The stance increasingly taken by male writers of the later seventeenth century was that, with only rare exceptions, women were excluded by Appollo's law from Parnassus as from the French throne. Each woman writer as she appeared therefore had to prove herself the exception to Apollo's rule. Frequently, too, writers who invoke the Salic Law of Wit assume that there can be only one exception at a time. So Cowley said Orinda did "cancel great Apollo's Salick Law," and George Jenkins made the same claim for Behn. But the law was never entirely canceled, so that each woman writer was almost certain to be lampooned in poems about sessions of the poets who would be judged by Apollo. As we recall, Winchilsea was replying to Apollo's law in her "Circuit of Apollo." Winchilsea's Apollo makes exceptions for all the female poets she mentions in the poem. *A Journal from Parnassus* (1688) describes Behn as too immodest for a woman and not witty enough for a man. Other poems of the genre call Cavendish a madwoman, and Manley and Pix are judged not equal to Orinda or Sappho. The parodies tended to pit women against one another in their assumption that there could be but one exception to the Salic Law at a time. In these poems women are excluded from the ranks of the poets for the same reason they are excluded from war: they will distract men from their true occupation. The continuing attack on women writers may be traced from *The Female Vertuosos* (1693) through *The Female Wits* (1696), and *Animadversions on Congreve's Late Answer to Collier* (1698) to *Three Hours After Marriage* (1717) by Pope, Gay, and Arbuthnot.[44]

The intent of this criticism seems not only to divide men from women but also to divide women from one another, projecting male competition upon them as they vie with one another to be the exception to Apollo's law. That such criticism tended to deal not with an author's work but with her personal life should not surprise us. The spate of women writers in the seventeenth century, including playwrights, occurs simultaneously with the appearance of actresses on the stage. The Restoration made both actresses and women playwrights possible, and shifts in sexual ideology, as Katherine Maus has suggested, may account for the increased tendency to receive both actresses and women writers as women first and artists second, if at all.[45] The confusion of artistic transgression and sexual transgression was constant in the thought of the time, and if one tired of saying women could not write, one could always call those who did whores, especially if they sold their writing, which was easily equated with themselves.[46]

In dealing with this criticism, the women who also wrote for the public theater used a variety of defensive strategies—including undoing and the exploitation of female stereotypes. Manley said *The Lost Lover* was written in seven days and that the warmth of passion in *The Royal Mischief* was appropriate for a woman writer. Pix believed that as a woman she should deal with the romantic side of history in her tragedies. Stage reform, an avowed aim of Trotter and Pix, exploits the increasing emphasis on women's moral role in a corrupting society. In Pix's plays, especially, reformation of characters like the rake and the unhappy wife conforms to sentimental values of virtue and innocence.

Yet, like the writers in the Orinda tradition, these women made a lineage to which they could refer instantly. As Laurie Finke has shown, the Female Wits created a tradition to which they could refer, even if it was only a decade old. "They seem," she says, "obsessed with creating precursors, with legitimizing female art by establishing a lineage that stretches back to the Greek poetess Sappho, through Katherine Philips (Chaste Orinda) and Aphra Behn (Fair Astrea), to themselves."[47] Manley tended to follow Behn in her assertiveness, whereas Trotter and Pix mix their styles between Orinda and Behn. All three dramatists found support in other women for taking the privilege of writing. All frequently dedicated their plays to important women, who were for them examples of what the whole sex could achieve. In addition, their prologues and epilogues reveal that, far from being divided from one another by vying to be the sole exception to Apollo's law, the Female Wits not only supported one another's work but enjoyed friendships with, and the support of, contemporary male writers. Many of the prologues and epilogues use a new strategy in defending female authors. Instead of viewing one another as exceptions to their sex, according to Apollo's rule, the women writers see one another as examples and champions of the whole sex. Here is Manley's tribute to Trotter's *Agnes de Castro,* which inspired Manley's writing and was based on a work by Behn:

> *Orinda,* and the Fair *Astrea* gone
> Not one was found to fill the Vacant Throne:
> Aspiring Man had quite regain'd the Sway,

Again had Taught us humbly to Obey;
Till you (Natures third start, in favour of our Kind)
With stronger Arms, their Empire have disjoyn'd,
And snatch't a Lawrel which they thought their Prize,
Thus Conqueror, with your Wit, as with your Eyes.
Fired by the bold Example, I would try
To turn our Sexes weaker Destiny.
O! How I long in the Poetic Race,
To loose the Reins, and give their Glory Chase;
For thus Encourag'd, and thus led by you,
Methinks we might more Crowns than theirs Subdue.[48]

Trotter's tragedy *The Fatal Friendship,* dedicated to Princess Anne, was greeted with a dedicatory poem, using a male voice, that pictured Trotter as destroying the Salic Law of Wit on behalf of the entire sex:

In Body weak, more Impotent of mind—
Thus some have represented Woman-kind;
But you your Sexes Champion are come forth
To fight their Quarrel, and assert their Worth.
Our Salique Law of Wit you have destroy'd,
Establish'd Female Claim, and Triumph'd o'er our Pride.[49]

Catherine Trotter's last play, *The Revolution of Sweden*, contains a dedication to Lady Harriet Goldolphin as an example who "might incite some greater Geniuses among us to exert themselves, and change our Emulation of a Neighboring Nation's Fopperies, to the commendable Ambition of Rivalling them in their illustrious Women; Numbers we know among them, have made considerable Progress in the most difficult Sciences, several have gain'd the Prizes of Poesie from their Academies, and some have been chosen Members of their Societies."[50]

In her prologue to *The Lost Lover,* Delariviere Manley declared that her audience expected her to fail: "The very Name you'll cry boads Impotence. / To Fringe and Tea they sho'd confine their Sence, / And not outstrip the bounds of Providence."[51] If the play succeeded, however, her audience would be sure that her lover had written it. (That was not a problem because the play failed.) For *The Royal Mischief,* Manley's tragedy also published in 1696, both Catherine Trotter and Mary Pix wrote important tributes, important because of the attitudes they reveal about women's privilege of writing. Both Pix and Trotter see Manley as representative of the sex; she may be the best, but she is not unique, according to Pix:

So you, the unequalled wonder of the age,
Pride of our sex, and glory of the stage,
Have charmed our hearts with your immortal lays,
And tuned us all with everlasting praise.
You snatch laurels with undisputed right,
And conquer when you but begin to fight.

Trotter, better educated and temperamentally more assertive than Pix, made even stronger claims for Manley's achievement—that she has entirely defeated male competition on behalf of all women:

For us you've vanquished, though the toil was yours,
You were our champion, and the glory ours.
Well you've maintained our equal right in fame,
To which vain man had once engrossed the claim.
. . . .
The men, o'ercome, will quit the field
Where they have lost their hearts, the laurel yield.[52]

One of the most interesting texts in this literature is Matthew Prior's epilogue to Manley's last play, *Lucius, the First Christian King of Britain* (1717). Here Prior brings together the two parts of the debate: he claims that either the Salic Law be condemned and Manley's play be praised, or women will take revenge on men by writing and talking more than they already have. But the tone is deeply ambiguous:

If *Petrarch's* Muse did Laura's Wit rehearse,
And Cowley flatter'd dear Orinda's verse,
She hopes from you—Pox take her Hopes and Fears,
I plead her Sex's Claim, what matters Hers?
By our full Pow'r of Beauty, we think fit
To damn this Salique Law, impos'd on Wit.
We'll try the Empire You so long have boasted;
And if we are not praised, we'll not be Toasted.
Approve what One of us presents to Night,
Or every mortal woman here shall write;
Rural, Pathetick, Narrative, Sublime.
. . . .
As long as we have Eyes, or Hands, or Breath,
We'll look, or Write, or Talk you all to Death
Unless ye yield for Better or for Worse.[53]

There is the suggestion of a misogynous stereotype in the threat that betrays the male behind the woman's voice. Prior had been supportive of Manley's work before, however; he had written a prologue for the *Royal Mischief* (1686), which he called "This early offspring of a Virgin Wit," again slightly ambiguous praise. His friendship with Manley is interesting, when one considers his attack on Aphra Behn in *Satyr on the Modern Translators* in 1683, where he calls her

> Our blind translatress *Behn.*
> The Female Wit, who next convicted stands,
> Not for abusing *Ovid's* verse, but Sand's:
> She might have learn'd from the ill-borrowed Grace,
> (Which little helps the ruine of her Face)
> That Wit, like Beauty, triumphs o're the Heart,
> When more of Nature's seen, and less of Art.[54]

The lines are occasioned by Dryden's having included Behn's "Epistle of Oenone to Paris" in his translation of Ovid's *Heroides,* in which Dryden admitted that Behn probably did not know Latin: "But if she does not, I am afraid she has given us occasion to be ashamed who do."[55] Prior's differing attitudes toward the two women writers reveal how unsettled were attitudes toward them during the time of the Female Wits. Behn was invading a sacred grove of antique learning and was therefore to be attacked as a woman. Manley was a political ally who had also worked with Prior and Swift on the *Examiner,* and besides, Manley was writing for the popular stage.

Although the Female Wits had, among them, a considerable circle of male friends and supporters, the commitments have at times an ambiguous ring to them, similar to that in Prior's tributes to Manley. Wycherley's prologue to Catherine Trotter Cockburn's *Agnes de Castro* published anonymously, almost invites the audience to react to the play stereotypically:

> Think not the Ladies Wit or Honour less,
> Because she seeks those who have less to please;
> Let not her aim, to please the Publick now,
> Design'd her Credit, but your Scandal grow,
> Make not her proffer'd favour, her Disgrace,
> Nay, though it should not please, th'Intention praise,
> 'Tis merit only, to desire to please;
> Then be not, as poor Women often find,

Less kind to her, but as she's more inclin'd,
At venture of her Fame, to please Mankind.

The sexual analogy is very clear in the last lines, and the negative construction of the poem becomes virtually an invitation to behave precisely as one has been told not to, especially because the prohibitions spell out in detail how one might react according to contemporary stereotypes. With a friend like the author of *A Country Wife,* Trotter hardly needed enemies.

Fortunately, Trotter had many other male supporters—among the dramatists, Congreve and Farquhar. Congreve tried to advise her about the action and characters of *The Revolution of Sweden* and remarked tactfully about the heroic women: "You are the best judge, whether those of your own sex will approve as much of the heroic virtue of Constantia and Christina, as if they had been engaged in some *belle passion;* for my part, I like them as they are."[56] Trotter was enough a feminist reformer to leave them "as they are," but her difference from Congreve's astute advice is instructive. As the foremost playwright for Lincoln's Inn Fields, Congreve defended Mary Pix against George Powell when in 1697 he plagiarized her *Deceiver Deceived* in a play Powell called *Imposture Defeated.* Congreve's partisanship for the Female Wits is certified by *Animadversions on Mr Congreve's late Answer to Mr Collier* (1698), which contains vicious parody on both Pix and Trotter.[57]

Because Trotter continued her writing career in philosophical and theological works after she stopped writing for the stage, she developed a new set of relationships with eminent men. She championed Locke's work, and he was grateful. She wrote religious tracts admired by Burnet and Warburton; she corresponded with Leibnitz. For a career interrupted by twenty years of child-rearing, it is an impressive record.[58]

Manley too enjoyed considerable support among the male great of the time. She had the duke of Devonshire and Sir Thomas Shipworth as patrons. She had both Swift and Steele as friends. She quarreled with Steele, but they made up; she dedicated *Lucius* to him, and he wrote the prologue. In the meantime, she had been working with Swift on Tory pamphlets and succeeded him as editor of the *Examiner.*[59] As an ardent Tory, she enjoyed the patronage of Harley for a time, of which more in chapter 5.

As the reader already may have concluded, this account reveals that men tended to support women's privilege to write when their interests or values coincided with those of the woman in question, but not out of principle or conviction. One searches in vain for a male feminist before Defoe, and his attitudes are often ambiguous. It is possible, however, that a long, interesting work defending women's right to education was written by a man (Mr. F.), even though parts of it claim to be the work of "a young lady." *Triumphs of Female wit, In Some Pindarick Odes. Or, the Emulation. Together*

With an Answer to an Objector against Female Ingenuity, and the Capacity of Learning and *A Preface to the Masculine Sex, by a young Lady* both appeared in 1683. The speaker in the *Preface* understands that her arguments will be considered unnatural and unreasonable, but she believes that women's complacency is responsible for their being confined to the kitchen during the day and "at Night to the ungratifying Divertisement of an unperforming Husband." Her argument is based on the assumption that nature has furnished woman with "Body and Mind as the best composed of you all." Therefore, if education were added to woman's natural capacity, "on my conscience we should out-do you in the trade of Ingenuity, and soon get a stock of acquired Excellency wherewith to set up for accomplish'd Professors of Arts and Sciences." Women, she argues, who are allowed freedom to be learned will become models for the sex.[60]

In "The Emulation" a young lady recapitulates the argument of the *Preface* by transforming questions of nature into issues of social custom. Men deprive women of the privileges they used to enjoy because men fear women will once again "ambitious be to reign / And to invade the Dominions of the Brain." But women want knowledge only to control their passions, to spend their time to best advantage. The arguments are similar to those made by Chudleigh and Astell in very different contexts, and we should recall that Egerton's poem about women's oppression, which makes many of the same arguments, is also called "The Emulation." The satiric ending of the poem identifies men's values as inspired by "Battle, Wench, or Vice," and women's as coming from "Charms of Wit, of Parts, and Poetry."[61]

The answer poem first invokes Apollo's Salic Law. It also reminds the fair that they have produced no art, which is too hard for them, and if they try to create, they may miscarry: "Your power not equal to your will." A studious life, the poem suggests, does not conduce to faith; learning brings doubt and lack of ease. Knowledge does not subdue passion but raises anxiety.

The rebuttal asks if Apollo denied the charms of Orinda's poetry. Women, it suggests, are not ambitious, but have a right to learning: "These lawful Longings we will ne're suppress . . . We'll so direct, with prudent Care, our Flight, / T'enjoy at once the *Tree of Knowledge* and *of Life*." The poem ends by asserting that the number of smart and virtuous women exceeds the number of similar men:

> Know Sir, that Women, witty, wise, and fair,
>   Than worthy Men more plenty are:
>   For we not only Men excell
> In choicer Gifts, but Wit to use 'em well.[62]

The end of the poem declares it was "Written by Mr. F." This, of course, may be a pose to avoid accusation of narrow self-interest. We also know or suspect that several popular works in the Renaissance controversy about women were authored by men who assume a woman's voice. This work seems little different from those. It mixes genders in the variety of its claims of authorship in order to capitalize on the reader's assumptions about a vested interest in each part. Once a discourse is established, each gender may easily emulate the voice of the other. This poem, if written entirely by a man using both voices, is a harbinger of eighteenth-century fiction written by men in a female voice. It is also evidence of support for women's achievements in the era of the Female Wits.

Behn's Drama

Behn's poetry would have made her remarkable in itself, but her career as the first woman professional playwright in England is even more extraordinary. As Nancy Cotton says,

> Playwrighting is in many ways the most difficult of all literary endeavors because of its public, collaborative nature. A dramatist must fit a play to a particular audience, a particular kind of theater, contemporary theatrical conventions, and, in the repertory system that obtained from Shakespeare's day until the end of the nineteenth century, a specific group of actors. Thus, theatrical apprenticeship of some sort is indispensable. The successful playwright, moreover, needs publicity, financial backing, and professional contracts. In a period when theatrical apprenticeship, money and contracts were virtually impossible for women to obtain, in a period when, indeed, public life was improper for them, many women nonetheless wrote plays and a number of them succeeded as professional playwrights.[63]

Of those covered in Cotton's study, *Women Playwrights in England c. 1363–1750*, Aphra Behn is unquestionably the most outstanding. In a London that had only two theaters, she wrote at least seventeen plays, fifteen of which were produced in her lifetime, two posthumously. Two more plays have been lost, and four anonymous dramas are assigned to her. All this in nineteen years, along with poetry, translation, and voluminous fiction. With the exception of a few plays, such as *Abdelazar,* that were clearly written to appeal to a lingering taste for melodrama, most of Behn's comedies demonstrate a genuine gift for "the Spanish-type comedy of intrigue, one of the most commercially successful genres of the day."[64] She began her career with two plays (*The Forc'd Marriage* and *The Amorous Prince*) in the style of Beaumont and Fletcher, but with *The Dutch Lover,* she turned to the comedy of intrigue, which proved her metier.

Readers of Behn's drama have three critical resources to assist them: Cotton's study, which relates her work to that of other women playwrights and deals primarily with evaluation of the plays, but not to the exclusion of their sexual politics; F. M. Link's *Aphra Behn,* which offers a developmental analysis of the plays in chronological order, as well as a description of their sources; and Angeline Goreau's *Reconstructing Aphra,* a social biography that relates the drama to Behn's life and times, but offers several detailed readings of individual plays and commentary about their themes.[65] Yet, more needs to be said about how the themes, character relationships, and structures of Behn's plays relate to her ideas about women, the prevailing sexual ideology, and the plays of women who succeeded her.

Behn's drama raised questions about marriage and the family, but, as successful stage plays, could hardly be expected to subvert entirely the social assumptions of their audiences. Behn was able, however, to use cavalier sexual ideology, popular in the seventies, to expose the most oppressive characteristics of marriage and patriarchal relationships in her time. Although the libertine cavalier vision of male-female relationships was fraught with hazards for women, it did offer a new perspective from which to criticize marriage; and so a portion of Behn's audience could be counted upon to agree with cavalier attitudes and to be at least superficially skeptical about the worldly aspect of the marriage relationship: the property and ambition continually cited in her poetry as hostile to love. As a result, two of Behn's first four plays deal with forced marriage: *The Forc'd Marriage* (1670) and *The Town Fop* (1676). *The Forc'd Marriage* is a Jacobean tragicomedy dealing with love and honor. Goreau describes the predicament of the heroine, Erminia, who has been forced to marry Alcippus while in love with the prince: "Honor for the King, the father, and the husband lies in defending an obligation they have freely taken upon themselves; whereas honor for Erminia means carrying out a promise that has been made in her absence, without her approval. She is blackmailed by their contention that their honor depends upon hers; *she* must protect their name."[66] Her predicament paralyzes Erminia, who cannot rebel against her father or betray her love; she is rescued by Alcippus's change of heart, to the distress of Goreau. Behn's strategy in this apprentice work is to use a rebellious double for Erminia in the subplot. In a Shakespearean effect, Aminta acts out the suppressed impulses of Erminia when Aminta upbraids her lover, Alcander, for his past loves and seeks to retain control over their relationship:

174

I have too much betray'd my Passion for him,
—I must recal it, if I can I must:—
I will—for should I yield, my power's o'erthrown,
And what's a Woman when that glory's gone?

(3:344)

Before she submits to him, Aminta demands proof of Alcander's love, and her acceptance of him indicates her feisty spirit; she is told,

Give him your hand, Aminta, and conclude,
'Tis time this haughty humour were subdu'd.
By your submission, whatsoe'er he seem,
In time you'll make the greater Slave of him.
Am. Well, not from the hope of that, but from my love,
His change of humour I'm content to prove.
Here take me, Alcander;
Whilst to Inconstancy I bid adieu,
I find variety enough in you.

(3:380)

The presence of Aminta in the play suggests the way in which Behn will use the cavalier vision to forge a new sense of female independence in her later plays. It also implies that Erminia's predicament can be taken as tacit criticism of the powerful males in *The Forc'd Marriage,* and that the happy conclusion may be the result of a change in male attitudes; but it is a tender fantasy that justifies lovers' wishes over patriarchal authority. To dismiss Behn's dramatic conclusions because they are the outcome of chance or coincidence, rather than decisions, is to miss the fact that they invariably endorse youthful desire over patriarchal authority while remaining within the dramatic conventions of the time.

In *The Town Fop,* Behn uses as a source a Jacobean play, George Wilkins' *The Miseries of Enforc'd Marriage.* Here she follows the basic structure of the old play, in which the enforced husband rebels against the union and becomes a prodigal, but with a difference.[67] In the source the enforced couple are reconciled and the squandered fortune restored. Behn does not sanction a loveless match: her enforced wife divorces her husband to marry her beloved, and the husband is free to marry his former betrothed. Far from serving its old function of reconciling the audience to an enforced marriage, in Behn's hands the structure subverts such unions.

175

The play is unusual in another respect: it contains two of Behn's feisty heroines, who reappear often in her plays. When Bellmour refuses to consummate their marriage, Diana is far from passive: she pursues a man who will kill Bellmour in return for her sexual favors. Bellmour's betrothed, Celinda, pretends that she has died after the enforced marriage and assumes a disguise to protect Bellmour from her brother, who believes himself betrayed by Bellmour's marriage. The men in this play, and in many of Behn's, do not compare well with the women: Bellmour agrees to marry, for example to save his inheritance. In general, Behn's men are more self-seeking than her women, who believe more deeply in love, and often, as here, are active in pursuit of it.

The Amorous Prince (1671) and *The Dutch Lover* (1673) represent men as often cynically promiscuous and women as needing to be assertive in coping with their potential victimization. In *The Amorous Prince,* Cloris's innocent, natural love is contrasted with the corrupt games of the amoral, profligate Prince Frederick, who must repent his bad old ways before he can marry her. In the meantime, however, Cloris feigns death and disguises herself as Philibert to protect Frederick, nursing him when he is wounded. The process of the drama is a cure of Frederick so that he can be united with Cloris. The epilogue makes clear that the play insists on the superiority of natural love to urbane love games; Cloris says,

> Ladies, the Prince was kind at last,
> But all the danger is not past;
> I cannot happy be till you approve
> My hasty condescension to his love.
> 'Twas want of wit, not virtue, was my crime;
> And that's, I vow, the author's fault, not mine.
> She might have made the women pitiless,
> But that had harder been to me than this;
> She might have made our Lovers constant too,
> A work which Heaven it self can scarcely do;
> But simple nature never taught the way
> To hide those passions which she must obey.
>   (4:212–13)

The play clearly invites the audience to question the social values by which desire, a natural good, is modified or distorted.

The Dutch Lover sustains the contrast between natural love and social institutions through a seemingly incestuous love that turns out to be permissible. The power of love to transform character is revealed by Antonio's conversion to love for Hippolyta, whose name evokes memories of the Amazonian queen. In revenge against her brother, Antonio has ravished Hippolyta, who hides out in a Venetian whorehouse. She then disguises herself as a man and fights several duels, one with her beloved. Although she is assertive, Hippolyta is haunted by guilt for having been raped, and she seems fixed eternally in her relationship with Antonio. The men are driven by selfish motives: Alonzo seeks an ambitious marriage; Marcil would force Hippolyta's marriage to Alonzo; Antonio and Marcil seek revenge; all blame Hippolyta for Antonio's brutal treatment of her. The play also represents men as seeing all women as the same: they are a species and not human individuals. Antonio tells Euphimia: "Faith, Madam, Man is a strange un-govern'd thing; yet I in the whole course of my Life have taken the best care I could, to make as few Mistakes as possible; and treating all Women-kind alike, we seldom err; for where we find one as you profess to be, we happily light on a hundred of the sociable and reasonable sort" (1:239).

At the end the play implies that women may be more constant in their affections than men:

> The Ladies too in Blushes do confess
> Equal Desires; which yet they'll not confess.
> Theirs, tho' less fierce, more constant will abide;
> But ours less current grow the more they're try'd.
> (1:329)

One consequence of all women being the same to men in these plays is that, despite their acknowledged need for sexual conquest, the men in Behn's mature drama seem curiously passive in significant sexual relationships. The differences in attitudes of the genders toward one another account for this effect because, for women, men are individuals to whom one bonds strongly, even outside marriage, whereas for men one virtually anonymous sexual conquest succeeds another. Thus women are assertive in working out the relationships with which the plays conclude, but the men are simply available in the plot to mate with the desiring women. This effect is particularly notable in both parts of *The Rover, Sir Patient Fancy, The Feign'd Curtesans, The Young King, The Widow Ranter,* and *The Younger Brother.*

The most interesting examples are both parts of *The Rover,* Behn's most famous play.[68] In the first part, the Rover, Willmore, is so attractive to the famous courtesan Angellica Bianca that she yields to him despite his inability to pay her fee. He immediately begins a courtship of the chaste but witty Hellena, and the rest of the play develops a rivalry between the women. Willmore patiently explains to Angellica that he was never made to be faithful:

By heaven thou art brave, and I admire thee strangely.
I wish I were that dull, that constant thing,
Which thou wouldst have, and nature never meant me:
I must, like cheerful birds, sing in all groves
And perch in every bough,
Billing the next kind she that flies to meet me.

(5:297–302)

Both Willmore and Angellica perceive one another as pursuing money through sexuality, while each seeks—momentarily, at least—to love freely. When Angellica offers to kill Willmore because he has betrayed her for Hellena, he offers to repay her for her charity to him, further enraging her. For her part Angellica implies that Willmore loves Hellena for her "two hundred thousand crowns" (4.2.185). Still furious, Angellica retreats, making way for the cool and witty Hellena in disguise, who outmaneuvers the Rover into defending her and marrying her: "Faith, Sir, I can boast of nothing but a sword which does me right where-e'er I come, and has defended a worst cause than a woman's: and since I lov'd her before I either knew her birth or name, I must pursue my resolution, and marry her" (5.515–19). Because he did not know Hellena's identity when he loved her first, Willmore has loved her freely; but, of course, the comedic plot supports their union with her fortune.

As Cotton suggests, Hellena wins the Rover not through her honor but through her wit. In her disguise as a gypsy and her anonymity, she remains as free as the Rover until the end. Hellena may have been destined for a convent at the beginning of the action, but she understands the consequences for her of the Rover's sexual ideology:

Marriage is as certain a bane to love, as lending money is to friendship: I'll neither ask nor give a vow, tho' I could be content to have the pleasure of working that great miracle of making a maid a mother, if you durst venture; 'tis upse gipsy that, and if I miss, I'll lose my labour.
Hell. And if you do not lose, what shall I get? A cradle full of noise and mischief, with a pack of repentence at my back? Can you teach me to weave incle to pass my time with? 'Tis upse gipsy that too.
Will. I can teach thee to weave a true love's knot better.
Hell. So can my dog.
Will. Well, I can see we are both upon our guards. (5. 453–59)

Because she is not made vulnerable by her marginal status in society, Hellena does not become angry, as Angellica does, but keeps control of her situation, and therefore is a genuine match for the Rover, who, like most

178

rakes, strives at all costs to maintain control of the relationship. Behn presents Angellica sympathetically; but her selling sexuality is a violation of the libertine ideology, and she is therefore in a classic double-bind: outcast from conventional society as a prostitute, and scorned by the rake for not giving love freely. Her rage at Willmore is justified, and she is another complex example of the way in which Behn could use the libertine mode of thought to comment on the social conventions of her time. The play implies that women only win a rover if they retain control of themselves and their fortunes—as long as they can, that is, until the marriage that concludes the comedy. The fact that, as Link suggests, Angellica "does not quite fit the comic world of the play" reveals that Behn's sympathies do not entirely accord with the libertine discourse in which she is writing.[69]

If one compares *The Rover, Part I* with Behn's source, Thomas Killigrew's *Thomaso* (1654), the difference in Behn's perspective on sexually active women from that of a male writer becomes clear. When Killigrew's Angelica Bianca understands that Thomaso will never marry her because she is a whore, she begins to plot against him. She then becomes a symbol of the eventual degradation of the rake's sexual freedom. Thomaso says, "It vexes me she should be guilty of so mean an action, because I thought her of a gallant temper, but she's a common Whore; and this life of mine, that which some men may pass some months in for humour, but no trade for men of honour."[70] Killigrew's Angelica is a mirror of disapproved libertine behavior, but the play also simply punishes her for sexuality it approves in the male: the play makes clear "its desire to punish in the female what can be forgiven in the male rake."[71] Because Behn was strongly male-identified, the mirroring effect possibly attracted her to Killigrew's play, but she could not tolerate his punishment of the sexually active woman. Nor is *The Rover* uncritical of the libertine ideology. Although Willmore is witty and attractive, the attitudes of Blunt represent the grim side of the cavalier code and its class distinctions: a whore may be raped and abused, but a girl of property must be respected.

Although a courtesan may be bested in *The Rover, Part I,* she has a successor in *Part II* who achieves with Willmore a relationship that represents both independence and equality. Willmore continues as a rake (he is now a widower), but the successors to Angellica and Hellena have different roles in the Rover's life. The courtesan, La Nuche, lacks Angellica's anger, and so she remains in control of the intrigue, the effect of which is to establish that for both Beaumond and Willmore one beautiful woman is just like another: "I mean, do ye know who she is? . . . Nor care; 'tis the last Question I ever ask a fine Woman" (1:206–7). This play, as Link suggests, makes a much firmer contrast between the ethic of love and that of interest:

La Nuche. What shall I do?
Here's a powerful interest prostrate at my Feet.
                              [Pointing to *Beau.*
Glory, and all that Vanity can boast;
—But there—Love unadorn'd, no covering but his Wings.
                              [Pointing to *Will.*
(1:193)

When La Nuche is attracted to Beaumond's wealth, the Rover scorns her: "Death, hadst thou lov'd my Friend for his own Value, I had esteem'd thee; but when his Youth and Beauty cou'd not plead, to be the mercenary Conquest of his Presents, was poor, below thy Wit: I cou'd have conquer'd so, but I scorn thee at that rate—my Purse shall never be my Pimp" (1:194).

Moments later the Rover declares La Nuche a whore because she will sell herself for money. But she recaptures Willmore through a bed trick—because he has mistaken her for Ariadne in the dark: "Put up your Sword, this lady's innocent, at least in what concerns this Evening's business; I own—with Pride I own I am the woman that pleas'd so well to Night" (1:207). For her gallant gesture ("this dear lying Virtue") of saving Ariadne's "honor," so that she may be safely married to the wealthy Beaumond, Willmore agrees to live with La Nuche:

> *La Nu.* And you it seems mistook me for this lady; I favour'd your Design to gain your Heart, for I was told, That if this Night I lost you, I shou'd never regain you: now I am yours, and o'er the habitable World will follow you, and live and starve by turns, as Fortune pleases.
> *Will.* Nay, by this light, Child, I knew when once thou'dst try'd me, thou'dst ne'er part with me—give me thy Hand, no Poverty shall part us [*Kisses her.*—so—now here's a Bargin made without a formal Foppery of Marriage.
> *La Nu.* Nay, faith Captain, she that will not take thy word as soon as the Parson's of the Parish, deserves not the Blessing.
> *Will.* Thou art reform'd, and I adore the Change. (1:207–8)

By equating the women, Behn makes a number of ironic points about sexual relationships. First, men's lack of willingness to control a need for conquest gives women the capacity to determine relationships. Second, when interest is involved, as it invariably is in marriage, there is no difference between the wife and the whore—both sell themselves, but men continue to make social distinctions that harm both the wife and the whore. Finally, Behn's parody on the rake's conventional reform in La Nuche's contrasts the ethic of love to the ethic of interest and flouts the double standard.

The effect is complex and deeply interrogatory of both the genre and the social values in which it is implicated.

One understands the attraction the figure of the courtesan had for Behn. The prostitute is honest about selling sexual favors; the "honest" woman is not. The prostitute is not coy but forthright about sexuality. The prostitute is independent: she may sell her favors, but she is not the medium of exchange between men because she does not become a man's possession. La Nuche makes her own decisions, and she can therefore choose the cavalier ideology that love is free and renounce the interest that is built into marriage. The prostitute, then, is part of Behn's critique of the social structures governing sexuality and gender relationships. During the course of her career as a dramatist, Behn moved from criticizing forced marriages to questioning the very grounds of the institution if the mates married for property.

In *The Feign'd Courtesans* (1679), honest noblewomen disguise themselves as courtesans in order to escape oppressive lives and pursue the men they love. Frank Galliard is the rake of this play, and leaves the disguised Cornelia in a fury when she tells him she is honest and of quality:

> *Cor.* I cannot repent of my fixt Resolves for Virtue!
> —But if you could but—love me—honorably
> For I assum'd this Habit and this Dress—
> *Gal.* To cheat me of my Heart the readiest way: and now, like gaming Rooks, unwilling to give o'er till you have hook'd in my last Stake, my Body too, you cozen me with Honesty.—Oh, damn the Dice—I'll have no more on't, I, the Game's too deep for me, unless you play'd upon the square, or I could cheat like you.—Farewell, Quality. (2:381)

But the next minute he returns and mistakenly believes Cornelia has been with Sir Signal Buffon. Ironically, then Galliard reproaches her for promiscuity, but he finally consents to marry Cornelia at the urging of his friend Sir Harry Fillamour because she is witty:

> *Gal.* Gad, I thank ye for that,—I hope you'll ask my leave first, I'm finely drawn in, i' faith—Have I been dreaming all this night of the possession of a new gotten Mistress, to wake and find myself noos'd to a dull Wife in the morning?
> *Fil.* Thou talk'st like a Man that never knew the Pleasure thou despisest; faith, try it, Frank, and thou wilt hate thy past loose way of living.
> *Cor.* And to encourage a young Setter-up, I do here promise to be the most Mistress-like Wife,—You know, Signior, I have learnt the trade, though I had not stock to practise; and we'll be as expensive,

insolent, vain, extravagant and inconstant, as if you had only the keeping part and another the assignations. What think ye, Sir?
Fil. Faith, she pleads well, and ought to carry the Cause.
Gal. She speaks Reason, and I'm resolv'd to trust good Nature:—Give
me thy dear hand. (2:408–9)

Behn would permit women to be conventional if they were witty enough
to have a healthy skepticism about social institutions and had enough energy to be assertive in the inevitable marriage.

Her attack on property as the basis for marriage continued in *The False
Count* (1681), where Julia is the victim of a forced marriage to a jealous old
merchant. In a fantasy of disguise, her betrothed lover convinces the old
husband that he has been captured by a Turkish sultan, and under a pretended threat of death, the old husband resigns Julia to her lover. The men
in the play clearly perceive Julia as property to be exchanged:

Bal. O horrid! What, intreat his Wife to be a Whore?
Car. Sir, you are mistaken, she was my Wife in sight of Heaven before;
and I but seized my own.
Fran. Oh,—Sir, she's at your Service still.
Car. I thank you, Sir, and take her as my own.
Bal. Hold, my Honour's concerned.
Fran. Not at all, Father mine, she's my Wife, my Lumber now, and
I hope, I may dispose of my Goods and Chattels—if he takes her we're
upon equal terms, for he makes himself my Cuckold, as he had already
made me his;—for, if my memory fail me not, we did once upon a
time consummate, as my daughter has it. (3:173)

This exercise in patriarchal family politics is made almost amusing and bear-
able by serving the cause of true love Julia and Carlos, and the Turkish fantasy is so outlandish that one feels a distance from the transactions like that
when listening to comic opera. Yet the basic assumptions of the audience,
if the structures are to be amusing, seem abhorrent.

Because she believed in sexual freedom and questioned marriage as an
institution, Behn frequently celebrated extramarital relationships in her
plays: two examples are *Sir Patient Fancy* (1678) and *The Lucky Chance*
(1686). Sir Patient is Molière's imaginary invalid, who has taken a young
wife. She pretends to share his pious views and humors his hypochondria
while intriguing with the penniless Wittmore. When Sir Patient settles
money on her, Lucia plans to support Wittmore and their love affair. At
the end a tolerant Sir Patient determines to abandon his piety, turn spark,
and take a mistress:

You see what a fine City-Wife can do
Of the true-breed; instruct her Husband too:
I wish all civil Cuckolds in the Nation
Would take example by my Reformation.

(4:115)

If a marriage is based on property, one need not be true to it; truth is only necessary where love is present. Plays in which young women are tied to old husbands idealize the stable extramarital affair, in which an equal, mutual relationship is possible. It creates a space outside the social structures where love can be as nearly free as possible.

Less innocent is *The Lucky Change; or An Alderman's Bargin,* which is based on Shirley's *The Lady of Pleasure.* Though it is true that the young lovers, Bellmour and Leticia, Gayman and Julia, defeat the old ones, Sir Feeble Fainwoud and Sir Cautious Fulbank, the device of gambling for a night with Julia inspires her anger at both her lover and her husband for the bed trick they arrange. The device reveals the mercenary imperatives of even the most cheerful and attractive males. Behn gives Gayman a legacy at the end to free him from property concerns, but their odor lingers even after the cheerful unions of the young lovers, one within marriage and the other outside.

The Young King (1679), *The Widow Ranter* (1689), and *The Younger Brother* (1696) are tied together by representing women with aggressive, largely male characteristics. As Cotton suggests, the Amazonian Cleomena in *The Young King* is an androgynous mirror of her lover, Thersander, and their marriage reconciles the conflicts between their countries, Dacia and Scythia.[72] The Widow Ranter is also a warrior who disguises herself as a man to follow her beloved General Daring into battle. The widow wins Daring from a younger woman and fights by his side on an equal basis, postponing marriage, which he proposes, until the wars are over. Her name suggests the sexual license associated with the religious sect.

In *The Younger Brother,* Mirtilla is a unique character, a female rover, a beautiful jilt who moves from one man to another, much as the males do.[73] She is amoral and cynical but also, like Willmore, a means by which hypocrisy may be exposed. Mirtilla sees no contradiction between her self-conscious duplicity and worldly hypocrisy; she likens her conquest of the Prince to male ambition and competition:

Geo. Thous own'st the Conquest then?
Mir. With as much Vanity as thou wouldst do, if thou hadst won his Sword: Hast thou took care wisely to teach me all the Arts of life,

and dost thou now upbraid my Industry? Look round the World, and thou shalt see, *Legere,* Ambition still supplies the place of Love. The worn-out Lady, that can serve your Interest, you swear has Beauties that out-charm Fifteen; and for the Vanity of Quality, you feign and languish, lye, protest, and flatter—All Things in Nature cheat, or else are cheated. (4:369–70)

Behn's application of a single standard for roving males and females is full of irony. George Marteen wants revenge on Mirtilla for betraying him, not through her marriage, but because of loving the Prince, yet George himself is busy planning to wed his father's fiancée Teresia. At the end, after Mirtilla has confessed her passion for the disguised Olivia to the Prince, he takes her from her husband because of having saved her in a fire, and the most generous and tolerant male gets the fascinating heroine:

> *Prince.* 'Tis true, she was once your Wife; but I have preserv'd her from the Flames, and I have most Right to her.
> *Sir Morg.* That's a hard Case, Sir, that a Man must lose his Wife, because another has more Right to her than himself; Is that Law, Sir?
> *Prince.* Lovers' Law, Sir. (4:396–97)

Behn assumed that love is powerful: repeatedly the young lovers defeat the old ones, who are more powerful in terms of wealth and station. In *The Emperor of the Moon* (1687), her last play, the young lovers join a wily servant in creating a masquerade that cures a Neapolitan philosopher of his fantasies about the moon. By fulfilling the patriarch's fantasies of power, his daughter, niece, and their lovers fulfill their desires. The play is light-hearted because Baliardo's blocking of the marriages results from his own obsessions, not ambition or money as in countless other plays. Yet Behn's basic pattern of love triumphant is consistent to the end.

The Drama of the Female Wits

Delariviere Manley is the heir to Behn who is closest to her in attitudes, themes, and life-style. Like Behn, Manley broke new ground: she was the first female political journalist, the first female author of a best-seller, and the first to challenge the double standard overtly. Like Behn she was vilified for the immortality of her life, and the attacks on her were more vicious than on the other Wits, possibly because her views about sexuality were more frank and her plays and fiction overtly feminist. She repeatedly said or demonstrated that desire is nature's strongest force and that passion is the greatest joy of which the human being is capable. Of Manley's four

184

plays, *The Royal Mischief* (1696), *The Lost Lover* (1696), *Almyna* (1706), and *Lucius, the First Christian King of Britain* (1717), two represent strong women who are frank about their sexuality. Both *The Royal Mischief* and *Almyna* use exotic Near Eastern settings to convey a tacit judgment on male oppression of women in the world of the play. Although Homais is the femme fatale of *The Royal Mischief* and seduces the Prince of Colchis, the source of her obsessive passion is her aged husband's confinement of her. Her husband tries to win her love by keeping her from seeing more youthful lovers, and she tells him:

> My lord, you moralise too far. Forgive
> My sex's frailty. I'm a woman, made
> Passionate by want of liberty.
> I'll learn to wear my fetters lighter,
> And if you please, will suit my welcome to it.
>   (*FW*, 218)

Homais's husband assumes that women, not fully human, are the possessions of men. Instead, the play demonstrates that Homais, like some of Behn's women, has the energy that drives the action; but all women, the play asserts, are lovers at heart:

> This is the general character. Nature
> Has lent that common softness to the sex.
> They're lovers all, or else they are not women,
> Though I must own a husband may not
> Always be the object of desire.
>   (*FW*, 227)

If her marriage is oppressive, Manley implies, a woman will love elsewhere, and the implication of the Near Eastern setting is that marriage is oppressive as an institution.

The decisions of several powerful men have rendered Homais vengeful by frustrating her love. For example, an early lover, Ismael, is now driven by ambition to help seduce Homais's love, the Prince of Colchis, who is unhappily married for political reasons to a virtuous wife who is accused of taking a lover. She reflects upon the code by which the mere accusation ruins her reputation forever and the mixture of political and erotic motives for the action:

Hark, they have got the Princess, Must I go?
How the World will condemn thee for this flight,
And yet I take it with my husband's uncle,
One deeply wronged like me; the cause is common.
Now should I fall till time has cleared my virtue,
My fame must perish with me. The standard
Which the world condemns or clears by
Is not our innocence, but our success.

(FW, 249)

Although some of the devices and gestures Manley includes in the action seem exotic, they are within the conventions of Dryden's heroic drama. And Homais, with her vision of reigning in Hell over those who oppressed her, retains vitality to the end. However mawkish some of its effects, *The Royal Mischief* makes searching comment on sexual politics. If marriages are made by men for political ambition and women are therefore oppressed in marriage, their desire may become destructive of harmless victims. The exotic setting, conventional in heroic drama, serves Manley well: she can show gender relations as profoundly oppressive without offending her audience.

In *Almyna* the title character is equal to the challenge of male oppression, but she is not married as the play opens. Again Manley uses a Near Eastern setting to critique male oppression of women without offending her audience directly. The Sultan's first wife was unfaithful, and, as a result, he executes successive wives because he is convinced by the Koran that women have mortal souls. The Sultan tells his brother, who loves Almyna, that she cannot do other than love him:

Appears she cold; 'tis strong Dissimulation,
For they, by nature, much o're match our fire.
Born to no other end, but propagation
Instinct to them, as to their fellow Brutes,
Goads on, to Multiply.[74]

Almyna, as we soon discover, is a living contradiction of the Sultan's ideas. Superbly educated, she believes she was born for higher things than simply marrying Abdalla; instead she will marry the Sultan and heroically end his practice of wife-killing:

Start not at my Request, it comes from Heav'n,
From thence derived, to save the innocent Lives

186

Of Virgin daughters, and their Parents' tears.
To stop the course of such Barbarity.

(P. 28)

In the meantime, the Sultan is beginning to have doubts: he dreams that the Prophet judges him for murdering his queens. In a long speech based on the defenses of women, laced with many examples of heroic women in history, Almyna convinces the Sultan that women have souls. He tests her courage, however, by pretending that she will be the last wife to be executed. When she faces death heroically, the Sultan declares:

How far thy bravery of Soul cou'd reach
Quite vanquish'd, by thy heroick Deeds
We gain in losing of so false a Cause.
Henceforth be it not once imagin'd
That women have not Souls, divine as we.
Who doubts, let 'em look here, for Confutation,
And reverence with us *Almyna's* Vertue.

(P. 46)

Almyna is a champion of her sex, by now a familiar figure in women's writing of the late seventeenth century.

In her only comedy, *The Lost Lover,* Manley continues her critique of mating arrangements. The heroes, Wilmore and Wildman, are slightly rakish, as their names suggest. Wildman is rebuffed by his former lover, Olivia, and Wilmore casts off his old Love, Belira, to pursue Marina: "Be wise *Belira*! We live not now in those Romantick constant days, where their first Mistress was their last. I lik'd you once, and still esteem you, but Vows that are made in Love, are writ in sand."[75] Although Wilmore is the stereotypic inconstant man, he does love Marina, whose mother finally resolves the plot by giving her daughter the liberty of choice in marriage. So even though Manley retains the rakish heroes and the theme of interest-forced marriage, her comedy presages eighteenth-century freedom of choice for children. In fact, the changes in her tragedies during the ten years between *The Royal Mischief* and *Almyna* show less alteration in Manley's personal values than differences of genre: she moves from heroic tragedy to tragicomedy, but her concerns about sexual politics remain constant. The vocabulary changes according to the genre.

Part of the reason that Almyna can be a heroic figure is that she is very well educated and thus feels a match for the Sultan. One of the problems that Manley constantly raised about claiming the privilege of writing was women's lack of education. One of her first assertions about plans for authorship is the poem, already quoted, honoring Catherine Trotter's play *Agnes de Castro,* in which Manley sees Trotter as a "third start," after Orinda and Behn, and Trotter's examples as giving Manley courage to write. In assessing Manley's deference to Trotter, we should recall that of the Female Wits Trotter was the best educated. Thus Manley had some reason to see her as a potential leader among women writers. As things turned out, Manley continued to be productive, whereas Trotter, after writing five plays and a novel, married the Reverend Cockburn and was silent for twenty years.

In the preface to *The Lost Lover,* Manley confessed that writing for the stage may not have been good for women, "to whom all Advantages but meer Nature, are refused; If we happen to have a Genius to Poetry, it presently shoots to a fond desire of Imitation."[76] Without an education or an apprenticeship available to them, women were extremely vulnerable in writing for the stage, and Manley seems to have felt less vulnerable writing journalism and fiction, where her relative want of learning would not be so visible. Like Behn, Manley was certainly vilified for her immoral character, but such was the code of the day that she could defend herself only about literary questions, such as the "warmth" of *The Royal Mischief.* Her defenses remind one of Behn's defenses of her bawdry because they have the same contradictory qualities. First, Manley said that she thought representations of love rather than ambition would be more acceptable to an audience from a woman author. Then she argued that Dryden used as much warmth in *Aurenge-Zebe.* But, even with contradictions, Manley defends her privilege of writing on any subject and thus holds ground for all women in a long-standing struggle.

Manley suffered more from the effect of *The Female Wits* than did her colleagues, Trotter and Pix. *The Royal Mischief* is the play parodied within the lampoon, and the portrait of Marsilia seems more negative than those of Mrs. Wellfed (Pix) and Calista (Trotter). Cotton believes that *The Female Wits* drove Manley from the stage, and she may be right.[77] Yet Manley's later behavior with regard to *The New Atalantis* (admitting and defending her authorship of an anonymous work) and her quarrel with Steele do not suggest a temperament so easily daunted by public exposure; but these incidents occurred more than a decade after *The Female Wits.* Gwendolyn Needham thought Manley was little hurt by the lampoon.[78] The truth is guesswork. What is certain is that, like Aphra Behn, she suffered much vilification for the way she wrote and the way she lived. It was the price she paid for making several benchmarks for women in English history.

Catherine Trotter Cockburn (1679–1749) and Mary Pix (1666–1709) were the other dramatists who followed Aphra Behn. Although all the Female Wits were supportive of one another, Pix and Trotter were more distant from Behn than Manley, and each had an individual voice. Trotter was the most confident of her abilities, and her feminism became more definite as her career progressed, until, that is, she married the Reverend Cockburn. Mary Pix was always humble about her limitations as a writer and tended to imitate the fads of the times, but with a perceptible sympathy toward women. Trotter does not seem to have lost her dedication to writing, even after marriage and child-rearing; for when her children were grown, she returned to writing theological treatises. There she continued her commitment to better education for all women. For example, she protests the limitations on the education of women in a poem appended to *Remarks upon the Principles and Reasoning of Dr. Rutherford's Essay on the Nature and Obligation of Virtue* (1747). Because of her own distinction as an intellectual correspondent and controversialist, her biographer Thomas Birch describes her as an honor to her sex who has "raised our ideas of their intellectual powers."[79]

Trotter's career began in 1693, when she was just fourteen, with *Olinda's Adventures,* a novel discussed in chapter 4. At sixteen she published her first play, *Agnes de Castro,* anonymously, a tragedy based on a novel of the same title by Aphra Behn. The play need hardly detain us: it is, as Nancy Cotton wryly observes, "a Senecan tragedy a hundred years out of date."[80] More interesting is the fact of Trotter's having written and published the play. Although she was conforming enough to publish anonymously, the style and presentation of the play promoted Trotter as a learned lady. That gesture and the composition of a play, rather than more decorous poetry or even another novel, are definitely transgressive of social boundaries. There is an Orinda-like cast to Trotter's style, yet her source and genre mark her as primarily descended from Behn.

Trotter was undeterred by the parody of her as Calista, the pretentious, catty pedant in *The Female Wits.* She enjoyed considerable encouragement from the foremost dramatists of the time, as we have seen. In 1698 Betterton's company produced *Fatal Friendship,* for which Farquhar had high praise. It is a blank verse tragedy written expressly to reform the stage; Collier's *A Short View of the Immorality and Profaneness of the English Stage* appeared in the same year. Trotter said her goal was the irreproachable, classical aim, "to discourage Vice, and to recommend a firm unshaken Virtue."[81] If one compares the action of *Fatal Friendship* with that of *Agnes de Castro,* however, it becomes clear that Trotter did not have to alter her dramaturgy greatly to suit the reform movement, for in both plays the major characters act from innocent motives. The difference is that in *Agnes* the very nobility of the Prince, Agnes, and the Princess incites the malice of Alvaro and Elvira, whereas in *Fatal Friendship* all the characters act from noble motives, but from cross-purposes, so as to produce the tragedy. The play suggests that we bring disaster upon ourselves as we fail to trust providence and trust ourselves instead: "let the most resolute / Learn from this story to distrust themselves" (*FW,* 207).

More interesting than Trotter's announced moral intentions, however, are the play's subtexts, which fit the sexual politics we have been exploring. One is a preoccupation with money. As Fidelis Morgan says, "The *Fatal Friendship*'s plot is extraordinary, for a tragedy, in its ingenious obsession with money, its advantages, and the problems resulting from the lack of it" (*FW,* 25). Bellgard, for example, would force his sister Felicia, who is in love with, and secretly married to, the impoverished Gramont, a second son, to marry Gramont's wealthy father: "I would prevent your ruin and my own," Bellgard tells her. Driven by the need for money, the men make decisions that cause them and the women to suffer and are ultimately fatal to the central characters. The action, with its mercenary element and its frequent secrecy, demonstrates that interest is the enemy of desire, as are the wealthy patriarchal figures. Their secrets are the means by which the powerless seek to avoid oppression. In these themes *Fatal Friendship* greatly resembles the fiction produced by the followers of Behn.

Trotter's next two plays continued her preoccupation with mating arrangements. *Love at a Loss* (1700), her only comedy, deals with three women who almost lose the men they love through folly: coquettishness, flirtation, premarital sex. With all its pointing sensible morals, the play again has subtexts that connect it with women's fiction. The women are active in the courtships, but their ignorance of the world leads them to risk their reputations, as in much eighteenth-century fiction. The men flirt with being predatory, but they are reformed rakes of sentimental drama. *The Unhappy Penitent* (1701) is a moralized tragedy, which recalls *Fatal Friendship.* Here again we have a secret marriage as the result of a long delay in a marriage contract, with slander and confusion sown by an unrequited suitor. The heroine, Margarite of Flanders, is accused of whoredom, and having been cleared of the accusation, remains true to her vow to enter a convent, renouncing her beloved husband. Although the overt morality depends upon the keeping of contracts, the play has a subtext similar to that in *Love at a Loss:* women's reputations can be ruined by their innocent errors; and to that in *Fatal Friendship:* women will suffer from men's errors in mating arrangements. Trotter also resembles Aphra Behn in being drawn to plots and dramatic gestures that involve oath-taking and the multiple questions that arise in remaining true to one's word. The attractiveness of this theme for both male and female writers in the period is well documented by Susan Staves in *Players' Scepters.*[82]

Trotter's last play, *The Revolution of Sweden* (1706), resembles Manley's *Almyna,* which appeared in the same year, as an overtly feminist play. Trotter had admitted in her dedication to *The Unhappy Penitent* that she took unhappy love as her theme to comply with the effeminate taste of her age.

In *The Revolution,* she wanted better things for her heroines. She announced that the play incites the audience to a particular virtue, "a disinterested and resolute Care of the Publick Good," and two heroines represent this value.[83] Christina is married to a traitor and fights in disguise for the Swedes as they drive the Danes from their country. She extols women's courage, which is only concealed by their being excluded from war by custom and opinion: "but where our Honour's plac'd we oft / Have shown in its Defence a no less Manly daring" (p. 17). Constantia, also devoted to the public good, denounces her husband to the king for treachery; her husband, proved innocent, approves her action as an example for men. It becomes clear to the reader, as it did to Congreve, that Trotter's belief in women's capacities exceeded her artistry in this play: the action is confusing and filled with long boring speeches. Congreve, who read a draft of the play, was tactful about the serious heroines, but warned that the play seemed "too full of business" and the last act "will have many harangues in it, which are dangerous in a catastrophe."[84] Yet the evidence of Trotter's growing commitment to women's achievements and ambitions, especially in intellectual endeavors, is significant, especially at the same time that Manley was making similar claims. In their assertions of women's rights to better education, to serious intellectual activity, and to a share in public life, both Manley and Trotter were true heirs of Aphra Behn.

Mary Pix (1666–1709), on the other hand, was often apologetic about her lack of learning, but she had a genuine gift for comedy. She had enough success on the stage to write more plays for the Restoration theater than any woman but Behn, but she seems not to have trusted her talent for comedy and so produced a good many heroic tragedies that make dull reading today. She wrote six tragedies: *Ibrahim* (1696), *Queen Catherine* (1698), *The False Friend* (1699), *The Czar of Moscovy* (1701), *Double Distress* (1701), and *The Conquest of Spain* (1705). The last two were clearly derived from Fletcher's *A King and No King* and *The Loyal Subject.* One of the major defects of Pix's serious drama is her unwillingness to go beyond her sphere and deal with the stuff of tragedy: war and matters of state. As the Prologue to *The False Friend* suggests, she wrote to reform the age, but in a manner befitting her gender:

> Amongst Reformers of this Vitious Age,
> Who think it Duty to Refine the Stage:
> A Woman, to Contribute, does Intend,
> In Hopes a Moral Play your Lives will Mend.
> Matters of State, she'll not pretend to Teach;
> Or treat of War, or things above her Reach:
> Nor Scourge your Folly's, with keen Satyrs Rage;

But try if good Example will Engage.
For Precepts oft do fail from Vice to win,
And Punishments but harden you in Sin.
Therefore (*Male Judges*) She prescribes no Rules,
And knows 'tis vain to make Wise Men of Fools.
Lest all those Wholesom Laws that she can give,
You'd think too much below you to receive.
–That part then of the Reformation,
Which she believes the fittest for her Station;
Is, to show Man the surest way to Charm:
And all those Virtues, Women most Adorn.[85]

Pix's attitudes are indicative of the way in which the Restoration era was turning into the Augustan. The assertiveness of Behn, Manley, and Trotter gradually became a reluctance to exceed more narrowly defined female roles that were gradually constrained to the personal sphere. Perceptible too is a growing polarization of the genders, with women as agents of men's moral reform. All these characteristics mark a gradual but profound change in sexual ideology from that of the Reformation and its aftermath to ideas of domestic sentiment in the eighteenth and nineteenth centuries. Because she was more sensitive to the attitudes of the age, Pix was far less feminist than Behn, Manley, and Trotter. Her characteristic tone is apologetic: "The Author on her weakness, not her strength relies." And she frequently pleads for male chivalry to the "imperfect Woman."[86] As a result of these limiting attitudes, Pix turns historical drama into romantic intrigue. Of *Queen Catherine* Nancy Cotton says, "The play reduces the Wars of the Roses to a quarrel over thwarted love."[87] And the same may be said for *The Czar of Moscovy,* on the theme of the false Demetrius. Although she seems to follow Manley's Homais in her portrait of Shaker Para in *Ibrahim,* her *False Friend,* with its endorsement of parental authority in mating arrangements, seems almost an answer to Manley's *The Lost Lover.* In *The Conquest of Spain,* a father, whose daughter has been raped by the king, remains loyal to the ruler, who is eventually deposed for the crime. Both Trotter and Manley had found strong female characters to celebrate the triumph of public values over private limitations, but Pix chose not to share their attitude.

Yet if Pix was less feminist than her colleagues in her serious plays, she exploited to good effect the passionate emotions usually associated with women. *Ibrahim* was very successful on the stage, and a contemporary quoted by Cotton describes the reason: "This Play, if it want the Harmony of Numbers, and the Sublimity of Expression, has yet the Quality, that at least ballances that Defect, I mean the Passions; for the distress of Morena never fail'd to bring Tears into the Eyes of the Audience; which few Plays, if any since Otway's have done."[88] Pix's later tragedies, *Queen Catherine, The Czar of Moscovy,* and *The Double Distress,* are full of operatic effects: mad scenes, rapes or threats of rapes, scenes of rant, and lyric love scenes. Cotton observes, "The theaters probably continued to produce these plays because Pix had a knack for alternating scenes of rant with melting love scenes in which a mighty hero languishes at his lady's feet. However silly such scenes seem on the page, they act well, and audiences continued to like them."[89]

Yet for all her differences from the other Female Wits, Pix was nonetheless a daughter of Behn. She signed her work, composed as a professional, and wrote several excellent comedies that explore major themes of Aphra's: forced marriage, the conflict between love and interest, and the defects of the marriage relationship. Pix's first comedy, *The Spanish Wives* (1696), sounds the familiar theme of a forced marriage for one of the wives, but with a difference: Elenora's former suitor rescues her from imprisonment and obtains a divorce for her. The Spanish setting works for Pix as Turkish settings worked for Manley: they convey socially sanctioned male oppression of women without overt criticism of English society. But the Governor of Barcelona is wiser than his countrymen and "gives his Wife more liberty than is usual in Spain."[90] She repays his faith in her by resisting the temptation to be unfaithful with a young English suitor. Both plots would have pleased Aphra Behn, for even if the style of the play is farcical, its sexual politics are enlightened.

Pix's next comedy, *The Innocent Mistress* (1697), unites two favorite themes: forced marriage and a younger son. Ironically, Sir Charles Beauclair has come into his estate after his marriage to a rich, tyrannical widow. He has since fallen in love with a spirited but virtuous woman, who renounces him just before his wife's former husband (Flywife) appears and releases the lovers to each other. The play is jammed with interesting characters: a teenage alcoholic with a weight problem, an independent woman who reforms her rake by seducing her competition in disguise, the wife deserter and his cunning but gullible mistress, an angry "Widow" and her foolish brother, a decent country squire who rescues his beloved with an elaborate murder plot. The intrigue is extremely complex and amusing, but Pix is careful to keep her hero and heroine entirely innocent: he has never consummated his forced marriage and she renounces even their platonic relationship. Pix's ideal is clear: as one character says of Bellinda: "How strong are the efforts of honour where a good education grounds the mind in virtue" (*FW,* 297). The play is sentimental about Bellinda and Sir Charles, but it is hardly sentimental about marriage.

Pix's next comedy, *The Deceiver Deceived* (1697), was plagiarized by one George Powell in *The Imposture Defeated* at Drury Lane, an incident Cotton describes in detail.[91] Of interest here is how Powell's treatment of the central action helps us define Pix's approach to sexual politics. In both plays a Venetian senator pretends to be blind to avoid the expense of a presidency; his wife and daughter take advantage of the situation to pursue lovers; and the daughter's suitor succeeds in getting the girl and a dowry from the father. The wife's situation reveals that Pix wrote in the new sentimental vein, whereas Powell adhered to Restoration hard comedy. In Powell's version the wife is lustful, and the revelation of the husband's deception comes just at the moment when she is *in flagrante delicto*. In Pix the wife preserves her honor during a flirtation with a former lover. She is unhappily married, but not unfaithful. Powell looks back through Restoration comedy to the Renaissance; Pix looks forward to the sentimental comedy of the eighteenth century. The artistic problem is that the device of the tricker tricked is central to hard comedy, and Pix's treatment of the wife makes the husband's cure of his blindness fall flat.

Pix was more successful in choosing her plots in the remaining comedies. Her next, *The Beau Defeated* (1700), presents two contrasting widows, each of whom has definite goals in remarrying. Lady Landsworth wishes to marry a poor, virtuous man who is unaware that she is rich. She finds him by going, masked, to the theater, where he concludes she is a prostitute and she thinks him a libertine. The other widow, who vows to marry quality, assumes pretentious manners and employs a retinue to instruct her in corrupt activities of upper-class life. In an echo of Behn's *False Count*, she is about to marry a disguised servant when she is saved by her friends and ends with a good, upright country squire. The play concludes with praise for London citizens:

> The glory of the world our British nobles are,
> The ladies, too, renowned and chaste and fair,
> But to our citizens, Augusta's sons,
> The conquering wealth of the Indias runs.
>
> (*FW*, 48)

In this theme Pix anticipates Centlivre. Pix's widows recall the assertive women in Behn's plays in that their decisions determine the course of the action; being widows, they are immune from the exchange and alliance systems that afflict the young. Although she was never the critic of social institutions that the other writers were, Pix clearly delighted in representing women who sought to control their lives.

In her next comedy, *The Different Widows* (1703), Pix presents sisters who are also contrasting widows. Laby Bellmont, the sensible widow, has a rakish son whom she matches with the rich and witty Angelica, who reforms him. Sir James and Angelica are Restoration characters settled in the service of sentimental action. The more hilarious and farcical plot involves Lady Gaylove, who refuses to admit that she is aging and therefore sequesters her grown son and daughter, keeping them ignorant and childishly dressed for twenty years. They are rescued by the daughter's suitor, but the son remains a simpleton. The play is packed with farcical intrigue, but the central actions focus again on two women who, whatever their excesses, seek to control their families.

Pix's last comedy, *The Adventures in Madrid* (1706), is also sentimental but with women in command. Two Englishmen, visiting the embassy in Madrid, are repeatedly tricked by women living in a neighboring house. "In a typically Pix fashion, the seemingly erring wife is actually virtuous."[92] The play has a tragicomic subplot in which old Gomez has usurped his nephew's estate and forced his niece to act as his wife. The nephew rescues his sister, has his uncle arrested, and the lovers are united at the end. Here as elsewhere Pix finds a way to end a forced marriage, but usually without divorce.

The general characteristics of Pix's drama deserve comment for their contribution to the sexual ideology at the end of the seventeenth century. Although she sentimentalizes the action of Restoration intrigues by keeping both sexes virtuous, she delights in active, lively, independent women who make the action work. Consequently, such characters frequently are widows whose wealth gives them autonomy. Pix's ideal relationship is a marriage for love, not the extramarital liaison: in this she looks forward to the later century. She does not make forced marriage, a frequent feature of her plays, into a critique of the institution in the manner of Behn, but she will not tolerate such relationships and finds ways to end them in play after play. We have three measures within the drama of the shift in sexual ideology during the seventeenth century: by the end of the century, most of the cuckholds are gone, as the hard patriarchal marriage of which they are a product gave way to more sentimental relationships; plays of forced marriage no longer reconcile the mates to the relationship, as they did in the Jacobean drama, but bring it to an end, even through divorce; children more and more frequently make their own marriage choices, whatever Lord Halifax may have claimed for parents in his famous work *Advice for a Daughter* (1688). As aristocrats took refuge in images of the arrogant will of the rake while the social institutions that supported their actual lives crumbled around them, parents, or at least fathers, were occasionally still trying to assert an authority over their children's marriage choices that was rapidly vanishing, both in art and life.

Susanna Centlivre (1669–1723)
and the Eighteenth Century

Susanna Centlivre was the last of Aphra Behn's descendents in the drama, and in certain ways, the culmination of the traditions of the Female Wits. She used the comedy of intrigue and reform to continue and explore the values established by Aphra Behn and developed by Manley, Trotter, and Pix. In addition, she showed the influence of the feminist ideas expressed by Mary Astell and other writers during the reign of Queen Anne (1702–14), and contributed to the developing sexual and mercantile ideology of the eighteenth century. For example, although Behn and the Female Wits had been Tories, Centlivre was an ardent Whig, who threw her sympathies in with the newly wealthy classes that would gradually come to dominate the government and social thought of England for the new century. Centlivre's political and sexual ideology were cut from a single fabric: she challenged established authority in the Stuart monarchy or oppressive fathers not in the name of political or sexual freedom but for the sake of solid merchant values. Her vision of marriage is one in which money supports love and in which choices are left to the partners for the sake of the future, not for the sake of inherited property from the past. Centlivre's ideal is a society governed by a limited monarchy and the modern party system gradually dominated by merchants, financiers, and industrialists. Behn's code of gallantry and wit, with its aristocratic overtones and its ideal of love free from interest, has given way to the identity of love and interest, in plays that distinguish privilege, not between aristocrats and merchants, but between the middling and the wealthy merchant. Within this altered social code, Centlivre shows herself an heir to Behn in her endorsement of education for women, in her frequent representation of independent, autonomous women who triumph over oppressive fathers or guardians, women who sometimes reform the men they love. Yet all the actions take place within a mercantile vision that supports marriage for love as the fulfillment of desire and maintains women's fidelity—and most males' too—within the marriage bond. The degree to which her continuing earlier feminist commitments linked Centlivre with Aphra Behn may be seen in the fact that even though her plays (after *The Perjur'd Husband,* 1700) were chaste and so was her life, she was still identified with Manley and Behn by John Duncombe in *The Feminiad* (1754):

> The modest Muse a veil of pity throws
> O'er Vice's friends and Virtue's foes;

Abash'd she views the bold unblushing mein
Of modern Manley, Centlivre, and Behn.[93]

When one considers the fact that Centlivre's best plays—*The Busy Body,
The Wonder, A Bold Stroke for a Wife*—were continuously performed in the
eighteenth century and that Garrick first began to play Felix in *The Wonder*
in 1756, one has some measure of the fact that a slur at a woman's private
life or her sexual habits was then as now the best way to denigrate a writer:
one had simply to make the accusation, for to prove a negative is virtually
impossible and certainly impractical.

One of Centlivre's favorite themes was challenging the authority of par-
ents. Her plays show more clearly than most the degree to which the
Puritan overthrow of established authority and its descendents in the anti-
Jacobite movement in the late seventeenth century were a source of inspiration for those who sought to relieve the oppression of women. A
significant number of Centlivre's plays—*The Beau's Duel* (1702), *The Stolen
Heiress* (1702), *Love's Contrivance* (1703), *The Bassett Table* (1705), *The Busy
Body* (1709), *The Wonder* (1714), and *A Bold Stroke for a Wife* (1718)—represent parental authority as oppressive and sometimes tyrannous. The victims are usually daughters, but occasionally sons as well, and the plays
invariably present the success of the intrigue in which the young people,
led by men or women, triumph over the old ones. The plays overtly endorse the right of children to make marriage choices. Renaissance and early
seventeenth-century plays frequently present the fantasy that the children's
choices and the parents' coincide, or that the parent, as in *Midsummer
Night's Dream,* is persuaded to accede by some higher authority. From
Jacobean times forward, the conflict between parents and children about
marriage choices was frequently represented in the play of enforced marriage, a tradition that Behn and the Wits carried into the late seventeenth
century. By Centlivre's time the enforced unions and cynical structures of
the *mal mariée,* which usually justify cuckoldry, have changed to love intrigues in which children trick authorities, and the plays not only let them
get away with it but consciously reprimand the parents. In *The Busy Body,*
Sir Jealous Traffick tells the audience, "By my Example let all Parents move /
And never strive to cross their Children's Love; / But still submit that Care
to Providence above."[94]

Some of the old structures persist in Centlivre's first play, *The Perjur'd Husband* (1700), which presents the Pizaltos: he, an old lecherous husband pursuing the witty maid Lucy, while his young wife cuckolds him with the
Frenchman Ludovico. After Pizalto, cuckolds dissappear from Centlivre's
vocabulary, but the plot involving the Pizaltos reveals by parallelism the concealed libertine nature of Bassino, the title character of the play. Although

some Centlivre males are rakish and many are lively and resourceful, none is allowed to be a true libertine. With *Love at a Venture* (1706), Centlivre returns momentarily to a version of gay comedy, in which Bellair is quite rakish (he assumes three identities and woos two heroines at once). Yet at the end, Bellair marries the serious Camilla, whose life he has saved before knowing her identity. He loves her enough to risk not only his life but his fortune for her. Bellair is also never allowed to cuckold Sir Paul Cautious despite elaborate intrigues with Sir Paul's wife. And so, in Centlivre's plays, rakish characters are disciplined, so that they eventually prove worthy of a serious mate. Similarly coquettes are disciplined too, although they are relatively scarce in Centlivre. Lady Reveller in *The Basset Table* and Lucinda who poses as a prude in *The Platonic Lady* (1706), qualify; but most of Centlivre's heroines are honest and straightforward in dealing with the men they love, and they are self-conscious about being so. Examples of such heroines are numerous: Clarinda in *The Beau's Duel,* Angelica in *The Gamester,* Valeria and Lady Lucy in *The Basset Table,* Miranda and Isabinda in *The Busy Body,* and Isabella in *The Wonder.* These women are assertive, but not transgressive in the way of Manley and Behn.

Centlivre frequently represented the oppression of women, usually as daughters who were confined by their fathers or guardians and intended to marry rich, old merchants, who might be foreign as well. Clarinda, in *The Beau's Duel,* is intended for Sir William Mode by her father, Careful, who must be tricked into marrying a fake Quaker in order to extract his agreement that Clarinda may have her inheritance even though she has married the man of her choice. Gravello pressures Lucasia, from *The Stolen Heiress,* to marry Pirro, who values only wealth; so she elopes with her beloved Palente, who is then sentenced to death (in Sicily) for kidnapping an heiress. Lucasia's brother reveals that she is not an heiress and that Pirro is corrupt. At the end Palente beomes an heir and is therefore acceptable to Gravello. The Sicilian atmosphere makes the play heavy with oppression. Gone are the days when love and money were enemies; now one follows the other.

Love's Contrivance is more cheerful, but the actions of the father, Selfwill, are just as tyrannous as the others: he had agreed to a match of Lucinda with Bellmie, whom she loves; but as the play opens, he rejects Bellmie in favor of Sir Toby Doubtful's greater fortune. Selfwill separates love and marriage in the old-fashioned way, and then betrays Lucinda after she has obeyed him:

> *Luc.* . . . I hope you won't be so barbarous as to force my inclinations: I have ever been a dutiful Child to you, never thought of Marriage till you yourself persuaded me. You bad me encourage *Bellmie's* Suit, as a Man you design'd for my Husband: In Obedience to you I strove

198

to love him, and by Degrees he gain'd my heart, which now is unalterably his; I ne'er can love but him.

Self. You can't—with all my heart, love him on, I don't bid you hate him,
nor love Sir Toby: You say Duty to me gave the first Impression of your
love to Bellmie, then let your Duty give the second, at my Command,
to *Sir Toby;* for d'ye see, I am resolv'd you shall ne'er see *Bellmie,* till you
are his Wife, and so consider on't; d'ye hear, to-morrow's the Day. (1:2)

Lucinda copes with this forced union through a series of ruses: she cannot
speak; then she arranges a proviso scene in which she makes outrageous
demands of Sir Toby, including a French coach, all of which make Sir Toby
skeptical about marriage; and after consulting an astrologer (Bellmie in
disguise), he concludes that Lucinda is not for him. Unlike some of the
other fathers, Selfwill is not gracious at the end but flounces out, declaring
that no penny of his will go to Lucinda. The atmosphere of the play is light-
ened considerably by a gay couple, Octavio and Belliza, who have an excellent slanging match when they first meet (1:16–25) and enjoy a love chase
until the end of the action.

After *Love's Contrivance* Centlivre turned to reform comedy in *The Gamester*
and *The Basset Table* and then wrote some of her best comedies in the humane intrigue mode: *The Busy Body, The Wonder,* and *A Bold Stroke for a
Wife.* But whatever comic vein she mined, oppressive fathers were part of
her dramatic vocabulary. In *The Basset Table,* Sir Richard Plainman tries to
force his daughter Valeria to marry Captain Hearty of the navy and breed
Englishmen to fight the French. Valeria loves science first and Ensign Lovely
of the army; he, with the aid of Hearty, tricks Sir Richard out of his daughter.
The Busy Body and *The Wonder* draw on Mediterranean cultures to suggest
the oppression of women by tyrannous fathers. In *The Busy Body,* Sir Jealous
Traffick imprisons his daughter Isabinda in the manner he learned from
long residence in Spain. The maid Patch says of Sir Jealous, "Oh, Madam,
its his living so long in *Spain;* he vows he'll spend half his Estate, but he'll
be a Parliament-Man, on Purpose to bring in a Bill for Women to wear
Veils, and the other odious Spanish Customs.—He swears it is the Height of
Impudence to have a Woman seen bare-fac'd, even at Church, and scarce
believes there's a true begotten Child in the City" (2:8). The implication
that sexual morality is culture-bound is unmistakable in Patch's comment
and in the various foreign settings of the Behn tradition: the Near East,
Spain, Sicily—all cultures noted for their oppression of women and all used
for two purposes in these plays. First, to demonstrate that the treatment
of women is culture-specific, that their oppression, not being universal, is
not inevitable. Second, to avoid negative reaction from English audiences,
if native social customs were criticized. Instead, extremes of which the English were not generally guilty could be rejected.

Charles Gripe must rescue Isabinda from the prison of her father's house. But all patriarchal oppression is not learned in Spain, for Sir Francis Gripe would marry his ward, who has £30,000, rather than allow her to marry her choice. Miranda, the ward, must trick Sir Francis into letting her marry as she pleases. Unlike Selfwill, Sir Francis and Sir Jealous are reconciled to the children's unions.

The Wonder is set in Lisbon, which Centlivre uses to explain the tyrannic behavior of Don Pedro, who would force his daughter into a convent, and of Don Lopez, who would force his daughter to marry a rich old fool. Both daughters evade their fates by drastic action: one jumps from her balcony and hides from her father; the other carries her own difficult courtship to a happy conclusion. The setting is made to account for much of the oppression of women: "Tempers are hotter, honor more sacred, jealousy more rife than in London. Father and brothers exercise despotic control over their wives, daughters, and sisters. Disguise and secret assignations are accepted as everyday occurences."[95] The code is made clear through one character's observation: "Liberty is the idol of the English, under whose Banner all the Nation Lists" (3:2). And another: "What pleasant Lives Women lead in England, where Duty wears no Fetter but Inclination" (3:6). Through her setting Centlivre can satirize patriarchal oppression, call it culture-specific, and flatter her compatriots simultaneously.

If their fathers may seek to victimize them, Centlivre's women are often extraordinary people. Although Clarinda (*The Beau's Duel*) is honest and resourceful, the most interesting woman in the play is Mrs. Plotwell, the former mistress of Bellmain and still his friend. Formerly a kept woman, she has recently come into a fortune that allows her to turn virtuous: "I am no more what you once knew me; since your Abode in Ireland, my Uncle, who kept from me my Estate, is dead, thank Heaven, and I am now Mistress of a Fortune sufficient for my Use; and, had I possess't it sooner, I never had been what I was: But now, I scorn Mankind on Terms like those; all innocent Diversions I freely take; I keep the best Company, pay and receive Visits from the highest Quality, people who are better bred than to examine into past Conduct" (1:19).

Mrs. Plotwell genially agrees to masquerade as a Quaker and "marry" Careful, who settles all his estate on Plotwell to spite his daughter; but when Plotwell becomes a shrew, he agrees to accept his daughter's marriage choice. Several aspects of Plotwell's character are of interest: she clearly exemplifies the principle that reform is possible in women, that they are not ruined for life if once they sell sex; that a woman's ruin is a social fact, which can be viewed as irrevocable or forgotten, depending on circumstances and the woman's attitude toward the condition. She also shows the economic basis for prostitution, and her attitude at the end of the play also indicates how much a woman with the strength and means to choose a virtuous life still internalizes the notion of a single, unalterable "ruin":

> I am pleas'd that I have done you Service, and henceforth shall devote myself to Virtue, and I hope Heaven will pardon the Follies of my past Life. . . . Virtue, though shining Jewel of my Sex–thou precious Thing, that none knows how to value as they ought while they enjoy it, but like Spend-thrift Heirs, when they have wasted all their Store, wou'd give the World they cou'd retrieve their lost Estate: Therefore beware, you happy Maids, how you listen to the deluding Tongues of Men, 'tis only they have the Power to betray you. (1:54–55)

Angelica from *The Gamester* is closer to a stereotype than Plotwell because Angelica's role is to reform Valere, the title character. She manages this by gambling with her lover while disguised and winning her portrait from him. An interesting touch in this play is Centlivre's use of shock to change the attitudes not just of the gamester but of his female couterpart Lady Wealthy, and of Angelica herself. Angelica is shocked by Valere's father's harsh attitudes toward her lover into seeing that she should forgive him. Then his father follows her example. Lady Wealthy has been shocked earlier by Lovewell's generosity into dealing with her lover honestly, instead of flirting with others to make him jealous. Shock supplies Centlivre with a device to motivate reforms in her comedies.

Valeria, from *The Basset Table,* is Centlivre's most interesting female character. She is a trained and systematic Margaret Cavendish, committed to the study of nature and to the education of women, according to the proposal of Mary Astell. Early in the play, Lady Reveller, who is not educated and is greatly addicted to gambling, mocks Valeria with Mary Astell's dream: "Well, cousin, might I advise, you should bestow your Fortune in founding a College for the study of Philosophy, where none but Women should be admitted; and to immortalize your Name, they should be called *Valerians,* ha, ha, ha" (1:19). Valeria retorts, "What you make a Jest of, I'd execute, were Fortune in my Power." Although most of the shallower characters make fun of her, it seems that Valeria is not, as some critics have claimed, a satiric portrait of Mary Astell. Valeria is already in love as the play opens, and she marries a man who encourages her experiments with nature, even if he occasionally mocks her to male company. Valeria is cheerful and courageous in her predicament, trapped between a bigoted and oppressive father who sees her only as a breeder of sons for England and the captain he intends to be her husband, a person appalled at her discourse–"She's fitter for *Moorfields* than Matrimony." The captain is instantly attracted to the frivolous Lady Reveller, but he is willing to help Ensign Lovely gain Valeria's

201

hand by tricking her father. Like the other Centlivre heroines, Valeria is not a coquette. When her scientific zeal makes Lovely wonder if she cares for him she declares, "Have I not told you twenty Times I love you?—for I hate Disguise; your Temper being adapted to mine, gave my Soul the first Impression;—You know my Father's positive,—but do not believe he shall force me to any Thing that does not love Philosophy" (1. 30). Valeria refuses to elope with Lovely because she is afraid her father will destroy her scientific equipment, but her father proves her wrong with regard to a forced marriage to the captain. As a result of Sir Richard's heaviness with Valeria, the audience may feel sympathy with the trick that Lovely and the captain play on him. Declaring she can love none but Lovely, Valeria refuses to look at her forced husband until he remarks, "Will not *Valeria* look upon me? She us'd to be more kind when we fish'd for Eels in Vinegar." The play ends with a vindiction of the union of Valeria and Lovely; Sir James tells Sir Richard:

> . . . I have no Reason to doubt you should repent it; he is a Gentleman, tho' a younger Brother; he loves your Daughter, and she him, which has the best Face of Happiness in a marry'd State; you like a Man of Honour, and he has as much as any one, that I assure you, Sir Richard.
> *Sir Rich.* Well, since what's past is past Recall I had as good be satisfied as not; therefore take her and bless ye together (1:94).

Centlivre saw no bar to married happiness in Valeria's learning or scientific pursuits; she and Lovely have the best relationship in the play.

As Lock suggests, *The Basset Table* also demonstrates how education is an important protection for women from the temptations of gambling. Lady Lucy and Valeria, both of whom are educated, are not tempted to play basset, or, if they play, do not become addicted to the game. Lady Lucy enjoys the theater more than gaming: "I had rather be noted every Night in the Front Box than, by my Absence, once be suspected of Gaming; one ruins my Estate and Character, the other diverts my Temper, and improves my Mind" (1. 7). Lady Reveller and Mrs. Sago, who lack education or any drive for it, are both addicts of basset and therefore are in the power of Sir James. Lady Lucy may be a bit prudish, but she is a good match for Sir James in her self-control. Mrs. Sago is smart, but her narrow background leads her only to copy Lady Reveller in everything; but, as Sir James observes, she has a fertile, if unimproved, brain. Centlivre dramatized the temptations of idleness and shallowness that dogged the eighteenth-century woman, and she made gambling a code for these weaknesses, just as the Bluestockings at the end of the eighteenth century made a point of holding soirées without card-playing to assert more serious intellectual values.

Miranda, from *The Busy Body*, rescues herself from a particularly difficult situation, for she is the ward of a guardian who would marry her himself. She has been meeting Sir George Airy in St. James Park incognita, and he also wishes to court Miranda officially. The incognita scene establishes Miranda and Sir George as a gay couple after she tricks him, and we understand that she can cope with both her guardian, whom she pretends to love, and the slightly rakish Sir George. In order to marry Sir George, she persuades her guardian to give his written consent that she will marry him. Again an oppressive authority is tricked in favor of a young person's marriage choice. The theme is reinforced by a similar action in the subplot. Although Miranda is not straightforward and verbally honest, her circumstances are such that the audience feels sympathy with her tricks and her consequent ability to control her life.

The heroine of *The Wonder*, Violante, is nearly as extraordinary as Valeria, for not only does Centlivre create the strong female bond between Violante and Isabella that accounts for Violante's keeping Isabella's secret, but Violante's relationship to her jealous lover Felix is genuinely passionate. Their scenes give reality to the risks Violante takes with Felix because she trusts their love: she vows to keep Isabella's secret "and trust to love, my Love to reconcile." That Centlivre understood Violante's action as violating a central stereotype about women is clear from the title: *The Wonder: A Woman keeps a Secret*. The end of the play sets Violante up as both the example and vindication of women: "No more let us thy Sex's Conduct blame, / Since thou'rt Proof to their eternal Fame, / That Man has no Advantage but the Name" (3:79).

In Centlivre's plays these extraordinary women who flout stereotypes achieve relatively equal relationships (which are almost always well financed) in marriage, unions that replace the more fragile equality achieved by the wit and poise of the earlier gay couples. Centlivre habitually used two couples in a pattern that J. H. Smith identifies as characteristic of her age: "The really popular and productive combinations after 1700 were those in which lively hero was paired with serious heroine, lively heroine with serious hero."[96] In these relationships any rakish or coquettish tendencies of the lively men and women may be disciplined, and the relationship made to seem quite stable and humane.

Centlivre's women are as frequent leaders of intrigue as men, and they are only occasionally morally superior agents of male reform, as in *The Gamester*. Only two of Centlivre's plays are overtly reform plays, and both address the vice of gambling—*The Gamester* and *The Basset Table*. With her next play, *Love at a Venture*, she returned to the familiar intrigue comedy in which the rake marries and his less honest ventures do not come to fruition. In their variety and sameness, Centlivre's plays are characteristic of their age, as described by Hume:

This survey has taken us to the end of the Carolean tradition and into the Augustan period, and is therefore complete. Looking back, one sees that underlying the obvious diminution of smut and cynicism is a more profound change in the whole philosophy reflected in the plays. At the extremes, the difference is easy to see: Steele's outlook is not Etherege's, and the value-systems implicit in the plays naturally differ. Similarly if less spectacularly Cibber refines upon Shadwell's reform pattern, Centlivre moralizes Behn's racy intrigues, Addison regularizes and democratizes Dryden's classic-stoic mode. Translating such particulars into broadly ideological terms, one may say that we have seen what is, philosophically speaking, an aristocratic Tory drama give way to one which is increasingly bourgeois and Whig.[97]

Centlivre contributes to the changes in sexual ideology already described. Forced marriage plays yield to plays in which children trick parents or guardians into letting them have their marriage choices. The father replaces the husband as the oppressor of women, who intrigue to marry happily instead of cuckolding their husbands. Toleration of trickery and forms of male-male rivalry are the most significant markers for changes in sexual ideology from the sixties and seventies into the beginning of the eighteenth century. Earlier the most frequent victim of trickery is the oppressive husband, who is cuckolded by a clever rival or wife, and the play tolerates the trick because the marriage is unhappy. The social triangle is husband-wife-lover. By Centlivre's time the cuckolds and the unhappy marriages diminish in number, and a frequent social triangle is father-daughter-lover. The lover's or daughter's trick is justified because the father is oppressive about the child's marriage choice. The emphasis in the drama has shifted from the consequences after marriage of parental control of the unions to the necessity of the children's love choice before marriage. There was questioning of partiarchal authority in both cases, but the shift in concern was quite definite in the period from the Restoration to the death of Anne. Centlivre's plays clearly demonstrate that shift, and the effect is to problematize the parent-child relationship, rather than the marriage.

As we observed at the beginning of this section, Susanna Centlivre is the last of the artistic heirs of Aphra Behn. Her approach to the privilege of writing was the familiar one for a woman who wrote for money. She claimed her work at first in both *The Perjur'd Husband* and *The Beau's Duel,* but attempted to conceal identity and sex in *The Stolen Heiress* (1702). Centlivre continued the protection of anonymity in *Love's Contrivance* (1703), but later claimed authorship of the play in the Dedication to *The Platonic Lady* (1706), where she said of *Love's Contrivance,* "thus passing for a Man's it has been play'd at least a hundred times." This dedication, "To all the Generous Encouragers of Female Ingenuity," is Centlivre's most overt feminist statement, in which she explains why she did not sign *Love's Contrivance* or *The Gamester*:

> A play secretly introduc'd to the House, whilst the Author remains unknown, is approv'd by every Body: the Actors cry it up, and are in expectation of a great Run; the Bookseller of a Second edition, and the Scribler of a Sixth Night: But if by chance the Plot's discover'd, and the Brat found Fatherless, immediately it flags in the Opinion of those that extoll'd it before, and the Bookseller falls in his price, with this Reason only, *It is a Woman's.* Thus they alter their Judgment, by the esteem they have for the Author, tho' the Play is still the same. They ne'er reflect, that we have had some Male-Productions of this kind, void of Plot and Wit, and full as insipid as ever a Woman's of us all. (2:Sig. A2)

Centlivre ponders the source of the wrath against women's writing. Is it "because they meddle with things out of their Sphere?" She answers, with Aphra Behn, "since the Poet is born, why not a Woman as well as a Man?" She does not derogate genius, but protests at the "ill-natur'd Criticks," who accuse her of plagiarism. "Nay, even my own Sex, which shou'd assert our prerogative against such Detractors, are often backward to encourage a Female Pen." Centlivre ends her dedication with a paean of praise for the great women of England, from whom she derives inspiration:

> Wou'd these profest Enemies but consider what Examples we have of Women that excell'd in all Arts; in Musick, Painting, Poetry; also in War; Nay, to our immortal Priase, what Empresses and Queens have fill'd the World? What cannot *England* boast from Women? The mighty *Romans* felt the Power of *Boadicea's* Arm; *Eliza* made *Spain* tremble; but ANN, the greatest of the Three, has shook the Man that aim'd at Universal Sway. After naming this Miracle, the Glory of our Sex, sure none will spitefully cavil at the following scenes, purely because a Woman writ 'em. (2:Sig. A2ᵛ2)

Two observations need to be made here. The first is that Anne's presence on the throne of England was a genuine inspiration to many women writers before Centlivre, as we have seen. Second, women writers in the Behn tradition retained a firm sense of their own artistic capacities because, writing for the stage as professionals, they did not internalize their inferiority or otherness to the extent that the writers in the Orinda tradition did. As a result, despite continuing prejudice and the Salic Law of Wit, they could build on the successes they achieved. This is precisely what happened to Centlivre. Her next few plays after *The Gamester,* a success, were published by "the author of *The Gamester.*" Later, even though she signed dedications from *The Busy Body* on, the title page reminded the reader that she was the author of *The Gamester* and *The Busy Body*. In short, Centlivre identified herself as the author of successful plays; and when she had another hit, she added that to her identification for the reader. Orinda's daughters also published in that fashion, as the author of *The Spleen,* or the Pindarick Lady, but in a more guarded way.

Once she had dedicated *The Wonder* to the duke of Cambridge, who would become George I, Centlivre wanted to remind those in power that she had been sympathetic to the Hanoverians before George had officially assumed the throne. From this point on, Centlivre was intent on achieving political advantage from the new regime; that she received very little recognition was not from lack of trying. Everything she wrote after the death of Anne was touched by politics, and she composed many poems in the hope of reward for her loyal support of the Whigs for many years; but Hanoverian largesse seems to have been limited to royal command benefit performances of *The Wonder, The Cruel Gift* and *The Busy Body,* and a handsome present. Were these limits the result of Centlivre's being a woman? Bowyer thought so: "Many of the literary Whigs—Addison, Steele, Philips, Burnet, Budgell, and others—were provided for under the new regime. Unfortunately, however, Susanna was a woman, and the political plums were not thought proper for a woman's table."[98] One of the ironies of this entire study is the persistence (even growth) of the idea that politics were beyond "woman's sphere," when virtually every writer covered here wrote about politics. Still, in an effort to contain women in their prescribed roles, society could withhold political rewards.

Although Centlivre wrote an amusing poem, *A Woman's Curse* (1720), about her personal life in order to gain advantage from her Whig support, she is like the daughters of Behn and unlike the daughters of Orinda in blending her poetry very little into her personal life. This is natural for a playwright, but even Centlivre's poetry is largely devoted to public life as well. In these gestures the daughters of Behn are, like her, more strongly male identified than the daughters of Orinda.

As I have said, Centlivre was accused of being loose morally, although there is little evidence that she was; and her plays were unlike Behn's in hewing to conventional mores. In these patterns Centlivre is of an era different from Behn's: she could not, if she had wished to, continue to turn the cavalier libertine philosophy to the service of a feminist vision. The accusations of immorality in the middle of the eighteenth century seem to have come from a recognition on the part of later writers of the female writing traditions that Centlivre drew upon.

In her Whig and mercantile sympathies, Centlivre is also clearly an Augustan writer. Behn herself was aristocratic in sympathy; Manley was an ardent Tory; only Mary Pix wavered slightly with her praise for the London citizens in *The Beau Defeated*. But Centlivre's mercantile and Whig commitments were definite and consistent. So, as John Loftis asserts, her plays grow stronger as the age progresses because her personal ideology was both consistent and consonant with the developments of the age.[99] This outcome is one that might be expected for the daughters of Behn, products as they were of the city and devoted as they were to politics. With much of the rest of England, they would contribute to the gradual development of the Whig mercantile hegemony.

Centlivre's middle-class orientation and her moral conformity did not mean, however, that her portraits of women were less active or assertive than those of Behn or the Wits. Her heroines, Valeria, Angelica, or Violante, are the equals of any earlier. I believe, however, that these feisty heroines come less from Centlivre's individual feminism than from the importance of "the Ladies" as an audience in the theater and a dramatic trend that features important women's roles in the plays of Centlivre's male counterparts, as described by J. H. Smith.[100] The shifts from hard to humane comedy, the gradual disappearance of cuckolding with its male ethos, the growing sense of women as a moral force in society, the decline of the libertine ideology, and, above all, ladies in the boxes, all contributed to the taste for strong but virtuous heroines who marry heart's desire at the end of the play. The rake, the coquette, the gay couple are all casualties of these developments, as the tastes of the new female audience carry the day in drama and in fiction too.

With all these changes, Centlivre profited little from her commitments or her sympathies. Although her plays held the boards constantly in the eighteenth century, their history is unpredictable and related less to audience tastes than to theatrical conditions, such as the fact that Garrick loved the part of Felix in *The Wonder*. Unlike the daughters of Orinda, who often used protective coloring and therefore concealed themselves more from the public until our era, the daughters of Behn attempted public recognition, but were often subject to historical vagaries beyond antifeminism or changes in public taste. They are to be admired for the risks they took and what they achieved for themselves and for women who came after them.

Chapter Four

Fiction

The fiction written by both the descendents of Behn and of Orinda takes its basic shape from an important translated work, Guilleraques's *Love Letters of a Portuguese Nun* (1669).[1] Robert Day describes the work, which was translated into English ten times before 1740:

> The letters purported to be five actual epistles written by a Portuguese nun, Marianna Alcoforado, to a French officer, the comte de Chamilly, who had loved and deserted her, and it has been definitely proved only in the present century that they are a literary fabrication. . . . In their own day, however, their authenticity was generally credited, and they were almost universally regarded as containing the accents of genuine and heartrending passion. The multitude of references to the letters, both in French and English, leaves no room for doubt of the enthusiasm which they generated.[2]

The letters, unaccompanied by a narrative, gradually re-create for the reader an intense passionate relationship between the nun and the French nobleman who has abandoned her. As Lawrence Lipking has pointed out, abandonment and separation are major themes in women's writing, but we need to ask ourselves about why the theme becomes so prominent a fantasy in amatory fiction of the seventeenth century. The answer lies partly in the sexual ideology of the time. As we have seen in earlier discussions, the libertine philosophy assumes a predatory, constantly roving male. It uses heterosexual relationships to maintain homosocial bonds, and therefore women circulate among men or are cast off when no longer desired. Eve Sedgwick's *Between Men* is useful in reading this literature.[3] In this way of thinking, marriage is the enemy of love, and the ideal heterosexual relationship is extramarital, free of interest or ambition, which plague the marriage relationship. Grafted onto this male-centered ideology in the fiction is a female sexuality which assumes that women are capable of enormous and lasting passion if once aroused by a desired lover, but that if their desire is satisfied outside marriage, the relationship men most desire, the women are ruined socially. They are ostracized, usually confined in the country while their lovers circulate freely. Both genders internalize the notion of the ruined woman and the double standard that goes with it so that both men and women assume that the man will reject the woman as society does. The woman suffers an additional double bind in that she is kept innocent to avoid her passionate arousal, with the result that she lacks defenses against the male's seductive wiles. This effect is reinforced by the socioeconomic status of the lovers: he is usually an aristocrat, in keeping with his libertine views, and she is usually country gentry, in keeping with her enforced innocence.

Abandonment is not always the disastrous result it may first appear to be. Once experienced, some women defy their "ruin" and become almost as predatory as the men. A few die innocent victims, but most survive and frequently in female communities, such as the nunnery of the Portuguese letters. The amatory novellas explore multiple strategies for the survival of abandoned women. More important for literary history, as Lipking says, "Abandonment may also be the secret of literature."[4] The deserted woman re-creates her passionate experience for the voyeuristic reader because the event is the most important in her life, and yet her voice is not subdued by marriage: she is still her own person. She is alone, to be sure, but still herself, bonded with her gender and able to display her experience of female passion:

> I do not know what 'tis I write for. Perhaps you'll pity me; but what good will that pity do me? I'll none on't. Oh how I hate myself, when I consider what I have forfeited to oblige you! I have blasted my Reputation, I have lost my Parents; I have exposed myself to the Laws of my Country against Persons of my Profession; and finally, to your Ingratitude, the worst of my Misfortune. But why do I pretend to Remorse, when at this instant, I should be glad with all my Soul, if I had run Ten Thousand greater hazzards for your dear Sake? And for the danger of my Life and Honour; the very thought on't is a kind of doleful Pleasure to me, and all's no more than the delivery of what's your own, and what I hold most precious, into your Disposition; and I do not know how all these Risques could have been better employ'd.[5]

The fiction most clearly reveals how some of the fantasies written for women fit the central fantasies represented to men: the woman is willing to sacrifice everything for the overwhelming experience of being with this man for however brief a time. She is willing to sacrifice her whole life just to share a brief sexual experience with him. No wonder male writers found this fantasy attractive! Yet because she has been abandoned, the woman has not only a room but a life of her own.

The fiction that most clearly develops the libertine ideology just described is that written by Aphra Behn, Delariviere Manley, the anonymous author of *Letters of Love and Gallantry,* Mary Hearne, and Eliza Haywood, although signs of eighteenth-century change are also noticeable in Haywood's work, where the extramarital liaison gives way to marriage for love, which may demand many adjustments but is both lovers' basic goal. The theme of money and the mercantile world becomes increasingly important as the enemy of both love and happy marriage.

Another group of writers—Mary Davys, Catherine Trotter, and the authors of *The Perfidious P* and of *Lindamira*—use their basic structures of amatory fiction without allowing immorality to thrive. Their books are stories of the education of a heroine in choosing wisely where to place her love in order to marry happily. This educational theme is important, for it represents a fundamental social meaning of the fiction for its large and growing female audience. Increasingly isolated in homes of small nuclear families, a status often represented in fiction by spatial confinement, marriageable women knew little of the world, of males, of their own sexuality. They and their world were increasingly convinced, however, of the new conclusions about marriage: children and not parents should make their marriages, and marriages for love were the only happy unions. The fiction described here, which women's increasing idleness gave them leisure to devour, provided them with examples of misguided parents, of inconstant lovers and their wiles, of the disaster of being ruined, of the power of aroused female sexuality, and of the power of love to lead one to a happy marriage.

The fiction of Orinda's daughters, Jane Barker, Penelope Aubin, and Elizabeth Singer Rowe, uses the amatory structures of Behn and her followers to convince the reader that life is not a tragedy of female innocence corrupted by the male aristocrat but a melodrama, in which married love is not only protected by providence but also may conquer death. A happy marriage, which children know best how to make, is the closest thing to heaven on earth. By the third decade of the eighteenth century, Haywood and Rowe are certain, in their different ways, about the power of love: to transform marriage in Haywood's work and to transcend death in Rowe's.

In *The Rise of the Woman Novelist* (1986), Jane Spencer demonstrates some of the continuities between the three groups of writers described here and the traditions in eighteenth-century women's fiction. The seduction fantasies of Behn and her followers, themselves politically conservative, are revised into novels of protest at women's condition by such radicals as Elizabeth Inchbald, Mary Hays, and Mary Wollstonecraft. The effects of Trotter, Davys, *Lindamira,* and *Perfidious P* are continued in the reformed and educated heroines of Burney, Charlotte Smith, and Maria Edgeworth.⁶ I would add that the fantasies of eighteenth-century romances may be related to those of Aubin and Barker in *Exilius* and Rowe's effects are strongly echoed in the work of Harriet Beecher Stowe. Whatever the orientation of the fiction–soft pornographic, educational and reforming, or polemical–it all graphically defined the predicament of women and conveyed changes in the sexual ideology through its fantasies and representations, sometimes directly as in the effects of forced marriages, but sometimes subtly as in the misguided decisions of parents in *Exilius*. As the seventeenth century turned into the eighteenth, the survival of ruined women–or women abandoned for any reason–became a distinctive feature of the fiction and, one might say, a tacit reply to the articulated and often internalized double standard. Although Delariviere Manley might condemn the double standard overtly, such a gesture was not available to the more conservative Jane Barker, who instead represents abandoned women rescued by Galesia and her landlady in *A Patch-Work Screen* and a veritable symposium of women telling and listening to stories of such women in *A Lining*. Manley describes a lesbian cabal in *New Atalantis,* and Elizabeth Rowe represents a female utopian family in *Letters Moral and Entertaining*. Again and again the fiction, whatever its moral stripe, represents women caring for women. Men, on the other hand, are not represented as being so generous with their emotions. They are predatory rakes early in the fiction, and later often agents of interest or ambition or both. In these fantasies of popular art, neither gender is rendered with great depth or complexity. One has to understand that the characters serve the purposes of the fantasies–to mediate the female readers' relationship to a world with which they must cope, a world in which males did, in fact, control property, could entertain ambition, did move freely, and enjoy the better half of the double standard of sexual morality. The rake is a stereotype, to be sure, but the fiction presents him as an extreme case of those males who use women. The stories represent plenty of males who value women, and such men are also valued and honored. The fiction represents situations that may be a threat to women readers to help them deal with possible situations. The fiction is hardly anti-male, but it is critical of men who use women. Bonding with women, except for Manley's lesbian cabal, is a refuge after male abandonment, a survival strategy, as it were.

Behn, Her Daughters, and the Gospel of Love: Delariviere Manley, Mary Hearne (fl. 1718–19), Eliza Haywood (1693–1756)

Included in *The Histories and Novels of the Late Ingenious Mrs. Behn* are *Love-letters to a Gentleman,* which closely imitates the *Portuguese Letters.* Some biographers have accepted Behn's letters as autobiographical, but one does not have to enter the debate on either side to see that the letters, which have no narrative frame, allow the passionate expression of a woman whose sexuality has been liberated by Lycidas, whereas he is cool, prudent, and manipulative:

> I burst to speak with you, to know a Thousand Things; but particularly, how you came to be so barbarous, as to carry away all that cou'd make my Satisfaction: You carry'd away my Letter, and you carry'd away *Lycidas*; I will not call him mine, because he has so unkindly taken himself back. 'Twas with that Design you came; for I saw all Night with what reluctancy you spoke, how coldly you entertain'd me, and with what pain and uneasiness you gave me the only Conversation I value in the World. I am asham'd to tell you this: I know your peevish Vertue will misinterpret me: But take it how you will, think of it as you please; I am undone, and will be free; I will tell you, you did not use me well: I am ruin'd, and will rail at you.[7]

As the letters develop, and they are all from Astrea to Lycidas, one sees Lycidas constantly judging Astrea, finding fault with her, to maintain control of the relationship: "You wou'd have me give, and you, like a Miser, wou'd distribute nothing. Greedy Lycidas! Unconscionable! and Ungenerous! You wou'd not be in Love for all the World, yet wish I were so" (p. 406). Occasionally, we learn that Lycidas is loving, but soon he is again prescribing "Laws and Rules" for Astrea. Although Astrea is intelligent and proud, she also clearly loves Lycidas far more than he loves her, and the letters are therefore an agonized record of her growing realization that she is being abandoned and must give up her commitment to him: "My Soul is ready to burst with Pride and Indignation; and at the same time. Love, with all his Softness assails me, and will make me write" (p. 412). As Lycidas creates greater and greater distance between them, Astrea wants him to be honest, but then reproaches his candor: "You prudently (but truly) told me your Business wou'd permit you to come every Night, but your Inclinations wou'd not. At least this was honest, but very unkind, and not over civil" (p. 415). As the sequence ends, then, Astrea hopes for further meetings with Lycidas, but the reader knows the affair is over. It is easy to see why critics and biographers have tied this short letter sequence to Behn's life: Lycidas's behavior squares with what we know of John Hoyle, and one can imagine Behn was entirely capable of the feelings expressed by the persona Astrea.[8] Yet this identification, dangerous for the biographer to use as evidence, makes a profound impression on the reader, especially in an era like the seventeenth century, when historical narratives were valued far above fiction, which frequently, as here in one kind of reading, presented itself as true to life. Whatever the verifiable historical truth of the *Letters,* their impact is intensified by their putative relation to Aphra Behn's life. The feelings are those of romance, and yet we accept them because they actually occurred. The process is also reversible: a contemporary female reader could have her sexual feelings aroused and learn to become as large a self as Astrea. The effect of the narrative is slightly larger than life because Astrea was clearly a playwright and frequently held soirées to which several male friends might come (p. 410). Yet her behavior is not so exalted that the ordinary woman reader might not develop her image of what a woman's erotic life might be by reading the *Letters.* The work does not deny the pain, the social penalty, or personal risk of aroused female sexuality, but it asserts that sexuality and describes how it feels.

Another dimension of the *Letters'* resemblence to life is also important. Because the persona of the letter-writer, Astrea, is very like Aphra Behn— has, in fact, her classical pseudonym—she writes as the financially independent, free woman that Behn was. Therefore Astrea does not assume the dependent stance that either a married woman or an unmarried, conventional virgin might take in relation to Lycidas. They have entered the relationship independently, and although he attempts to rule her, the letters make clear that he does not succeed. She has reminded us that she is socially ruined, but as they part, we have little sense that, like Goldsmith's lovely lady's, her life has ended. Instead we sense that another lover will emerge in her life, perhaps one of the men trying to convince her that Lycidas was not handsome. The Portuguese nun has survived to tell a woman's story of love and assert her identity; Astrea does not need to carry the letters to that conclusion to make her identity clear; both women write fully and intensely about women's sexuality and women's predicament, but always with individuality too:

> If Aphra Behn understood even before her affair with John Hoyle began that he would keep her at a distance, perhaps that was, in a sense, what she wanted. She might have chosen a man who was not a wit, but none of the forms that a conventionally reciprocated relationship took in her age would have permitted her the freedom she required. Had she been a wife, she would have had to worry about compromising the family honor by her writing; and even as a mistress, she would have had to play the sort of feminine games she detested. Loving a

man who loved her wholly in return would have made it more difficult to oppose him. In choosing John Hoyle, she could give herself
entirely to her passion without bearing the usual consequences, maintain her ideal of love without living it out in social convention.[9]

As important for my argument here is Behn's long epistolary novel, *Love-
Letters Between a Nobleman and his Sister* (1684, 1685, 1687), which Day
describes as "significant for its technical innovations, its length, and its popularity." He calls it "a pioneering scandal novel – its first part being an epistolary novel of outstanding technical virtuosity with strong romantic and
even 'Gothic' tendencies; and it is the first lengthy and original piece of
English fiction to adopt the method of the *Portuguese Letters*."[10]

Love-Letters has three parts, and the first, most artistically coherent and
interesting part, is entirely epistolary. As the letters begin, Philander is
married to Myrtilla, but is abandoning her to seek an incestuous relationship with her sister Sylvia. (As suggested by the title, relations with a spouse's
family were legally incestuous until the nineteenth century. The source
of the idea is that man and wife are one flesh.) The premises of the libertine ideology are established early in the work, when Philander writes
to Sylvia that a wife (her sister) should not stand in the way of their love
because the wife is only property.[11] After resistance to many of Philander's
letters, Sylvia finally agrees to a liaison, which is only consummated after several humorous episodes in which the sisters' parents are involved
during Philander's attempts to enter their house. The satire on parents,
a constant theme in this fiction, may be seen in Philander's meeting a "rival" entering the house at night, only to have encountered a lover of Sylvia's mother; her father, moreover, propositions Philander when he is disguised as a maid to gain access to Sylvia. The end of the first part is exciting. Sylvia's parents arrange a forced marriage for her and the rich but
repellant Foscario. Philander kills Foscario as Sylvia escapes to Paris with
Philander's valet. Philander is arrested and imprisoned for the murder, and
Sylvia marries the valet to escape her parents' authority. The story ends
with both as fugitives: Philander flees to Holland to join Sylvia, who is
disguised as a boy. In the meantime, the wife-sister continues her affair with
the highborn Cesario.

Philander's further roving in Parts 2 and 3 are part of the libertine paradigm. He quickly tires of Sylvia once he has gained her. In subsequent parts
they separate, and he spends energy seducing Calista, who ends in a nunnery. Sylvia is an excellent example of the unleashing of female sexuality
that results from seduction: gradually over Parts 2 and 3, despite the fact
that she has the devoted Octavio to love her and to propose marriage, Sylvia
becomes a rake. At the end of the narrative, Octavio, having taken holy
orders, offers Sylvia a pension if she will stop taking lovers, but she thinks

only of using the money for new clothes, the better to seduce her latest conquest.

The work of Eve Sedgwick and René Girard is helpful in analyzing the homosocial bonds and triangulated desire characteristic of the libertine ideology that governs the narrative.[12] Male desire for a woman is virtually always inspired by a rival. For example, Philander's original passion for Sylvia is much inflamed by seeing an imagined rival (actually her mother's lover) in the garden. Philander has long tired of Sylvia in Part 3, but his desire for her is rekindled by jealousy:

> At this *Philander* grew into a violent Rage, sometimes against *Octavio* for his Treasons against Friendship; sometimes he felt the old Flame revive, raised and blown Jealousy, and was raving to imagine any other should possess the lovely *Sylvia*. He now beholds her with all those Charms that first fired him, and thinks, if she be criminal, it was only the Effects of the greatest Love, which always hurries Women on to the highest Revenges. In vain he seeks to extinguish his returning Flame by the Thought of *Calista*; yet, at that Thought, he starts like one awakened from a Dream of Honour, to fall asleep again, and dream of Love. Before it was Rage and Pride, but now it was Tenderness and Grief, softer Passions, and more insupportable. New Wounds smart most, but old Ones are most dangerous. (2:122–23)

The strength of homosocial bonds may also be seen in the fact that Philander is most attracted to Sylvia and Calista when they are disguised as men (2:77–78); and because Calista is Octavio's sister, her resemblence to Octavio increases Philander's desire: "I never saw any Thing more resembling my dear *Octavio,* than the lovely *Calista*. Your very Feature, your very Smile and Air; so that, if possible, that increased my Adoration and Esteem for her: thus compleated, I armed her, and buckled on her Sword, and she would needs have one of my Pistols too, that stuck in my Belt; and now she appeared all lovely Man" (2:78). Sylvia shows her sensitivity to this aspect of male sexuality by dressing as a man to receive her new lover at the end of the narrative (2:234).

The effect is reinforced by the effeminizing of the male when he seeks to circulate easily among women. When Philander first gains access to Sylvia's bed, her father interrupts them, and so Philander must be disguised as a maid, whom her father immediately propositions. In Part 3 Octavio is so overwhelmed by his love for Sylvia that he neglects all the interest, politics, and business that are the affairs of men. Behn says, "For while thus he lived retired, scarce visiting any one, or permitting any one to visit him, they charge him with a thousand Crimes of having given himself over to Effeminacy; as indeed he grew too lazy in her Arms; neglecting Glory,

Arms, and Power, for the more real Joys of Life" (2:39). As a constant and generous lover, Octavio suffers a fate that echoes his sister's: he goes to a monastery, just as she has gone to a convent. In contrast, the rake Philander ends back in court and finds any semblence of a stable relationship as unwelcome as marriage. During a temporary reconciliation with Sylvia late in the narrative, Philander discovers he is still as tired of her as if they were married: "He had all the Night a full Possession of *Silvia*, and found in the Morning he was not so violently concern'd as he was overnight. It was but a Repetition of what he had been feasted with before; 'twas no new Treat, but like Matrimony, went dully down" (2:127). Such a man is well received by other men; at the end he "came to Court in as much Splendor as ever, being well understood by all good Men" (2:234).

Behn's representation of the libertine ideology is thorough, and in its homosocial dimension unique in the fiction of seventeenth-century women. It is another manifestation of how strongly she was male-identified. Her portrait of Sylvia also bears out male identification as Sylvia adopts the male ideology and gradually becomes a female rake. In this, Sylvia is distinctive in such fiction, for the women in Manley, Hearne, or Haywood may circulate from one lover to another but they are not predatory. Behn not only represented the libertine ideology uniquely in women's fiction, but she also held the conservative social views associated with it. Consequently, although she frequently represents aroused female sexuality in her short fiction, she never reconciles the social structures of the stories to those representations.

For example, Isabella, in *The History of the Nun: or, The Fair Vow-Breaker* (1689), illustrates the power of female sexuality: when she falls in love after having taken holy orders, nothing stops her elopement with Henault, and, after his supposed death, her union with an earlier lover, Villenoys. When Henault returns, she kills him and then ensures Villenoys's death as well. The story is artistically flawed because Behn masks her favorite theme of the power of love with a moral about Isabella's broken vows, possibly because of political implications about vow-breaking.[13] Ardelia, in *The Nun; or the Perjured Beauty* (1698), is another such character, but Behn does not know how to handle her inconstancy and amorality. These stories reveal that, far from challenging social convention through female sexuality, Behn simply placed female sexuality within the representation of social structures to which it is alien without an effort toward reconciliation. In the novellas she did not resolve the conflict between the romance structures she had used effectively in *Letters* and *Love-Letters* and the moral themes that she tried to graft onto them.

One can see clearly in still another novella how Behn evaded the consequences of her romance structures. *The Adventure of the Black Lady* is the story of Bellamora, who comes to London searching for Madame Brightly but finds instead the sister of Fondlove, who has gotten Bellamora preg-

216

nant. The sister finds a place for Bellamora to stay in London and sends for Fondlove, who comes to marry her before the child is born. When the Overseers of the Poor comes searching for a just-delivered Black Lady, they are shown a black cat who has just had kittens. Behn's humor hardly disguises the gloss this tale puts on many other stories of pregnant women, deserted by lover and family, hounded and abused by officers of any community where they might give birth. The intertextuality of the story is so strong that it can hardly be received as other than an ironically romantic fantasy. A further example is *The Fair Jilt* (1688), in which Miranda, a femme fatale, ruins one man after another and attempts to have her sister murdered. Although Miranda is irresistible to most men, only Prince Tarquin really loves her; and paradoxically, each time she tries to harm someone, her victims are spared by lucky chance. She and Tarquin are finally united in Holland, where they can make a new life. Through the magic of coincidence, the couple are exempt from the consequences of Miranda's actions and motives.

Two of Behn's stories illustrate a theme that will become increasingly important in women's fiction: the mistakes parents make about enforcing their children's matches. Such errors are made and corrected in *The Unhappy Mistake* (1700) and *The Wandering Beauty* (1698). The latter, an artistic triumph, depicts a daughter who runs away to avoid a forced marriage – Behn's bête noire in the drama – and so Arabella becomes a maid to Sir Christian Kindly's daughter. Although Arabella's disguise crosses social boundaries, her marriage does not. After some happy years, Sir Lucius Lovewell seeks Arabella's hand. She accepts him and returns home for her parents' blessing. In *The Unhappy Mistake*, Miles Hardyman's father prevents his marriage to Diana Constance, but after denouncing his patrimony and winning renown as a soldier in France, Miles inherits his father's title, his estate, and wins the lady. Parents seldom win in Behn's work, and those who would force desire must change. If they do not repent, children simply make the right choices with the author's approval. As in Elizabethan and Jacobean literature, the children always choose a mate of the proper social status. This theme will have many variations and transformations in women's fiction yet to be described.

The next important volume of fiction in the Behn tradition was *Letters of Love and Gallantry. And several other Subjects* (1694). This work claimed to be "written by Ladies," and is dedicated to "the Beaux," who "published our favours as soon as you receive them," and so the authors ironically present them the letters. The authors almost uniformly assume that men are predatory and will abandon women who yield to them or who believe their promises. Intrigue is defined as "the essential part of a Beau," so that the reader expects men to be aggressive in pursuit of desire.[14] One letter expresses the paradigm played out in the others; its title reads, "From a Lady to a Gentlemen who promising her Marriage, Debauch'd her, and then left her, taking a Journey beyond the Sea" (2:123). Women understand that if they yield to their suitors, they will undoubtedly lose them. Again and again, women hope for "friendship," a relationship without the dangerous physical side, but men create a double bind: they will settle for nothing less than a sexual relationship and instantly abandon women to their ruin.

The *Letters* give two characters of ruined women, with variations depending on class. The coquette "marries a Soldier that beats her, first gets all she has (which is but little) and then Runs away and leaves her to the wide World; she repents her ill spent life; makes a general Lamentation to all her Relations, who usually are of the best Quality" (2:150). The coquette's family scorn her and say she deserves her condition. The country lady is ostentatious in dress and behaves ridiculously in church; she meets a Covent Garden beau, who "carries her out to some place, debauches her as easily as he got her out. In a little time she finds herself with Child" (2:156). The lady is then sent back to the country and married to an alderman's son. The collection trades on popular stereotypes, but it also clearly defines woman's predicament in relation to the libertine ideology. One lady drily writes her suitor that she is sure he is merely testing her and that her honor "is more Sacred to you than the Humour of being Immodest can be pleasant" (2:130). Although some of the letters strive for an urbane tone, all the men are self-seeking, and the world is one women dare not trust. Part of the effect of the work—and others like it—is to warn women that they should not move from the domestic sphere, that the world is a dangerous place in which only men may move freely. The poise and urbanity of some of the letters does not conceal the suffering and cruelty that is represented in the fiction and that corresponds to accounts from life. The sexual risks of venturing into the world also become a figure for economic venturing in a frightening mercantile world, in which older, stable relationships and class structures were changing from the world of the early Stuarts.

In this context the fiction of Delariviere Manley seems as extraordinary as her life. She took about as many risks as one could and survive, and her fiction is not less varied and exotic than her life. Manley wrote in the Behn tradition, in the libertine ideology, but without Behn's male identification. Like Behn, she celebrates female sexuality, sees men as predatory, and interest as the enemy of love. Her feminism, however, makes her critical of the double standard and of the double bind that keeps women innocent, uneducated, and therefore vulnerable, easy prey. Although she was conservative politically, Manley was more radically feminist than Behn. Manley's fiction is important because it was immensely popular through the first half of the eighteenth century and perpetuated as well by Eliza Haywood's imitations of several of her works. It is Manley who began the use of amatory fiction to educate her female readership about the socioeconomic terms of love and marriage in their world. The venturing, acquisitive spirit leads to sin in Manley's fiction, and loving pleasure for its own sake is idealized. The way in which she contributes to the contemporary sexual ideology is best seen in three of her works: *Secret Memoirs and Manners of several Persons of Quality of Both Sexes from the New Atalantis* (1709), *The Adventures of Rivella* (1714), and *The Power of Love* (1720).

New Atalantis contains an allegorical frame in which Lady Intelligence relates stories to Virtue and to Astrea, who has returned to earth to see if humans have improved; all three make moral judgments about the stories as they proceed. We rapidly discover that interest has not only destroyed love in marriage, but material calculation and ambition—which are largely male attributes that a few women imitate—have destroyed love, including extramarital relationships. Manley thus attaches the libertine ideology to the growing spirit of mercantile culture, with which as a Tory Manley had little sympathy.

In one of the stories, Fortunatus is cunningly ambitious and wishes to be rid of his mistress, whose compulsive sexuality evokes the Restoration court. Fortunatus substitutes another man in her bed and is therefore able to accuse her of infidelity. Thus the adulterous duchess seems the victim of her lover's deceit. In Manley's works men rove, not simply for pleasure but for power and wealth as well. And innocent women end tragically, as does Charlot, raped by her guardian, without practical social protections: "She dy'd a true Landmark, to warn all believing Virgins from Shipwrecking their Honour upon (that dangerous Coast of Rocks) the Vows and pretended Passion of Mankind."[15] Charlot could not protect herself, moreover, because her guardian had kept her wholly innocent of "this entirely corrupted Age" (1:328). Charlot's unhappy end also justifies Manley's soft pornographic literature for what it can teach the isolated female reader about the sexual ideology of the age. The impact of the story for first readers would surely have been intensified by the fact that it was based, as Spencer shows, "on a real intrigue."[16]

From Manley's fiction one would learn, for example, to look for the workings of interest and money behind the words of men, but quite indirectly in some cases. When a baroness has been betrayed by a prince who has made a precontract with her and now denies it, a friend coolly advises her that she is ruined:

> There's something unaccountable, 'tis one of the *Arcana's* of Nature, not yet found out, why our Sex cool and neglect yours, after possession, and never, if we can avoid it (and have our Senses about us) chuse our selves Wives from those who have most obliged us; 'tis, I confess, the grand Specifick of Ingratitude, but it seems so in-born in all, that I wonder there are still Women that confide in our false

Oaths and Promises, and that Mothers do not early, as they ought, warn their Virgin-Daughters from Love and Flattery, the Rocks upon which the most deserving are generally lost; Chastity is recommended as the greatest Ornament of your Sex, as Valour is of ours, because of the difficulty there is in maintaining 'em, tho' I do not think the Comparison equal, because Courage we see in-born to many, whilst Chastity must be acquir'd, because it moves directly against the prior Law of Nature, and has the whole Artillery of *Venus* to contend against. (1:416–17)

When the count tells the baroness that she should detest the prince and seek satisfaction elsewhere, Astrea is impressed with the count's advice until Lady Intelligence reveals his hidden motives:

All this fine Advice tends only to his own Interest; he does not despair of getting the *Baroness* for his Wife, and can you blame him then for making her vertuous; her Fortune is convenient for him; a concealed Mortgage eats up the Profits of his whole Estate; he will not be long in a Condition to support his Title without a Dowry; this Lady is by much the richest in all the Province; she will do his Business, if he can accomplish her, and has let him into a dangerous Secret, if she be wise, she will never marry him after, lest he upbraid her with it: See her indiscretion, he will be provoked at her Refusal, as she will still refuse him, because she has an Adversion to his Person, and would rather chuse a favorite Domestick for her Master; and consequently he'll divulge her Secret at the expence of the World's Opinion, both of her Conduct and Honour. (1:418–19).

No sooner do the allegorical trio lose sight of the count and the baroness than they see a woman in white nailed dead to the gibbet, and they learn from a countrywoman that she was a gentleman's daughter who was "abus'd by a young Soldier of Fortune (quarter'd near her Father's *Villa*) whom she fell in love with" (1:421). This fiction never denies the risks for women in its central fascination with love in all its many guises, joys, and defeats. It presents a world that must be deciphered by the reader, just as Intelligence, Virtue, and Astrea help one another decode human behavior.

In *New Atalantis* men frequently echo the count in holding women responsible for believing men's hypocritical lies told to gain sexual favors. As Mosco tells Zara, "You will object the Promises I made you, it would be much greater Madness to perform 'em, neither did I think you seriously expected it; no wise Woman reckons upon the performance of those extravagant things that are said to gain her" (1:512–13). When Zara protests, Mosco concludes that she is insane and so abandons her. She commits suicide, and he makes off with her fortune.

The interest that ruins love also ruins marriage: "Were Marriages not the Result of *Interest,* but Inclination! were nothing but *generous Love*! the *Fire* of *Virtue*! the *warmth* of *Beauty*! and the *Shine* of *Merit*! consulted in that Divine Union, guilty Pleasures wou'd be no more. But *Avarice*! contemptible *Covetousness*! sordid Desire of *Gain*! not only mingles with the more *Generous Native Sentiments,* but have quite extinguish'd the very Glimmerings of that informing *Light*" (1:535). These considerations justify, at least in part, most of the extramarital affairs in Manley's work. Marriage may be sacred, but if it is loveless, both partners rove. The problem is that roving is permitted only for the male, and yet passion is as strong for the woman as for the man. We see the power of love in the Duchess of the Fortunatus story and many other times throughout *New Atalantis.* As Elenora says of her mercenary suitor: "Don Antonio had still the Assurance to sollicite me; I yet loved him, tho' I hated him; a *Paradox* that may easily be reconcil'd by those that know our Passions are *involuntary,* and the Opposition of *Reason* and *Inclination*" (1:634). Manley's soft pornographic situations constantly assume that female sexuality, once aroused, is overwhelmingly passionate.

Because Manley saw little difference in the passion of the genders, she also saw little difference in the morality that should apply to their sexual behavior. As a result, she was critical of the double standard of sexual morality, both as it applied to her characters and to her own persona. Virtue says of a wealthy noblewoman, "Her seeming Ingenuity has made a Party for her in my Breast; I will do all that is possible to recover her to Virtue; I'll try if the Maxim not be false; that a Woman once departing from me, never returns, till old Age and Wrinkles have fitted her for nothing else. I will endeavour to warm her to my Precepts, and so render her as renown'd for her return to Virtue, as she is for Beauty" (1:419). This is only one of many comments Manley makes throughout her writings questioning the double standard.

In her fictional autobiography, *The Adventures of Rivella,* Manley describes her persona through a male narrator: "Her Vertues are her own, her Vices occasion'd by her Misfortunes; and yet as I have often heard her say, *If she had been a man, she had been without Fault*: But the Charter of that Sex being much more confin'd than ours, what is not a Crime in Men is scandalous and unpardonable in Woman" (2:743). Somewhat later in *Rivella,* Manley comments again about the double standard, echoing Virtue's observation in *New Atalantis,* but in relation to Christian redemption of Original Sin. Women, Manley understood, are treated more strictly about their chastity than are human beings in general about all their crimes:

Rivella is certainly much indebted, continu'd *Lovemore,* to a Liberal Education, and those early Precepts of Vertue taught her and practised in her Father's House. There was then such a Foundation laid,

that tho' Youth, Misfortunes, and Love, for several Years have interrupted so fair a Building, yet some Time since, she is returned with
the greatest Application to repair that Loss and Defect; if not with
relation to this World (where Women have found it impossible to be
reinstated) yet of the next, which was mercifully told us, *Mankind can
commit no Crimes but what upon Conversion may be forgiven.* (2:748)

Manley was the earliest woman to challenge the double standard directly.
Although Behn frequently wrote as if men and women were equal sexually
and morally, the only other writers of the time to challenge this long-held
custom were some of the dissenting sects; but their challenge was based on
religious grounds, not on a sense of sexual and social equality. And because
Manley's sexual ideology, like that of the cavaliers, was more radical than
her politics, she did not advocate social change that would alter the double
standard.

Just as interesting from a feminist perspective is Manley's description in
New Atalantis of a lesbian cabal, or what we would call a community. The
cabal excludes men because they are unfair to women: "They have wisely
excluded that rapacious *Sex,* who make a Prey of the Honour of Ladies,
find their greatest Satisfaction (some few excepted) in boasting their good
Fortune. The very *Chocolate-Houses* being Witnesses of their Self-love, where
promiscuously, among the known and the unknown, they expose the Letters of the Fair, explain the Misterious, and refine upon the happy Part,
in their redundancy of *Vanity,* consulting nothing but what may feed the
insatiable *Hydra!*" (1:577).

The lesbian group have a pleasant retreat to which they repair, a lodging
"in a place obscure and pleasant, with a Magazine of good Wine and Necessary Conveniences, as to Chambers of *Repose,* a tolerable *Garden,* and the
Country in Prospect" (1: 578). Although Manley makes the physical relationships among the women clear enough, the society also informs women
about dealing with the snares of men and allows married women to receive
loving care, "an Article in this well-bred wilfully-undistinguishing Age,
which the Husband seems to be rarely sollicitous of" (1:579). The society
has, moreover, utopian aspects in that all a woman's property is shared with
her lover: "In this little *Commonwealth* is no *Property*; whatever a *Lady* possesses, is, *sans ceremone,* at the service, and for the use of her *Fair Friend,*
without the vain *nice* scruple of being oblig'd. . . . Mutual *Love* bestows
all things in *common*" (1:589). Astrea's judgment about the community is
indicative of its function in Manley's fiction. If the cabal fosters only tender
friendship, she calls it an imitation of "immortal Joys." But, she says, "if
they carry it a length beyond what *Nature* design'd, and fortifie themselves
by these new-form'd Amities against the *Hymenal* union, or give their *Husbands* but a second place in their *Affections* and *Cares*; 'tis wrong and to be

blam'd" (1:590). Astrea concludes that the cabal will become the subject of "new invented Satyr, *fanciful Jealousies* and *impure* Distrusts, in that nice unforgiving Sex: who *Arbitrarily* decide, that Woman was only created (with all her *Beauty, Softness, Passions* and compleat *Tenderness*) to adorn the *Husband's* Reign, perfect his *Happiness,* and propogate the *Kind*" (1:590).

It would be gratifying to discover in Manley a liberated vision of female sexuality that could encompass a lesbian dimension, for the relationships in the cabal are clearly physical. But Manley was too committed to Nature, "who has the Trick of making them doat on the opposite improving *Sex*," for such a vision of sexuality. The physical relationships of the cabal are part of a larger critique of male-female relationships throughout *New Atalantis* and its soft pornography, just as the lesbian commonwealth also critiques property relationships of loving couples and just as Astrea's judgment about the community moves from sexuality to a comment about male oppression of women. Again, Manley wants changes in individual attitudes, but not in social institutions.

The Power of Love, a selection of seven stories from Painter's *Palace of Pleasure,* also reveals Manley's version of the current sexual ideology.[17] Most of the stories deal with unhappy marriages, which are the enemy of love; yet cuckoldry is not a theme. Instead infidelity is avoided or punished, even though two sets of stories are labeled "The Wife's Resentment" and "The Husband's Resentment." The power of love is illustrated in "The Perjur'd Beauty," where Victoria, a nun, elopes with Romeo, and they are both eventually executed. The most revealing story in the collection is "The Happy Fugitives," in which Ardelesia, daughter of the Frankish king, runs away with the duke of Saxony's son, and they live happily in a rustic setting. Their son is Beraldus of the Forest, through whom they are eventually reunited with their fathers. The combination of this pastoral story, where love is life-giving and free from corrupt social pressures, with the many stories of conventional marriages, where either the husband or wife is deeply unhappy or where lovers are betrayed, reveals once again Manley's basic idea that love is the greatest good for humankind if it is free from social corruption. The power of love is amply demonstrated in one story after another, but society invariably renders the outcome unhappy. Where the result is happy, Manley creates an erotic space for idealized characters, rather than advocating social change.

Manley's self-portrait in *The Adventures of Rivella,* a fictional autobiography in which a male narrator tells her story, is written from a similar conviction about love. After hearing Rivella's story from Lovemore, his listener D'Aumont exclaims, "*Allon's* let us go my dear *Lovemore,* interrupted young *D'Aumont,* let us not lose a Moment before we are acquainted with the only Person of her Sex that knows how to *Live,* and of whom we may say, in relation to Love, since she has so peculiar a Genius for, and has made such noble

223

Discoveries in that Passion, that it would have been a *Fault in her, not to have been Faulty*" (2:856).

Manley begins *Rivella,* as we have seen, by questioning the double standard, and so she claims for herself the sexual morality that would have applied to a rake while still reminding the reader of what conventional judgments about her life would be. Rivella is known as the author of the *Atalantis,* who "has carried the Passion farther than could be readily conceiv'd . . . [her characters] are such Representatives of Nature, that must warm the coldest Reader; it raises high Ideas of the Dignity of Human Kind, and informs us that we have in our Composition, wherewith to taste sublime, and transporting Joys: After perusing her Inchanting Description, which of us have not gone in Search of Raptures which she every where tells us, as happy Mortals, we are capable of tasting" (2:740).

Manley's fiction has, then, one classic function of soft pornography: to inform the naïve reader of the joys of sex. In addition, Rivella's history of male friends and lovers is depicted as gradually educating her through experience with Sir Peter, Lord Crafty, Tim Double, the Baron, Oswald, her husband, and Cleander for whom she sacrifices her love in order that he may marry a fortune (2:843–44). As author and example, Rivella is the apostle of love, which may compel sacrifices, but is also a sublime experience:

> Then to have rais'd your Passions in her Favour; I should have brought you to her Table well furnish'd and well serv'd; have shown you her sparkling Wit and easy Gaiety, when at Meat with Persons of Conversation and Humour: From thence carried you (in the Heat of Summer after Dinner) within the Nymphs Alcove, to a Bed nicely sheeted and strew'd with *Roses, Jessamins,* or *Orange-flowers,* suited to the variety of the Season; her Pillows neatly trim'd with Lace or Muslin, stuck round with Junquils, or other natural Garden Sweets, for she uses no Perfumes, and there have have given you leave to fancy your self the happy Man, with whom she chose to repose herself, during the Heat of the Day, in a state of Sweetness and Tranquility. (2:855–56)

So long as love is removed from the world of interest and property, so long as it is in a power-free, natural setting, it is the central joy of being human. Although Manley maintains throughout her work that sex and sexuality are natural, her composition of soft pornographic literature reveals the extent to which she also understood that such behaviors are culturally derived, that she was, in fact, using the authority of nature to justify her vision of sexuality.

Mary Hearne is a follower of Manley in two short novels: *The Lover's Week* (1718) and *The Female Deserter* (1719). *The Lover's Week* is dedicated to Mrs. Manley, and both novels show men and women following out Manley's doctrine of love. *The Lover's Week* describes Philander's gradual seduction of Amaryllis, who writes why she is staying in the country to her friend Emilia. Amaryllis is a shallow person, compared with Rivella or many of Manley's women: "My dear *Emilia,* you know it is not in our Powers to act against our Inclinations, not being Mistress of those little Arts that, in my opinion, are too much used by our Sex."[18] Manley's heroines are strong, capable of difficult decisions, innocent or sensual; but Hearne's women are soft hedonists, who simply enjoy their love affairs without giving their lives much thought. Where Manley offers interesting ideas and characters, Hearne is a superior artist and psychologist. Soon we discover that Amaryllis is not so innocent and high-minded as she would like to appear, for her journey from her aunt's house to an assignation with Philander is extremely complex and involves her willing cooperation in a complicated series of maneuvers (pp. 14–17). When she meets Philander, Amaryllis is furious (one of many rages at him) because he has kept her out too late to return to her aunt's. Colonel P, Philander's friend, appears exactly at that minute to persuade Amaryllis to stay the night. Philander throws himself at her feet and pleads with her. Needless to say, she agrees. All these machinations suggest a design in which Amaryllis, despite her protest, is a willing participant. Yet because of Amaryllis's innocence of the world (we are aware that she is in a *bagnio* before she is, for example), the reader is never certain about trusting her disingenuousness. She describes the fact that Philander, having gained access to her room, sleeps there to guard her "treasure" until morning. She believes he was led to this compromising action by love: "When I consider'd it was love, which generally hurries us on without Consideration, that made him guilty of it, though not without sufficiently upbraiding him of ungenerously betraying me into a Fault which my Innocence and too good Opinion of him, had led me into" (p. 31). Hearne skillfully uses Amaryllis's anger at Philander to reveal her complicity with his scheming to seduce her. She blames him every time she colludes in her own ruin.

Amaryllis rapidly understands that she cannot return to her aunt's because that lady has gossiped about her. So Amaryllis goes to Colonel P's lodging and thence to a small country cottage twelve miles from the city; it is a lovely pastoral retreat, an erotic space:

> it is placed on a rising Hill, though not high enough to make it bleak, nor so low but you may see beneath it a pleasant Vale, enamel'd o'er with various Flowers of Nature's planting, which make a sweet and agreeable Prospect; nor is it so lonely, to make it melancholy, it being within a Mile and a half of a Market-Town, that in a quarter of an Hour's driving you may be as publick as you can wish; and, in short, is the most commodiously situated that can be imagin'd, having Gar-

dens, Orchards, and Fish-Ponds, with every thing that can conduce to make a Seat agreeable. (P. 47)

Although the retreat is very pleasant, Amaryllis is also careful to assure Philander that any place would be satisfactory to her so long as he was there: "But were it as mean as those rural Cottages inhabited by the meanest Shepherd, yet, blest with dear *Philander's* Company, I should esteem my-self more happy than in the greatest Spendor that could be invented" (p. 53). Philander too looks upon their retreat as a genuine pastoral withdrawal "from the Flatteries of the Court" (p. 52). They lead a pleasant social life, paying and receiving visits from neighbors, and Amaryllis ends by compar-ing herself implicitly to Katherine Hyde: "She is a Lady for whom I know you have a particular Value as well as myself; and all the World, who has the Honour to know her, must have an Esteem for her" (p. 55). The nar-rative ends with a poem by Prior about Katherine Hyde, which celebrates the triumph of desire over the parent:

> Fondness prevailed, *Mamma* gave way
>   *Kitty,* at Heart's Desire
> Obtains the Chariot for a Day
> And set the World on Fire.
> (P. 56)

The effect of this detailed description, the pastoral setting, the *haut monde* comparison, is to ratify Amaryllis's choice of true love rather than an un-happy marriage urged upon her by her aunt, who, like most of the authority figures in this fiction, cannot understand what is best for her niece: "Though I have exposed myself to the Censure of the World, I have this Satisfaction, that it is for the Man I like; on the other hand, had I taken my Aunt's Ad-vice, and married the Duke of A——, whom I could never have loved, I had not only made myself unhappy, but by my Indifference to him, should have given him, and all the World, reason to have been very free with my Character, and should have undergone the Scandal without having the Satisfaction" (p. 54).

Hearne's fiction makes clear the problem of perceiving marriage as the enemy of love, but her resolution of the paradox is to create an erotic space that insulates the lovers from a censorious world. The freight of detail Hearne loads on the simple narrative gives the relationship a substantial quality, but the social paradoxes that lie behind it are only avoided, not resolved.

Although Day calls *The Female Deserters* "decidedly inferior" to *The Lover's Week,* which he much admires, he seems not to have perceived Hearne's clever approach to her theme in the later book.[19] It is constructed through letters from Amaryllis to Emilia that describe her continuing affair with Philander, which encloses the affair of Calista and Torismond, which encloses the affair of Polydor and Isabella, who is serving in disguise as Calista's maid, an echo of Behn's *Wandering Beauty*. All three sets of lovers are trying to cope with parental objections to their unions: Amaryllis and Philander, Calista and Torismond succeed in remaining together, but Polydor and Isabella are betrayed to her father by a rival for her affections. Polydor is subsequently shipped out of England to keep the lovers separate. The gulf that divides them is parental consent, based on money. Their courtship, symbolically, takes place while their fathers are meeting about business:

> Thus, did we pass our Time in the absence of our Parents, and at length we became so Intimate as to own our Loves to be mutual: All the difficulty that now remain'd, was to get their Consent, nor had I much occasion to fear my Father's, the fortune of *Polydor* being so far superior to mine, whilst he on the other Hand hop'd Sir *Charles* would see with his Eyes, or if he should not at first yield, I am sure, says he, my Father rather than see me miserable, will give his Consent; but he was mistaken! and his fatal Resolution has I much fear made us both miserable as long as we live! (Pp. 38–39)

And so as Calista's maid, Isabella waits out the return of Polydor. Calista's father has, he thinks, isolated her from Torismond, but, although she finds ways of seeing her lover, Calista will not leave her family for him, and she assumes he will surely abandon her as soon as she yields to him. When she does so accidently (as things always happen in virtuous fiction), Torismond persuades her to stay with him instead of returning to the tyranny of her father. In conducting their courtship Torismond and Calista have the aid of her physician and Isabella, who preaches both the gospel of love and disdain for marriage which justify the liaison:

> *Torismond* is the only Man in the World with whom I could like to pass the rest of my Life, yet we must consider the Censures of the World: *Isabella* having a mind to persuade me to make that easie, which she foresaw was like to be my lot, used all the persuasive Arguments that could be to Reconcile me; and to what she had already said: Added, I beg Madam you would remember that it is not in your Power to live without *Torismond*; therefore You should not by the vulgar Notion of Marriage make your self uneasie, since that Ceremony is nothing but a piece of Formality, introduced on purpose to bring Profit to the Church; and I think that Love is much more to be Esteem'd, which has no other Motive but mutual Affection, rather

than when any Constraint is put upon our Passions, and I am sure it is for the generality more lasting. (Pp. 102–3)

Amaryllis finishes the narrative with the lines, "Among the many Pleasures which we Prove, / None are so real, as the Joys of Love." Although Hearne's novels are based on that assumption, they are not as romantic as Behn's or Manley's. A careful artist, Hearne has both Amaryllis and Calista express all the proper scruples about yielding to a lover and then discover joy in having yielded. This is primarily because, although Hearne's men scheme from time to time, they are not rakes. In Hearne's world, affairs have their domestic side: "we were no sooner come in, but somebody rap'd at the Gate, and to both our Satisfactions, it prov'd to be my *Philander,* and with him *Torismond,* after the first Transports of our meeting were over; *Philander* invited *Torismond* and *Calista* to stay and sup with us, and I began to enquire of them what News there was in Town, and particularly at Court, from whence they were just come" (p. 107). Hearne's distinctive contribution to amatory fiction, then, is to transfer the predatory burden from male lovers to parents and so to domesticate extramarital love affairs that she makes them seem not only real, but entirely possible and tranquilly happy.

Eliza Haywood (ca. 1693–1756) was the last of the "fair Triumvirate of Wit," which James Sterling describes in his verse tribute to the third edition of her *Secret Histories, Novels, and Poems* (1732). The other two of this group are Behn and Manley. Thus, Sterling accurately designates Haywood's literary antecedents because Haywood was not ashamed to imitate the work of either writer. Although she wrote very much in the tradition of Aphra Behn and Delariviere Manley, at the end of her career Haywood departed from their mode of fiction and journalism for one that was more directly aimed at reforming the morals of the mid-eighteenth century. In the prime of her career, however, Haywood exploited a libertine sexuality, attached to the acquisitive motives of men, who will ruin the hapless virgin:

> Honour's sworn Foe, the Libertine with Shames,
> Descends to curse the sordid lawless Flames;
> The tender Maid here learns Men's various Wiles,
> Rash Youth, hence dread the Wanton's venal Smiles—
> Sure 'twas by brutal Force of envious Man,
> First Learning's base Monopoly began.[20]

Haywood used this pattern, but she also clearly went beyond it in her depiction of women's predicament, for many of her heroines are boldly aggressive and seem a protest against the growing passivity and confinement of women in their sphere that characterizes the eighteenth century. Haywood was known as the champion of her sex, and she often depicted women's lot as bitterly unhappy. If she was as much the advocate of women as Manley, Haywood showed the impact of her era in treating marriage, not the love affair, as the ideal outcome of love. Money is a more frequent hidden motive in Haywood's fiction, always the enemy of love, and parents or other authority figures are invariably wrong about their children's choices in love. In some of Haywood's stories, women bond to help one another, though frequently they are brought together by male abuse, in one case from the same man. Haywood's work is a fascinating combination of a bleak perspective on women's lot and a frequent tendency to represent males' reforming in marriage at the end of narratives. Indeed, at the end of her career she wrote two long novels to encourage virtue in both sexes, while still exploring multiple options in the marriage relationship.

Early in her career, Haywood imitated Behn and Manley in writing stories of passion, replete with predatory males, often driven by ambition or interest, and innocent, victimized women. *Love in Excess* (1719) was one of Haywood's first works in the amatory mode; it has three parts, and the first two postpone Count D'Elmont's marrying a woman he loves. In the first part, D'Elmont loves Amena, but he allows himself to be married to Alovisa, who has a large fortune but whom he does not love. In the second part, D'Elmont falls in love with his ward, Melliora, but sees his marriage as an impediment to the fulfillment of his love. He writes to Amena that he is being punished for his betrayal of her: "My Crime is my punishment, I have offended against Love, and against thee."[21] Part Two has two themes: the overwhelming nature of love and the ways in which men manipulate women for male purposes. When D'Elmont tells Melliora that he loves her, he exclaims about love's power: "Every other Passion that finds Entrance in the Soul, Art, and Discretion, may Disguise, but Love, tho'it may be feign'd, can never be Conceal'd, not only the Eyes . . . but every feature, every faculty betrays it" (2:25). At the end of *Love in Excess,* passion is called an influence "against which, no Laws, no Rules, no Force of Reason, or Philosophy, are sufficient grounds" (3:14–15).

D'Elmont and his friend Baron D'Espernay are attractive men, but they are also callous and scheming. They plot to arrange for Melliora's rape: "that on the first opportunity *Melliora* shou'd fall a Sacrifice to Love" (2:44). Because he loves Alovisa, the baron helps D'Elmont with his plot to have Melliora; yet the baron does not consider that he is helping to ruin his beloved's marriage. His is the sort of love, Haywood says, "which considers more it's own Gratification than the Interest, or quiet of the object Beloved" (2:73). Haywood's critique of male behavior is consistent: she comments that although D'Elmont would be unfaithful to Alovisa, he blames her for his transgression: "Man is too Arbitrary a Creature to bear the least Contradiction, where he pretends an absolute Authority, and that Wife who thinks by ill humour and perpetual Taunts, to make him weary of what she wou'd reclaim him from, only renders herself more hateful, and makes that justifiable which before was blameable in him" (2:19).

In Part Three when still another woman is pursuing D'Elmont, who is constant (for a man) to Melliora, Haywood says, "tho' no Man that ever liv'd, was less addicted to loose Desire—in fine, he was still a Man! . . . So he gave his Hands and Eyes a full Enjoyment of all those Charms" (3:94). The final effect of the work is mixed because although it acknowledges the power of love, and although it contains rakish, self-centered men and innocent, victimized women, all of the principals marry at the end. Haywood uses a pattern that is to become common in eighteenth- and nineteenth-century fiction that is too chaste for love affairs: the mistaken first marriage in which one learns one's identity and that of one's beloved, whom one marries after the first marriage mercifully ends. Although Haywood's men are eventually aimed toward marriage, they are predatory and materialistic; and she is actively critical, even of their minor behaviors.

Haywood continued the epistolary genre by paraphrasing Boursault's *Lettres nouvelles* as *Letters from a Lady of Quality to a Chevalier* (1721), which expresses the complex and ambivalent feelings of a married woman for her lover, who finally abandons her. Her struggle is to remain faithful to her marriage and yet love. She is possessed by her passion for her lover, yet bound by society to her husband: in this predicament Haywood represents one of the many double binds confronting women in the fiction of this era. Women are constantly tempted to love, but ever constrained from fulfilling desire, both by society and by the lover himself. As she continued to work in this vein, Haywood tried to capitalize on Manley's success with *New Atalantis* by imitating it in *Memoirs of a Certain Island Adjacent to the Kingdom of Utopia* (1725). Like *Atalantis*, *Memoirs* has an allegorical frame in which Love tells a series of stories to Pecunia and Fortune. The work has two parts, and each is unified by sexual politics and setting. "Volume 1 is set in the country and is concerned primarily with evil, unruly, aggressive women; volume 2 takes place in the city, specifically amid the life of the court and the palace, and focuses on men."[22] Haywood's women are frequently much more aggressive than those depicted by any of her female colleagues, except possibly Manley's Homais; and so Schofield may be right that Haywood's portraits of such women are "actualizations of her own aggressive desires and wishes."[23] Certainly these representations and others like them, as we shall see, are Haywood's distinctive contribution to amatory fiction. Although Haywood's God of Love labels Flirtillara, Clarismonda, and Wyaria as evil, he frequently also reveals a bias toward women, even in Volume 1: "When a Courtezan, celebrated for her Charms, receives the Addresses of a Man who, perhaps,

230

to her own knowledge, has been the Undoer of a thousand poor unhappy Creatures, whose artless Innocence required no more than Love for Love; why should she not set a Value on herself, make him bid high for her Possession, revenge her Sex's injuries, and pay at once for all!" (1:11).

Such small victories, which leave untouched the social structures that oppress women, are characteristics of Haywood's popular art: she invests her individual anger in a genre that represents women as victims rather than victors, and she depicts them as sinful and despised if they transgress social boundaries. She accepts the genre that she inherited and the modified Restoration sexual ideology that came with it. Haywood shares neither Behn's male-identified perspective, in which independent women are free to love if they can create a suitable erotic space, nor Manley's sense that only the double standard need be changed for a woman who knew how to truly love to be valued. Both visions empower women, but Haywood, writing when women's world and roles were shrinking and when marriage had replaced an asocial relationship as the goal of love, saw no such alternatives. Because of this assumption, Haywood's fiction represents money as more important than it has been in earlier fiction and women as never free from social judgment but fixed in a small number of stereotypes. Behn's and Manley's amatory fiction is admonitory but liberating; Haywood's is essentially negative. In Volume 2, for example, we are treated to a catalog of rapes by rakes and libertines; no man remains with the woman he has violated or with his child by her. Yet the fiction does not call for another way of perceiving the sexual relationship, as in Mary Hearne or Manley. Instead, women are described as fixed in detestable patterns, and the only tolerable male-female relationship—a love marriage—is available to but a few. I quote at length:

> Behold! *Said the Divine Inspirer of the softest Passion,* in these two Ladies, the Dispositions which are ordinarily to be found in Womankind.—That Sex is for the most part in Extremes; either Pride or Ambition puffs up their giddy Souls, and renders them regardless of any other Merit than Grandeur; or devoting themselves to loose Desires, become a Prey to every Object, without distinction, which seems agreeable to the present Inclination.—How detestable to the Gods, and all good Men, are either of these Temperaments.—The former, indeed, is accounted by the World as the most prudent because Men are generally too ungrateful for the Favours they receive from pure Attention, and for the most part use those Women worst who love them best; but the latter is of that odious to Nature, that the very Wretch who lives but by the shameful Trade, abhors it, and loaths and scorns his dissolute Benefactress.—So certain is it, that tho' the Act is still the same in all, the chastest Matron and the Lewdest

Prostitute; yet *Love,* as it alone can give a *Sanction* to the rewarded Flame, alone renders it a joy.—My influence is superior to the Law; where I with mutual Ardor inspire the mingling Souls, the Bodies cannot sin; but without me, even the Marriage-bed is unhallow'd and prophane." (2:24)

After the series of appalling stories, it seems highly unlikely that Haywood's putative ideal of a love-marriage will impress the reader, even though she is careful to distinguish between men of sense and fools:

His fine Sense will represent to him, in such lively Colours, the monstrousness of using a Woman cruelly, only because she has shewn too great a Regard for him, that it is next to an Impossibility he can be guilty of it; and if, like *Doriless,* conscious that he cannot return the Affection she has for him with equal Fervor, will, to make up that Deficiency, the more industriously study to oblige her in any other Affair of life, in which it may happen in his power to do it.—Fools are ever refractory, self-opinionated, and churlish; and when once the Passion of Desire is extinct, the woman who has favour'd them may bid adieu to all dependence on their Friendship:—Yet will not that unheeding Sex take Warning by the multiplicity of Examples which both History and daily Experience furnishes for their Observation. (2:269–70)

Haywood's parting shot seems to reveal that she was aware of framing her angry narratives in an ideology of love and marriage with which the stories of rape and abandonment do not cohere.

The Secret History of the Present Intrigues of the Court of Carimania (1727) was as popular as *Memoirs.* A simple scandal chronicle, it is more obvious and not so infused with Haywood's anger. The central character, Theodore (George II), is a straightforward rake, married to a wise spouse who deals effectively with his multiple infidelities, and strongly attached to a mistress, to whom he is also repeatedly unfaithful. The mistress has a masculine temperament and "free from the Vanity and Tenaciousness of her Sex, could consent to see the Man most dear to her in a Rival's Arms" (p. 24). Her tactics are effective, for after each dalliance, Theodore returns to her more passionate than ever. Haywood admires both wife and mistress for their ability to cope with Theodore's behavior, but she offers no social insights beyond the analyses of the status quo. In fact, the behavior of both the wife and the mistress conforms to advice in all marriage manuals, courtesy books, and other literature of socialization. This is ironic because *Carimania* is the work that earned for her Pope's malevolence and the satire in *The Dunciad,* which drove her to publish anonymously for almost ten years, "but her novels remained as popular and powerful as ever."[24]

Reflections on the Various Effects of Love (1726), a collection of short essays, poems, and stories, reveals that at this point in her career Haywood still tended to accept the libertine stereotypes: a woman loves wholly while a man "has still an Eye to Interest and Ambition."[25] The volume contains many poems and stories of abandonment. Haywood perceives a lucky few who achieve her ideal, a mutually loving and satisfying relationship as the happy exceptions to the vast majority, who are quite miserable:

> Love is therefore, for many Reasons, dangerous to the softer Sex; they cannot arm themselves too much against it, and for whatever Delights it affords to the Successful few, it pays a double Portion of Wretchedness to the numerous Unfortunate,—Insensibility, is, with all the Deficiencies imputed to it, a State of Ease and Tranquility; and I cannot think a Woman prudent who, if she can avoid it, quits a certain *good* for the Prospect of an uncertain *better.* That Heaven which Lovers talk so much of, is indeed, too much a real Heaven to be frequently found on Earth; and for one Example of two Persons, who with equal Ardour and equal Tenderness regard each other, we shall find ten thousand of the contrary,—even among those, whose Choice seem'd wholly guided by Inclination." (P. 56)

Although her vision of women's lives continued to be bleak throughout her career, Haywood's faith in marriage-for-love grew as time went on, or she wrote to please an audience whose values had gradually changed. *Love-Letters on All Occasions* (1730) pretends to be a work collected by Haywood, and many of the letters conform to a familiar pattern, but with Haywood's characteristic additions. Most men are predatory and tire of women who yield to them, as with Myrtilla and Sarpedon: 'Tis not yet one poor Month since, deceived by your fictitious Vows, I yielded up my Honour, and am already abandoned to Despair and Shame, cruel Requital for such Love as mine."[26] Yet other letters depict relationships that are lasting, and these will result in marriage, an idealized state that dominates the bleaker libertine vision: "Marriage has in it all we can conceive of Heaven, when the Persons so united have but one Will to actuate them both, one Principle to direct them, and one Interest to follow. With such the word *Duty* is of no force, they make it their Study to please each other, not so much because they ought to do so, as because it is a pleasure to themselves" (pp. 216–17).

Haywood's ideas about marriage continued to develop throughout her career and form her major contribution to the sexual ideology of her time. Because marriage was more important to Haywood than to Behn, Manley, or Hearne, the mercenary motives of men and of parents loom large in her fiction as the enemies of love and of women. In *The Unequal Conflict* (1725), for example, Philenia is in love with Fillamour, but is intended by her parents for Coeurdemont. A friend tries to help Philenia by creating a fiction that Fillamour will rescue Philenia and by engineering her escape from her parents. *But* Fillamour, unable to "forget he was a man," marries a wealthy match arranged by his uncle, and later rapes Philenia. In a sequel, *The Fatal Fondness,* the friend marries Coeurdemont, and Philenia kills herself when she finds Fillamour dying, stabbed by a jealous lover. Despite all the story's romantic trappings, its depiction of Philenia's predicament is bleak, and Fillamour's crucial decision is based on money.

An even more corrupt pattern is represented in *The Mercenary Lover* (1726), where Clitander is not satisfied with the fortune of one sister, Miranda, but lusts for the additional fortune and body of the other, Althea. Both women are innocent, and so it is not long before he has violated Althea. She becomes pregnant, but he attempts to have her sign away her fortune, even that part intended for their child. As a result of her suspicions, Clitander finally poisons Althea.

More complex motives of ambition dominate *The Life of Madam de Villesache* (1727), where the villain is Henrietta's father and not her husband. She loves Clermont, a wealthy farmer, and secretly marries him; but her father hales her off to court, where she too easily forgets her country husband. Afraid to confront her father, she marries his choice, a marquis. Clermont soon appears and gets Henrietta pregnant. The marquis discovers them; Clermont dies in prison; Henrietta stands trial for adultery, but the father conceals her marriage to Clermont to secure the estate and title for the child. So the marquis brutally murders Henrietta and the unborn child: "he rip'd her open with an unmanly Brutality, and taking hence the Innocent unborn, stuck it on the point of his remorseless Sword, then threw it down in Scorn by the Bleeding Parent."[27] Haywood is quite astonishing in the bitterness of her representations of males, which joins oddly with her esteem for the marriage relationship.

Money is a fascinating subtext of *Philidore and Placentia,* a story that primarily explores male mythmaking about women, as both Philidore and a eunuch prefer their images of beloved objects to the real women, whose behavior does not coincide at all with the male ideas. Money is Haywood's means of resolving her Pygmalion-like story, for Placentia, who has been represented as aggressive, loses her fortune when her brother returns to claim the inheritance, and, at the end of the story, Philidore inherits a fortune because his uncle dies. As soon as Philidore is richer than Placentia, he can not only save her from slavery but also give up the fictions he had created about her.

Placentia is one of many aggressive women Haywood created in her fiction as she struggled to define women's predicament. In *The Injur'd Husband* (1723) the Baroness Tortillée has married a foolish, wealthy husband in order to gratify her desire for money, and so she pursues a series of affairs until she falls seriously in love with Beauclair, who is rescued by his true love. By splitting the female figure, Haywood expresses woman's transgression only to contain it socially and to show that approved female aggression takes place on behalf of love. Beauclair is forgiven his lapse in the arms of the baroness, the male being free to err.

Gigantilla, heroine of *The Perplex'd Dutchess* (1728), is a female Tamburlaine, who would destroy her rivals to be a duchess and gain wealth and power. Like Tamburlaine, she is never satisfied, "the Fears of losing what by such indirect Means she had acquir'd empoisoned all the Felicities of her Life,"[28] and, like Tamburlaine, she is eventually overtaken by a "Power Supreme." The crucial difference from the Elizabethan conquerer should not be lost on us, however: Gigantilla loses her power when her husband dies and is succeeded by his virtuous brother. To attain her goals, even a very transgressive woman must use her beauty, dissembled love, deceit, and conspiracy to manipulate men. By representing a woman who wants power, Haywood shows how powerless women really are.

Lasselia (1723) depicts a heroine who, rejecting an affair with the king, retires to the country and an affair with a married man. After the affair is discovered, she retires to a convent. Lasselia is like many heroines of the amatory fiction, who survive in female communities after society has rejected their transgressions. Although Haywood thought of women's situation as truly grim, she also frequently represented them bonding, often because of their negative experiences with men. Her most bitter work about women's lives is *The Fruitless Inquiry* (1727), a fable in which a widow is told that she can regain her only son by having a shirt made for him by a woman who is perfectly contented. The story in a male writer's hands has obvious misogynous potential, which Haywood avoids by showing woman after woman in circumstances not of her making: forced marriage, deceitful or criminal mates, disinherited children, and jealous husbands. There is some blaming of victims: "Is there a fate upon us to be wretched? Must we labour under woes for our own formation, when Fortune contributes all she can to make us happy?"[29] But the general effect is to subvert the announced intent of the fable: to urge women to be contented with their lives because happiness is not possible in mortal existence, and peace of mind is an interior condition. Although the frame ends happily in that Miramillia regains her son, Haywood leads the reader to feminist conclusions: that women's lot is generally oppressed and that much representation of that lot is contrived to lead women to accept their oppression and call it good and just.

Although she dwells on women's oppression more than any other writer of fiction, Haywood fills out her representation of women's predicament with a number of stories of women's survival.[30] One of the most interesting is the early *The British Recluse* (1722), for although it depends upon a coincidence—a meeting of two women seduced by the same man—the conclusion in which they decide to live together involves not only their survival, but female bonding as well: "both their Resolutions of abandoning the World continuing, the *Recluse* and she [Bellinda] took a House about seventy Miles distant from *London,* where they still live in perfect Tranquility, happy in the real Friendship of each other, despising the uncertain *Pleasures,* and free from all the *Hurries* and *Disquiets* which attend the Gaieties of the Town."[31] An interesting sidelight of the story is the way in which Lysander blames Cleomira, the recluse, for having caused the end of his love for her. He says, "Had your Passion, at least the Show of it, been less violent, mine might have had a longer Continuance; and as there is nothing more unnatural, than that a Woman shou'd expect a Man can be in *Love* with her always, the best Way to retain his Complaisance is, not to take Notice of his Alteration. That I once lov'd, I shall ever acknowledge, and desire you wou'd be as just in assuring yourself, that your own Mismanagement was the Cause I cou'd do so no longer" (pp. 62–63). Haywood's fiction may not be the most subtle ever written, but her eye for male foibles in the gender relations of her era was very acute.

As we have noticed, Haywood wrote a different kind of fiction and nonfiction after she was defamed by Pope in *The Dunciad* (1728; 1743) and after the publication of *Pamela* in 1740.[32] From 1741 until her death, she wrote novels that conform to the Richardsonian pattern of the triumph of good over evil, with moral instruction and good works as part of the mode. Haywood's three important fictions of this time are *The Fortunate Foundlings* (1744), *The History of Miss Betsy Thoughtless* (1753), and *The History of Jemmy and Jenny Jessamy* (1753). Gone are the earlier rebellions. In *Fortunate Foundlings* the chaste heroine refuses all suitors until she marries a true gallant; her former suitor wins a desirable lady after proving himself in subsequent adventures. "By recounting the deeds and adventures of Louisa, Horatio, and Charlotta, Haywood is able to give examples of both male and female virtue."[33] Betsy Thoughtless is a vain, fanciful, but curious heroine, who turns into a woman of sense at the end of long volumes. She is at first a heedless and willful person, who throws away her chance for a good man who marries another. After a series of loves, she marries a man who cannot make her happy, nor she, him. Marriage becomes "an Egyptian Bondage," and Betsy leaves Munden, only to be hideously exploited and return to find that Munden has taken a mistress. Munden grants her a separation without support, but when he is mortally ill, she nurses him until his death and in the process begins to understand her own vanity and pride. In the meantime, Trueworth's wife has conveniently died, and so he and the reformed Betsy may marry at the end. The familiar nineteenth-century pattern is perceptible here, as in *Love in Excess,* where mistaken alliances provide the insights necessary to true relationships at the end of the narrative. Spencer sees Betsy's development of self-knowledge as anticipating *Pride and Prejudice*.[34]

Haywood's later writings about manners, *The Female Spectator* (1744–46) and *The Epistles for the Ladies* (1749), have the clear intent to inform and reform the manners of the age. Haywood's putative audience is women. In both works the ideal relationship is a relatively equal marriage, and a great deal of the writing revolves on how to make a happy marriage. The first book of *The Female Spectator* covers such topics as being sure of one's feelings and those of the beloved, parents' tendency to force marriage, country women dealing with gallantry, coping with rape or marriage to another. The theme of the second book is marriage and how to make a good marriage, which is central to human happiness; there is

> no one Thing on which the Happiness of Mankind so much depends; it is indeed the Fountain-Head of all the Comforts we can enjoy ourselves, and of those we transmit to our Posterity.—It is the Bond which unites not only two Persons, but whole Families in one common inseparable Interest.—It is that which prevents those numberless Irregularities and Confusions, that would else overthrow all Order, and destroy Society; but then not to pervert the Intention of so necessary and glorious an Institution, and rob it of every Blessing it is full of, lies only in ourselves.[35]

Haywood values mutuality in marriage: "a Parity of Sentiment is the Cement of that lasting Friendship, as well as mutual Confidence, in which the Comforts of a married State chiefly consist." (1:92–93). The succeeding books of *The Female Spectator* tend to relate their specific themes to the relations between the genders. For example, the theme of Book 3 is avarice, and the first story involves a forced marriage because of wealth and portions. Another story represents a young man who refuses to be dependent on his beloved even though she is an heiress and they love one another (1:179). Book 4 is devoted to conversation and many of the issues relate to gender: that an immoderate desire for company is bad, that widows should not be in a hurry to remarry. Book 5 deals with raising children and their ingratitude, and so on. Almost every theme is made relevant to gender relations. Book 10 is interesting because it joins its theme, jealousy, to the education of women. The argument for women's education gives examples of learned women; it defends the size and capacity of women's brains; it advocates philosophy, mathematics, and history as subjects for women to study; it explains marital discord through educational discrepancy: "It is entirely owing to a narrow Education that we either give our Husbands room to find fault with our Conduct, or that we have Leisure to pry too scrutinously into theirs" (2:245). If the elite ratify learning for women, the argu-

237

ment continues, then others will follow: "If the married Ladies of Distinction begin the Change, and bring Learning into Fashion, the younger will never cease solliciting their Parents and Guardians for the Means of following it" (2:246). The writer acknowledges that most men fear women's learning because it would make them too nearly equal with men, but ends with the idea that knowledge makes the bad no worse and the good better. With Milton, the author praises a marital union of hearts and minds.

Other comments of interest here are a fictional letter from a man who believes avocations for women "can alone render them what *They* wish to be, *our Equals* and what *we* heartily wish them to be, *our Helpmates*" (2:256). The female spectator observes, "The great Number of Separations and Divorces, which we see of late, is a Testimony that few Ladies are educated in such a Manner as to have good Qualities sufficient to enable them to bear so great a Disregard of themselves" (3:29). In this context many examples are offered of wives who through patience with their husband's infidelities brought their mates back to a decent marriage.

Another topic of concern is the power of parents in the marriage choice. It is unnatural for parents who have loved their children during infancy and youth to make them miserable for the rest of their lives by forcing marriage "only to gratify some sordid Interest of their own" (3:106). Although the essays urge that "obedience to Parents is an indispensible Duty," they also suggest that when a parent would force marriage, disobedience is no crime (3:316). Haywood openly articulated what was hidden in the fantasies since the days of Elizabeth.

Haywood's *Epistles for the Ladies* also is concerned frequently with the parents' role in marriage choice. Some letters show the sad effects of marrying without parental consent, but others show the need for children to follow their own choices. The problems of making love and marriage choices are, in fact, the subjects of most of the letters; a substantial minority concern the ingredients of happy marriages. Haywood's ideal of the happy marriage led her to be more radical about divorce and separation than earlier writers. Certain epistles (58 and 59) are written to and from a wife who decides to separate from her brutal and nasty husband. She says, "I reflect, that the same ordinance, which made me a *wife,* was never intended to make me a victim of a husband's unreasonable passions; that God, who gave the sovereignty to *man,* made *woman* a *help-mate,* not a *vassal*; that the second institution, which subjected me to *Manilius,* commanded him to love and to cherish me; and he has in every respect so palpably violated the sacred covenant, I have no reason to condemn myself for the part I have acted."[36] She receives a letter of support from a woman friend in return, one that counsels her to conquer her tender feelings so that she will not stay in the destructive relationship. Still another letter is from a wife who has been living abroad to remain separated from her husband, and she is now pleased because her husband is living openly with his mistress, and so the wife may return to England and yet remain separated (1:307).

Marriage lay at the center of Eliza Haywood's thinking, and this fact accounts for her distinctive voice in amatory fiction. She appropriated but could not extend the basic paradigm of the innocent female victimized by the predatory libertine. Because her thinking was based on the institution in which women were subordinate, she had trouble imagining them as successfully empowered in their own right or truly independent. Instead, where her work deals with their predicament, it is a bleak chronicle of their oppression by ruthless males and parents. Only a lucky few achieve an equal and mutual relationship, though such is the idea by which she measures gender relations. If her ideal does not empower women, however, it does release a new critique of marriage, in which unhappy marriages should be abandoned, even by the wife. Her last works, *The Wife* and *The Husband,* end that way and demonstrate that she never shrank from the consequences of her thinking within the conceptual framework she accepted.

Possibly one of the reasons that Haywood could approve the social structures of her time is that ideas about marriage and courtship had changed substantially from those with which the seventeenth-century writers coped. Her writing shows clearly the progress toward a marriage of relative equals, both in behavior and affection, a loving relationship, as little based on property as possible, and one largely arranged by the partners themselves. Even if the social reality fell short of that ideal, as many of Haywood's bleak representations suggest, the mere existence of the ideal was advantageous for women. The other outstanding characteristic of Eliza Haywood's work is that as much as she accepted the constraints of her society, she also wrote consistently to aid women in their struggle for survival within existing social structures. The purposes that Ann Messenger has identified in *The Female Spectator,* in short, also may be applied to Haywood's fiction: she was not out to change the world or to inspire her women readers to try to change it, but she was the champion of her sex in teaching them how to survive within social codes.

Between Orinda and Behn—Educating the Heroine: Trotter, *Perfidious P, Lindamira,* and Mary Davys (1674–1727)

The work of Eliza Haywood brings to an end fiction written in the tradition of Aphra Behn, and we now turn to a group of writers, Catherine Trotter Cockburn, the authors of *The Perfidious P* and of *The Adventures of Lindamira,* and Mary Davys, who used the libertine paradigm without allowing immorality to prosper. The work of this group accented the heroine's education in finding heart's desire. These writers focused on the experience of the innocent, often mistaken heroine to guide the female reader who was increasingly restricted from venturing into a capitalist, mercantile world that was full of risk or so represented to women. The adventures of the fictional heroines could compensate and educate the reader who feared to enter into a world safe only for male entrepreneurs.

Catherine Trotter wrote the first of these novels, *Olinda's Adventures* (1693). The novel first appeared in Briscoe's miscellany, *Familiar Letters of Love, Gallantry and Several Other Subjects. All Written by Ladies.* The work is entirely epistolary, and the recipient of the letters is Cleander. Olinda's adventures are arranged so that she never marries or is seduced, but moves from interest in one man after another as each one is fortuitously removed from her life. Olinda appears naïve, but she proves capable of coping with each situation as it comes along. Her first suitor is Berontus, a tradesman. He gets her mother's consent, although Olinda cannot love him; he finally loses his fortune, and the match breaks up when he marries a woman with a large fortune. Money is a not-so-subtle subtext in the relationships, but it is seldom the overt motive it was in Haywood.

Olinda's next suitor is an old Dutchman, whose son might have made a better match. Then a gay blade in the army tries to defame Olinda, and she takes revenge on him. Next she begins secret meetings with the love of her life, Cloridon, a married man. Cloridon is rich and powerful, and the fact that he helps two of Olinda's needy friends inspires considerable anxiety in the experienced reader of amatory fiction. But he is soon called away to Flanders, and Antonio becomes his rival for Olinda. Antonio has the support of Olinda's mother, but he earns Olinda's anger by trying to make her believe Cloridon has been untrue to her. When Cloridon appears suddenly at her house, Olinda hides him in the closet when Antonio calls. Olinda will intrigue, but not yield: "In this age, kindness is a more effectual way to cure Love."[37] When Cloridon begins to test her love, Olinda rejects his advances, even when he tries to trick her: "I find by Experience 'tis but bravely, heartily, and throughly Resolving upon a thing, and 'tis half done: There's no Passion, no Temptation so strong, but Resolution can be overcome: All is to be able to Resolve; there's the Point, for one must lose a little of the first Ardour before one can do that; and many of our Sex have ruin'd themselves for want of time to think. Tis not a constant settled purpose of Virtue will do; there must be particular Resolutions for a particular Attack" (p. 182).

In the meantime, Olinda goes to the theater and to Bath, where she meets some sparks, and one of them, Orontes, proposes to her. He also has her mother's support: the wedding is planned, but only delayed at the urging of Cloridon, who finds a sinecure to remove Orontes from the scene.

Olinda's last letter is addressed to Cloridon, urging that they behave so that his wife will not be offended; but when we learn his wife has died, the way is clear for their union. The adventures from which Olinda learns so much come to her, but because the males represent a range of class and type, the reader has a sense of scope rather than repetition in the suitors. Where, in Behn and her followers, aristocrats habitually used their power to seduce women who attracted them, here the lover uses his power to facilitate their union. The mother is as continuously mistaken as all parents in drama and amatory fiction. But the most powerful effect is the learning process that Olinda experiences.

The Perfidious P (1702) features a triangle in which Corydon eventually abandons his mistress Clarinda for a decorous widow, who refuses to yield until marriage. In a familiar pattern of this fiction, Clarinda is sent to the country to avoid scandal, and Corydon is identified with ambition at court. Yet the emphasis of the novel is less on Corydon's desertion of Clarinda, despite the title, than on the contrast between the experienced but restrained widow and the innocent but fallen and scorned Clarinda. The implications of the narrative are at least two: men behave according to decipherable patterns, and experience or knowledge, not innocence, can prevent a woman's losing her social status. (This is a subtext in *Olinda* as well.) Clearly if the reader is a young woman, she should read novels like this to avoid Clarinda's fate. Reading amatory fiction is a way out of the double bind of female innocence. The implication may also result in young female readers buying a good deal of this kind of fiction.

Lindamira, the author of the letters that form *The Adventures of Lindamira, A Lady of Quality* (1702), begins her story as something of a coquette: she poses a bit for her female reader Indamora in saying, "'In fine,' said I, 'Valeria, I think my happiness would consist in having an absolute empire over the heart of a virtuous person.'"[38] Because of Lindamira's tone and the silliness of her suitors, especially Sir Formal Trifle, we do not take her adventures seriously at first. Even her mother, who will not force Lindamira's inclinations, is satirical about marriage; she says, "Few men have loved their wives as well as their mistresses, and that marriage quite altered the constitution of their souls, and as saintlike, complaisant, and obliging as they appeared during their courtship, they became tyrants instead of husbands, and did so ill-use their power that they treated their wives like slaves, and had not that tenderness and affection for 'em as might justly be expected" (p. 20). From this we expect a worthy exception to emerge and, after some minor complications, settle down with Lindamira. But soon Lindamira falls in love with Colonel Harnando, a married man and a gallant, and then we expect her to be ruined instantly, especially because she is separated from her wise friend Valeria. But having resisted Harnando, she falls in love with Cleomidon, but resists him so that he can marry a fortune in Cleodora. Now not only do Lindamira's adventures become complex, but her character has deepened as the story develops: the shallow girl has become capable of sacrifice.

Colonel Harnando's wife dies, and he revives his interest in Lindamira just at the time that Cleomidon's wife also dies. Cleomidon's mother-in-law and aunt by marriage, who wishes to gain his inheritance from his wife, begins a rumor that he has remarried because he believed Lindamira had married Harnando, as indeed she was disposed to do. Both discover at the eleventh hour that the rumors are untrue, and they marry. In Lindamira's world innocence and insouciance are not enough, for gradually her suitors transform from Trifles and Spintexts into powerful men with complex motives and complicated lives. Lindamira seems to have a chance for married happiness because she has grown up through her adventures, including the death of her mother. At the end she has little in common with the girl who spoke of "absolute empire over the heart of a virtuous person." Again we also notice the tendency of virtuous amatory fiction to use several marriages, rather than affairs, to help the central character define a good relationship.

Mary Davys contributed *The Reform'd Coquet* (1724) and *Familiar Letters Betwixt a Gentleman and a Lady* (1725) to the amatory fiction of the period, and she used the formulas with wit and spirit. Amoranda, the heroine of *The Reform'd Coquet*, develops from a vain and heedless girl into one much wiser by the end of the action. At first she seems a likely victim of Lord Lofty, but she is rescued by an agent of her guardian. Later she is almost kidnapped, but arranges for disguises that foil the plan. She then discovers that Lord Lofty has debauched and deserted Altemira, and she tricks Lord Lofty into marrying Altemira, a result he claims to welcome because his conscience had been hurting about his treatment of his bride. Amoranda is much more active and resourceful than Lindamira and Olinda, and her adventures are more exotic.

In subsequent action Biranthus abducts Amoranda in revenge for having been defeated by Amoranda's protector. Although one gentleman hears Amoranda's cries for help, he does not rescue her. Instead she is eventually rescued by a stranger, who turns out to be the same man who had deserted her, and he strangely resembles her protector: "I think the upper part of your Face like his, and there is some resemblence in your Voices too, but that you speak slower, and have a little Lisp."[39] As the reader by now strongly suspects, Formator turns out to be the rescuer and Amoranda's guardian. The splitting of the figure, however, allows the unusual effect of Amoranda's falling in love with her guardian. His constant protection of her, despite her considerable resourcefulness, suggests that her vanity, not any lack of wit, makes her vulnerable to male threats; her guardian tells her,

> I came to you, disguised like an old Man, for two reasons: First, I
> thought the sage Advice you stood in need of, would sound more

natural, and be better received from an old mouth, than a young one; next I thought you would be more open and free, in declaring your real Sentiments of every thing to me, as I was, than as I am. How good an effect my Project has met with, you are not, I hope, insensible; and I beg you will give me leave to remind you of the vast difference there is betwixt your Behaviour then, and now. (Pp. 159–60)

Davy's fiction splits both the male and the female figure: the male between the man of sense, who aids and values the virtuous woman and who carries the approval of parental authority, and the predatory male, who will ruin any woman if she is guileless enough to let him and who enjoys the specious power of wealth and social status. Amoranda manipulates Lord Lofty into reforming from the predatory male to the married man. Her own history is a reform from the vain coquette, deeply affected by male flattery, to a woman of sense, who can value and understand a similar male. The book is dedicated to the Ladies of Great Britain, who are counselled by the author to emulate the reformed Amoranda: "When you grow weary of Flattery, and begin to listen to matrimonial Addresses, chuse a Man with fine Sense, as well as a fine Wigg, and let him have some Merit, as well as much Embroidery: this will make Coxcombs give ground, and Men of Sense will equally admire your Conduct with your Beauty" (p. viii). The fiction prepares the imputed woman reader to face the most important decision of her life and make a prudent choice—that is, to control her life as much as possible within the extremely narrow confines of society. To do this, she cannot be a child-woman, however clever, but must be mature and wise. Then she will repel the wrong kind of man and attract the right kind. We notice that the narrative assumes that Amoranda will make her own marriage choice; fortunately, of course, her uncle's choice is the guardian she loves, affirming once again that children's choices should be decisive. The effect comes from the romance tradition, where desire naturally conforms to authority.

Davys's *Familiar Letters Betwixt a Gentleman and a Lady* reveals the same perspective. Both Berina and Artander are spirited young people who have many interests and much to write about besides their friendship. In fact, it is not until one of the later letters that Artander writes about love. Before that they write of coquettes and prudes, of politics—she a Whig and he a Tory—of the Irish and their rebellion, of Artander's adventures in his village and its environs (including the rescue of a woman dwelling in a cave), of the generosity and greed of physicians, of dancing and gaming as pastimes, of local scandals. Berina has all the poise and intelligence that are lacking in the early Armoranda, and because they have been friends first and then become lovers, this pair seem closer to equals and more destined to respect one another than others in this fictional tradition.

In an excess of love, Artander pledges to Berina "that your least Inclination shall be a Command."[40] Berina then turns the tables on him, saying that marriage is a bitter cup, but urging Artander to assert himself: "I should despise a Husband as much as a king who wou'd give up his own Prerogative, or unman himself to make his Wife the Head" (p. 303). She says that she has a friend who will make the perfect wife for him. In her next letter, she reproaches him for imitating the style of the lover without the substance: "But me thinks you are like a half-bred Player; you over-act your Part: The next time you put on the lover, do it with an easier Air; 'tis quite out of fashion to talk of Dying, and Sighing, and Killing Eyes, and such stuff; you should say, Damn it, Madam, you are a tolerable sort of a Woman, and, if you are willing, I don't much care if I do you the Honour to marry you" (p. 306). The satire and irony, of course, cut both ways—toward the extreme affectation and toward the brutally downright.

Berina is like the witty women in the gay couples of the stage; she takes risks, testing whether Artander can love her unconventional spirit, and so despite her assertions about women's weakness, she is assertive and her temperament will match Artander's. Yet both Davys's works have in common with those of the other writers in this group that they drive toward marriage and provide for their imputed audience of women models for making the crucial decision of their lives within the prescribed social confines.

Orinda's Daughters and Providence: Barker, Penelope Aubin (ca. 1685–1731), Rowe

Three writers of fiction may accurately be described as Orinda's daughters: Jane Barker, Penelope Aubin, and Elizabeth Singer Rowe. They put the amatory structures we have been investigating to a different use, for through romance they show the reader not only moral patterns in human life but a larger providential design as well. These writers translate the predatory world of the romances into a moral and spiritual obstacle course in which their persecuted heroines struggle to fulfill a destiny that may be a commitment to married love or to a single life lived according to personal values. These writers' fantasies are not tragic but melodramatic, in that forces of good eventually triumph. Men are sometimes allies and sometimes the enemy, for the threat represented by the corrupting rake has now been subsumed by larger forces within the heroine's world. Barker, Aubin, and Rowe are definitely, but subtly, concerned about children obeying parents and parental authority about marriage choices. Although their fictions ostensibly endorse filial obedience, the larger patterns they represent, as we shall see, cause the reader to question parental wisdom in choosing suitable mates for their children. These fictions illustrate the waning of parental authority in the work of writers who overtly wish to sustain it, but the same works do not, except occasionally in Barker, mediate marriage choices because they have larger spiritual work to do.

Jane Barker, whose poetry is discussed in chapter 2, above, contributed four major pieces to this fiction: *Love Intrigues* (1713), *Exilius* (1715), *A Patch-Work Screen for the Ladies* (1723), and *Lining for the Patch-Work Screen* (1726). *Love Intrigues* is the closest of her works—or any of the fiction by this group—to the Behn tradition. It is clearly written to represent a young woman's predicament as she is courted by a man who toys with her emotions, attempts to get her to agree to a hasty marriage, swears everlasting devotion and urgent desire, but then leaves her for long periods and finally never asks her parents for her hand in marriage. The writer of a poem of praise for the novel suggests its monitory function; the novel describes,

> The Charms of Nature, and those painted true.
> By what strange Springs our real Passions move,
> How vain are all Disguises when we Love;
> What Wiles and Stratagems the Men secure,
> And what the tortur'd Female Hearts endure;
> Compell'd to stifle what they feign would tell,
> While Truth commands, but Honour must rebel.[41]

Galesia is indeed constrained by her sense of propriety in not revealing her passion for Bosvil, either to him or to her mother, but the reader has a sense that the revelation would have made little difference to the inconstant Bosvil. When he presses Galesia for a "speedy Marriage," she rebukes him for treating her like a mistress, and he responds passionately but with patent hypocrisy:

Sure, dear Cousin, said I, (with a Tone wholly confus'd) you forget in whose Company you are, and believe your self with fair Mrs. *Lowland*: if such an amorous Slumber has cast you into this *Delerium*, pray awake, and behold before you, your Cousin *Galesia* with whom I converse at present: her reserv'd Behaviour, with which she treats me her faithful Lover, is a sufficient Demonstration, that it is the prudent, vertuous, chast *Galesia*! It is this reserved Mein, Madam, which has often deter'd me, and commanded my Tongue to a respectful Silence; whilst my poor Heart, over-charg'd with Passion, only eas'd with Sighs, and my Looks were the only Language whereby to express my interiour Thoughts. (P. 28)

Here Barker anticipates Haywood in demonstrating the ways men blame their perfidy on women. Although Galesia is the stereotypically innocent young woman, she is responsible for her involvement with Bosvil and her survival after the relationship: both occur because of Orinda. As Margaret Doody has said and as we noticed in chapter 2, modeling on Orinda went on throughout Jane Barker's fiction: *Love Intrigues* is "related to Lucasia," for example (Sig. B).[42] As the story opens, the reader is aware that Galesia has been made very vulnerable to fantasies of love by her reading, which also has made her equally eager to imitate Orinda in writing poetry and to write her commitment to single life upon a tree, the old pastoral lover's gesture:

> Then gentle Maid cast off thy Chain,
> Which links thee to thy faithless Swain,
> And vow a Virgin to remain.
>
> Write, write thy Vow upon this Tree,
> By us it shall recorded be;
> And thou enjoy Eternity.
>
> (P. 14)

When she is actually abandoned by Bosvil, Galesia

> resolved to espouse a Book, and spend my Days in Study: This Fancy having once taken Root, grew apace, and branch'd it self forth in a thousand vain conceits. I imagined my self the *Orinda*, or *Sapho* of my Time, and amongst my little Reading, the Character of the Faithful Shepperdess in the Play pleas'd me extreamly; I resolved to imitate her, not only in perpetual Chastity, but in learning the Use of Simples for the Good of my Country Neighbors. Thus I thought to become *Apollo's* Darling Daughter, and Maid of Honour to the Muses. In order to do this I got my Brother (who was not yet return'd to *Oxford*) to set me in the way to learn my Grammar, which he willingly did, thinking it only a Vapour of Fancy. (P. 15)

Literature has a double meaning for Galesia: it feeds her fantasies of love and models her behavior in life, but it also changes the meaning of Bosvil's desertion. Writing gives Galesia a means of surviving her abandonment: like the Portuguese nun, Galesia has a voice, in part, because her relationship to Bosvil does not culminate in marriage. The relationship has ended, but the emotions remain to be explored and analyzed.

Throughout the process of the novel, which is, of course, narrated by

Galesia, both she and Bosvil appear to be imitating romances, largely because of Galesia's innocence of the world. Thus the text is a mirror of the social transaction of amatory fiction: a female reader, largely without access to the world, learns about it and models her behavior through reading. We feel for Galesia as she tries to cope with Bosvil's actions, in this case, informing a friend that he will not introduce him to Galesia because "he design'd his Cousin *Galesia* for himself":

> This Transaction, tho' coming to me by a third hand, gave me a strong Belief of *Bosvil's* Sincerity; and made me interpret every little dubious Word, which he sometimes mix'd with his fond Actions, to be Demonstrations of a real Passion; not doubting but a little time wou'd ripen the same into an open Declaration to my Parents, as well as formerly to me, and now lately to young *Brafort*. In the mean time attributing this Delay to his Prudence, in acquainting himself with my Humour, and Inclinations, before he gave himself irrevocably to me; which made me regulate my Behaviour with discreetest Precautions my poor inexperienced Thoughts cou'd dictate. My Grammar Rules now became harsh Impertinences, for I thought I had learnt *Amo* and *Amor,* by a shorter and surer Method; and the only Syntax I studied, was how to make suitable Answers to my Father, and him, when the long'd-for Question shou'd be propos'd; that I might not betray my Weakness.
> (P. 21)

Here Barker clearly presents the central function of amatory fiction: to teach its readers the complex codes of the grammar of love, to provide in Foucault's terms, a discourse of sexuality in which any subject may find a syntax. Although the narrative frequently implies that Galesia's prudence with Bosvil is a cause of his cooling toward her, the reader can only conclude that her reserve has saved Galesia from being ruined and that she is blaming herself as a victim. The novel is a fascinating and complex representation of a woman's predicament, in which she escapes the fate of a Haywood heroine because of the particular literary models she has chosen. Barker is simply more explicit than her contemporaries in showing how her characters model their behavior on what they read.

Exilius or, the Banish'd Roman (1715) was Jane Barker's reply to tales of gallantry. As her subtitle informs the reader, Barker wrote "for the Instruction of Some Young *Ladies* of Quality," to stem the tide of libertinism with a concept of heroic love that would fulfill itself in marriage:

> Thus it has far'd with this kind of Heroick Love of late; it has been as it were rallied out of Practice, and its Professors laughed out of Countenance, whilst Interest and loose Gallantry have been set up in its Place, and monopolized all its Business and Effects. How far

this has been an Inlet to that Deluge of Libertinism which has over-flow'd the Age, the many unhappy Marriages and unkind Separations may inform us, and at the same time show how proper an Ingredient Love is, towards the making of a happy Marriage: for where Love is not the Cement, as well as Interest the Foundation, the Superstructure of Conjugal Faith, seldom stands long, the first Wind that blows . . . will go near to shake, if not quite overthrow the Fabrick.[43]

Romances, Barker tells her reader, are therefore justified in demonstrating how heroic love is to be achieved. To represent the value of heroic love, four sets of Roman mates—Cordiala and Scipio, Clelia and Marcellus, Clarinthia and Asiaticus, and Scipiana and Exilius—have complicated and far-flung adventures that culminate in their unions. *Exilius* is written "after the Manner of Telemachus," which implies that it celebrates the manly virtues Odysseus's son defended in his scenes with Penelope. Thus, drawing on the epic sources of romance, Barker makes marriage of the four couples into their destinies, like the founding of Rome or the conquest of Jerusalem. For example, Clelia has the approval of Jupiter's oracle for her love of Marcellus. In these stories men and women are allies as they struggle against obstacles to their destined mates. Their commitment to one another does not begin with marriage, for it has already been amply demonstrated. Interest and marriage bonds are no longer the enemies of love but, with it, support the ideal relationship.

Another important theme in *Exilius* is obedience to parental authority and its relation to heroic love. *Exilius* overtly and repeatedly condemns filial disobedience. Daughters who defy their fathers end up married to monsters or fish: "In this I could not but again admire the exact justice of Heaven, in thus punishing her Lewdness and Disobedience to her Parents. She that refus'd the honest Esposals provided by her Father, became Wife to a monster; she that disgrac'd herself and her Friends by unlawful Lust, was a Prostitute to a Fish" (2:72). Still, as Doody points out, the woman's predicament as a fish's spouse is not as bleak as one might expect: "There are delicate ambiguities to the moral fable; although the author seems officially to present the undersea world as the domain of the inhumane and lustful, the world under water has its attractions and advantages. The comic, the grotesque, and the beautiful combine in a manner that complicates interpretation and resists simple moral exemplification."[44] And, paradoxically, *Exilius* leaves the reader skeptical of parental authority in relation to genuine heroic love of the sort experienced by the four central couples. If parents become tyrannical in opposing a destined heroic love, as they invariably do, then children are justified by the romance in opposing them. Parents do not come off very well in this novel: at least they are blind to the destined loves of their children, and at worst they oppose them because of incestu-

248

ous longings. The children's relationships are only unsuitable, but never adulterous or lustful; and so the effect on the reader is to inspire skepticism about parental authority in filial marriage choices, which should be left to providential design, sensed and understood only by the children. Just as Barker's fantasies support and interrogate social structures, so the narrative is more subtle than first appears about both supporting and subverting parental authority.

A Patch-Work Screen for the Ladies (1723) continues Galesia's story from *Love Intrigues*. Barker proves herself a true daughter of Orinda by using undoing generously in the address to the reader. She has chosen a patchwork screen as a metaphor for her narratives, she says, "the better to recommend it to my Female Readers, as well in their Discourse, as in their Needle-Work," for "whenever one sees a Set of Ladies together, their Sentiments are as differently mix'd as the Patches in their Work."[45] Then she exclaims, characteristically, "Forgive me, kind Reader, for carrying the Metaphor too high; by which means I am out of my Sphere, and so can say nothing of the *Male Patch-Workers*" (p. vi). Barker's fiction is that Galesia has become a virgin recluse who passes her time in retreat, reading, writing poetry, telling stories, and rescuing women in distress. Barker records the stories in a work that gives the appearance of fragmentation, "but in a *Patch-Work* there is no Harm done" (p. viii).

The patches present Galesia's story as well as those she tells the narrator. Both Galesia and the narrator are personae for Barker. We learn that Galesia has been engaged to a young man whom she did not greatly fancy but who was much favored by her parents. At the last minute, he was arrested for robbery, and so she escaped that union. Galesia and her mother move to the city, and a friend tries to persuade Galesia to marry an old man; but she is now too wise for that (p. 54). Her mother also urges Galesia to marry, but her "Reflections on Bosvil's Baseness, gave me a secret Disgust against Matrimony" (p. 79). Later, when another suitor has committed suicide after a violent argument with his mistress, Galesia wonders if fate is persecuting her; but at this time, as at all other moments of despair, she is comforted by thoughts of Katherine Philips and her poem, "A Virgin Life." Galesia concludes that fate has designed her for a single life (p. 89).

Orinda, then, is the inspiration for Galesia, as she writes poetry in her garrett, eschewing ambition or wealth for the sake of virtue:

> The Pleasure of [retreat] was greatly improv'd by reading Mrs. *Phillips*. I began to emulate her Wit, and aspir'd to imitate her Writings; in doing of which, I think, I deserv'd *Arachne's* Fate, or at least to be transform'd into one of the lowest of Mack-Fleckno's Followers: Her noble Genius being inimitable; especially in Praise of a Country-Life, and Contempt of human Greatness . . . Her Poetry I found so inter-

woven with Vertue and Honour, that each Line was like a Ladder to climb, not only to Parnassus, but to Heaven. (P. 3)

Galesia becomes a learned woman (she is interested in Harvey's theories of circulation of the blood, for example). Although her brother, like Barker's, humors Galesia's interests, the rest of the world finds her unfit company, "for the Unlearned fear'd and the Learned scorn'd my Conversation; at least, I fancy'd so: a Learned Woman, being at best but like a Forc'd Plant, that never has its due or proper Relish, but is wither'd by the first Blast that Envy or Tribulation blows over her Endeavours" (p. 11). Barker portrayed Galesia and her mother as further internalizing this view of learned women, who are not made attractive by learning, "but live in a Stoical Dulness or humersome Stupidity" (p. 79). Again there is tension between the values Barker herself held and those she represented in her fiction. In the early eighteenth century, to be sure, a learned woman was often regarded as an oddity, but Orinda was certainly not rejected by society because of her achievements.

A *Patch-Work* exhibits parents in very much the way they appeared in *Exilius*: lacking in understanding of their children's welfare. Galesia's parents favored her marriage to the robber, for example, and her mother favored her marriage to the suicide. In a telling example of Galesia's stories, a father forces his daughter to marry a man other than the lawyer she desires. The husband goes bankrupt, whereas the lawyer grows to fame. Wherever parents set their judgment ahead of the inclination of their children, the outcome in both the short and long run is bad for the children.

Another important pattern in Barker's fiction is the woman rescuer. One of Galesia's stories tells of a goldsmith who seduces an innocent girl and then denies her. Galesia gets her into a hospital and thence to a plantation (p. 54). Belinda is a similar example. A married man preaches to her of platonic love, but she soon finds herself pregnant; and when he deserts her, Galesia and her landlady come to her rescue. The culmination of this theme is the story of "The Unaccountable Wife," which paradoxically conforms to and violates all contemporary codes for female behavior. It begins with a wife's toleration of her husband's open affair with their servant. When the husband tries to get rid of the servant, however, the wife does the servant's work, much to the disapproval of their friends. Both wife and servant finally leave for the servant's hovel in the country. There the neighbors try to get rid of them "to prevent a Parish charge" (p. 103). A lady of quality sees them being driven from town and shelters them in her house. They return to the husband because he is ill, and he soon dies. The queen eventually offers the wife a pension, but she refuses it and ends her life a beggar. The narrator attributes the "unaccountable" actions to infatuation, yet to a reader familiar with women's discourses, the story is full of resonances about women's predicament, and one of its points is the lack of social understanding of contradictions in codes of behavior. For example, the women live out the opening line of Mary Chudleigh's famous poem "Wife and Servant are the same." One also recalls the many pleas in advice books for wives to tolerate their husbands' extramarital affairs, rather than disturb their marriages. The problem with social acceptance of these terms is that the women, as in a comedy, have followed them to their logical extreme and thereby expose the social system. The husband wanted to cast off only the awkward member of the triangle, not both women. The social system (i.e., the Poor Law) will not tolerate two unattached, unemployed women in the servant's former village. The wife's refusal of the pension is a rejection of her social station and illuminates the condition of all less fortunate women. Unaccountable in contemporary terms is the fact that the wife calls the servant the only friend she has. Women wooed by the same man and bonding across class lines are simply not to be understood. The story is a powerful indictment of the status of women in Barker's society, but it is presented without rancor: rather, its effect is to interrogate the social structure through irony, not anger.

The Lining of the Patch-Work Screen: Designed for the Farther Entertainment of the Ladies (1726) extends the reader's sense that women help women. Barker creates this impression partly by having a group of women who listen to Galesia and contribute stories to the text, but her most effective device is to use several stories of the Behn tradition for new purposes. The Portuguese nun reappears, as does Behn's fair vow-breaker, but she now accidentally sews her first husband's shroud to the second husband's coat. The old stories from the libertine tradition refined and set in a moral framework impress the reader with the scope of the female community and its strong internal bonds.

Penelope Aubin (ca. 1685–1731) combines the familiar theme of persecuted female innocence with popular travel literature to produce a fiction in which Providence protects her heroines in a hostile world.[46] Her novels show a melodrama in which good innocence is narrowly preserved, and the characters' own commitment to marriage, like Providence, transcends all obstacles. Aubin's fiction also continues the pattern of filial obedience combined with parental misjudgment about a child's marital choice. The structures do not question parental authority, but simply prove it wrong. The general purpose of Aubin's fiction is to use romance and travel structures to illustrate providential workings for the reader. As she says in *The Life of Charlotta DuPont* (1736):

> Thus divine Providence having by various Trials and strange Vicissitudes of Fortune, proved the Faith and Patience of these heroick Christians, whom neither Slavery nor the Fear of Death could prevail with to for-

sake their Faith, or distrust their God, they were all happily preserv'd and deliver'd out of their Troubles, and at last brought Home to their own Native Lands. *Charlotta,* whose filial Piety and Extraordinary Virtues make her justly claim the first Place in our Esteem, as well as in this History, had the satisfaction of seeing her dear Father die in Peace in a good old Age; was blest with an excellent Husband, and many Children fair and virtuous as herself: Nor was her Prosperity interrupted by any Misfortune.[47]

Aubin urged her readers to recognize the larger providential design in human existence, rather than simply focusing upon the morality of individual decisions. Of Barker's work, only *Exilius* exhibits this pattern. In Aubin the effect of the narrative is to show the reader models of lives conducted within the cosmic design. The travel element, which Aubin distinctively engrafts onto amatory fiction, provides her with the larger scope to illustrate the pattern. *Charlotta* contains an action that extends from Europe to the West Indies and South America, but it is also interesting for the way in which a single action—here the seduction of Dorinda, who becomes Charlotta's stepmother—reverberates within the lives of many others. Aubin demonstrates the impossibility of limiting or even understanding the consequences of our action for others. Along the way, she also comments at length on the double standard and the libertine ideology. I quote at length to give the flavor of her writing:

He went to his own Home to his Wife and Family, and the poor distracted *Dorinda* was conducted with her Maid to a handsome Chamber. . . . It is impossible to describe in Words what she felt when she consider'd, that she had left her tender Parents, blasted the reputable Family she belong'd to, since none but must guess the Cause of her sudden Flight; that she was now in a strange Place, and in the Hands of those she knew nothing of; that in case *Leander,* from whom she had little Cause to expect any good, refus'd to marry and take Care of her, she was ruin'd to all Intents and Purposes; could no more return to Her Home and Family, nor had with her half enough to provide for her long and the helpless Infant she was likely to bring into the World. She shed a Flood of Tears, and wish'd for Death a thousand Times, and pass'd the Night without closing her Eyes. Thus by one imprudent Action we often ruin the Peace and Quiet of our Lives for ever, and by one false Step undo our selves. I wish Mankind would but reflect how barbarous a deed it is, how much below a Man, nay how like a Devil 'tis, to debauch a young inexperienc'd Virgin, and expose to Ruin and an endless train of Miseries, the Person whom his Persuasions hath drawn to gratify his Desire, and to oblige him at the Expence of her own Peace and Honour. And surely if our Laws be just, that punish that Man with Death who kills another, he certainly merits that or something worse, that is, eternal Infamy, who betrays the foolish Maid that credits his Oaths and Vows, and abandons her to Shame and Misery. And if Women were not infatuated, doubtless every Maid would look on the Man that proposes such a Question to her, as her mortal Enemy, and from that Moment banish him from her Heart and Company. (Pp. 13–14)

From Dorinda's seduction results her cynical marriage to DuPont, whose daughter Charlotta Dorinda ships to Virginia and thence to the West Indies. Thus Aubin shows a single action rippling out into countless other lives totally unknown to the perpetrator. For Aubin there is little glamor or freedom in the libertine code, and her sense is also that the ruined woman does not recover morally from her one experience of debauchery and abandonment. Having been harmed, she will harm others. A far cry from Behn and Manley.

Aubin published *The Life of Madam de Beaumont* in 1721, and it appears, like Barker's *Exilius,* to have been a reply to the literature of gallantry; for she says drily that there are two remarkable elements in it: the heroines are virtuous and the hero is faithful to his wife. The story is exotic and does not pretend to be true. Exiled from her French husband, Madame de Beaumont has lived for fourteen years in a cave on the Welsh coast with her daughter Belinda; Madame has refused a large settlement to turn Catholic: "He that would keep his Integrity, must dwell in a Cell."[48] Belinda soon marries a Welsh country gentleman, whose rakish cousin and heir soon begins to threaten their happiness; and in the course of the narrative, Belinda is saved from ruin numerous times, sometimes by Providence, sometimes by male virtue, which exists here as it has in Davys. At the end, having remained true to his destined union with Madame, Belinda's father returns with her husband to rejoin his family: "Thus Providence does, with unexpected Accidents, try Men's Faith, frustrate their Designs, and lead them thro a Series of Misfortunes, to manifest its Power in their Deliverance" (p. 142).

A third work of Aubin's illustrates clearly how her sexual ideology has developed from the libertine vision: her translation of *The Illustrious French Lovers* (1737), a series of eight stories, the morals of which she extracts at the beginning of the two volumes. What strikes one first is the pragmatism of the stories, until one recalls that they are translations from the French. One story advises parents not to give children their fortunes before death; another shows how a virtuous, prudent maid may get a superior husband; still another demonstrates how the whole world slights a woman bereft of husband and betrayed by mercenary relatives. Despite her belief in Providence, Aubin is like other writers of amatory fiction in seeing the world as a dangerous and hostile place in which women must beward of parents who might force marriage or libertines who are everywhere: "an Advertisement to all Womankind, to be ever upon their Guard; and the more Beauty and Merit a Woman has, the more doubtful and Cautious she must be of giving any Opportunities to the faithless Sex, who always plot the Fair Ones ruine, not trusting to her own Virtue alone."[49]

Although Aubin is conventional in her view of parents' marriage choices and predatory males, she has more faith than her colleagues in women's moral power, and so she sees hope for a rake in the influence of a good woman: "his Conversion to Virtue, after having acted the Part of a Rake and a Hero before, shew the Power a virtuous Woman, who has sense, may gain over the most vitious Man" (p. xi). Similarly, a young woman who has been ruined may repair her fault through being faithful to her lover: "and by her Constancy to her first Engagement, shew that it was no vitious Inclination that induced her to oblige him, but only Love, and the entire Confidence she had in him: which, if he proves a Villain to her, will make her pitied, and him scorn'd and despised" (p. ix). Aubin here shows the beginnings of an idea about women that is to grow powerful in the eighteenth and nineteenth centuries: the notion that the love of a virtuous woman is socially and morally transforming.[50] The idea that women could be a powerful influence for good on those around them possibly compensated, however slightly, for their limited mobility, their scant actual power, and the narrowing scope of their lives.

Aubin dedicated *Charlotta* to Elizabeth Singer Rowe and called her "my much Honoured Friend." The preface to a posthumous collection of Aubin's fiction also claims friendship with Rowe, though Jane Spencer casts doubt on the possibility of close ties between the two writers. She believes that Aubin was probably trying to capitalize on Rowe's fame, even though Rowe's fiction had not yet been published: "The dedication is no evidence of acquaintance between the two women, but strong evidence of the power of Rowe's name to guarantee the religious and virtuous character of any woman writer who could manage to appear associated with her."[51]

Rowe used amatory fiction for sacred purposes. In her two works of epistolary fiction, *Friendship in Death in Twenty Letters from the Dead to the Living* (1728) and *Letters Moral and Entertaining* (1728); 1731; 1732), Rowe demonstrates how love transcends the grave and how sexual passion may be transformed into the love of God. *Friendship in Death* presents the departed as still caring for the living and looking after them; in this way Rowe's fiction extends earthly domesticity into the hereafter. *Friendship in Death* gives earthly characters and its readers not only assurance of immortality but also that living according to a sentimental Christian morality will earn heavenly bliss, that life need not be a tragedy, but can be a melodrama in which the good finally prevail. The transcendent vision of *Friendship in Death* helps the reader find the meaning in the frequent renunciations of relationships in *Letters,* the many times characters may be consumed with passion but do not yield to it, the many reforms of evil characters. The prospect of immortality transforms a lack of earthly fulfillment into eternal bliss and substitutes spiritual love for desire.

The dead in *Friendship in Death* care deeply for the living, and the dead wish to guide the living to make correct choices, both in terms of earthly pragmatism and in terms of achieving heavenly bliss. A dead husband instructs his wife about how to escape captivity by the Bassa in Spain; Clerimont writes to his former ward Leonora that she can avoid marrying her brother's choice Cassander ("another Name for Misery") by revealing Cassander's guilty secret, a young and beautiful Italian wife.[52] Cleander writes to his brother practical advice that he press his suit of Bellamira, the best of women, and break "all Engagements with the lewd and infamous Amoret" (p. 47). Other writers alert their living relations to exchanged babies and possible incest or the need to care for an infant daughter. In short, life on earth is continuous with life in heaven, and the dead watch over the living, judging and guiding their actions in light of earthly values as well as eternal life. There is no perceptible distinction between one and the other.

Letters Moral and Entertaining begins with Philario's forced marriage to a girl of ten "only to secure her vast fortune."[53] Defiant, he courted Amasia, who was forbidden by her dying mother to respond to Philario. He waited until her mother's funeral was past, invaded Amasia's room, and raped her. In his absence Amasia is ill and dies, haunted by her mother's shade, but hoping for Philario's aid. Amasia believes herself "cited to the supreme tribunal," and Philario is powerless to help her (p. 7). Another letter from Amoret confesses to her friend a fatal secret, her passion for Sebastian. The whole letter seems modeled on a libertine seduction: "Time and place, the evening gloom and verdant shade, every circumstance conspired to my undoing. The whispering gales, the falling fountains, the green retreats and flow'ry scenes heighten'd the soft temptation. All nature seem'd to sooth the tender passion, and gave my charming seducer new advantages, his form, his aspect acquir'd unusual graces, and his language was all enchantment" (p. 29). Yet Rowe frames the seduction with intimations of immortality that allow the reader to evaluate the erotic experience from the prospect of eternity: "O celestial life! How do these peaceful scenes sooth and flatter my soul! through what enchanting paths does my imagination stray! Ye vain grandeurs of the world adieu! Adieu ye idle amusements, and fantastick pleasures! What shadows do you now appear! How unsubstantial to these serious prospects of bliss" (p. 29).

Another writer, seeking to disuade a friend from the libertine way of life, demonstrates how Rowe substitutes eternal bliss for erotic fulfillment:

This is the supream excellence after which my soul aspires; if 'tis imaginary, the mind must yet be enlarged by grasping at the enjoyment of infinite happiness: for I dare confess my end is the same as yours, 'tis pleasure we both pursue; and as at present it consists chiefly in expectation, mine must surpass yours by proportion to its object.

You have set your night for the Opera, to hear Faustina sing; I expect the period, when the curtain of mortality shall be drawn, and the scenes of eternal glories open, and angels solace me with celestial harmony. (P. 33)

Viewing their actions *sub specie eternitas* allows Rowe's characters to reform, to resist passion, to endure hardships. It also allows them to accept the death of a loved one. Yet Rowe is not unrealistic: her Cleora acknowledges the loss of Addison, "especially in an age like this, where so little honour, friendship and sincerity are to be found" (p. 115).

Like Aubin, Rowe represented a virtuous woman as a potentially transforming presence in the lives of others, as her letter to Cleora shows; but Rowe is somewhat more sophisticated in that she understands that such influence is partly a creation from within the person being transformed: "I must confess you have given me a sort of imaginary character, and I am a heroine of your own making; as great minds always suppose they find in others the same virtues they really possess themselves" (p. 104).

Rowe creates an ideal society of women similar to Delariviere Manley's, though without lesbian overtones and feminist critique. Rowe's pastoral group is simply utopian, an account of how one family may seek earthly happiness and tranquillity. The family—a mother and two daughters—lives in a modest house located in a beautiful valley beside a lovely river. They are cultured, surrounded by a library of music, maps, history, divinity, travels, philosophy, and drama. As the narrator enters, he sees the mother, "a grave well-looking woman of about fifty, who was reading aloud to two very beautiful young ones, who were at work, embroidering flowers on white silk; they were dress'd alike in white satin waistcoats and brown lutestring petticoats and upon their heads fine lac'd caps, made like those of the common peasants. They had an air of innocence and modesty greater than ever I saw" (p. 133).

The family have adopted their retreat after the death of their husband-father, who left large debts and whose family refused to help his widow and children. By living austerely, the widow has managed to pay off the debts, "but had found so much peace in that solitude, that she was loth to quit it, and had the pleasure to find both her daughters in the same mind" (p. 135). They spend their days in devotions, in pursuit of the arts, in helping the poor, in reading to one another while the others work. In this first encounter with the family, the narrator reveals that the mother resists the intrusion of love into their idyl: she becomes ill when the older daughter falls in love with Alphonso. The daughter renounces her love, and the mother recovers! Lest the reader too quickly conclude Rowe's rustic family have taken vows of chastity and poverty, subsequent letters in the next volume reveal that Rosella has not only married Alphonso, but he has come into considerable wealth, and so they all are living more elegantly. The narrator has returned to the retreat to claim the younger daughter as his bride. Rowe's ideals of female behavior seem to require the capacity for renunciation without the fact. Most significant about this family is, however, that the mother has created an existence, a retired life of which Orinda and the poets wrote, a life that many English gentry women might emulate: it is not unlike the life led by Elizabeth Carter or Hannah More, somewhat later in the century, or by Rowe herself for that matter. The model is developed in detail, far beyond concepts or maxims. Because the vision is centered in the family domestic scene, it is an amazing harbinger of similar scenes in American nineteenth-century fiction.

Although Rowe, like Milton, made a place for sexual love in her ideal life and although she wrote a letter that culminates in the line, "GOD himself is Love," we should not conclude that she was as tolerant of the fallen woman as Penelope Aubin (3:167). *Letters* ends with a vision of several of the most famous women lovers of all time consigned to hell, which is "no fiction pious men adore," but an affirmed reality in which Helen of Troy, Thaïs, Cleopatra, and Ovid's Julia all mourn their heavy doom and stand as examples to many "a lovely guiltless maid" (3:253). The fate of these famous women is, for Rowe, simply the other side of her proleptic vision of the ineffable pleasure that awaits for eternity all those who resist illicit earthly pleasure.

Rowe's work may be profitably compared to that of Harriet Beecher Stowe. Although feminist critics have studied Stowe's work in detail, it has not been compared to Rowe's, possibly because they are separated by a century and nationality. A sentimental, proleptic vision is common to both writers, a vision that extends the structures of feeling and behaving from the present to the hereafter. Consequently they are preoccupied with death not as a catastrophe but as a deliverance. Both represent life as a melodrama in which the good enjoy bliss for eternity, and both extend domestic values into the hereafter, which forms a continuity with earthly existence. Both writers also fuse religious and social values; they attempt to constrain social behavior with religious motives. Stowe is more overtly political, Rowe more social, but both use religious concepts to motivate social change. Finally, both see women as an important moral force and create female utopias, in which men are not centrally involved and in which women's values and customs are critical: it is a small step from Honoria's retreat to Rachel Halliday's Indiana kitchen.[54]

It is truly provocative to see Rowe as a precursor of Stowe and similar American authors, for they seem to develop from the seventeenth-century Puritan tradition, yet additional similarities of their cultural situations are uncanny. Both were enormously popular. *Uncle Tom's Cabin* was the first American novel to sell more than a million copies, and if Lincoln's quip is half true, its influence was acknowledged. Yet its popularity puzzles critics: "And no wonder. The modernist literary aesthetic cannot account for the unprecedented and persistent popularity of a book like *Uncle Tom's Cabin*, for this novel operates according to principles quite other than those that have been responsible for determining the currently sanctified American literary classics."[55] Because the English tradition is longer and more complex, Rowe's popularity is even more embarassing, even to one of the few critics to study her with respect. John Richetti acknowledges that she was the most famous of the women writers before Richardson and Fielding, included in a small library with Shakespeare, Milton, Dryden, and Pope:

> It is hard to understand why. Her most popular work is a deadening book, written in ecstatic and inflated prose and full of the most explicit and tedious moralizing about the pains of a life of sin and the comforts of living virtuously. Its situations and characters are mechanical and verbose, and strike any modern reader as almost comically unreal. Worst of all, perhaps, Mrs. Rowe's book reeks of what must be called morbidity about death, which we are reminded on every page is always menacing us and can never for a moment be lost sight of."[56]

From these comments, it seems clear that the aesthetic criteria used to judge Rowe's work are different from those accepted by her wide eighteenth-century audience. In fact, the same may be said for most of the fiction writers covered in this chapter. Writing for a popular audience a fiction that has ample social work to do in mediating women's predicament in a world of male interest, these writers make little effort to imbed their themes or to mystify the reader. That the work of Behn, Manley, Haywood, Hearne, Rowe, and the others lived for the eighteenth century is a fact beyond dispute: our task is to join Jane Tompkins in finding ways to read their popular art again. One way is to understand the cultural function it was created to perform.

Chapter Five

Politics

The substantial body of poetry, prose, and drama women wrote about public life in this period has been almost entirely neglected, partly because of the stereotypical attitude, sometimes fostered by the authors themselves, that politics was none of their business. It is the purpose of this chapter to open this field of women's writing. As we have noticed before, women's views and actions were largely formed by the classes from which they came; and during the seventeenth century, women of the radical Puritan sects made unique protests to Parliament, actions that did not result in social gains for women, partly because the Commonwealth did not survive. After the Restoration the women writers with whom this book is concerned began to write political poetry. They did not advocate changes in society: they supported, with a few exceptions, the Stuart monarchy and the values with which it was associated. Still, their political writing forms a substantial achievement for women at a time when participation in public life was barred to them, and married women had no legal existence.

Women Petitioners and Parliaments of Women

Before we turn to the contributions made by women writers to the political literature of the seventeenth century, some description of women's political activity and the reactions it inspired will give the reader a sense of the scope of women's involvement in public life, activities that were truly extraordinary and unsurpassed until the nineteenth century. For information about radical women's political activity in this time, we are indebted to two women historians: Ellen A. McArthur, who wrote "Women Petitioners and the Long Parliament" in 1909, and Patricia Higgins, who in 1973 wrote "The Reactions of Women, with special reference to women petitioners" in order to supplement McArthur's study. Their essays reveal that women petitioned and marched on Parliament many times in the decade between 1642 and 1653, submitting petitions with thousands of signatures and staging demonstrations with from 5,000 to 10,000 participants. Sometimes, as in the 1648 demonstration for the release of John Lilburne, they had the help of men; sometimes they had male participants donning women's clothing; sometimes their critics thought all their activity was inspired by males; but their numbers and their courage were such that to the public they were known as the Women Petitioners.

First, we should understand that the women petitioners came from a small, radical, largely sectarian minority of the London population: "For most women, especially those living outside London, life continued as usual or with only minor interruptions."[1] Yet the scope of the petitioners' activity is truly impressive, in view of the fact that some were injured, some imprisoned, and some killed by guards. Their first attempt to influence Parliament took place on 31 January 1642, when they requested control of the decay of trade that was causing the starving of their children. On 4 February 1642, they were back, protesting the Papists within the House of Lords and among the bishops, and asking, as they had before, for protection of the Protestants in Ireland. A few days later, on 10 February, they asked Parliament to petition the queen to stay in England and that Parliament put down the seditious tumults that were driving her from the country. From January through August of 1643, thousands of women repeatedly petitioned Parliament for peace. These demonstrations were dispersed by guards, women were imprisoned, and they were questioned about having been directed by male conspirators.

In several years these activities were followed by the demonstrations to free the Levellers: in 1646 and 1647 women petitioned for the release of John Lilburne. In 1648 the women were joined by men as 10,000 demonstrated for Lilburne's release, which was followed in 1649 by a petition for the release of Lilburne, Walwyn, Prince, and Overton. Throughout the year there were petitions on behalf of the imprisoned Levellers, which continued sporadically through 1653. The most successful petition advocated reform in the debt imprisonment laws, which Parliament did revise. A 1653 petition for the release of John Lilburne contained language that asserted women's right to petition, at just about the end of the activity. Lilburne was not released as a result of the petitions, but banished by Parliament in 1652; and when he returned to England in 1653 illegally, he was tried and again imprisoned. Although the Levellers did petition on his behalf into the newly established Protectorate, the general demonstrations ceased.[2]

What did not cease were the ideas and the rhetoric of the movement, which lasted into the 1680s. As Patricia Higgins observes, the petitioners frequently accepted their own inferior status, sometimes, it seems, as a rhetorical strategy. Generally this ploy did not work, for they were frequently told to go home, were smeared as whores or at best locquacious busybodies. In their turn, however, the women trotted out the familiar examples of Esther and Boedica, not to mention Semiramis, as women who had a part in public life. More important, however, seem their claims of equality with men. Their justification for such claims are two: the equality of souls in Christ, a powerful argument in a society dominated by Puritans; and their equal interest in the Commonwealth, for which women had worked and sacrificed a great deal.[3] A gesture that indicates significant assumption of equality in the time was a petition by maidservants to enjoy the same holidays as apprentices.[4] Still, most of the women's petitions were made on behalf of others: their starving children, political prisoners, those in debtors prison, their husbands and sons, and such. The rhetoric of the petitions often reveals their origins among the radical sects, and is inconsistent with regard to the status of women; but it usually deals with their highly contradictory and ambivalent situation during the years of the Commonwealth.

There is a contradiction between the female petitioners' admissions of the inferiority of their sex and the intellectual case they made for the equality of the sexes. It is not wholly surprising, however, for the society in which these women lived was excessively patriarchal; and like the women writers, they sought to undo their transgression wherever possible. The religious and political crisis inspired the women, stimulated them into undertaking unconventional actions and into forming their own opinions on religion and politics. In such an atmosphere, strange speculations and new ideas germinated and flourished. Though they did not overtly challenge masculine superiority, women tentatively put forward justifications for their involvement in politics based on the equal rights of men and women. They did not abandon their customary deference to men and to male-dominated society, but they perceived that "ye weaker Sex" had rights that in a crisis of church or Commonwealth it could assert. It was said of one woman during the civil war that she had been "found playing the good huswife at home (a thing out of fashion)."[5]

Although the demonstrations lasted only a dozen years, the ideas of equality and of women's role in public life endured, and not just in women's writing. Out of the petitions to Parliament grew a subgenre: "the parliament of women," a phrase, in fact, used by the duke of Lenox when confronted by four hundred women coming to the House of Lords in January 1642: "Away with these women, wee were best to have a parliament of Women."[6] The phrase, of course, goes back to Aristophanes' *Ecclesiazusae*. The seventeenth-century parliaments imitate Aristophanes' play only in the concept of the chaos that accompanies women in charge of government and in the ample use of bawdry.[7] The appearance of the subgenre roughly coincides with the petitioners' activity, and so many parliaments of women or ladies were written that to review all of them would take this study beyond its scope; instead we will glance at the first and the last for a sense of their spirit and range.

The earliest *Parliament of Women* (1640) appeared before the petitions and is not very impressive, but it is lively satire with interesting implications. It is set in ancient Rome, and it motivates the parliament by having a son who has attended the Senate with his father taunt his curious mother by telling her that the Senate was debating whether men should be allowed two wives. The mother instantly gathers a group of women, highborn and tradeswomen, who spend their deliberations on grievances against their husbands, and the laws passed by the women are largely ribald slapstick: the work amounts to the wives' revenge. What the satire reveals, however, is a spirit of equality, beginning with a law that women may have two husbands, but moving to the details of the marriage relationship.

> . . . Why should wee toyle and turmoyle for our horne-headed, and hard-headed husbands, and not taste of the sweet as well as of the sower, of the gaine as the paine, the pleasure as the puzle. If the husbands be ours, their Cash and Coyne ours, and all their moveables (howsoever seldom in motion ours too) and at our command; then why should we be niggards, and not spend freely of our owne? or why, when they be prodigall abroad should we be penurious at home? nay, let us eate good fare, keepe good fires, want nothing that women would have, good cates after good company: we can then bed any God-speed without good gossips. It is fit we should bee merry, so it fall within compasse of meanes.[8]

The Parliament of Women published in 1684 is far more complex, subtle, and allusive. The setting is not remote ancient Rome, but contemporary England: just determining the site of the parliament alludes to the Gunpowder Plot, for example.[9] The participants adopt male attire, which they have stolen while their husbands slept off a night's drinking. Whatever satiric intent about women *The Parliament* may have, it also refers specifically to their oppression. As Penthesilea, the speaker of the Upper House, says, "You all know how we have suffered for a long time under the Oppression of men, who have all this while taken upon them to govern the Business of the World, in their Councils, Assemblies and Cabals while we ti'd to our Distaffs, and our Needles, have slothfully deserted our own Cause. . . . We have no share in the Government of the Common-wealth, that Men only make use of us, as we make use of our Bed-pans and Close-stools" (pp. 5–6).

262

In keeping with its double purpose of satirizing women while defining their predicament, *The Parliament* represents a speaker making serious political and social observations while being interrupted by members of the assembly who have personal grievances against their husbands or who wish to exchange recipes for pudding. Speakers or details of the setting constantly allude to famous moments of women's aggression, not always positive ones: the mace is a truncheon used by the Bacchae and adorned with vine leaves, for example. The discourse abounds with stories of women's violence against men, but also looks to equality, both parodic and serious:

> . . . We have little reason to be so serv'd; for by the Confession of men themselves we are their Equals. And if they confess us to be their Equals, you may be certain there's more in it then we are at present aware of; they look upon Women as a Company of easie Souls, soon contented, and therefore allow us to be their Equals; to keep us from prying Farther into the knowledge of that superioritie, which they are too guilty sensible to be our due, therefore I say again, there must be something in this condescension of theirs; the Cat did not winck for nothing: for which reason I humbly move that the Ancient Records may be searched in the Raigns of. *Penthesilea, Semiramis, Boadicea,* etc to the end we may no longer be kept in the Dark, but may be able to assert our Right by way of claim. (Pp. 42–43)

The Parliament is well aware of the impact of education upon women: it contains an amusing account of a pornographic curriculum offered girls in a boarding school, including works in Latin "beyond her Spheare too" (p. 31). One woman claims to have lost her virginity just from hearing Aretino read aloud! Indeed, the best speakers spend their time reading history instead of sewing. As in so much of the controversial writing about women, the edge cuts both ways: reading may be said to corrupt or liberate, depending on how the reader values women, but the text never finally rests on a single perspective. Still, by making one parodic point after another about reasons why women should rule instead of men, it cleverly ridicules the arguments justifying male domination, such as physical superiority, the ways of nature, or examples of conquest.

Two of the longest and most interesting arguments reveal the extent to which the author of *The Parliament* understands the predicament of women, even if he or she will not take a stand on the question; both have to do with women as property. The first is a debate about whether prostitutes should be allowed to join the parliament, and one speaker argues to include them because they are indistinguishable from aristocratic ladies, who must also sell their bodies and become the property of the male (p. 120). The second is an allied idea: cuckoldry, one speaker avers, depends on the male's understanding that his wife is his property (p. 126). The satiric tone and technique should not conceal the acuity of the observations about women's condition. The rhetoric of *The Parliament* is a means of undoing its ideological implications.

Once the crisis in English society ended, women's part in public life was, as usual, severely diminished; and as we have observed, the major demonstrations were led by a minority of radical sectarians, who sought not political office but influence over the institutions of the Commonwealth. After the Restoration, which brought an end to radical activity, women's political voice is that of the conservative women writers who not only support the Stuart monarchy but also, with a few exceptions, resist the changes occurring in their time.

That women's political writing has been neglected is obvious, and my purpose here is not only to outline the contributions women made to the vast corpus of political poetry written in the seventeenth century but also to define their distinctive approach to political issues, both as a group and as individuals. Both the heirs of Orinda and of Astrea share with modern audiences the assumption that "politics is not the Business of a Woman."[10] Although this statement was no more accurate then than it is now, the stereotype was carefully guarded then as now. Indeed, the stereotype flourished even during the brilliant reign of Elizabeth I and continued during the less brilliant days of Good Queen Anne. Nonetheless, just as Elizabeth's rule held off the development of patriarchal political theory for a generation in England, so Anne's rule was inspirational to many of the women writers of her time. Although the presence of a woman on the throne may have far more complex effects upon her society than feminist historians and critics have assumed in the past, those effects should nevertheless be reckoned carefully.

Orinda and Daughters:
Chudleigh, Egerton, Winchilsea, Rowe, Aubin,
Barker, Masters, Barber

Orinda and her daughters assume that they are writing for a coterie with values much like their own, instead of a popular audience. Therefore, these writers use poetry to guide the reader in thinking and feeling about public events, rather than taking up one cause or party against another. Because Philips and her followers usually wrote for a coterie audience, they did not use the rhetoric appropriate for political verse in London at the moment when they wrote, as did Behn: they use instead a verse of personal reaction to events of state. They also use rather simple poems of iambic pentameter couplets, and only occasionally the more highly formal genres, such as Pindarics. Frequently they seek to disarm rather than impress the reader; but they are seriously engaged with political themes. They may use undoing, but, as with the privilege of writing, they use it to balance their intrusion into public life.

Orinda and her followers tend to follow class lines in their political orientation, with exceptions, Royalist before the Restoration and Tory afterward. Because they are not part of the city, journalistic, and theatrical worlds, they are exempt from the pressures of imprisonment or suppression that plagued Behn, Manley, or Centlivre. Yet they gradually exhibit the same skepticism about authority that we see in the Behn tradition, and in Mary Astell this skepticism became a genuine conservative critique of Puritan thought. Although Queen Anne was generally spared criticism by Manley and Centlivre, to have a woman on the throne seems to have been a genuine inspiration not only to Astell but to Chudleigh, Egerton, and Rowe. For the most part, Orinda's progeny do not write plays, although Philips herself and Winchelsea are exceptions. And Philips's translation of Corneille's *Pompey* may have been an attempt to appeal to Charles II's French tastes.[11]

Katherine Philips's volume of *Poems* (1664) begins with a series of political poems, about which she used her familiar rhetorical strategy of undoing. The first poem concerns the execution and slandering ("double murther") of Charles I and is written to answer "a Libellous Copy of Rimes by Vavasor Powell." Orinda begins the poem by explaining that she thinks "not of the State," but that Charles' memory is "a cause / That will excuse the breach in Nature's laws," that is, presumably, a woman's writing about politics. Thus her concern for Charles is more personal than a matter of state and so urgent as to be excusable. The theme of the execution and execration of Charles as unnatural actions runs throughout the poem, as does the doubleness of Charles's misery (unfaithful friends and ignoble enemies) and of the Puritan actions: "Slander must follow Treason." Philips ends the poem with a critique of the Christianity of the Commonwealth saints:

> *Christ will be King,* but I ne're understood
> His Subjects built his Kingdom up with blood,
> Except their own; or that he would dispense
> With his commands, though for his own defence.
> Oh! to what height of horrour are they come
> Who dare pull down a crown, tear up a Tomb![12]

In the poems that follow, which celebrate the Restoration, Philips frequently uses biblical analogies, usually from the Old Testament, analogies that formed a verbal battleground for Puritan and Royalist. Thus in the poem "On the numerous Access of the *English* to wait upon the King in Flanders," she seeks to mystify Charles's presence by asserting that where he is, England is, and that as long as he stays in Belgium, England will be emptied of people. When he comes to England, he will heal her woes:

> For *England* (though grown old with woes) will see
> Her long deny'd and Sovereign Remedy.
> So when old *Jacob* could but credit give
> That his prodigious *Joseph* still did live,
> (*Joseph* that was preserved to restore
> Their lives that would have taken his before)
> *It is enough,* (said he) *To Egypt I*
> *Will go, and see him once before I die.*
>
> (p. 2)

"Arion on a Dolphin" represents Charles as Defender of the Faith, who will rise above punishing those "who did themselves and him oppose" (p. 4). Indeed, Charles is the great Protestant monarch, who will lead the world, as Sheba's queen resorted to Judah's court:

> Discovered *Rome* will hate your Crown,
> But she shall tremble at your Frown.
> For *England* shall (rul'd and restor'd by You)
> The suppliant world protect, or else subdue.
>
> (p. 5)

In still another poem Philips likens the fair weather at the coronation to the parting of the Red Sea for the Hebrews' crossing (p. 5).

Although she began this series of poems with a denial of her political interests, Philips continues political themes in celebrating the arrival of Catherine of Braganza to marry Charles II. She comments on how the marriage will change the balance of power in Europe and ends, like Shakespeare's Henry V courting Katherine, with a vision of their son subduing England's enemies. Unhappily the vision was unfulfilled in both cases:

> And till they give him leisure to subdue,
> His enemies must owe their Peace to you.

266

Whilst he and you mixing illustrious Rays,
As much above our wishes as our praise,
Such Hero's shall produce, as even they
Without regret or blushes shall obey.

(p. 7)

Orinda's constant vision of Charles is an aggressive ruler who will dominate not only his own kingdom, but all of Europe.

When we observe Orinda using undoing to balance her assertive stances in political poetry, we should remember that her royalist sympathies and joy at the Restoration were at variance from the sentiments of her husband and his family. In fact, James Philips enjoyed political favor and prosperity during the Commonwealth and therefore had to retire from public life after the Restoration. The complexities of the Philips's private and public relationships and opinions reveal, as few things could, the radical disruptions of authority and settled patterns of behavior during the civil war. In fact, one of Orinda's most moving civil war poems seems to have been written after Charles's defeat at Worcester in 1651 and then doubtless suppressed. The title is simply "On the 3. of September, 1651." The poem sees the passing of English royalty, mustering all its strength and support in one last supreme effort, only to take all the heroes with it: "Their weight sinks others." The world is collapsing, and so the poet distrusts all worldly vanities, calling for qualities that survive a time of total uncertainty: "Oh give me Vertue then, which sums up all, / And firmly stands when Crowns and Scepters fall" (p. 14).

After the Restoration, however, Orinda's *Letters to Poliarchus* are full of cheerful, practical interest in Welsh politics and in pursuing her husband's interests through the Court of Claims in Ireland. Both James and Katherine Philips had urged Poliachus (Sir Charles Cotterell) to run for office as burgess of Cardigan and its parliamentary seat. Her letters are frequently about this campaign, for Cotterell was unexpectedly opposed by Sir Francis Lloyd, and Cotterell won the seat only by taking the election to a committee.[13] Orinda's letters to Poliarchus also reveal her fascination with the court cases she listened to while waiting to press her husband's claims.

Lady Mary Chudleigh is an example of the meaning that Queen Anne's reign had for women writers. Although she was retiring, Chudleigh, we recall, shared with Mary Astell very strong convictions about improving women's lot in marriage and how they conducted their lives in order to have better control over them. Chudleigh's combination of rage and caution led her to look for a protector, one she found in Queen Anne, to whom she dedicated *Poems on Several Occasions* (1703). We note the characteristic undoing of the gesture: "The Address has too much Confidence; the Ambition is too aspiring; But to whom should a Woman unknown to the World, and who has not Merit enough to defend her from the Censure of Criticks, fly for Protection, but to Your Majesty? The Greatest, the Best, and the most Illustrious Person of Your Sex and Age."[14]

In her later work, *Essays upon Several Subjects in Prose and Verse* (1710), where Chudleigh's whole purpose is to persuade women to improve control of their lives through knowledge and command of their passions, Queen Anne is an important example for both women's capacity for learning and the ability to control anger. Chudleigh's argument about women's learning follows the practice of the defenses of women in accumulating many illustrious examples, and among the learned queens, Anne is the living instance.[15] Later in the work, one of the most interesting essays is "Of Anger," which Chudleigh sees as an emotion particularly harmful to, and prevalent in, women because it comes from powerlessness. There Queen Anne is the only female example – among many males – of the capacity to control rage. (pp. 132–33) For Chudleigh, as for other women writers, Anne had as much significance in sexual politics as in matters of state.

Sarah Fyge Field Egerton is more fierce than Chudleigh in her poem addressed to Queen Anne on the occasion of the war with France, a theme that allows her to combine anti-French sentiments with ardent feminism:

> Revenge on your proud Foes, their *Salick* Law,
> With your fair Hand, their boasted Greatness awe.
> Why are we barr'd, or why I Woman made,
> Whose Sex forbids to Fight, and to Invade,
> Or give my Queen, more than my Wish for Aid?
> I shall not tremble, at the Launce, or Sword.
> Will strait turn Amazon, but speak the Word;
> Scarce can I curb, my eager loyal Soul,
> For you I'd fight, Mankind from Pole to Pole,
> Till al the Kingdoms, in one Empire meet,
> Then lay the Gown at your Imperial Feet.[16]

Although Egerton wrote a few poems of state, such as her *Ode on the Death of King William,* her remarkable verse is devoted to feminist sexual politics and a pastoral critique of society.

Anne Finch, the countess of Winchilsea, followed a Renaissance aristocratic political code into the eighteenth century. She believed in hereditary privilege that exacted civic service. Profoundly loyal to the Stuarts, she envisioned a heaven in which an apotheosis of Charles I would take place: "With Christs there Charles's Crown shall meet / Which Martirdom adorns."[17] In addition, she saw herself as virtually alone in composing an elegy for James II: "Which does an abler Writer ask / But abler Writers will the Work refuse." Winchilsea praised James's military career "for keeping England then, superior to the Dutch," his provident ways, "which kept the Treasury full yett not the subject bare," and finally his personal conduct of the kingship:

> You who subordinate in Publick Cares
> For his Inspection modell'd the Affaires
> Remember still how easy Your Accesse
> No Pleasures kept him from your sight
> No late Debauch, no Revel of the Night
> No distant slothfull Seat e're serv'd as a Recesse
> Open to all but when the Seaman came
> Known by his Face and greeted by his Name.[18]

The end of the elegy follows the convention of broadening the canvas beyond the deceased into a plea for a legitimate dynasty and Britain's internal peace: "may Rightfull Kings procure Thee lasting Peace."

As the reader may conclude from the elegy for James, Winchilsea was deeply concerned about public officials' responsiveness to those they governed. A most unusual poem in the Wellesley Manuscript illustrates this interest. The poem describes an incident in which a woman becomes the advocate for her friend to a lord who pretends to be too busy and important to deal with her. The narrator resolves to pursue the cause despite the rebuff. The poem is written in crude couplets, but is full of dramatic interest, partly for its sexual politics—the suitor is a flighty woman the lord would send to his wife—and partly for its searing portrait of the oppressive lord, especially from a poet of conservative political values. The suitor sums up her judgment of the lord:

> . . . with a Roman virtue scorn
> The Land depraved where I was born
> Where men new wealthy grown and great
> En bagatell our sufferings treat
> Yet still I will your cause pursue
> Th' unrighteous Judge the harden'd Jew
> As soon might be at rest as I
> Will leave them till they all comply
> Or if no good from thence I draw
> They are still Jews without the Law.
>
> (p. 79)

Winchilsea was no friend of rebellion, which she compared to a hurricane (pp. 252–62), and she believed the established order preserves each kind from oppression (pp. 177–78). Like Ben Jonson she placed her political faith in royal prerogative and the ancient privilege of landed aristocrats, as she expressed most clearly in her elegy "Upon the Death of Sir William Twisden." In the venerable mode of the pastoral elegy, Winchilsea laments for all of Kent "that Twisden is no more, their Matchlesse Patriot's dead." The poem celebrates Twisden as the perfect example of a statesman:

> He, whose lov'd Country was his cheifest care,
> Might find her very Archives there,
> Her ancient Stattutes, in their first design,
> Prerogative, and Priviledge to joyn,
> The perfect draught of all-preserving Law.
> . . . .
> Well did we in our far applauded Kent,
> Whilst Pious, Wise, Heroick, and refin'd,
> Whilst those strong Rayes, of our old Vertue shin'd,
> Make him our choice, the Whole to represent;
> The worthyest pattern of a Publick Mind.
>
> (P. 63)

Winchilsea goes on to mystify Twisden's good breeding and education: "With Him, we the Traditions loose, / Of great, and of Illustrious Men, / Which his Discourse, reviv'd to us again." In a final tribute, Winchilsea equates Twisden to the most famous Renaissance Kentish courtier-statesman, Sir Philip Sidney, a gesture that not only praises Twisden but also evokes the tradition dearest to Winchilsea, all the values Sidney had come to symbolize, whether he actually possessed them or not.

> No lesse Applause, no lesse exalted Verse,
> Then once adorn'd our boasted Sydney's Hearse,
> Shou'd to his Character, do equal right;
> Shou'd of this second Astrophel endite,
> "As much the Poet's Friend, as much the World's delight."
>
> (P. 67)

In still another genre, a country-house poem, Winchilsea symbolizes England's greatness as a country and race through exalting Longleat, the

270

seat of the Thynne's, viscounts of Weymouth, who were friends and patrons of Rowe as well. "To the Honorable the Lady Worsley at Longleate" is written in the tradition of the country-house poems of Jonson and Marvell.[19] The poem modulates its focus through beginning with an implicit contrast between the poet's humble retreat, "fitt only for the Wretch opress'd by Fate," and the grandeur of Longleat:

> The real splendours of our fam'd Long-leate
> Which above Metaphor itts Structure reares
> Tho all Enchantment to our sight appears
> Magnificantly Great the Eye to fill
> Minutly finish'd for our nices[t] skill
> Long-leate that justly has all Praise engross'd
> The strangers wonder and our Nations boast.
>
> (P. 53)

As the poem moves from a description of Italianate fountains to carefully trimmed terraces and then to the prospect of the whole estate, Winchilsea develops her opening assertion that the beauty of the house and grounds defies description. Then, in its second movement, when the poem continues to celebrate the family who live at Longleate, the poet reverts to English country values: these are people "Who from abroad shall no Examples need / Of men Recorded or who them Exceed / To urdge their Virtue or exalt their Fame" (p. 54). In fact, the end of the poem compares Longleat to prelapsarian Eden, evoking through the Golden Age a statement about English aristocrats as morally comparable to Adam and Eve; the poem moves to this hyperbolic comparison so easily that one finds it not the least grandiose because it concentrates on the setting as a compliment to the people:

> So Paradice did wond'rous Things disclose
> Yett surely not from them itts Name arose
> Not from the Fruits in such Profusion found
> Or early Beauties of th'enammell'd Ground
> Not from the Trees in their first leaves arraid
> Or Birds uncurs'd that Warbl'd in their Shade
> Not from the streams that in new channells rol'd
> O're radiant Beds of uncorrupting Gold
> These might surprise but 'twas th'accomplish'd Pair
> That gave the Title and that made itt fair.

All lesser Thoughts Immagination Balk
"Twas Paradice in some expanded Walk
To see Her motions, and attend his Talk.

(P. 55)

The poem is the pastoral art at its most deliberately political, where no overt public theme is articulated, but political values are embedded in the celebration of the place and its inhabitants through codes used for public commentary since antiquity. So gracefully submerged in the description of house, grounds, and paradise is the assertion about Winchilsea's aristocratic models that the political ideology all but disappears.[20]

Although Winchilsea held with antique traditional values, her political vision was always practical too, as we see in her poem about the pompous lord or her tributes to James II's sobriety, frugality, and accessibility. The extent of her practicality is nowhere better demonstrated, however, than in the last poem in the Wellesley Manuscript. There "A Contemplation" represents her fantasy of a heaven in which political retribution takes place, as with Charles's apotheosis. Both Winchilsea's husband and her best friend, Lady Tufton, are benefactors of her vision, which seems both personal and political:

The Lord to whom my life is joyn'd
For Conscience here oppres't
Shall there full retribution find

There Coventry of Tufton's Line
For piety renown'd
Shall in transcending Virtues shine
And equally be Crown'd.

(P. 145)

She imagines, moreover, a fate for monuments to past and present state corruption and profiteering—Hampton Court and Blenheim:

And Mammon wert thou well employ'd
What Measures might be wonne
Whilst Woolsey's Pallace leyes destroy'd
And Marlborough's is not done.

(P. 145)

The range of Winchilsea's political commentary is quite remarkable, though the most audacious, later poems remained unpublished in the Wellesley Manuscript.

Although Winchilsea and Elizabeth Singer Rowe were literary friends, as we see from a poem addressed to Philomela in the Wellesley Manuscript, their politics were very different and may have kept them distant personally. Whereas Winchilsea was loyal to the Stuarts, Rowe was full of praise for William and Mary, especially for William's anti-Catholic policies toward Louis XIV of France and his allies. What William saw as a policy preserving the Low Countries and opposing any single domination of Europe, Rowe saw as a holy war. The Jacobite war against William, however, she thought should end at once. Rowe's religious values naturally were part of her politics, but they did not make her pacifist; they encouraged religious analogies in her political poetry and determined the cause she deemed just.

At the center of Rowe's anonymous volume of poetry, *Poems on Several Occasions Written by Philomela,* is a series of political poems, largely Pindarics, which were written for the *Athenian Mercury,* published weekly by John Dunton from 1689 to 1696, as we remember from chapter 2. Rowe's poems depend on biblical analogies and a fictional dialogue between the Athenians, her readers, and a heroic female poet, a kind of literary Joan of Arc. The first poem, "A Pindaric Poem on Habakkuk," announces the theme of the group; it refers to Jehovah's coming from Teman in answer to Habakkuk's prayer and putting the Ethiops and the Midems in confusion with floods and earthquakes to stop their fighting (Hab. 1–3). The poem calls upon God to repeat that action with William's enemies: "So now, great God, wrapt in avenging Thunder, / Meet thine and William's Foes, and tread them groveling under."[21] The religious differences that accompanied the Jacobite conflicts with William III allowed Rowe to dress political conflicts in the religious terms that were profoundly meaningful to her. The next poem, "The Athenians to the Compiler of the Pindarick Now Recited," represents the ideal choric reaction to the poet's theme, which is a holy war, waged by William and his allies against Roman Catholic Europe:

> Begin, begin, thy *Noble Choice,*
> *Great William* claims the *Lyre,* and claims thy *Voice,*
> All like *himself* the *Hero* shew,
> Which *none* but *thou* canst do.
>
> (P. 23)

The poem exalts the poet as a religious and political prophet with a tradition descending from Orinda:

273

Thus Sing, *Bright Maid*! thus and yet *louder*
  Sing,
Thy *God* and *King*!
Cherish that Noble *Flame* which warms thy *Breast*,
And be by *future* Worlds *admir'd* and *bless'd*:
The *present Ages* short-liv'd *Glories* scorn,
And into *wide Eternity* be born!
There Chast *Orinda's* Soul shall meet with *thine*,
  More *Noble*, more *Divine*;
And in the *Heaven of Poetry* for ever shine:
  There all the *glorious few*,
  To *Loyalty* and *Virtue* true,
    Like *her* and *you*.

(P. 25)

In the next poem, "A Poetical Question concerning the Jacobites, sent to the Athenians," Rowe again excoriates James's supporters as "ungrateful Vipers" while exalting William, "A Prince as Great, and wonderous Good, as e're / The sacred Burden of a Crown did wear" (p. 27). The special configuration of English politics in the last years of the seventeenth century, with conflicts that were both political and religious, allowed Rowe to transform her piety into political zeal.

A few years later, in 1707, Penelope Aubin was idealizing "The Stuarts" in the same hyperbolic manner. In 1708 her Pindaric "The Ecstasy," presented to Queen Anne, celebrated England's victory over France, and "The Welcome" marked Marlborough's triumphant return to England.[22] Jane Barker was also a Jacobite, but her political work, "A Collection of Poems Referring to the Times," remains in manuscript unavailable to me at this writing.[23] Several decades later Mary Masters expressed similar themes about the Hanoverians. In "Upon his late Majesty's going to Sea, in June 1724," Masters portrays the alliance of Britain and Prussia as waging a holy war against the Catholic nations of Europe. A succeeding poem exhorts a fellow poet, moreover, to leave love poetry and celebrate the coronation of George II.[24]

Of all the poets in the Orinda tradition, none wrote such interesting political verse as Mary Barber, largely because she was commenting on the Irish scene and had a general sympathy with the oppressed. Constantia Grierson accurately described her friends' nature:

Her tender Care, and Grief for the Distrest;
Her Joy unfeign'd, to see true Merit blest;

274

Her Soul so form'd for every social Care;
A Friend so gen'rous, ardent, and sincere.[25]

Barber cared deeply about Ireland and publicly castigated England's oppression. In fact, she says, conditions in Ireland were so bad the sun was ashamed to shine there:

> There he sometimes shines;
> But oft'ner hides his Head, and pines
> On happier Climes to look, not see
> Such dismail Scenes of Poverty
> Nor seen an Isle, by Nature Bless'd,
> By ill-judg'd Policy oppress'd;
> Her Trade usurp'd by foreign Lands,
> Whilst Albion fast ties up her Hands:
> Nor sees her Sons in Science skill'd,
> And yet her Posts by Strangers fill'd.
> (Pp. 196–97)

To balance this condemnation of policies and the conditions they created, Barber was eloquent in her praise of Carteret and Swift for their attempts to relieve Ireland, and she wrote many occasional poems celebrating the noble families of Ireland and the virtue of her many friends: "For, O Hibernia, when I quit thy Coast, / Such friends I leave, as few could ever boast" (p. 263). It was clearly the English, not the Irish, that were responsible for the condition of Ireland. In a poem about an officer's widow deprived of her husband's pension, Barber therefore calls on Britain to change its ways before it is too late:

> *Britain*, for this impending Ruin dread;
> Their Woes call loud for Vengeance on thy Head:
> Nor wonder if Disasters wait your Fleets;
> Nor wonder at *Complaining in your Streets*:
> Be timely wise; arrest th' uplifted Hand,
> Ere Pestilence or Famine sweep the Land.
> (P. 240)

Because of her sensitivity to social conditions surrounding her, Barber suffered occasional attacks of conscience about devoting time to poetry instead of helping those in misery. She wrote to Lady Torrington:

Endless Anxiety I find,
Hath dire Effects upon the Mind:
A Life of unsuccessful Care
Too often sinks us to Dispair.
From such a Life as this, I chuse
To snatch some Moments for the Muse;
To slight Mortality, and soar
To Worlds where Anguish is no more;
Forget *Irene's* wretched State,
Tho' doomed to share her cruel Fate;
Destin'd to pass my joyless Days,
Where Poverty, relentless, preys;
And form'd, unhappily, to grieve
For Miseries I can't relieve.

(P. 33)

The poem ends with Barber's consolation that even if she does not have wealth to share with others, she can occasionally "help a Wretch by what I write." Barber wrote three kinds of poetry for helping others. First, there are numerous poems that celebrate others' acts of social conscience and generosity. These usually had a double function: they publicized both the deed and the doer as examples for others. She wrote "To Lady Elizabeth Germain":

Thrice happy Fair! indulgent Heav'n
To thee was doubly kind:
To others only *Hearts* are giv'n:
Thy *Fortune* suits thy Mind.

(Pp. 118–19)

Second, Barber wrote a good deal of socially conscious satire, such as, for example, "An Unanswerable Apology for the Rich," in which she describes the conspicuous consumption of the rich, who never give to charity, even as they grow richer: "Would Heav'n but send ten thousand more, / He'd give—just as he did before" (p. 17). Third, Barber used occasions for direct commentary on political policy, such as the poems about Irish conditions quoted above. Another interesting example is an antislavery poem, "On seeing the *Captives,* lately redeem'd from Barbary by his Majesty," in which she says,

276

> Now, Slavery! no more thy rigid Hand
> Shall drag the Trader to thy fatal Strand:
> No more in Iron Bonds the Wretched groan;
> Secur'd, Britannia, by thy Guardian Throne.
>
> (P. 281)

Penelope Aubin's *Charlotta du Pont* (1723) declares, "The selling of human Creatures is a Crime my Soul abhors; and wealth so got ne'er thrives."[26] The occasional earlier protests against slavery were to be echoed by some of the Bluestockings at the end of the eighteenth century before the crescendo of outrage in the nineteenth century. Women may be proud of their long record of abhorrence at slavery and will doubtless find other sources of pride as we learn more about what we have been, and done, and written.

Behn and Daughters: Manley, Centlivre, Haywood, Trotter, Davys

Aphra Behn and her followers used the familiar genres and discourses of their time to write about politics for a general audience. They used Pindarics to impress the reader, or plays and scandal novels to reach as wide an audience as possible. Because they wrote for money and lived in the city, Behn and Manley were vulnerable if they opposed authority, and both were imprisoned for political crimes. Centlivre also took considerable risk in an early dedication to the man who became George I. The jeopardy in which they lived makes their record of loyalty even more impressive than it otherwise would be.

One of the clearest notes sounded in the political writing of Aphra Behn, Mary Manley, and Susanna Centlivre is recorded in the following quotation.

> Long may [Astrea] scourge this mad rebellious age,
> And stem the torrent of fanatic rage,
> That once had almost overwhelmed the stage.
>
> . . . .
>
> But while that spurious race played their parts
> To alienate their Prince's subjects' hearts,
> Her loyal muse still tuned her loudest strings,
> To sing the praises of the best of kings.[27]

Whatever their political stripes—Whig or Tory—Behn and her heirs who wrote serious political poetry tended to remain firmly loyal to original commitments, whatever changes occur in the possession of power. Their record of loyalty is quite striking in a time of tremendous governmental instability and a time when famous male writers altered their political views substantially.

Aphra Behn's political poetry is a record of loyalty: she believed that the Stuarts were the rightful rulers of England, that only they could unite the divided people, and that their enemies were her enemies. Yet she did not extract from herself changing commitments as the Stuarts changed. She did not, like Dryden, change her faith, nor did she admire any change of allegiance. Neither did she alter her loyalties after the exile of James II, the arrival of Mary, or the advent of William. She tried to get patronage for her support and eloquence, but need did not change her convictions.

Behn wrote about politics in fiction, plays, and poetry, but first in plays. Behn was like all conservatives in seeing a better time in the past: the prologue to *The Young King* (1679), a play that represents transvestite adventures, alludes to a fight between Jack Churchill, later the duke of Marlborough, and Orange Betty at the Duke's Theater. This incident Behn makes into a symbol of the degenerate state of men in her time. The prologue ends with a tribute to the king, who is forced to keep the peace because of the sorry state of his troops: "This is the Fruit of Idleness and Ease; / Heaven bless the King that keeps the Land in Peace, / Or he'll be sweetly served by such as these."[28] In view of Marlborough's later achievements, the prologue is deeply ironic. Behn had no hesitation in dedicating *The Rover, Part II* (1681) to the duke of York at a time when he was not at all popular. For her he was "gracious Off-spring of this Royal Martyr," and she somewhat fulsomely celebrates his devotion to his country: "How careless since Your Glorious Restauration You have been, of your Life for the Service of Your mistaken Country, the whole World knows, and all brave men admire" (1:114). Behn certainly deserved York's patronage, which she enjoyed at this time, but she never altered her course for advantage.

In prologues to *The Rover, Part II* and her next play, *The False Count*, Behn begins an analogy that she would extend in *The Roundheads* (1681): a comparison of the Whigs to the defeated Puritans of the Commonwealth. "Poets," she says,

> have caught to the disease o' the age
> That pest, of not being quiet when they're well,
> That restless fever, in the brethren, Zeal;
> In public spirits call'd, good o' th' Commonweal.
>
> (1:115)

The epilogue accuses her fellow poets of disloyalty to Charles, who may go begging like them because Parliament was holding the Royal Subsidy until the Exclusion Bill passed. In the prologue to *The False Count* Behn pretends she has converted to Whiggery, and she portrays the Whigs as keeping up the Civil war and threatening the monarch. She liked the analogy because it implied their ultimate defeat: "Ye furious Guelphs and Gibelines of Wit, / Who for the cause, and crimes of Forty-One / So furiously maintain the quarrel on" (3:99). The identification of the Whigs with the good old cause implies not just political disagreement but betrayal of the king, as well as their eventual defeat. *The Roundheads* continues the identification throughout the entire play, as the events of 1659–60 after Cromwell's death are made satiric analogues to the Whigs. The play is a crude combination of political lampoon and love intrigue, which pull apart from one another: the two sides of Lady Lambert's character – the ambitious political wife and the heroine of the love intrigue – do not cohere. The play's success, however, suggests that it served its political purpose.

The City Heiress (1682) also contains satire on the Whigs, but here political commentary is successfully blended with a love intrigue. Sir Timothy Treatall is the comic butt: his miserly Whig tendencies contrast nicely with his nephew's cavalier Tory ways. The contrast is broadly ideological – the mercantile interests competing with the gay, aristocratic posture of Wilding; and, of course, this particular conflict was one that Behn used throughout her drama, one that carried on the tradition of Middleton and Massinger. Shortly after this play, Behn's political activities resulted in her arrest. In August 1682 she had written an epilogue to *Romulus and Hersilla* that criticized Monmouth for desertion of the king, and Charles, acting on paternal sentiment, had Behn and the actress who spoke the lines arrested. She wrote no plays for four years.

Despite the arrest, she was not through with Monmouth. Two years later, having turned to fiction, Behn produced *Love-Letters Between a Nobleman and his Sister* (1684), which, in addition to being one of the formative works in amatory fiction described above, is also a roman à clef, referring to Lord Grey of Werk; his wife, who was Monmouth's mistress; Lady Henrietta, who was Grey's sister-in-law; and their tangled love affairs. Lord Grey used his wife's affair with Monmouth to justify his legally incestuous love affair with her sister, who had been secretly married to Grey's servant in order to prevent her father's claims on her. The father did bring a case to court, but Grey and Henrietta were never sentenced. At the beginning of the narrative, the love intrigue is framed by a description of the involvement of Monmouth and Grey in the Rye House Plot to assassinate the king. One of the conspirators was executed, but Monmouth and Grey survived. Angeline Goreau comments, "It was exactly the sort of story to appeal to Mrs.

Behn—romance, parental disobedience, defiance of social codes, political intrigue, incest, disguise, escape, betrayal."[29] The love intrigue is unusual for Behn in that Philander (Grey) is an unsympathetic rake. We gradually understand that Behn's portrait of him was more than simply her judgment of his abandonment of Sylvia, for Behn shows Sylvia coping with that behavior, even though she is corrupted by the abandonment. The political intrigue that frames the love story holds, I believe, the answer to the negative portrait of Philander. The final episodes of the political narrative at the end of Part 3 (1687) give an accurate picture of Monmouth's rebellion against James II and defeat at Sedgemoor. The exact part Grey had in the defeat is not clear, but he certainly turned state's informant to save his life, and Monmouth went to his death. It was the kind of betrayal Behn despised, whatever her initial attitudes toward Monmouth, and when she pictures Philander prospering at the court, in which he is warmly welcome, while all those whose lives he has corrupted are ruined, destroyed, or in orders, Behn's irony is clear. The real political events—and some private intrigues—make the romance a history, and the political and personal themes reinforce one another.

In her last years, Behn wrote a series of state poems on many of the most important political events of the age. Several of these, especially those about Charles, James, and Queen Catherine, contain the inflated rhetoric expected for such occasions: it is the rhetoric that represents the ideology associated with the Stuarts from 1603. Virtually every poet who wrote for the Stuarts—Jonson, Shakespeare, Donne—used the familiar pretenses that the Stuarts were gods who made the sun shine and the wind blow. It is not clear whether even the Stuarts themselves understood the effect of the topoi, but writing for them seems to have required such grandiose gestures, especially after the Restoration, with the problem of the succession and the need to deny the failures of the past. Behn's Pindarics on the death of Charles, to Queen Catherine, and on James's coronation, all compare their subjects to divinity. Charles is compared to Christ: "A Bleeding Victim to attone for all," Catherine to Mary, and James to God.[30] Yet through the inflated language, there is a firm thematic core, one that implicitly makes sense in the context: the continuity of rule and the consequent order of the kingdom. The poem about Charles's death dwells on the succession, surely the issue that preoccupied him at the end; the poet tells that the heavens assure the event:

> Officious Angels catch his dying Sighs,
> And bear 'em up in Triumph to the Skys,
> Each forms a Soul! of the Divinest dress!
> For the *New-born Kings,* and *Heroes* to possess.

280

> The last that from the sacred *Fabrick flew*,
> Made CHARLES a God! and JAMES a *Monarch* too.
>
> (P. 5)

Queen Catherine survives, Behn asserts, to give the society order and unity in a time of fear and plotting, probably an exaggeration, but the poem served to remind readers of the need for unity behind the royal family. The poem for James's coronation also emphasized the monarch's making peace with dissenters in his realm, good advice, if little heeded, and the loyalty of the aristocrats to the new ruler, surely more wish than expectation.

The history of political poetry is frequently the chronicle of poets' changing allegiances, and the Restoration is a particularly complex period for such changes; but for Aphra Behn, political and religious issues were a matter of personal commitment, as we see in her last political poems, which witness her commitments poignantly. In 1689, the year of her death, Behn wrote "A Congratulatory Poem to her Sacred Majesty Queen Mary upon her Arrival in England." Behn does not pretend that it is easy for her to accept her country's rejection of James II and so she cannot easily "bless Britain's faithless shore." She comes to accept Mary when she understands that Mary will unite the divided country behind the virtues of her father and the Stuart line – Mary is acceptable because she is a Stuart:

> The Murmuring World till now divided lay,
> Vainly debating whom they shou'd Obey,
> Till You Great Cesar's Off-spring blest our Isle,
> The differing Multitudes to Reconcile;
> Thus Stiff-neckt Isreal in defiance stood,
> Till they beheld the Prophet of their God.[31]

With this analogy Behn could accept the Glorious Revolution, but she was never persuaded, even by Bishop Burnet, to praise William III, as we have seen. In *A Pindaric Poem to the Reverend Doctor Burnet* (1689), she was restrained, she reminded Burnet, by the same loyalty that animated all her political writing and kept her from trimming to political winds:

> But Loyalty Commands with Pious Force,
> That stops me in the thriving Course,

The Brieze that wafts the Crowding Nations o're
Leaves me unpity'd far behind
On the Forsaken Barren shore.

. . . .

Thus while the Chosen Seed possess the Promis'd Land,
I like the Excluded Prophet stand,
The Fruitful Happy Soil can only see,
But am forbid by Fates Decree
To share the Triumph of the joyful Victory

(6:409)

Her personal integrity was identical with loyalty to the Stuarts, despite her poverty and neglect. In months she was dead.

In our time commentary on Behn's poetry and drama is beginning to appreciate how thoroughly political much of her work is. For example, Maureen Duffy reads many occasional verses that are not overtly political in their context to demonstrate connections to public life and intrigue.[32] Duffy's review of a 1984 production of *The Luckey Chance* also emphasizes its political implications.[33] George Guffy reads *Oroonoko* as a defense of the power of legitimate kings, which creates a parallel between Oroonoko and James II, England and Surinam.[34] Continued historical study of Behn's writing will doubtless reveal more ways in which it is implicated in the public life of her time.

Political writing was more central to Delariviere Manley's career than for any writer in this study. Others, including Behn, wrote about politics, but Manley was a professional political writer for about a decade (1705–14), and her importance in that arena would be acknowledged even if her other writing did not exist. She was as ardent a Tory as Behn, loyal by inheritance, "a perfect Bigot from a long untainted Descent of Loyal Ancestors and consequently immovable."[35] A comparison to Swift, with whom Manley collaborated, reveals her resistance to the temptations of preferment: he changed parties, but she remained a lifelong Tory. Manley wrote two kinds of political works: scandal novels and essays. The novels, which we have already read as amatory fiction, combined with her having been "ruined" at an early age to earn her a bad reputation, one that, as Gwendolyn Needham has shown, has quite eclipsed her work as a political writer.[36] I would add that her reputation as a political writer for the *Examiner* has simply been overwhelmed by Swift's canonical fame. Because much of this work is anonymous or of uncertain authorship, we have only a series of pamphlets on which to base Manley's reputation as a political writer. A full account of Manley's achievements may be found in Needham's study.

There is still plenty of interest in Manley's scandal novels, their impact on the political scene, and the trouble they created for her. They are *The Secret History of Queen Zarah and the Zarazians* (1705), *Secret Memoirs and Manners of Several Persons of Quality, of Both Sexes. From the New Atalantis* (1709); and *Memoirs of Europe Towards the Close of the Eighth Century* (1710). *Queen Zarah* was published as campaign literature during the parliamentary elections of 1705 and reissued in 1711 when the Tories were campaigning against Marlborough. To understand the success of Manley's rhetorical strategies, we should recall her predicament as a Tory defender of the Stuarts during the reign of Queen Anne, the last of the Stuarts; that is, criticizing the Whigs without being critical of the queen. This circumstance was further complicated by Marlborough's being a military hero. Manley threads her way through these complexities by making Sarah Churchill, duchess of Marlborough, the villain, an evil influence over the pious young queen, "the best Woman in the World," and by praising Hippolito's military service while depicting him as seduced into marriage by Zarah at sixteen. Zarah is in complete control of the government: "The Government of the Kingdom was in a Manner in her Hands, and whoever expected Favours or Rewards, must apply themselves to Zarah, by whom all was granted, as the Pipe that convey's the Royal Bounty to the Subject, past Ages have furnish'd us with Examples of this Nature, Posterity may see the like, but not to equal this; for it may be said, without Exaggerating upon the subject too much, Albania [the queen] took the Crown from her own Head to put it upon Zarah's."[37]

Zarah, with the help of Volpone, uses constant graft to influence elections and is the chief pro-Whig influence on the queen. Manley's portrait of Zarah is a skillful mixture of factual description and fictional vilification; and though it was deemed effective enough to be revived, it did not work in 1705, for the Whigs were elected. Zarah was, however, the name the public identified with the Duchess of Marlborough, and the book went through five editions between 1708 and 1712.

Manley's *New Atalantis* was even more successful, as a book and as a political weapon. As one may recall from chapter 4, *Atalantis* is a general commentary on English society with an allegorical frame involving Astrea, Virtue, and Intelligence, who tour Angila and its capitol New Atalantis. Here again Manley attacks the Marlboroughs and Goldolphin, retelling scandals of the reigns up to 1709, including exposure of the Whig intrigues since 1705. She extols Harley and Mrs. Masham as the new saviors of the country. *Atalantis* had considerably more impact than *Zarah*:

There is no doubt about the political effectiveness of the *New Atalantis*. Its help in undermining public confidence in the Whigs came at the psychologically right time for the Tories, who were striving to overthrow the ministry. Their goal was achieved in August 1710, when

Goldolphin was dismissed and Harley assumed leadership. Though discounting truth in the writings of a woman of "no character," G. M. Trevelyan has found that the most harmful publication to the ministry in 1709 was the *New Atalantis*.[38]

Needham goes on to remark that proof of the harm done the Whigs' cause by the book was their immediate prosecution of the publisher, printer, and supposed author of the second volume. As soon as Manley admitted authorship, the printer and publisher were spared. For what happened next, we are dependent on her *Adventures of Rivella*, hardly an unbiased source. The government, as always, wondered about her sources; she portrays herself as using escape wit worthy of Falstaff in saying she wrote by inspiration: "she said then it must be by *Inspiration*, because knowing her own Innocence she could account for it no other way."[39] The charges were finally dismissed in 1710. Suffering imprisonment and standing up to authorities should not be trivialized, however proud Manley was of her wit; we know how Defoe was punished. Both a letter to Harley and Swift's journal testify to Manley's hardships in the incident.

Whatever she endured, Manley quickly produced a sequel, *Memoirs of Europe*, a copy of which she presented to Harley, possibly in hope of reward; and another volume of *Memoirs* followed within a year. Although *Memoirs* has less immediate appeal to the modern reader, who may lack detailed knowledge of the contemporary scene, Manley's own audience might easily have found it exciting for her detailed knowledge of political intrigue.

> She reveals, for example, what went on in the inner councils of the Whig Junto concerning Sacheverell's famous trial. She correctly depicts Lord Somers as arguing against the trial and trying to restrain Wharton, Sunderland, and Goldolphin. She accurately describes the political furore over Mrs. Masham's rise as the Queen's favorite and the acrimonious spirit of the Duchess of Marlborough's final scenes with Mrs. Masham and with Anne. Mrs. Manley covers all highlights of the party conflict, such as the Greg affair which forced Harley's resignation, the question of Marlborough's being made Captain-General for life, and the army appointment of John Hill (Mrs. Masham's brother).[40]

The work served the Tories well; in one section Manley attacks both Lord Wharton and Richard Steele, who dismissed her as a frustrated lover, but they were reconciled toward the end of her life.[41]

Memoirs was the last scandal fiction Manley wrote because after the Tories came to power in 1710, she wrote essays and pamphlets exclusively. One of Manley's pamphlets that earned Swift's admiration was *A New Vindication of the Duke of Marlborough* (1711), in which she pretends to be a supporter of Marlborough, demonstrating that his record does not need the defense written by Dr. Hare in *Bouchain: or a Dialogue between the Medley and the Examiner.* As Manley shows that the Duke needs no vindication, she can emphasize his worst actions: "How seasonably did he decline King James's service, when the papists and dissenters were united in interests to destroy the church; King James, to whom the Duke of Marlborough was engaged by the highest gratitude."[42] The Whigs quickly replied to this clever pamphlet with *The Duke of M——h's Vindication. In Answer to a Pamphlet falsely so called* (1712). The campaign of which Manley's works were a significant part finally succeeded in driving England's hero and his duchess into exile in 1712.

Manley's last pamphlet was, appropriately, a defense of Queen Anne because the Whigs had shown undue excitement at a rumor of the queen's death. In *A Modest Inquiry into the Reasons of the Joy expressed by a Certain Sett of People, upon the Spreading of a Report of her Majesty's Death* (1714), Manley uses a dialogue about Anne between a foreign visitor and an Englishman. Why should people rejoice at her death? Was she a tyrant? The Englishman then has the opportunity to praise Anne, whom he compares to Elizabeth because Ann has preserved the Protestant succession. It was a comparison Anne herself made more than once. When the Tories fell at Anne's death a few months later, the Whig hegemony began, and Manley's political writing came to an end. Though she was not well rewarded financially for her political writing, Manley was proud of having served "her Country and the Antient Constitution."[43] But after the Tory fall, she quickly changed her theme, taking refuge in the stereotype about women and politics, quoted earlier, but doubtless she feared retaliation for her past work from the Whigs and she needed to sell books to survive.

Susanna Centlivre was as ardent and loyal a Whig as Manley and Behn were Tories, and she used epilogues and dedications, as well as a few poems, to express her views. The epilogue to *The Busy Body* (1709), represents her reservations about making peace in the War of the Spanish Succession:

> Some snivling Cits, would have a peace for spight,
> To starve those Warriours who so bravely fight.
> Still of a foe upon his Knees affraid;
> Whose well-bang'd Troops want Money, Heart, and Bread.[44]

Centlivre next had trouble with the Tory government because of a Whiggish epilogue (a defense of Marlborough) to *The Perplexed Lover* (1712), which was published with the play but not spoken in performance. Centlivre's most significant political gestures occurred during the succession anxieties when Anne was dangerously ill in 1713. In the midst of the controversy about the Hanoverian succession, Centlivre dedicated *The Wonder* (1714) to the duke of Cambridge, the future George I:

> The Dedication was a bold move politically; Steele apparently advised against it. In the event, the gamble paid off handsomely: Jacobite hopes evaporated when Queen Anne died on August 1 and—Sophia having died shortly before Anne—George I was proclaimed without opposition. Centlivre's loyalty was not forgotten. The Prince of Wales, as the Duke became, had command performances of *The Wonder, The Cruel Gift,* and *The Busy Body;* on March 17, 1720 the King himself commanded a performance of *The Busy Body* for the author's benefit.[45]

Two of Centlivre's plays are distinctively political: *The Gotham Election* (1714) and *The Artifice* (1722). Both are most interesting for the way in which they tie political issues to questions of patriarchal authority. In the first play, a Tory rascal, who is pro-French and a Jacobite, uses bribery and the sale of pensions to rig the election in Gotham. Tickup, the Tory, has the support of the mayor and Lady Worthy, as he opposes Sir John Worthy and Sir Roger Trusty. The mayor has a daughter, Lucy, whom he wishes to send to a convent in France so that he can use her fortune; but she saves herself from his tyranny by putting herself into the protection of Friendly, an agent of Trusty. Thus Centlivre attaches political values to questions of parental authority. The middle of the play contains a fascinating debate between Sir Roger Trusty and Alderman Credulous, which begins with the parental issue:

> *Ald.* Ay, ay, Sir Roger, we Fathers know what's good for our Children, better than they do themselves; they have nought to do but to submit to our Pleasures; passive Obedience is as absolutely necessary in our Wives and Children as in Subjects to the Monarch; is not your Opinion the same, Sir Roger?
> *Sir Rog.* Yes, whilst Husbands, Fathers and Monarchs exact nothing from us, contrary to our Religion and Laws: But pray, Mr. *Alderman,* how come you so passive? I remember you wore other Principles in Eighty Eight—this is not natural, Alderman.[46]

That the Mayor would have Lucy violate her religion represents a clear breach of authority and justifies her seeking protection from his tyranny. In a gesture that combines an assertion of the inclination of children with the definition of good political authority, Lucy tells Friendly that she will not return to her father: ". . . This Day I am of Age, and I chuse you for my Guardian,—and if you can bring me unquestionable Proofs of your being an honest Man;—that you have always been a Lover of your Country;—a true Assertor of her Laws and Privileges; and that you'd spend every Shilling of my Portion in Defence of Liberty and Property against *Perkin* and the Pope, I'll sign, seal, and deliver myself into your hands in the next Hour" (3:69–70).

So intermingled are the issues of state, religious, and gender politics that we never do find out who won the election, but we end the play firm in our understanding that Friendly has won Lucy and defeated her father. Lucy says, "This is my Maxim, in a marry'd Life, / Who hates his Country, ne'er can love his Wife" (3:72). Lock's reading of this marriage as a political allegory seems strained, but Centlivre's blend of kinds of authority articulates the Whig, mercantile ideology.[47]

The Artifice, though basically a comedy of love intrigue and cuckoldry, contains substantial satire on the Catholic clergy, Jacobites, and Non-Jurors, which may be related to the discovery of the Jacobite plot to restore the Stuarts and to Atterbury's trial. The play presents two wives who outwit their husbands and a mercenary father who would force his daughter's marriage. Sir Philip Moneylove has favored Sir John Freeman for his daughter Olivia until Freeman lost his fortune to his brother Ned. Ned, in his turn, has tried to abandon his Dutch wife and mother of his child, but she, with the aid of John and Olivia, tricks Ned into marrying her in England and resigning the estate to John. Ned, in the meantime, is trying to cuckold old Watchit with his young and lively wife. When this intrigue fails, Ned and the Watchits all reform. To fuel anti-Catholic satire, Mrs. Watchit is made a Catholic, and her husband masquerades as her confessor to discover her affairs with Ned. This incident allows Mrs. Watchit to turn tables on her husband and Centlivre to indulge in anticlerical lampoon. The implications of the lines of action are clearly to question paternal and spousal authority, and this Centlivre's contemporary political enemies seemed to have understood; for one wrote, in gross exaggeration, "the whole scope of the Play is to encourage Adultery; to ridicule the Clergy; and to set Women above the arbitrary Power of their Husbands."[48]

Centlivre's poetry is a much smaller part of her work than is Behn's, and it is mostly political. Her best state poems were written after the death of Anne, when the Whig hegemony had begun. Among these are *A Poem Humbly Presented to his Most Sacred Majesty, An Epistle to Mrs. Wallup, On the Right Hon. Charles Earl of Halifax Being Made Knight of the Garter.*[49] All three poems extol George as deliverer of England from the evil Tories who misled Queen Anne and evoke the earlier days of William and Mary as the continuity for the new dynasty. Caroline is represented as the successor to Mary II, for example. The strategies that writers of all political stripes use to avoid negative representations about Anne are fascinating.

For all her support of the Hanoverians, Centlivre seems to have felt unrewarded—that a few command performances and some presents were not sufficient in relation to her efforts. Her complaints are expressed in an amusing poem with a clever rhetorical strategy. *A Woman's Case* (1720), addressed to Charles Joye, a director of the South Sea Company, asks for a block of stock as a reward for her past support of the Whigs.[50] The poem deftly puts Susannah's complaints in her husband's mouth. Joseph is as skeptical about the Whigs as about his wife's literary talents. He feared being fired (he was a royal cook) when Centlivre dedicated *The Wonder* to the duke of Cambridge; and when she received no reward for the gesture, Joseph cursed her scribbling. He promised reconciliation, however, if Joye would come through with the stock. It is a charming performance that capitalizes on stereotypes in a complex way, but there is no evidence that it succeeded. Behn, Manley, and Centlivre never received significant patronage for their political writing, but in a world where their loyalty could be depended upon, patrons had little motivation to reward them. Moreover, male writers were not rewarded handsomely either, except with preferments, most of which women were barred from. And so, for all three writers, loyalty to political commitment had to be its own reward.

Although Eliza Haywood imitated Manley's scandal novels in a series of works—*Memoirs of a Certain Island Adjacent to the Kingdom of Utopia* (1725), *Bath Intrigues* (1725), *Memoirs of Baron de Brosse* (1724), *The Secret History of the Present Intrigues of the Counrt of Carimania* (1726), *Letters from the Palace of Fame* (1727)—Haywood's interests in the scandal novel were different from those of Behn or Manley. She used verifiable intrigues not to expose the politics of state or party but to expose the sexual politics of the whole society. The first volume, *Memoirs,* is set in the country and devoted to the corruption of women; the second, set in the court, depicts rakes and libertines who rape their way through life, abandoning one victim after another. Haywood's artistic purposes are similar to Manley's: she wants to expose social ills; but for Haywood the ill is a sexual, rather than political, ideology. *The Court of Carimania* is the closest to Manley's practices among Haywood's works, but even though it depicts the court of George II and the king's affair with Henrietta Howard, it has sexual reform as its purpose, not political motives. Both Manley and Haywood were feminists, as we have seen; but for Haywood women's problems superseded all other reform: Thus was she called "the champion of her sex."

For Catherine Trotter Cockburn, too, the theme of public good in *The Revolution of Sweden* is subordinated to the way the behavior of both genders may be related to the theme. Gustavus has a virtuous wife who rivals his country, and a heroine sacrifices her love for the public good:

> Nor will she [the author] less we hope engage the Fair,
> Since Publick Good is now that Sexes Care,
> They must a Noble Heroine approve,

Parting with Life, nay what we prize above
To save the Nation, vanquishing her love.
This pattern may prevail to disingage
All the Fair Politicians of the Age,
From every Byas that our Feuds increase,
Renouncing Private Ends, for Publick Peace.

Here a general concern for public welfare is focused on the value of women's participation in public life and their ability to subordinate private interest for the public good—to be heroes in the antique sense and to meet the challenge of any public office. Trotter is quite radical in this vision of women: few men have found this idea of female behavior acceptable, and Amazons, who have committed their lives to female power, have always had an ambiguous reputation. Yet Trotter's vision of women's part in public life was inspired by the example of Queen Anne:

Nor can the vainest, haughtiest Man, disdain
A woman's Precepts in Great Anna's Reign;
If by a Woman you to right are taught,
Think on that Source from whence th'Instruction's brought.[51]

Still a third version of feminist political writing is Mary Davy's *Familiar Letters,* where an essentially egalitarian couple have opposing political views: Berina is a Whig and Artander a Tory. They debate the political issues as part of their courtship, and unfortunately break off when Berina becomes angry in her arguments and Artander fears a misunderstanding. Although Davys envisions a loving and equal couple exchanging political opinions, she evades genuine conflict between them.

Striking about women's political writing is that it contains no concrete political issues for women. Although they voice a desire to have a part in public life, all is written about the world as they find it, and much is written and done on behalf of others. If, for the modern feminist, the personal is political, for her early counterpart the political was personal. Hence the importance of Queen Anne as inspiration and example. Her reign was testimony that a woman could rule: it was a vision of what might be, but it changed little for all women.

Chapter Six

Pastoral and Country Life

In *Reason's Disciples* Hilda Smith provides a lengthy discussion of the use of the pastoral by Orinda and her followers. She emphasizes their themes of retreat to the country, refuge in nature, platonic female friendships, classical pseudonyms, and virtuous moral stances, especially in Philips, Winchilsea, Chudleigh, Rowe, and Egerton.[1] Although Smith's discussions of these poets are valuable as far as they go, there is more to be said for two reasons: the pastoral and retirement traditions and these writers' use of them are more complex than Smith represents, and she does not explore the uses of the pastoral tradition by Behn. Moreover, Behn's followers' use of the pastoral has been entirely neglected. Because Smith has written extensively of the theme of friendship in retirement in the poems of Philips and her school, I will concentrate my discussion on other themes in their work. But first, the complexities of the pastoral and retirement traditions.

In this chapter we will deal with two distinct but related traditions in classical and English poetry: the pastoral, which evolves from the eclogues of Theocritus and Virgil, and retirement poetry, which develops from Horace's second epode and, secondarily, Virgil's Georgics. Likening all ways of life to the shepherds', the pastoral represents an idealized nature that responds to human needs and emotions, a setting in which shepherds are carefree and revel in *otium,* a satisfied ease in which they are untroubled by striving. Pastoral looks back to the Golden Age or other prelapsarian myths to contrast with the corruption of present civilization. Retirement poetry, as we saw in chapter 2, above, focuses on the contentment and happiness the husbandman can achieve in country life, where his humble and obscure place meets his simple needs and where he is free of the conflicts and stress of city life. The pastoral, with its artifice and retrospective gaze, appeals to

290

the aristocrat; and retirement poetry originates in the voice of a usurer Alphinus. So Aphra Behn is drawn to the pastoral, whereas Orinda and her followers come, as we have seen, out of the retirement tradition. Although many of Orinda's followers also use pastoral conventions, Behn's heirs, with the exception of Egerton, are not drawn to retirement themes.

Behn and Daughters:
Hearne, Egerton, Manley, Haywood

Aphra Behn's most important pastoral poem is called, appropriately, "The Golden Age," and it announces that it is a paraphrase of a French translation. These gestures prepare the reader for a poem that exhibits the full scope of the pastoral mode, and indeed all the major characteristics of the Golden Age are represented: shepherds make love by streams in an eternal spring with calm air and bright skies. In the Golden Age, no agriculture is necessary, nor laws, nor states, nor rulers, nor religion, nor property, nor rights, nor ambition, fame, honor.[2] Love is entirely free and therefore true:

> The lovers thus, thus uncontroul'd did meet
> Thus all their Joyes and Vows of Love repeat:
>   Joyes which were everlasting, ever new
>   And every Vow inviolably true:
> Not kept in fear of Gods, no fond Religions cause,
> Nor in obedience to the duller Laws.
> Those Fopperies of the Gown were not then known,
> Those vain, those Politick Curbs to keep man in,
> Who by a fond mistake Created that a Sin,
> Which freborn we, by right of Nature claim our own.
>
> (6:141)

Angeline Goreau sees a conflict between the characteristics of the Golden Age and Behn's Tory values.[3] But these features are conventions of an antique pastoral tradition, as much a part of Gonzalo's ideal commonwealth in *The Tempest* as of Hesiod's *Works and Days*, Ovid's *Metamorphoses*, or Jonson's *The Golden Age Restored*. The revolutionary vision of society Goreau attributes to Behn is characteristic of an era *before* history, an ideal from which all history has lapsed, and should not therefore be juxtaposed to Behn's Tory politics. The myth of the Golden Age may serve any political persuasion, but is especially compatible with the conservative vision that looks back to a better time. Because Behn was always critical of the effect of property and ambition upon sexual relationships, the ethos of the Golden Age was an ideal vehicle for her criticism of society; but as the myth represents a nostalgic, idealized vision, it could, in fact, blend with her conservatism about contemporary politics.

Behn's individual contribution to the many versions of the myth in Renaissance and seventeenth-century poetry is the condemnation of honor as an instrument to shame women and the use of sexual relations in the mythic time to critique seventeenth-century constraints:

> Oh cursed Honour! thou who first didst damn,
> A Woman to the Sin of shame;
> Honour! that rob'st us of our Gust,
> Honour! that hinder'd mankind first,
> At Loves Eternal Spring to quench his amorous thirst.
> . . . .
> Honour! that put'st our words that should be free
> Into a set Formality.
> Thou base Debaucher of the generous Heart,
> That teachest all our Looks and Actions Art;
> What Love design'd a sacred Gift,
> What Nature made to be posses't
> Mistaken Honour made a Theft.
>
> (6:142)

Behn specifically invokes the Golden Age as a setting for love:

> . . . let the Golden Age Reign:
> Let the young wishing Maid confess
> What all your Arts would keep conceal'd
> . . . She only shows the Jilt to teach me how,
> To turn the false Artillery on the Cunning Foe.
>
> (6:143)

The poem ends with a pessimistic recognition that because the Golden Age will not return, one must "the Gay hasty minutes prize." The freedom of the Golden Age stands, then as a tacit but unattainable contrast to the conditions that corrupt love in Behn's world: honor, property, interest, ambition, all the values she also criticizes in her fiction and drama.

Behn's poetry contains a number of examples of frank and free sexuality that is possible in a pastoral setting. "The Willing Mistress" does not stand upon her honor, safe in the shaded grove, secure from human eyes (6:163).

At the end of "To Mr. Creech (under the Name of Daphnis) on his Excellent Translation of Lucretius," the poet may entertain both love and poetry in a similar grove:

> The Shady Groves and Banks of Flowers
> The kind reposing Beds of Grass,
> Contribute to their Softer Hours.
> Mayst thou thy Muse and Mistress there Caress,
> And may one heighten to 'thers Happiness.
>
> (6:170)

The same kind of pastoral setting inspires the muse in Behn's reply poem to Mrs. Wharton about the death of Rochester (6:172). A carpe diem poem, "The Counsel," advises Sylvia to take refuge in a pastoral setting:

> Then haste, my Sylvia, to the Grove,
> Where all the Sweets of *May* conspire
> To teach us ev'ry Art of Love,
> And raise our Joys of Pleasure higher:
> Where while embracing we shall lie
> Loosly in Shades on Beds of Flow'rs,
> The duller World while we defie,
> Years will be Minutes, Ages Hours.
>
> (6:191)

For Behn the pastoral is not only a setting where love can be free but a place that positively nourishes love with all its arts and pleasures.

For Behn's followers the pastoral has two basic values: it may offer a setting in which love that is not socially approved may flourish, or it may offer model countercultures that contrast to contemporary society in one of the traditional functions of the pastoral. Because of the artifice of the genre, in which nature is acknowledged to be artfully constructed, pastoral always suggests the fragility of the vision it creates. In both of Mary Hearne's novels, *The Female Deserters* (1719) and *The Lover's Week* (1718), pastoral settings, complete with enameled flowers (*LW*, 47), are identified with happy but illicit love affairs that could not exist in the mainstream of society. These are not cuckolding relationship or casual loves but couples who establish a household in an isolated country setting so that, like Behn's lovers in a grove, they (especially the women) may be free from social judgment and immediate pressures of family. Hearne's exact use of pastoral vocabulary, a self-conscious adoption of the convention, suggests that the setting also works as an implicit critique of a society intolerant of loving relationships for the sake of interest, ambition, "the Flatteries of the Court" (*LW*, 52). The alternative offered by society in both novels—an unhappy forced marriage—contrasts invidiously with the fully realized love affairs represented in the novels. Hearne's use of the pastoral convention is as sophisticated in its way as Behn's, but because it does not call attention to itself and is simply imbedded in the fictional narrative, it has never attracted comment.

Sarah Fyge Field Egerton follows both Behn and Orinda in her use of pastoral and retirement themes. In a Pindaric ode, "The Extacy," she uses a pastoral theme, the Astrea myth, which contrasts conditions on earth to those of a timeless past. Astrea was, of course, the last deity to leave the earth; and now in Egerton's poem, she contemplates returning. After surveying conditions on earth, the goddess decides to remain in the higher realms, being driven from earth by war, cities full of envy, strife, deceits, and a court full of falsehood, lust, and ambition. If Astrea must descend to earth, a pastoral setting is the only one tolerable for her:

> If I must downwards fly
> I may Descend upon the blooming Plain,
> Bles'd with the harmless Nymph, and humble Swain,
> There let me ever undisturb'd remain.[4]

The contrast is typically pastoral: it critiques society through the creation of an artificially better nature.

Delariviere Manley and Eliza Haywood harbored strong feminist convictions about women's predicament, and they used pastoral gestures in which female characters reject society and create another mode of life in which they can, like Hearne's lovers, find happiness. We recall that Manley's fascinating lesbian cabal in *New Atalantis* exists in an obscure place in the country, that it is a commonwealth in which there is no property but a sharing of all possessions with one's lover. Manley is here using a specific characteristic of the Golden Age to criticize the property relationship within marriage. That her lesbians have a utopian community with accepted rules suggests Manley's use of the pastoral extends beyond Hearne's in its social critique. Her utopian counterculture is critical of specific social structures, such as property ownership, not simply of a society hostile to love in open relationships. We also recall that the one optimistic narrative in Manley's *Power of Love* is "The Happy Fugitives," a pastoral structure, in which royal children escape their father's oppression to live in an obscure location until they can be reconciled to their parents. Again the pastoral forms a critique of the unhappy marriages in the rest of the narratives of *The Power of Love,* where the characters remain bound in social conventions.

Eliza Haywood's characters in *The British Recluse* experience a similar need to reject an oppressive society and find peace in an alternative life-style, Two women have been seduced by the same man, they discover when they meet at an inn, and they decide to abandon the world to live together in friendship and tranquillity. These women's decisions form an implicit criticism of their oppression by males, but the pastoral is not used to form a counter-statement, as in Manley's work. Instead, the effect is closer to retirement themes. The use of the pastoral by the daughters of Behn ranges from Hearne's individual assertion against social convention to Manley's so-cial statements in countercultures to Haywood's simple rejection of an op-pressive society. What they have in common is that all the protests center in sexual relationships: the pastoral offers erotic space where sexual love or friendship may be free and true, as in the Golden Age. Or it offers a space free from oppression, especially after women have experienced it; but this is a survival strategy, not the ideal, which is still a male-female relationship that is as free as one might have in the Golden Age.

Orinda's Daughters and Pastoral Love: Killigrew, Egerton, Rowe

Although Orinda was reserved about writing of love, several of her fol-lowers often use the pastoral to write love poetry, and their practices con-trast with those of Behn's followers. For Killigrew, Egerton (here closer to Killigrew and Rowe) and Rowe, the pastoral is a means of mitigating the risks and inconstancy of love through the distancing effect of generic con-ventions. For example, Anne Killigrew wrote two pastoral dialogues in which love is the theme. In the first Amintor loves Alinda, who holds him at a distance because she believes that men in love are cruel and kill women. When he tells her the good reasons he loves her—her piety and strictness— she assures him that if she ever loves, she will love him; and as he begins to protest, she breaks away. The poem presents the predicament of the lovers without bitterness and with a grace that controls their gestures. In the second dialogue, an old man, Melibeous, tells to an audience of young lovers and nymphs the story of Rodanthe's seduction by a rover who de-serts her, "for he no sooner saw her Heart was gain'd, But he as soon the Victory disdain'd."[5] The woman and the nymphs are cautioned by the tale, but the man announces that Melibeous lacks compassion for youth. We then learn that this man has deserted other nymphs he has seduced. Again, although the mood Killigrew creates is characteristically skeptical, the frame within the poem allows detachment, and one enjoys the irony of the lover's comment.

Egerton is similar to Killigrew in the biting tone of many of her poems. In the center of *Poems on Several Occasions,* Egerton wrote a number of poems about love using pastoral conventions: "To Alexis," "A Song," "Love," "To One Who Said I Must Not Love," and "A Song." The poems are written from a woman's perspective; they become increasingly cynical about male inconstancy, though the speaker is tempted to infidelity too. The conventional names and situations check most tendencies to self-pity or vulnerability on the part of the speaker. The spirit is not that of the male rover, but it is often anti-romantic:

> How pleasant is Love
> When forbid or unknown;
> Was my Passion approv'd,
> It would quickly be gone.
> (Pp. 32–33)

Only where she might take full advantage of the distancing present in the fully articulated pastoral does Egerton allow herself to deal simply with inconstant love. In "The Fond Shepherdess," a pastoral dedicated to William Congreve, Egerton uses a dialogue between Daphne and Larinda, in which the latter confesses that she has been neglecting her flocks because Exalis has deserted her. When Daphne hears of all the gifts Larinda has given Exalis, Daphne counsels Larinda to avoid the pain of love, but Larinda replies that such is not possible. As she bids farewell to Daphne to seek Exalis, Larinda faints from grief, and the poem closes (pp. 106–9). Her strict adherence to the pastoral convention with its distancing allows a bitter spirit like Egerton to write about abandonment with restraint.

Elizabeth Rowe addressed some of her most interesting love poems to women, as we have seen. Relationships with men were too heavily freighted with power and the oppression of women, whereas Rowe repeatedly idealized equal, loving relationships with women. One of her most charming poems of this kind is a fully realized pastoral song addressed "To Madam S—— at the Court." The poet calls to Phillis to leave the court and rove the fields with her. They will spend the day in innocence, "untoucht with that mean influence / The duller world obey."[6] In an ironic touch, the poet promises to enchant Phillis and mermaids "while *William* is my theme." One cannot, apparently, really leave the court, even in secure Venerian groves.

Yet the lovers will try to re-create Elysium, repeating to one another the charms that introduced their loves:

> And like those happy lovers we,
> As careless and as blest;
> Shall in each others converse be
> Of the whole world possest.
>
> (P. 47)

The invitation, like the famous song it imitates, creates a space, as in Behn, where love can be free and innocent. Yet unlike Behn's, Rowe's poem also distances physical love and the reality of the emotions—all are subsumed in "harmless sports." The entire affair exists if Phillis accepts the invitation and if the setting proves to be like Elysium. Rowe used the pastoral as effectively as many of her predecessors to suggest more than she said about love. That her contemporaries understood her art is shown in that they associated Rowe with Sappho and Behn, as well as Orinda.

Orinda and Retirement:
Chudleigh, Egerton, Barker, Rowe, Winchilsea

As we have seen in chapter 2, above, the tradition of retirement was the central discourse in which Orinda and her followers were able to find a stance from which to create poetry. Although Orinda—and Egerton—had little fondness for the country in life, the themes of retirement were deeply attractive to a generation that had experienced the turmoil and loss of the civil war and the wrenching changes within society in the Restoration too. If Katherine Philips longed for London and the celebrity of successful production of *Pompey*, Orinda, her poetic persona, gave voice to a desire to be invulnerable to hardship and loss. Her "Invitation to the Country," addressed to Rosania, emphasizes the sense in which "Titles, Honours, and the World's Address / Are things too cheap to make up Happiness."[7] Philips's ideal became a self-sufficiency that looks on catastrophe unshaken:

> Man unconcern'd without himself may be
> His own both Prospect and Security.
> Kings may be Slaves by their own Passions hurl'd,
> But who commands himself commands the World.

297

A Country-life assists this study best,
Where no distractions do the Soul arrest:
There Heav'n and Earth lie open to our view,
There we search Nature and its Author too;
Possest with Freedom and a real State
Look down on Vice, and Vanity, and Fate.

(P. 104)

Orinda's daughters continue her use of the retirement ideology as a moral critique of society, but they develop the themes with individual emphasis. Chudleigh, Egerton, Barker, Rowe, and Winchilsea all use retreat to the country as an explicit judgment on the state of their society, just as Killigrew depicts the miseries of man mourned by the nymphs in Arcadia. For Chudleigh retirement is an ethical statement about her cultivation of self-sufficiency. Of her essays, she says, "The following Essays were the Products of my Retirement, some of the pleasing Opiates I made use of to lull my Mind to a delightful Rest, the ravishing Amusements of my leisure Hours, of my lonely Moments."[8] In the preface to her *Poems on Several Occasions* (1703), Chudleigh is more prescriptive in the self-sufficiency to which she hopes women will aspire, in which one is not vulnerable to loss or oppression:

> The way to be truly easie, to be always serene, to have our Passions under a due Government, to be wholly our own, and not to have it in the Power of Accidents, of things foreign to us to ruffle and disturb our Thoughts, is to retire into our selves, to live upon our own stock, to accustom our selves to our own Conversation, to be pleas'd with nothing but what strictly and properly speaking we may justly pretend a Right to; of which kind, such things can never be said to be, of which 'tis in the Power of Fortune to deprive us. (Sig. A4)

A poem in this volume is addressed to Eugenia, the person one imagines having authored the *Female Advocate; or, A Plea For the just Liberty of the Tender Sex, and particularly Married Women* (1700), a reply to Sprint, to whom Chudleigh herself also eloquently replied in *The Ladies Defence* (1721). The poem to Eugenia deals with the Golden Age when love, which is now turned into trade and art, was free. But instead of following out the pastoral vision of love in the Golden Age, the poem pictures the good person maintaining integrity alone:

> Those few who dare be good, must live alone
> To all Mankind, except themselves, unknown:

From a mad World, to some obscure Recess,
They must retire, to purchase Happiness.

(P. 31)

This statement is not simply an escape: it is a judgment on the world because it is the good people, the few, who will choose retirement, and Chudleigh's main purpose in writing is to prepare her female audience to make such a choice and to thrive in it. For Chudleigh the retired life is a moral ideal for which one prepares with care: "To render a private life truly easie, there must be Piety, as well as humane knowledge, uncorrupted Morals, as well as an Insight into Nature, a Regardlessness of Wealth, at least no eager Solicitude for it, a being wean'd from the World, from its Vanity, its Applause, its Censure, its Pomp, all that it has of inciting or disturbing, all that it can give, or take away" (p. 237).

Like Orinda, Chudleigh believed firmly in the self-sufficient ideal of the *beatus vir*, a person impervious to Fortune because not valuing what Fortune offers. Far more the scholar than Orinda, Chudleigh could imagine the pleasures of solitude and private life, and this seemed to Chudleigh a particularly important discipline for women. Her stance also makes a virtue of necessity: women restricted to the domestic sphere could cultivate themselves. In her multiple understandings of women's anger, of women's unrealized intellectual potential, and their need to control their lives, Chudleigh was a remarkable forerunner of modern feminist therapists.

For Egerton retirement to the country allowed the speaker to be serene "in safe Obscurity," but retreat also has a larger significance in creating a space for scholarly pursuits. "The Retreat" is such a place, which has been praised by poets as best place on earth; but it is also, as for Chudleigh, a place for discipline for the soul:

Here their great Souls, with Raptures fir'd
Philosophers of old in Solitude,
Their own resisting Passions first subdu'd;
Then with good Precepts civiliz'd the Rude.
They knew a Court or city would molest
The calm Conceptions of a studious Breast.
Here the Mantuan Swain gain'd all his Bays
To Solitude his unmatch'd Pen doth raise,
Deserved Trophies of immortal Praise.

(Pp. 32–33)

In *A Serious Proposal to the Ladies* (1964), Mary Astell envisioned her college for women as a religious retirement; she tells the ladies that they are invited to a "Happy Retreat! which will be the introducing you into such a *Paradise* as your Mother *Eve* forfeited, where you shall feast on Pleasures, that do not, like those of the World, disappoint your expectations, pall your Appetites, and . . . put you on the fruitless search after new Delights."[9] Astell's idea depends upon the assumption of retirement poetry that the country is the best setting for the sound development of young people.

In her fiction, Jane Barker frequently represents country solitude as preferable to life in London because a rural setting offers escape from the vanities and corruption of the city. A poem included in *A Patch-Work Screen* presents country lovers "in careless Consort," whereas those in town are "by Business, Families, and Fortune Ty'd; / Beset, beseig'd, attack'd on ev'ry side."[10] That country solitude is preferable to city life is one of the recurrent themes of *A Patch-Work Screen*. In "An Invitation to my Friends at Cambridge," Barker exhorts students to strive for solitude and innocence, because learning cannot take place where pride, avarice and ambition reign (p. 3).

Barker's voice is more practical and more escapist than those of her fellow poets. She makes no bones about preferring to live in a village because of the temptations London offers:

> Retire then all, whom Fortune don't oblige,
> To suffer the distresses of a *Siege*.
> Where strong temptation Vertue do's attaque,
> 'Tis ignoble an escape to make:
> But where no Conquest can be hop'd by fight,
> 'Tis honorable, sure, to scape by flight.
> rly to some calm retreat, where you may spend
> Your life in quietude with some kind Friend;
> In some small Village, and adjacent Grove.
>
> (Pp. 22–23)

Obeying the poem's injunctions, the reader will avoid party politics, sordid wealth, sophisticated wit, meals with wine, and beds of lust, and may instead spend time in contemplation of "God and Nature's Books" (p. 23). Although the poem gestures toward contemplation as a goal, one has the strong sense that Barker simply found the city a corrupt and hostile environment. From this perspective retirement is another means, like the sexual ideology of the fiction, these writers used to cope with social changes brought about by the growing mercantile enterprise in London. As women were gradually being driven from the economic scene and confined in private worlds, writers like Orinda's daughters sought to find the best values they could through a rejection of a society that held little congenial place for women. Moreover, they found in the retirement discourse a positive vision of a happy retreat to a better life. Barker's fictional image of Galesia as a rescuer of innocent women who are corrupted and abandoned by males in the city also conveys the same judgment on city life, always for Barker more practical than moral. The city was simply not a good place for good women. In Barker's view women could not thrive there any more than poetry could:

No more than Beauty, without Wealth, can move
    A Gallants heart to strokes of Love;
Than fair persuasions, without stripes, reduce
    The Birds of Bridewell, or of Stews;
Than Gypsies without Money can foreshow
    No more can Verse in *London* grow.

For, *Verse* is the tender'st Plant in th' Field of Wit,
    No Storm must ever blow o'er it;
A Very *Noli-me-tangere* it is,
    It shrivels with the touch of business;
But, *Heliotropian* like, it seeks the gleams
    Of Quietudes reviving Beams.
How shou'd it then endure this irksome shade
    Which is by noise of Plots and Bus'ness made?
                  (Pp. 108–9)

Elizabeth Rowe's fiction also frequently uses the pastoral code to suggest the moral superiority of country inhabitants. We recall that her utopian female family luxuriates in an idyllic country setting where it apparently never freezes or storms. The family lives so economically, moreover, that the mother is quickly able to repay the father's debts.[11] Another of Rowe's heroines, seduced by a false lover, finds refuge from the consequences of her ruin in the country. From the following quotation, we may see how Rowe's settings are morally encoded:

Let me be entertain'd with more pure and lasting joys, in some humble retreat, far from the noise and thoughtless amusements of the world! I ask not princely bowers, or artful walks; let me pass my hours in some unfrequented shade, where the images of vanity and sin never enter! Oh celestial life! How do these peaceful scenes sooth and flatter my soul! through what enchanting paths does my imagination stray!

Ye vain grandeurs of the world adieu! Adieu ye idle amusements, and fantastick pleasures! What shadows do you now appear! How unsubstantial to these serious prospects of bliss! Let me dwell unmolested here! Let me lose the remembrance of his busy world, and hear no more of its distracting follies! (p. 29)

The ideal marriages in Rowe's fiction exist in settings very similar to those in which Hearne's happy liaisons take place: country seats, located on gentle hills, with happy valleys beneath, complete with enameled flowers, purling streams, and the inviting shade of happy groves (pp. 133–34). Rowe's Silviana, daughter of a country clergyman, marries an earl and moves to London, and from there she writes to her friend about the fatigue of spending long hours at her toilet, and her clumsy innocence in dealing with gallants: "'tis only my affection for my Lord, that helps me to support this illustrious bondage, this splendid misery; but as sincerely as I love him, I cannot without a sigh recall the harmless freedom, the unmolested innocence, in which the earliest part of my life was past" (p. 176). In Rowe's fiction the city-country duality and contrast do a great deal of moral work. Because of her own reclusive inclinations, the retirement code seems almost an inevitable vehicle through which Rowe would express her pious view of contemporary manners without dropping the advantages of fiction over sermons. She was herself an example to her own time of a virtuous life in solitude:

> The love of solitude, which seems almost inseparable from a poetic genius, discovered itself very early in Mrs. Rowe, and never forsook her but with life itself. Before her marriage, though it cannot be doubted that she was often solicited to quit her beloved obscurity, yet she had only made a short visit to the town of a few weeks. After Mr. Rowe's decease, as a decent retreat seemed to her alone suited to a state of widowhood, her aversion to a public appearance in the world increased; and the approach of the decline of life determined her more strongly to devote the remainder of her days to retirement; nor could any arguments, or persuasions of her friends, prevail with Mrs. Rowe to alter her sentiments and conduct in this instance.[12]

Anne Finch, the countess of Winchelsea, was the most accomplished pastoralist, retirement poet, and nature poet among Orinda's followers. Wordsworth admired her nature poetry, with good reason. As we have seen, her personal retirement, like Cavendish's, was compelled by nonjuror status after 1688. Winchilsea wrote pastoral dialogues, pastoral elegies and country-house poems, which I have already discussed. Winchilsea loved nature and wrote many poems about trees, birds, and, specifically, nightingales, and about these subjects her poetry is genuinely distinctive. Her occasional poems about nature are also very fine.

The Wellesley Manuscript contains a charming poem that illustrates Winchilsea's delight in the English countryside: "A Ballad to Mrs Catherine
Fleming in London from Malshanger farm in Hampshire" (pp. 89–91). The
poet is careful to specify that she writes from a farm, not a villa or country
house. She celebrates the safety of the country, its lovely sounds and sights,
its wholesome foods, and refreshing surroundings. Only her friend, she
declares, could draw her away from this setting, as Orpheus moved the rocks
and trees with his song. Here the retirement ideology is carefully represented, yet, like her country-house poems, this one clothes ideology in the
freshness of observation.

Winchilsea's more familiar nature poems, such as "The Bird," "The Tree,"
and "To the Nightingale," have a similar celebrative approach to natural objects or creatures, and they have the additional intention of finding patterns
in nature that human beings may emulate or defining a resonance in nature
on which human values are based. Thus the noble tree ends its life heroically: the winds blow it down,

> Their scatter'd Strength together call
> And to the Clouds proclaim thy Fall;
> Who then their Ev'ning-Dews may spare,
> When thou no longer art their Care;
> But shalt, life ancient Heroes, burn,
> And some bright Hearth be made thy Urn.
> (P. 267)

Similarly, the poet imitates the song of the nightingale:

> This Moment is thy Time to sing,
> This Moment I attend to Praise,
> And set my Numbers to thy Layes.
> Free as thine shall be my Song;
> As thy Musiick, short, or long.
> (P. 267)[13]

"A Nocturnal Reverie," Winchilsea's most famous poem, takes an approach that looks forward to romantic poetry. Instead of using analogies
between humans and nature, the poem evokes a scene with elaborate detail

and considerable scope, and then concludes with an observation about human beings in relation to nature. The creatures, for example, celebrate while "Tyrant-Man do's sleep." The speaker's free soul becomes so tranquil, emptied of rage, that it both reaches the ineffable ("Something, too high for Syllables to speak") and resonates with the natural world "and thinks it like her Own" (p. 270). The effect is similar to Wordsworth, and so it was understandable that he would admire it, and it also is not far from the eighteenth-century sublime.

Winchilsea's effects that represent retirement themes most accurately occur in poems less successful than "A Nocturnal Reverie." One of these is "The Petition for an Absolute Retreat," which is inscribed to Winchilsea's friend, the countess of Thanet. Here the speaker longs for a retreat in which no intruders will bring idle gossip, where food will be simple country fare, clothing will be adjusted to the seasons, and perfumes be only those of the garden. The speaker's partner will help evoke prelapsarian Eden:

> Give me there (since Heaven has shown
> It was not Good to be alone)
> A *Partner* suited to my Mind,
> Solitary, pleas'd and kind;
> Who, partially, may something see
> Preferr'd to all the World in me;
> Slighting, by my humble Side,
> Fame and Splendor, Wealth and Pride.
> When but Two the Earth possesst,
> Twas their happiest Days, and best.
> (P. 72)

The next section of the poem focuses on the double theme of pastoral rejection of ambition and Ardelia's (Winchilsea) rescue from neglect by Arminda (Thanet):

> So the sad *Ardelia* lay;
> Blasted by a Storm of Fate,
> Felt, thro' all the British State
> Fall'n, neglected, lost, forgot,
> Dark Oblivion all her Lot;
> Faded till *Arminda's* Love
> (Guided by the Pow'rs above)

304

Warm'd anew her drooping Heart,
And Life diffus'd thro' every Part.
(P. 73)

The speaker likens her need for a friend that that of David after he had fled
Jerusalem. At the bottom of one's fortunes, however, one has consolation,
not only of friendship, but of humble station:

Where, may I remain secure,
Waste, in humble Joys and pure,
A Life, that can no Envy yield;
Want of Affluence my Shield.
(Pp. 74–75)

Thus, the poem cites traditional retirement values and two Roman heroes
who would have avoided disaster if they had not been ambitious: Crassus,
who should have stayed in his cave, and Sertorius, who should have stayed
in the Canaries or the Fortunate Isles. At the end of the poem, the speaker
appeals to fate for the contemplative mind to compensate for rejection of
world pleasures:

Give me, O indulgent Fate!
For all Pleasures left behind,
Contemplations of the Mind.
Let the Fair, the Gay, the Vain
Courtship and Applause obtain;
Let th'Ambitious rule the Earth;
Let the giddy Fool have Mirth;
Give the Epicure his Dish,
Ev'ry one their sev'ral Wish;
Whilst my Transports I employ
On that more extensive Joy.
(P. 77)

Here a celebration of simple pleasures with their implicit judgment of worldly
practices modulates to an explicit expression of differences in the material
life and the life of the mind, more simple but similar to those Milton achieves
in *L'Allegro* and *Il Penseroso*. Winchilsea's poetry comprehends the pastoral

genres, the retirement themes, and the nature poetry that continue in the eighteenth and nineteenth centuries.

The antique pastoral mode offers women writers a critique of their oppression through property and interest, especially with regard to love. In that tradition they could imagine a fragile space in which lovers could freely enjoy one another. Pastoral conventions could also allow poets to achieve distance on bitter or tender themes. The retirement tradition also allows women to imagine space, away from the burgeoning commercial and public life of the city, which held little place for them. In retreat they envision personal development through study and a simple existence that conduces to moral life. The scene is not yet domestic, and there is only a hint that women are morally superior to men; but both ideas may be glimpsed. A more subtle development lies in the keen observation of nature by Cavendish and Winchilsea. The overtly ideological representations of nature pastoral and retirement poetry gradually give way in Winchilsea to more concrete and detailed images, which are no less ideological, but aesthetically different.[14]

Conclusion

All women together ought to let flowers fall upon the tomb of Aphra Behn,
which is, most scandalously but rather appropriately, in Westminister Abbey,
for it was she who earned them the right to speak their minds. It is she—
shady and amorous as she was—who makes it not quite fantastic for me to
say to you tonight: Earn five hundred a year by your wits.
—Virginia Woolf (1928)

By far the most important conclusion of this study is to modify the long-
held belief summed up in Virginia Woolf's *A Room of One's Own*: "Towards
the end of the eighteenth century a change came about which, if I were
rewriting history, I should describe more fully and think of greater importance than the Crusades or the Wars of the Roses. The middle-class woman
began to write."[1] Now we must return to the middle of the seventeenth
century to write an accurate literary history for women in England. This
study is just the beginning of a process of revision, which has already been
proceeding apace in more specialized articles and books. The outlines and
individual interpretations presented here inevitably will be challenged as more
research is done into each writer and the relations among them. Yet their
achievements cannot be ignored while we strive to draw a more and more
accurate picture of what they thought, felt, and wrote. Inevitably, too,
speculations about "Why then?" will change as new historical information
becomes available, but Virginia Woolf's sense that we must reach backward
through our mothers is not invalidated by her lack of knowledge of, and
taste for, Manley or Haywood. In fact, she claims for Winchilsea, Cavendish, Dorothy Osborne, and Aphra Behn the sanction for the later, greater
women writers: "Without those forerunners, Jane Austen and the Brontës

and George Eliot could no more have written than Shakespeare could have written without Marlowe, or Marlowe without Chaucer" (p. 103). As one looks back at their achievements, the fact that women wrote in such a variety of genres, including drama to be staged, is most impressive. That is one of the uses of such an overview. Another is the ability to recognize their acuity in solving the problem of authority in taking the privilege of writing by quickly creating a tradition from Sappho and two contemporary models. As investigations continue, we have become aware of how the successors of Behn or Orinda became themselves models for later writers, of how, for example, Elizabeth Rowe inspired Elizabeth Carter.[2] A third use of an overview is to appreciate the scope of their protest and analysis of their own oppression. Feminist critics are no longer afraid of the anger and advocacy of women's writing. What alienated Woolf from Winchilsea reaches us today with special power.

A second important conclusion is the uninterrupted continuity between the seventeenth-century writers and their eighteenth-century descendents. In the middle of the eighteenth century, Eliza Haywood was still writing: her work showed one way in which the earlier seduction fantasies might be transformed to serve changes in gender ideology. Susanna Centlivre's plays were still being acted in the latter half of the eighteenth-century, partially because of Garrick's love of certain roles. In 1739 seventeenth-century feminism was alive and well as the Sophia pamphlets repeat the arguments of Poulain de La Barre's *The Woman as Good as the Man,* translated into English in 1677. The 1750s saw a revival of interest in women's writing. In 1752 George Ballard published his magisterial work *Memoirs of Several Ladies of Great Britain,* in which Cavendish, Philips, Killigrew, Chudleigh, Astell, and Winchilsea are represented. Duncombe's *Feminead* (1751; 1754; 1757) vilified Behn, Manley, and Centlivre, but saw Rowe as redeeming them. Duncombe also had high praise for Catherine Trotter Cockburn, whose collected works had just appeared. Theophilus Cibber included Manley and Behn among other women in *Lives of the Poets* (1753). In 1755 *Poems by Eminent Ladies,* compiled by George Coleman and Bonnell Thornton, was published; the volumes presented Barber, Behn, Chudleigh, Killigrew, Masters, Cavendish, Philips, Rowe, and Winchilsea.

Twenty years later Mary Scott wrote *The Female Advocate* (1774), in which she finds a great many women to praise for their genius, among them Cavendish, Killigrew, Philips, Barber, and Masters, and she also makes a strong plea for women's education.[3] As Jane Spencer has shown, the late eighteenth century regularly congratulated itself on the number and achievements of English women writers.[4] Doris Stenton observes, "It is a remarkable sign of the improvement in the education generally given to girls that from the 'forties of the eighteenth century a continually increasing number of women won for themselves a modest place in a national memory by their intellectual achievements."[5] Women continued to write for the stage: Elizabeth Cooper, Frances Sheridan, and Elizabeth Griffith wrote successful comedies. "In the 1780's the eccentric Lady Wallace was 'emulous of attaining the fame of Mrs. Behn and Mrs. Centlivre.'"[6] Late in the century, Elizabeth Inchbald wrote adaptations of foreign plays, Hannah Cowley wrote successful moral comedies, and Frances Brooke composed comic operas. Elizabeth Singer Rowe's poetry and prose remained very popular and much respected well into the nineteenth century.

Yet it must also be admitted that writing at the end of the century, Mary Wollstonecraft does not draw on the authority of the seventeenth-century feminists. For all the advocacy of women's education by the feminists and the women writers included in this volume, in 1774 the intellectually accomplished Laetitia Barbauld rejected the idea of a woman's academy with reasons vested in gender ideology. The project, she said, "appears to me better calculated to form such characters as the *Précieuses* or *Femmes Savantes* than good wives or agreeable companions."[7] Eighty years before, Mary Astell's similar proposal foundered for endowment because it too closely resembled a nunnery at a time of great anxiety about Roman Catholics. The feminists' critique of marriage, moreover, had brought no legal change in the status of women. So, although we may sympathize with Hilda Smith's desire to see linear progress in the feminist cause, the issues through which each epoch faces questions about the status and condition of women constantly change. For that reason it is difficult to see the seventeenth-century writers' efforts on behalf of women as truncated: they raised the questions about their oppression in terms that their culture could reckon, and they taught one another how to cope with their situation. By the time of Laetitia Barbauld, a different gender ideology prevents her from accepting an academy for girls, yet she herself is evidence of intellectual opportunity in her time. Not only are normative statements about "women" different from their personal experience of their society, but each culture will define the woman question through differing issues; and therefore feminists of each era can draw on the vision of their foremothers to a limited degree. Although the Sophia pamphlets created a stir in the middle of the eighteenth century, Ruth Perry says, "they belonged to an earlier period intellectually."[8]

In the gradualness of its social change, the eighteenth century is a contrast to the seventeenth. The trends apparent at the turn of the century continue in a relatively stable world. More and more, women lose their places in the economic and public world, and their restriction to the private and domestic sphere is greater than before. The ideology of femininity, glimpsed earlier, gradually becomes dominant, even for the Bluestockings. Slowly notions of equality of souls or female inferiority to males are replaced by concepts of difference: that women are not inferior or equal to men, but basically different from them according to nature. Men are active and amoral; women are passive and virtuous. Men are public beings; women are private. These assignments are not seen as cultural: they are believed to be inscribed by nature. These differences were presaged on the Restoration stage.[9] They also explain the intensity with which Behn, Manley, and Haywood were vilified in the eighteenth century and why the sexually transgressive Wollstonecraft suffered similar treatment. We will return to this question.

The gradual distinction between the writers who followed the chaste Orinda and those who followed Behn, whether they were "loose" or not, fits the general pattern of distinguishing among women on the basis of their sexual transgression. In this ideology women's passivity and virtue are identified with the domestic setting. Seventeenth-century retirement to the country is succeeded by retreat to the home. The novel gradually becomes the dominant genre for women, partially because it seems an accessible genre, but mostly because it brought income from an expanding audience. Women writing novels reveal one of the contradictions of the eighteenth century: several novelists were separated from their husbands in the century that began the celebration of marriage. So these women stay at home, but they write for money to support their families. In a sense, many eighteenth-century writers are domestic daughters of Aphra Behn. Yet the ideology of the fiction they create frequently glorifies woman's domestic mission.

In the eighteenth century, as we have seen, the novelists transform the three major traditions in seventeenth-century fiction. As Jane Spencer has shown, the fantasy of seduced heroines, widely adapted by earlier writers to a variety of uses, was transformed at the end of the eighteenth century into a protest against the ideology of femininity by the radicals Hays and Wollstonecraft. The reformed heroines of Trotter, Davys, and *Lindamira* have their descendents in certain of Burney's novels, the later Haywood, Smith's *Emmeline,* and Inchbald's *A Simple Story.* The cosmic romances of Aubin and Rowe are transformed into the gothic and the romances of escape. These continuities demonstrate that literature constantly transforms fundamental issues into terms acceptable to differing epochs. The rate of social change is gradual and not always progressive. But literature may keep certain basic kinds of questions – children's choice in marriage – continuously before audiences while at the same time transforming the fantasies about the issues to respond to – and shape – cultural conditions.

Before we can examine the outcomes of the feminist protest expressed by the writers included in this study, we need to acknowledge several facts demonstrated here. With the exception of Centlivre and Rowe, these writers were extremely conservative, Royalist or Tory in persuasion, and they therefore did not advocate social change, even when they might have been radical about sexuality or profoundly critical of marriage as an institution. Moreover, their political poetry was always written on behalf of others or to express loyalty to others. In short, their political poetry was not feminist; nor were their feminist writings political. With the exception of Astell's *Proposal to the Ladies,* even pleas for better education were not conceptualized concretely, but called for changes in male – and female – attitudes toward women's abilities. And ideas about education are always constrained by gender ideology: Astell described the preparation of single women to meet their Maker; Barbauld assumed education prepares a woman to attract and hold a mate. In general, as Stenton has taught us, women's education did improve during the eighteenth century, but it was often directed to narrow purposes defined by the feminine ideology.

Radical feminist claims survived the failure of the Commonwealth in polemic that lasted well into the eighteenth century. The notion of the equality of souls transcended sects for virtually all Protestants, including devout Anglicans like Astell. Cartesian ideas, such as faith in reason and the questioning of custom, also endured into the eighteenth century. Questioning of naturally determined genders gave way, however, to the increasing polarization of the feminine ideology. The late eighteenth and nineteenth centuries witness a triumph of essentialism in gender definitions. This is one change that makes certain seventeenth-century thinkers appealing to the modern reader because of their understanding that gender descriptions are cultural.

The relation between a writer's personal sexuality and her reputation continues to be problematic as epochs change. Intense cultural opposition to the woman writer whose personal life is – or can be called – transgressive of social boundaries transcends politics. Behn and Manley were pilloried for their personal lives; they were ardent conservatives but dramatized erotic relationships in writing. At the end of the eighteenth century, Hays and Wollstonecraft, radical politically and personally, were vilified for their lives. The common thread is sexual transgression, whether real or apparent, rather than political persuasion. Moreover, the disapproval of Aphra Behn herself and writers associated with her grows from the seventeenth to the eighteenth century. Except for occasional anthologies of women writers, the slow decline in visibility of most seventeenth-century women writers during the eighteenth and nineteenth centuries may be partly ascribed to their lack of conformity to the growing feminine ideology. Transgressive women were certainly not welcome to the late eighteenth- and nineteenth-century culture, but with the exception of Winchilsea in the Romantic era, even the Orinda group lost visibility during the strong gender polarization of later eras.

The critique of marriage continues into the eighteenth century, and it has

311

gradual consequences. Eliza Haywood's *Female Spectator* and *Epistles for the Ladies* accept the idea that marriage should be a mutually happy relationship, but also held that if the union proved intolerable for the wife, she should leave her husband and make her way in the world. Later fiction represents similar ideas, and though the laws had not changed substantially, more and more women were living apart from their husbands and managing to survive financially, sometimes through writing fiction. A pattern we have observed beginning in these early writers continued: the hero or heroine must marry more than once to achieve a happy relationship. The serial marriage fantasy replaces serial relationships in the earlier, more libertine fiction. Clearly, the problem of really understanding the other gender in a highly polarized society makes such fantasies compelling and fascinating.

The most gradual and lasting change in gender ideology is children's choice of marriage partner. This change began with Elizabethan fantasies of romentic love and protests against enforced marriage. It continued with variations on these themes in the seventeenth century. A notable effect in several works of fiction by such conservative writers as Jane Barker and Elizabeth Rowe is that parents really do not understand their children's right choices, and that if parents enforce their will upon marriage choices, the marriages will be unhappy. Fiction, of whatever stripe, is consistent in suggesting this conclusion, and so one is little surprised to read that the child's choice triumphed in the eighteenth century and thus brought about the multiplication of novels on a theme already announced and explored in women's fiction of the seventeenth century: how to know a good mate when you see him. Fiction also provides education in gender relations to women whose culture is determined to keep them "innocent" of the terms of their crucial choice in life. Little wonder the books are full of heroines who mistake their true feelings or their real chance for happiness.

As Lipking asserted, much of this poetry and fiction begins with loss, abandonment, and retirement from the world. Yet literature itself creates a bond to another, the reader, and gives the writer a temporary sense of not being alone. Through literature women have survived their isolation in the domestic scene and their exclusion from public life and the world of work. But the literature itself also represents women as surviving loss and abandonment through bonding with one another. Themes of friendship from Orinda through Haywood show women who survive through care for one another, and these representations are more important than the literary traditions and friendships the authors made in real life because the ordinary woman does not have to be an author in order to relate to the fictions.

Representations in fiction and poetry of women helping one another are a mirror of a major purpose these authors had in writing: educating one another about the terms of their predicament and strategies for endurance.

They wrote about education and for a female audience in order to change one another, not to change their society. Their goal was to help one another cope with their lives as they found them. They sought to change what their culture taught them they could control: themselves.

Self-deprecation was also a survival strategy, as we observe in the different treatment accorded Orinda and Behn, especially by misogynist writers like Gould. As claims for equality fade in meaning because of increased polarization of gender differences and the ideology of femininity becomes dominant, self-deprecation takes on greater importance, as we observe in the letters of Lady Mary Wortley Montague or the comments of Elizabeth Carter about her own accomplishments. But, as literary historians, we must be careful not to take women writers at their word. Orinda's self-effacement and retirement themes were contradicted by her public achievements that were extremely important to other women in the seventeenth century. Although an Egerton or a Chudleigh might apologize for taking the privilege of writing, both understood and analyzed women's oppression. Because they deal constantly with cultures hostile to their purposes as writers, women authors have an exceedingly complex relation to their audiences, a relation we are only beginning to understand. These writers provide rich examples to continue this exploration of the woman writer's relation to her audience and her culture.

Because, as we have already observed, culture constantly transforms issues of gender from one era to another, the historical study of literature has much to teach the feminist. More than polemic or politics, literary representations are continually transforming social issues into codes that their audiences can accept as not ideological, though, of course, they are. An obvious example is how the Female Wits used Turkish or Spanish settings to protest male oppressive behavior in their plays. Feminists interested in gender history need to understand many more subtle transformations of gender ideology in literature, not only to learn more about the relation between literature and society, but to understand larger questions of social change.

The writers in this work understood the necessity of creating authority in taking the privilege of writing. Both groups established a stance in a discourse—retirement or libertine—and appealed to a literary tradition of their own making. They may have apologized for publishing their work, but they found important patrons and willing publishers nonetheless. They wrote from a female perspective, they made distinctive use of genres, and certain themes attracted them: they despised ambition, interest, war, and slavery; they critiqued marriage, explored female sexuality, and sought to survive love. They refused to compete with other women and celebrated friendship with them instead. Only Cavendish felt exceptional, possibly because she was first. Some wrote distinctively about nature. They denied their right to comment on public life, but almost all wrote about politics, even as political journalists. They plumbed their own deprivation, but understood their anger and their melancholy too. Unable to change their society, they sought to change themselves through education and the cultivation of private life. They have waited long enough: it is time to acknowledge and explore the full scope and character of their achievements.

Notes

Preface

1. See Linda Alcoff, "Cultural Feminism versus Post-Structuralism: The Identity Crisis in Feminist Theory," *Signs* 13 (Spring 1988): 405–23.
2. Sandra M. Gilbert and Susan Gubar, *The Madwoman in the Attic* (New Haven, Conn.: Yale University Press, 1979), pp. 45–92.

Introduction

1. Hilda Smith, *Reason's Disciples: Seventeenth-Century English Feminists* (Urbana: University of Illinois Press, 1982): "A feminist ideology can incorporate a number of interests focusing on women and divergent viewpoints about women's position within a given time and place, but it must include some understanding of women as a group whose lives have differed from men's on account of their sex" (p. 6).
2. "These early English feminists were largely forgotten both because the social effect of their thought was limited and because its historical influence was truncated" (Smith, *Reason's Disciples*, p. 192). Smith attributes the end of seventeenth-century feminism to "both its inability to suggest broader political goals and the sentimental tendencies of eighteenth-century thought that undercut these writers' rationalist argument" (p. 201).
3. *First Feminists: British Women Writers, 1578–1799*, ed. Moira Ferguson (Bloomington: Indiana University Press; Old Westbury, N. Y.: Feminist Press, 1985).
4. John J. Richetti, *Popular Fiction before Richardson* (Oxford: Clarendon Press, 1969).
5. Lawrence Stone, *The Family, Sex, and Marriage in England, 1500–1800*, abridged ed. (New York: Harper and Row, 1977), chap. 8, "The Companionate Marriage."
6. Linda Woodbridge, *Women and the English Renaissance: Literature and the Nature of Womankind, 1540–1620* (Urbana: University of Illinois Press, 1984); Katherine U. Henderson and Barbara F. McManus, *Half Humankind: Contexts and Texts of the Controversy about Women in England, 1540–1640* (Urbana: University of Illinois Press, 1985). For another source of women's writing in the period, see *The Whole Duty of a Woman: Female Writers in Seventeenth-Century England*, ed. Angeline Goreau (New York: Doubleday, 1985).
7. From Patricia Crawford, "Women's Published Writings, 1600–1700," in *Women in English Society, 1500–1800*, ed. Mary Prior (London: Methuen, 1985), p. 212.
8. Catherine Belsey, *The Subject of Tragedy: Identity and Difference in Renaissance Drama* (London: Methuen, 1985), pp. 216–24.

315

9. See *Half Humankind*, pp. 306–25.

10. Moira Ferguson says, "Sustained polemic offers full-scale feminist polemic, which customarily calls for a change in women's condition. These began to appear when women had gained more self-confidence, greater access to printing and publishers, and more refined philosophical tools with which to analyse their situation" (*First Feminists*, pp. 28–29).

11. Although Ferguson claims a "comparative dearth of full-length feminist works after the early years of the eighteenth century" (p. 19), she omits to acknowledge how the work of Eliza Haywood, Susanna Centlivre, Mary Davys, and Jane Barker fit into the continuity of the feminist critique. Her excellent introduction suffers somewhat by its focus on polemical feminist works. She must omit fiction and drama, for example, because of length. Even so, she surely demonstrates secure outlines for the continuity I am claiming.

12. Recent writers about Cavendish attribute her rejection of contemporary discourse to her feminism, and she certainly scorned whatever excluded her. See Sylvia Bowerbank, "'The Spider's Delight': Margaret Cavendish and the 'Female Imagination,'" *ELR* 14 (Autumn 1984): 392–408; Lisa T. Sarasohn, "A Science Turned Upside Down: Feminism and the Natural Philosophy of Margaret Cavendish," *Huntington Library Quarterly* 47 (1984): 289–307.

13. Maren-Sofie Røstvig, *The Happy Man: Studies in the Metamorphoses of a Classical Ideal, 1600–1700* (Oxford: Basil Blackwell, 1954). Volume 2 covers the period 1700–1760.

14. For an excellent discussion of the libertine ideology in relation to seventeenth-century discourses of sexuality, see Harold M. Weber, *The Restoration Rake-Hero: Transformation in Sexual Understanding in Seventeenth-Century England* (Madison: University of Wisconsin Press, 1986).

15. Laurie A. Finke, "The Satire of Women Writers in *The Female Wits*," *Restoration* 8 (Fall 1984), 68.

16. For documentation of these patterns, see Mary Ann O'Donnell, *Aphra Behn: An Annotated Bibliography of Primary and Secondary Sources* (New York: Garland, 1986).

17. Robert Gould, *Poems, Chiefly Consisting of Satyrs and Satyrical Epistles* (London: n.p., 1689), pp. 65–66. For a discussion of Gould's satires of women, see Felicity Nussbaum, *The Brink of All We Hate: English Satires on Women, 1660–1750* (Lexington: University Press of Kentucky, 1984), pp. 25–34.

18. In writing about women's drama, Nancy Cotton observed these traditions in women's writing of the seventeenth century in *Women Playwrights in England c. 1363–1750* (Lewisburg, Pa.: Bucknell University Press, 1980), pp. 194–212. Although I had already noted the differences in the groups during my research, I am much indebted to Professor Cotton for confirmation of my ideas and for her excellent discussion of the Salic Law of Wit. Jane Spencer has also noted the modeling on Behn and Orinda by early women writers in *The Rise of the Woman Novelist from Aphra Behn to Jane Austen* (Oxford: Basil Blackwell, 1986), pp. 22–33.

19. See W. G. Day, "The Athenian Society: Poets' Reputations, 1692–1710," *Notes and Queries*, 216 [n.s. 18] (1971):329; *The Poems of Anne Countess of Winchilsea*, ed. Myra Reynolds (Chicago: University of Chicago Press, 1903), p. 92.

20. John Duncombe, *The Feminiad: A Poem* (London: For M. Cooper, 1754; rpt. Augustan Reprint Society, Los Angeles: Clark Library, 1981), ll. 139–42.

21. Undoing is a psychological defense as defined by Anna Freud in *The Ego and the Mechanisms of Defence*. The mechanism is a form of denial that a social transgression has occurred: a child who has cut another's hair may put it back. The effect is not remorse but compensation for the action. When an adult anticipates disapproval or has anxiety about an action—a woman publishing in the seventeenth century—the subject may minimize the transgression ("These are trifles."), displace responsibility for the action ("This patron urged me to publish, and I could not refuse."), or find an acceptable motive for the action ("I wrote these for my children only."). Through this means the transgression seems not to have happened. Anna Freud, *The Ego and the Mechanisms of Defence* (New York: International Universities Press, 1946), pp. 46–47; Joseph Sand-

ler with Anna Freud, *The Analyses of Defense: The Ego and the Mechanisms of Defense Revisited* (New York: International Universities Press, 1985), pp. 128–35.

22. Lawrence Lipking, "Aristotle's Sister: A Poetics of Abandonment," *Critical Inquiry* 10 (September 1983): 77.

23. Ann Messenger, "Educational Spectators: Richard Steele, Joseph Addison, and Eliza Haywood," in *His and Hers: Essays in Restoration and Eighteenth-Century Literature* (Lexington: University Press of Kentucky, 1986), pp. 108–47.

24. Antonia Fraser, *The Weaker Vessel* (New York: Knopf, 1984), shows how seventeenth-century England happened to provide unparalleled opportunities for women to be active in politics, war, religion, business and trades, as writers, midwives, and, for the first time, as actresses. Fraser's ending is bleak because she sees the early eighteenth century as a period of backlash: "It is however an almost universal fact of history that women have done well in war time when they have been able or compelled to act as substitutes for men. . . . It is another fact that the post-war period has generally seen a masculine retreat from the view of the female sex when the vacuum no longer needs to be filled. Post-Restoration England was no exception to this rule" (pp. 468–69). This study silently answers Fraser in two ways: First, I disagree with the masculinist biases in her judgments about many of the women she writes about, including her evaluation of the work of writers represented here. Second, although I think that even though women could not immediately build social and political gains after stability returned to English society, they maintained a continuity of thought and writing about their condition that should be made visible, and they wrote to show one another how to control their lives within social confines.

25. Stuart E. Prall, *The Bloodless Revolution: England, 1688* (Madison: University of Wisconsin Press, 1985), pp. viii–ix.

26. See Sara Heller Mendelson, "Stuart Women's Diaries and Occasional Memoirs," in *Women in English Society,* pp. 181–201.

27. Quoted in Susan Staves, *Players' Scepters: Fictions of Authority in the Restoration* (Lincoln: University of Nebraska Press, 1979), p. 6.

28. Ellen A. McArthur, "Women Petitioners and the Long Parliament," *English Historical Review* 24 (1909): 698–709; Patricia Higgins, "The Reactions of Women, with Special Reference to Women Petitioners," in *Politics, Religion, and the English Civil War,* ed. Brian Manning (London: Edward Arnold, 1973): 179–222; "Sharing in the Commonwealth," *Weaker Vessel,* pp. 222–43.

29. Staves, *Players' Scepters,* p. 2.

30. David Underdown, "Honest Radicals in the Counties, 1642–49," in *Puritans and Revolutionaries: Essays in Seventeenth-Century History Presented to Christopher Hill,* ed. Donald Pennington and Keith Thomas (Oxford: Clarendon Press, 1978), pp. 186–205; William Lamont, "Pamphleteering, the Protestant Consensus and the English Revolution," in *Freedom and the English Revolution: Essays in History and Literature,* ed. R. C. Richardson and G. M. Ridden (Manchester: Manchester University Press, 1986), pp. 72–89.

31. Lamont, "Pamphleteering," p. 89.

32. Underdown, "'Honest' Radicals," p. 186.

33. Stone, *Family,* pp. 186–88; Fraser, *Weaker Vessel,* pp. 9–25.

34. Richard Grassby, "Social Mobility and Business Enterprise in Seventeenth-century England," In *Puritans and Revolutionaries,* pp. 380–81.

35. For women's informal influence in a local community, see Mary Prior, "Women and the Urban Economy: Oxford 1500–1800," in *Women in English Society,* pp. 93–117.

36. Joan Thirsk, "Foreword," in *Women in Society,* p. 14.

37. Katherine E. Maus, "'Playhouse Flesh and Blood': Sexual Ideology and the Restoration Actress," *ELH* 46 (1979): 595–617.

38. Anna Maria à Schurman, The Learned Maid: or, Whether a Maid may be a Scholar?, trans. Clement Barksdale (London: John Radmayne, 1659), pp. 10, 15.

39. Bathsua Makin, *An essay to revive the antient education of gentlewomen* (London: By J. D. for Tho. Parkhurst, 1673), p. 4; excerpted in *The Whole Duty,* pp. 25–26.

40. Both Wooley and Masham are excerpted in *The Whole Duty,* pp. 27–31.

41. Elizabeth Elstob, *An English-Saxon Homily, on the birth-day of St. Gregory . . . Translated into Modern English* (London: W. Bowyer, 1709), Preface; excerpted in *First Feminists,* pp. 240–46.

42. Poulain de la Barre, *The Woman as Good as the Man,* trans. A. L. (1677), ed. Gerald Mac-Lean (Detroit, Mich.: Wayne State University Press, 1988).

43. *Poems of Winchilsea,* ed. Reynolds, p. 6.

44. Keith Thomas, "The Puritans and Adultery: The Act of 1650 Reconsidered," in *Puritans and Revolutionaries,* pp. 281–82.

45. Christopher Hill, *The World Turned Upside Down: Radical Ideas during the English Revolution* (London: Temple Smith, 1972), p. 257.

46. Weber, *Restoration Rake-Hero,* pp. 3–12; Staves, *Players' Scepters,* pp. 13–15, 115–18, 136–60.

47. Laura Brown, "The Defenceless Woman and the Development of English Tragedy," *SEL* 22 (1982): 429–43; Patricia Meyer Spacks, "'Ev'ry Woman is at Heart a Rake,'" *Eighteenth Century Studies* 8 (1974): 27–46.

48. Staves, *Players' Scepters,* pp. 152–57.

49. Ibid., pp. 148–51.

50. Mendelson, "Diaries," in *Women in Society,* pp. 193–94.

51. Stone, *Family,* pp. 217–24.

52. David Blewett, "Changing Attitudes toward Marriage in the Time of Defoe: The Case of Moll Flanders," *Huntington Library Quarterly* 44 (Spring 1981): 77–88.

53. Marilyn Williamson, *The Patriarchy of Shakespeare's Comedies* (Detroit, Mich.: Wayne State University Press, 1986), pp. 59–74.

54. Stone, *Family,* pp. 183–84.

55. Richetti, *Popular Fiction,* pp. 148–52.

56. Quoted by G. E. Aylmer, "Unbelief in Seventeenth-Century England," in *Puritans and Revolutionaries,* p. 42.

57. Staves, *Players' Scepters,* pp. 313–14.

58. L. L. Schucking, *The Puritan Family: A Social Study from Literary Sources,* trans. Brian Battershaw (New York: Schocken Books, 1970; first published in 1929); Randolph Trumbach, *The Rise of the Egalitarian Family: Aristocratic Kinship and Domestic Relations in Eighteenth Century England* (New York: Academic Press, 1978).

59. Belsey, *Subject of Tragedy,* p. 221.

Chapter One

1. Margaret Cavendish, *Poems and Fancies* (London: Printed by T. R. for J. Martin and J. Allestrye, 1653; facsimile ed., Menston: Scolar press, 1972), p. 214.

2. Douglas Grant provides a complete and accurate list of Cavendish's publications in *Margaret the First: A Biography of Margaret Cavendish Duchess of Newcastle 1623–1673* (London: Rupert Hart-Davis, 1957). Even if recent feminist scholarship has modified Grant's idealized portrait of Cavendish as a "champion of her sex," one still cannot study Cavendish seriously without using Grant's valuable work.

3. "An Epistle to Mistris Toppe," *Poems,* Sig. A5.

4. Sylvia Bowerbank, "The Spider's Delight: Margaret Cavendish and the 'Female Imagination'" *ELR* 14 (Autumn 1984): 396. Bowerbank documents the contemporary impression of Cavendish as mad.

5. Margaret, duchess of Newcastle, *A True Relation of my Birth, Breeding and Life,* ed. C. H. Firth (London: George Routledge, 1903), pp. 176–77. Cavendish's now famous autobiography was first published as the eleventh and last book of *Nature's Pictures Drawn by Fancy's Pencil to the Life* (London: Martin and Allestrye, 1656). Firth's publication of *A True Relation* with *The Life of William Cavendish* is a gesture that subordinates Cavendish's narrative about herself more than she did, although it echoes the practice of Lucy Hutchinson and Anne Fanshawe, who actually appended their memoirs to biographies of their husbands. Mary Mason argues from this connection that Cavendish "limns her own portrait in a double image, herself and her husband, the Duke

of Newcastle" ("The Other Voice: Autobiographies of Women Writers," in *Autobiography: Essays Theoretical and Critical*, ed. James Olney [Princeton, N.J.: Princeton University Press, 1980], p. 211). The issue is more complex, as I suggest later in this chapter.

6. *CCXI. Sociable Letters* (London: Printed by William Wilson, 1664; facsimile ed., Menston, England: Scolar Press, 1970), p. 52.

7. Dolores Paloma, "Margaret Cavendish: Defining the Female Self," *Women's Studies* 7 (1980): 56.

8. *A True Relation*, pp. 177–78.

9. *Observations upon Experimental Philosophy. To which is added, The Description of a new Blazing World* (London: A. Maxwell, 1666), p. 13.

10. *Playes written by . . . the Lady Marchioness of Newcastle* (London: by A. Warren for John Martyn, James Allestry, and Tho. Dicas, 1662), Sig. A⁸. A good introduction to the ideas in Cavendish's plays is "A Champion of the Learned Lady," chap. 2 in Jean Gagen, *The New Woman: Her Emergence in English Drama, 1600–1730* (New York: Twayne Publishers, 1954). Like Grant's, Gagen's image of Cavendish as an advocate for women needs to be set in the context of all her thinking and her whole career. Yet for the plays alone, this is a good summary.

11. *Plays, never before Printed* (London: A. Maxwell, 1668), p. 95.

12. *A True Relation*, pp. 167–68.

13. *Orations of Divers Sorts, Accomodated to Divers Places* (London: n. p., 1662), Sig. A2.

14. Grant, *Margaret the First*, pp. 192–95. For comments about Cavendish as a writer about science, see Gerald D. Meyer, *The Scientific Lady in England, 1650–1760: An Account of Her Rise, with Emphasis on the Major Roles of the Telescope and Microscope* (Berkeley: University of California Press, 1955), chap. 1, "The Fantastic Duchess of Newcastle."

15. Lisa T. Sarasohn, "A Science Turned Upside Down: Feminism and the Natural Philosophy of Margaret Cavendish," *Huntington Library Quarterly* 47 (1984): 291.

16. *The Worlds Olio* (London: J. Martin and J. Allestrye, 1655), Sig. E2ʳ ᵛ.

17. For the background of Margaret's ideas about nature, see Carolyn Merchant, *The Death of Nature: Women, Ecology, and the Scientific Revolution* (New York: Harper and Row, 1980).

18. "To the Most Famous Universities of England," in *The Philosophical and Physical Opinions* (London: J. Martin and J. Allestrye, 1655). This is reprinted (with the erroneous date of 1663, the later edition of *Opinions*) by Firth in *The Life of William Cavendish*, pp. 209–10.

19. *Orations*, p. 227. An excellent introduction to Cavendish's ideas about women is Mary Ann McGuire, "Margaret Cavendish, Duchess of Newcastle, on the Nature and Status of Women," *International Journal of Women's Studies*, vol. 1, no. 2 (1978), pp. 193–206. Although I agree generally with her argument, I think McGuire does not account enough for Cavendish's changes of opinion or psychological defenses. The range of Cavendish's views and her contradictions are all gathered for the reader from often inaccessible sources.

20. *Observations upon Experimental Philosophy* (London: By A. Maxwell, 1666). This and the following quotations are contained in the "Preface to the Reader" without pagination or signatures.

21. *Sociable Letters*, pp. 225–26.

22. Lawrence Lipking, "Aristotle's Sister: A Poetics of Abandonment," *Critical Inquiry* 10 (September, 1983): 77.

23. Virginia Woolf, *The Common Reader* (New York: Harcourt, Brace, 1925), pp. 111–12.

24. Sarasohn, "Science Upside Down," p. 302; Bowerbank says, "Her work represents, in a whimsical way, a groping toward an alternative vision to Salomon's House with its pretence to finding certain and objective knowledge. And she does attempt a relationship with nature that runs counter to the exploitive mastery proposed by Bacon; her approach is sensitive and reverent as well as subjective" ("Spider's Delight," p. 406).

25. Mason, "The Other Voice," in *Autobiography*, ed. Olney, p. 223.

26. Mary Beth Rose, "Gender, Genre, and History: Seventeenth-Century English Women and the Art of Autobiography," in *Women in the Middle Ages and the Renaissance: Literary & Historical Perspectives*, ed. Mary Beth Rose (Syracuse, N.Y.: Syracuse University Press, 1986).

27. *The Life of William Cavendish Duke of Newcastle*, ed. Firth, pp. 40–41. For a discussion of the differences between Margaret's rhetorical strategies in *The Life* and those of male

biographers of the seventeenth century, see Patricia Sullivan, "Female Writing beside the Rhetorical Tradition: Seventeenth Century British Biography and a Female Tradition in Rhetoric," *International Journal of Women's Studies*, vol. 3, no. 2 (1980), pp. 143–60.

28. Lipking, "Aristotle's Sister," p. 70.
29. *A True Relation*, p. 172.
30. Grant, *Margaret the First*, p. 179.
31. For both instances see James G. Turner, *The Politics of Landscape: Rural Scenery and Society in English Poetry, 1630–1660* (Cambridge, Mass.: Harvard University Press, 1979); "Thatcht House": p. 119; *Poems and Fancies*, p. 95; pastoral: p. 174, *Poems and Fancies*, p. 142.
32. *A True Relation*, p. 172.
33. *World's Olio*, p. 55.
34. *Playes* (1662), p. 333.
35. *The Life*, p. xxxviii.
36. *Playes* (1662), p. 158.
37. *Blazing World*, p. 92.
38. *Playes* (1662), p. 668.
39. Bathsua Makin, *An essay to revive the ancient education of gentlewomen* (London: By J. D. for Tho. Parkhurst, 1673), p. 10.

Chapter Two

1. Katherine Philips, *Letters from Orinda to Poliarchus* (London: By W. B. for Bernard Lintott, 1705), p. 233.
2. *Poems by the most deservedly Admired Mrs Katherine Philips The Matchless ORINDA To which is added Monsieur Corneille's Pompey & Horace Tragedies With several other Translations out of the FRENCH* (London: By J. M. for H. Herringman, 1667), sig. b.
3. Maren-Sofie Røstvig, *The Happy Man: Studies in the Metamorphoses of a Classical Ideal, 1600–1700* (Oxford: Blackwell, 1954), chap. 1.
4. Antony Low, "New Science and the Georgic Revolution in Seventeenth-Century English Literature," *English Literary Renaissance* 13 (Autumn 1983): 231–59.
5. James G. Turner, *The Politics of Landscape: Rural Scenery and Society in English Poetry, 1630–1660* (Cambridge, Mass.: Harvard University Press, 1979), p. 3.
6. See Røstvig, *Happy Man*, pp. 298–306.
7. Turner, *Politics*, p. 106.
8. Røstvig, *Happy Man*, p. 348.
9. Philip Souers, *The Matchless Orinda*, (Cambridge, Mass.: Harvard University Press, 1931), pp. 39–78.
10. Jeremy Taylor, *The Measures and Offices of Friendship*, 3d ed. (London: For R. Royston, 1662; repr., Delmar, N.Y.: Scholars Facsimiles and Reprints, 1984), p. 71.
11. See "Friendship's Mystery, To my dearest *Lucasia*," pp. 21–22; "Content, To my dearest Lucasia," pp. 22–25; "To the truly Noble Mrs. *Anne Owen*, on my first Approaches," pp. 33–34; "Lucasia," pp. 34–35; "Friendship in Embleme, or the Seal. To my dearest Lucasia," pp. 36–39; "Rosania shadowed whilest Mrs. Mary Awbrey," pp. 48–50; "To my excellent *Lucasia*, on our Friendship," pp. 51–52; "Injuria Amicitiae," pp. 53–55; "Parting with *Lucasia*, A song," pp. 65–66; "To Mrs. Mary Awbrey," pp. 70–71; "To Rosania, now *Mrs. Montagu*, being with her," pp. 56–58.
12. Lilliam Faderman, *Surpassing the Love of Man: Romantic Friendship and Love between Women from the Renaissance to the Present* (New York: William Morrow, 1981), p. 71.
13. Claudia Limbert, "Two Poems and a Prose Receipt: The Unpublished Juvenalia of Katherine Philips," *ELR* 16 (Spring 1986): 383–90.
14. Lawrence Lipking, "Aristotle's Sister: The Poetics of Abandonment," *Critical Inquiry* 10 (September 1983): 77.
15. Killigrew's fame through Dryden's *Ode* has made her a subject of derision by critics: Ann Messenger quotes a series of critics—Judson Jerome, Arthur Hoffman, David Vieth—

who agree that notwithstanding Dryden's praise, Killigrew's poetry is insignificant; see "A Problem of Praise," in *His and Hers: Essays in Restoration and Eighteenth-Century Literature* (Lexington: University Press of Kentucky, 1986), pp. 15–16.

16. *Poems by Mrs. Anne Killigrew* (London: Samuel Lowndes, 1686), facsimile by Richard Morton (Gainesville, Fla.: Scholars Facsimiles and Reprints, 1967).

17. Carol Barash has given the best account of Killigrew's attitudes toward her art in an as yet unpublished essay, "'Embolden'd thus, to Fame': Anne Killigrew and the Heroic Tradition," presented at the MLA Convention in New York, December 1986. Barash writes in part to answer Messenger's argument in *His and Hers*, pp. 14–40. I like Messenger's comments better than Barash does, though I disagree with some of Messenger's arguments, and I find confirmation in the views of both critics. Messenger's comments are largely stylistic, whereas Barash's and my own are largely thematic.

18. Dryden said, "Art she had none," and it falls to posterity who wish to praise her poetry to explain that line. I have two mitigating readings. The first is that although Ballard claims Killigrew had a polite education and reading of the Bible and the classics is evident in her verse, she did not have a formal, classical education. Second, she wrote without experience, having died at twenty-five. Dryden, who began composing late in life, may have believed the classical maxim that begins, *Ars longa, vita brevis*. Either of these characteristics would be enough to explain Dryden's line, without its being pejorative to Killigrew's poetry.

19. Ruth Perry, *The Celebrated Mary Astell: An Early English Feminist* (Chicago: University of Chicago Press, 1986). An earlier biography of Astell, still useful, is Florence Smith, *Mary Astell* (New York: Columbia University Press, 1916).

20. Mary Astell, *A Serious Proposal to the Ladies, For the Advancement of their true and greatest Interest* (London: R. Wilkin, 1694), p. 10. I am grateful to Ruth Perry for a reproduction of the British Museum copy of this title.

21. Joan K. Kinnaird, "Mary Astell and the Conservative Contribution to English Feminism," *Journal of English Studies* 19 (Fall 1979): 63.

22. Mary Astell, *Some Reflections upon Marriage, With Additions*, 4th ed. (London: William Parker, 1730; reprint, New York: Source Book Press, 1970), Appendix, pp. 97–99. The first edition is entitled *Some Reflections upon Marriage Occasioned by the Duke and Dutchess of Mazarone's Case which is also considered* (1700). The third edition was called *Reflections upon Marriage* (1706), to which was added a preface "in answer to some Objections." The 1706 edition is published in *The First English Feminist*, ed. Bridget Hill (Aldershot: Gower Publishing Co., 1986).

23. Perry, *Mary Astell*, p. 153.

24. Michael A. Seidel, "Poulain de la Barre's *The Woman as Good as the Man*," *Journal of the History of Ideas* 35 (1974): 499–508.

25. *An Essay In Defence of the Female Sex*. Written by a Lady (London: A. Roper, E. Wilkinson, and R. Clavel, 1696).

26. Hilda Smith, *Reason's Disciples: Seventeenth-Century English Feminists* (Urbana: University of Illinois Press, 1982), p. 145.

27. *Six Familiar Essays upon Marriage, Crosses in Love, Sickness, Death, Loyalty, and Friendship*. Written by a Lady (London: Thomas Bennet, 1696).

28. *A farther Essay Relating to the Female-Sex. Containing Six Characters and Six Perfections* (London: A. Roper and E. Wilkinson, 1696).

29. Writers about Chudleigh, even feminist writers, have often assumed that bitter personal experience inspired her critique of marriage, but there seems not to be much evidence for such conclusions. Chudleigh may partly have brought this impression upon herself by accusing Reverend Sprint of writing his sermon because of an unhappy experience with a woman. Such accusations are commonplace in controversy, of course. The issue should not prevent us from acknowledging Chudleigh's insights about how political the personal is, as family and marital structures oppress women and children. For Chudleigh's unhappy marriage, see Smith, *Reason's Disciples*, p. 163; for one reply to the idea, see Perry, *Mary Astell*, p. 5.

30. Lady Mary Chudleigh, *Poems on Several Occasions. Together with the Song of Three Children Paraphras'd* (London: Bernard Lintott, 1703).

31. Lady Mary Chudleigh, *Essays upon Subjects in Prose and Verse* (London: By T. H. ?
    R. Bonwicke, W. Freeman, T. Goodwin, J. Walthoe, M. Wotton, S. Manship, J. Nicho
    son, R. Parker, B. Tooke, and R. Smith, 1710), Sig. A4.
32. Røstvig, *Happy Man,* 1:417–18.
33. Chudleigh, *Essays,* p. 237; Røstvig, *Happy Man,* 1:418–30.
34. Perry gives a brief account of Astell's influence on Chudleigh in *Mary Astell,* pp. 106–8,
    490; Hilda Smith also discusses Astell and Chudleigh, *Reason's Disciples,* p. 187.
35. See Hilda Smith's discussion of Chudleigh's thought in *Reason's Disciples,* pp. 163–64.
36. *The Female Advocate: or, A Plea for the just Liberty of the Tender Sex, and particularly of Mar-
    ried Women. Being Reflection On a late Rude and Disingenuous Discourse Delivered by
    Mr. John Sprint, in a Sermon at a Wedding May 11th, at Sherburn in Dorsetshire, 1699.*
    By a Lady of Quality (London: Andrew Bell, 1700), p. vi.
37. Jane Barker, *Poetical Recreations Consisting of Original Poems, Songs, Odes, etc. With Several
    New Translations. In Two Parts* (London: Benjamin Crayle, 1688), p. 99.
38. See *First Feminists: British Women Writers, 1578–1799,* ed. Moira Ferguson (Bloomington:
    Indiana University Press; Old Westbury, N.Y.: Feminist Press, 1985), pp. 171–72. See
    also Margaret Doody, "Jane Barker," *British Novelists, 1660–1800,* ed. Martin C. Bat-
    testin (Detroit, Mich.: Gale, 1985), 39:24–30.
39. See *First Feminists,* pp. 171–72, and Doody, "Jane Barker," *British Novelists,* 39:24–30.
40. Lipking, "Aristotle's Sister, p. 77.
41. John J. Richetti, "Mrs. Elizabeth Rowe: The Novel as Polemic," *PMLA* 82 (December
    1967): 522. See also E. R. Napier, "Elizabeth Rowe," in *British Novelists, 1660–1800,*
    ed. Battestin, 39:409–13.
42. See *The Poetical Works of Mrs. Elizabeth Rowe Including the History of Joseph in Ten Books
    with an Account of her Life and Writings* (London: Sultaby, Evance & Fox and Baldwin,
    Cradock and Joy, 1820), pp. xxx–xxxii; the Wellesley Manuscript is Anne Finch (Kings-
    mill), countess of Winchilsea, Manuscript of Poems, held in the Special Collections
    of Wellesley College Library. The manuscript is described and excerpted by Elizabeth
    Hampsten, "Poems of Ann Finch," *Women's Studies* 7 (1980): 5–19; Katherine Rogers,
    Feminism in Eighteenth-Century England (Urbana: University of Illinois Press, 1982),
    pp. 256, 278.
43. Smith, *Disciples,* pp. 170–71.
44. Rogers, *Feminism,* p. 256.
45. Smith, *Disciples,* p. 199.
46. John Dunton, *Athenianism, or the New Projects of Mr. John Dunton* (London: R. Mor-
    phew, 1710), pp. 1–61.
47. *Poems on Several Occasions, as Philomela* (London: John Dunton, 1696), Sig. a2ᵛ
48. Richetti, "Elizabeth Rowe," p. 522.
49. See Ann Messenger, "Publishing without Perishing: Lady Winchilsea's *Miscellany Poems*
    of 1713," *Restoration* 5 (Spring 1981): 27–37; for the Wellesley Manuscript and Hamp-
    sten's description of its contents, see n. 42 above.
50. *The Poems of Anne Countess of Winchilsea,* ed. Myra Reynolds (Chicago: University of
    Chicago Press, 1903); all references to Winchilsea's work not otherwise identified are
    to this volume.
51. Lipking, "Aristotle's Sister," p. 77.
52. Reynolds, *Poems of Winchilsea,* p. lii.
53. Messenger, "Publishing without Perishing," pp. 32–33.
54. Ibid., p. 31.
55. Røstvig, *Happy Man,* 1:410–11.
56. See Reuben A. Brower, "Lady Winchilsea and the Poetic Tradition in the Seventeenth
    Century," *Studies in Philology* 42 (1945): 61–80; Katherine Rogers, "Anne Finch, Countess
    of Winchilsea: an Augustan Woman Poet," in *Shakespeare's Sisters: Feminist Essays on Women
    Poets,* ed. Sandra M. Gilbert and Susan Gubar (Bloomington: Indiana University Press,
    1979), pp. 32–46.
57. Mary Masters, *Poems on Several Occasions* (London: By T. Browne for the Author, 1733).
    All quotations refer to this volume.

58. Mary Barber, *Poems on Several Occasions* (London: C. Rivington, 1735); all quotations refer to this volume. A folio edition with the same contents had been published in 1734, also by Rivington.

59. Rogers, *Feminism,* p. 252.

60. These attitudes both confirm, and bring about, developments described by historians, especially, Randolph Trumbach, *The Rise of the Egalitarian Family: Aristocratic Kinship and Domestic Relations in Eighteenth century England* (New York: Academic Press, 1978); and Lawrence Stone, *The Family, Sex, and Marriage in England, 1500–1800,* abridged ed. (New York: Harper and Row, 1977), chap. 8, "The Companionate Marriage."

Chapter Three

1. Harold M. Weber, *The Restoration Rake-Hero: Transformations in Sexual Understanding in Seventeenth-Century England* (Madison: University of Wisconsin Press, 1986), pp. 3–11; Susan Staves, *Players' Scepters: Fictions of Authority in the Restoration* (Lincoln: University of Nebraska Press, 1979), pp. 111–90.

2. Weber, *Rake-Hero,* pp. 49–90; Barbara Rubin, "'Anti-Husbandry' and Self-Creation: A Comparison of the Restoration Rake and Baudelaire's Dandy, *Tulsa Studies in Literature and Language* 14 (1973): 583–92.

3. P. H. Hardacre, "The Royalists in Exile during the Puritan Revolution, 1642–1660," *Huntington Library Quarterly* 16 (1953): 353–70.

4. John Traugott, "The Rake's Progress from Court to Comedy: A Study in Comic Form," *Studies in English Literature,* 7 (1966): 381–407; K. Z. Keller, "Re-reading and Re-playing: An Approach to Restoration Comedy," *Restoration* 6 (1982): 64–71.

5. See Richard Quaintance, "French Sources of the Restoration 'Imperfect Enjoyment' Poem," *Philological Quarterly* 42 (1963): 190–99; Judith K. Gardiner, "Aphra Behn: Sexuality and Self-Respect," *Women's Studies* 7 (1980): 67–78.

6. Traugott, "Rake's Progress," pp. 388–92.

7. Rubin, "Anti-husbandry," pp. 584–88.

8. P. M. Spacks, "'Ev'ry Woman is at Heart a Rake,'" *Eighteenth-Century Studies* 8 (1974): 27–46.

9. For these changes see Robert D. Hume, *The Rakish Stage: Studies in English Drama, 1660–1800* (Carbondale: Southern Illinois University Press, 1983); Weber, *Rake-Hero,* and J. H. Smith, *The Gay Couple in Restoration Comedy* (Cambridge, Mass.: Harvard University Press, 1948).

10. Staves, *Players' Scepters,* pp. 111–89.

11. Hume, *Rakish Stage,* p. 184.

12. Smith, *Gay Couple,* pp. 135–37; R. D. Hume, *The Development of English Drama in the Late Seventeenth Century* (Oxford: Clarendon, 1976), pp. 492–94.

13. Hume, *Development,* p. 56.

14. Ibid., p. 57.

15. "To the Reader," *Sir Patient Fancy, The Works of Aphra Behn,* ed. Montague Summers (London: Heinemann, 1915), 4:7. All references to Behn's works are to this edition unless otherwise noted.

16. Hume, *Rakish Stage,* p. 62.

17. Nancy Cotton, *Women Playwrights in England c. 1363–1750* (Lewisburg, Pa.: Bucknell University Press, 1980), pp. 103–19.

18. See Weber, *Rake-Hero,* passim.

19. *Works of Behn,* 3:220.

20. Gardiner, "Sexuality," p. 68.

21. "Life of Mrs. Behn," in *The Histories and Novels of the Late Ingenious Mrs. Behn* (London: Samuel Briscoe, 1696), n.p.

22. Nancy Cotton describes the two traditions in *Playwrights,* pp. 194–212. Although my readings sometimes differ from hers, I found welcome confirmation in her work.

23. Mary Ann O'Donnell, *Aphra Behn: An Annotated Bibliography of Primary and Secondary Sources* (New York: Garland, 1986).

24. This passage is from Behn's translation of the sixth book of Cowley's *Sex Librii plantarum*, quoted in Angeline Goreau, *Reconstructing Aphra: A Social Biography of Aphra Behn* (New York: Dial Press, 1980), p. 292.

25. Anne Wharton, *The Temple of Death* (London: By T. Warren for Francis Saunders, 1695), p. 244.

26. For a complete account of this entire incident, see Goreau, *Aphra*, pp. 244–45.

27. Ibid., pp. 265–66.

28. Gardiner, "Sexuality," p. 68.

29. Ibid., p. 72.

30. Ibid.

31. See M. M., "Ephelia," *A Dictionary of British and American Women Writers, 1660–1800*, ed. Janet Todd (Totowa, N.J.: Rowman and Allanheld, 1985), pp. 115–16.

32. Edmund Gosse was responsible for the identification of Ephelia as Joan Philips, whom he also identified as Katherine Philips's daughter, with no apparent evidence (*Seventeenth Century Studies* [New York: Dodd, Mead, 1897], p. 255.) for information about Katherine Philips's daughter, see Philip Souers, *The Matchless Orinda* (Cambridge, Mass.: Harvard University Press, 1931), pp. 91–92. Maureen Mulvihill is presently working on the historical problem of Ephelia's identity.

33. Ephelia, *Female Poems on Several Occasions* (London: William Downing for James Courtney, 1679), pp. 72–73; also in *WD*, pp. 222–23.

34. Goreau, *Aphra*, p. 205.

35. Jeslyn Medoff, "New Light on Sarah Fyge (Field, Egerton)," *Tulsa Studies in Women's Literature* 1 (Fall 1982): 171.

36. Sarah Fyge Field Egerton, *Poems on Several Occasions* (London: J. Nutt, n.d.), Sig. A4.

37. Medoff, "New Light," p. 165.

38. Ibid., p. 164.

39. See Felicity Nussbaum, *The Brink of All We Hate: English Satires on Women 1660–1750* (Lexington: University Press of Kentucky, 1984), pp. 26–30.

40. James Olney, *Autobiography: Essays Theoretical and Critical* (Princeton, N.J.: Princeton University Press, 1980), p. 22.

41. Lawrence Lipking, "Aristotle's Sister: The Poetics of Abandonment," *Critical Inquiry* 10 (September 1983): 77.

42. Medoff, "New Light," p. 173.

43. Cotton, *Playwrights*, chap. 6.

44. Ibid., pp. 180–93.

45. Katherine E. Maus, "'Playhouse Flesh and Blood': Sexual Ideology and the Restoration Actress," *ELH* 46 (1979): 595–617.

46. See Nussbaum, *All We Hate*, pp. 36–37.

47. Laurie A. Finke, "The Satire of Women Writers in *The Female Wits*," *Restoration: Studies in English Literary Culture, 1660–1700* 8 (Fall 1984): 68.

48. Catherine Trotter Cockburn, *Agnes de Castro, A Tragedy* (London: H. Rhodes, R. Parker, S. Briscoe, 1696), poem signed De la Manley.

49. Catherine Trotter Cockburn, *Fatal Friendship. A Tragedy* (London: Francis Saunders, 1698), dedicatory poem.

50. Catherine Trotter Cockburn, *The Revolution of Sweden. A Tragedy* (London: James Knapton and George Strahan, 1706), Sig. A2.

51. Mary De la riviere Manley, *The Lost Lover: or, The Jealous Husband* (London: for R. Bently, F. Saunders, J. Knapton, R. Wellington, 1696), Sig. B.

52. *The Female Wits: Women Playwrights of the Restoration*, ed. Fidelis Morgan (London: Virago Press, 1981), p. 390.

53. Mary Manley, *Lucius: the First Christian King of Britain. A Tragedy* (London: J. Barber, 1717), p. 56.

54. *The Literary Works of Matthew Prior*, ed. H. B. Wright and M. K. Spears (Oxford: Clarendon, 1959), 2:824–25.

55. "Preface Concerning Ovid's Epistles," *The Poems of John Dryden*, ed. John Sargeaunt (Oxford: Oxford University Press, 1910), p. 511.

56. See Cotton, *Playwrights*, for a full account of the exchange between Congeve and Trotter, p. 108.

57. *Animadversions on Mr. Congeve's Late Answer to Mr. Collier* (London: for J. Nutt, 1698); excerpted in *Female Wits*, ed. Morgan, p. 389.

58. See Thomas Birch, "Life of the Author," in the first volume of *The Works of Catherine Trotter Cockburn, Theological, Moral, Dramatic, and Poetical* (London: J. & P. Knapton, 1751).

59. Gwendolyn B. Needham, "Mary de la Riviere Manley, Tory Defender," *Huntington Library Quarterly* 12 (1949): 253–88.

60. "A Preface to the Masculine Sex," *Triumphs of Female Wit, In Some Pindarick Odes. Or, The Emulation. Together With an Answer to an Objecter against Female Ingenuity, and Capacity of Learning. Also, A Preface to the Masculine Sex, by a Young Lady* (London: T. Malthus, J. Waltho, 1683), n.p.

61. Ibid., pp. 3–5.

62. Ibid., p. 20.

63. Cotton, *Playwrights,* p. 9.

64. Ibid., p. 60.

65. See Frederick M. Link, *Aphra Behn* (New York: Twayne, 1968).

66. Goreau, *Aphra,* pp. 126–27.

67. I have analyzed this pattern in the Jacobean play of forced marriage in *The Patriarchy of Shakespeare's Comedies* (Detroit, Mich.: Wayne State University Press, 1986), pp. 64–74.

68. Aphra Behn, *The Rover,* ed. F. M. Link (Lincoln: University of Nebraska Press, 1967). This edition contains only Part 1.

69. Ibid. p. xvi.

70. Quoted in Weber, *Rake-Hero,* p. 156; Weber compares *Rover II* invidiously with *Thomaso* and also presents an excellent analysis of *Thomaso.*

71. Ibid., p. 157.

72. Cotton, *Playwrights,* p. 68.

73. For a discussion of the female rover generally, see Weber, *Rake-Hero,* pp. 130–78.

74. Mary Delariviere Manley *Almyna: or, the Arabian Vow. A Tragedy* (London: William Turner, 1707), p. 13.

75. Mary Delariviere Manley, *The Lost Lover: or, The Jealous Husband* (London: for R. Bently, F. Saunders, J. Knapton, R. Wellington, 1696), p. 36.

76. Ibid., "Preface."

77. Cotton, *Playwrights,* p. 97.

78. Gwendolyn B. Needham, "Mrs. Manley: An Eighteenth-Century Wife of Bath," *Huntington Library Quarterly* 14 (1951): 265–66.

79. Thomas Birch, "Life of the Author," in *The Works of Catherine Trotter Cockburn, Theological, Moral, Dramatic, and Poetical* (London: J. & P. Knapton, 1751), 1:ii.

80. Cotton, *Playwrights,* p. 83.

81. Catherine Trotter Cockburn, *Fatal Friendship* (London: for Francis Saunders, 1698), Dedication.

82. Staves, *Players' Scepters,* pp. 192–252.

83. Cockburn, *Revolution of Sweden,* Sig. A2$^\mathrm{v}$.

84. Birch, "Life," *Works of Cockburn,* 1:xxiii.

85. Mary Pix, *The False Friend, Or, the Fate of Disobedience* (London: Richard Bassett, 1699), Prologue.

86. Mary Pix, *Ibrahim, The Thirteenth Emperor of the Turks: A Tragedy* (London: John Harding and Richard Wilkin, 1696), Epilogue and Sig. A2.

87. Cotton, *Playwrights,* p. 115.

88. Ibid., p. 89.

89. Ibid., p. 119.

90. Mary Pix, *The Spanish Wives* (London: R. Wellington, 1696), Dramatis Personae.

91. Cotton, *Playwrights,* pp. 111–14.

92. Ibid., p. 119.
93. Quoted in J. W. Bowyer, *The Celebrated Mrs. Centlivre* (Durham, N.C.: Duke University Press, 1952), p. 246.
94. *The Plays of Susanna Centlivre,* facsimile editions, ed. R. C. Frushell (New York: Garland, 1982), 2:72; citations are to volume number in edition and pagination of play texts.
95. F. P. Lock, *Susanna Centlivre* (New York: Twayne, 1979), p. 96.
96. Smith, *Gay Couple,* p. 198.
97. Hume, *Development,* pp. 493–94.
98. Bowyer, *Centlivre,* p. 154.
99. John Loftis, *Comedy and Society from Congreve to Fielding* (Stanford, Calif.: Stanford University Press, 1966), p. 86.
100. "In the first half of the eighteenth century it becomes the principal business of comedy (if this term may still be used to describe the plays) to empty these standard patterns to repress rakishness and coquetry, and to recommend contrary ideals" (Smith, *Gay Couple,* p. 199).

Chapter Four

1. *Five Love Letters from a Nun to a Cavalier,* trans. Roger L'Estrange, 3d ed. (London: R. Wellington, 1714).
2. Robert A. Day, *Told in Letters: Epistolary Fiction before Richardson* (Ann Arbor: University of Michigan Press, 1966), p. 33. Also useful for women's epistolary fiction, and especially why the fiction of letters appealed to women, is Ruth Perry, *Women, Letters, and the Novel* (New York: AMS Press, 1980).
3. Eve Kosofsky Sedgwick, *Between Men: English Literature and Homosocial Desire* (New York: Columbia University Press, 1985).
4. Lawrence Lipking, "Aristotle's Sister: The Poetics of Abandonment," *Critical Inquiry* 10 (1983): 75. I have modified Lipking's formulations, using John J. Richetti, *Popular Fiction before Richardson* (Oxford: Clarendon, 1969). Although Richetti's work is not feminist, it is so clear about the ideological basis of the popular works he describes that it is a substantial aid to present feminist concerns.
5. *Five Love Letters,* pp. 17–18.
6. Jane Spencer, *The Rise of the Woman Novelist from Aphra Behn to Jane Austen* (London: Basil Blackwell, 1986), passim.
7. *Love-Letters by Mrs. Behn, The Histories and Novels of the Late Ingenious Mrs. Behn* (London: S. Briscoe, 1696), pp. 403–4.
8. Angeline Goreau, *Reconstructing Aphra: A Social Biography of Aphra Behn* (New York: Dial Press, 1980), pp. 189–206.
9. Ibid., p. 205.
10. Day, *Told in Letters,* p. 159; *Love-Letters Between a Nobleman and his Sister* as a roman à clef will be discussed in chapter 5.
11. Aphra Behn, *Love-Letters Between a Nobleman and his Sister; with the History of their Adventures. In Three Parts,* 7th ed. (London: C. Hitch. L. Hawes, et al., 1759), 1:30.
12. René Girard, *Deceit, Desire, and the Novel: Self and Other in Literary Structures,* trans. Yvonne Freccero (Baltimore: Johns Hopkins University Press, 1965).
13. See Ann Messenger, "Novel into Play," in *His and Hers: Essays in Restoration and Eighteenth-Century Literature* (Lexington: University Press of Kentucky, 1986), pp. 46–53.
14. *Letters of Love & Gallantry And several other Subjects. Written by Ladies* (London: S. Briscoe, 1694), 2:108.
15. Mary Delariviere Manley, *Secret Memoirs and Manners of Several Persons of Quality of Both Sexes from the New Atalantis* (London: John Morphew and J. Warchward, 1709). Reprinted in *The Novels of Mary Delariviere Manley,* ed. Patricia Koster (Gainesville, Fla.: Scholars Facsimiles and Reprints, 1971), 1:355. *The Power of Love* is not included in this volume. Quotations from *New Atalantis* and *Rivella* refer to Koster.
16. Spencer, *Woman Novelist,* p. 114.

17. *The Power of Love: in Seven Novels* (London: John Barber and Joseph Morphew, 1720).
18. Mary Hearne, *The Lover's Week: or, the Six Days Adventures of Philander and Amaryllis. Written by a Young Lady* (London: E. Curll, 1718), p. 6.
19. Day, *Told in Letters*, p. 177; Mary Hearne, *The Female Deserters* (London: J. Roberts, 1719).
20. Quoted by George Whicher, *The Life and Romance of Mrs. Eliza Haywood* (New York: Columbia University Press, 1915), p. 16. Haywood's fiction is available in the following modern editions: *Four Novels of Eliza Haywood*, ed. Mary Ann Scholfield (Delmar, N.Y.: Scholars Facsimiles and Reprints, 1983), which contains *The Force of Nature* (1725), *Lassalia* (1723), *The Injur'd Husband* (1723), and *The Perplex'd Dutchess* (1727); and *The Secret History of the Present Intrigues of the Court of Caramania*, ed. Josephine Grieder (New York: Garland, 1972).
21. Eliza Haywood, *Love in Excess: or the Fatal Enquiry* (London: W. Chetwood, R. Franklin, J. Roberts, 1719), 2:17.
22. Mary Anne Schofield, *Quiet Rebellion: The Fictional Heroines of Eliza Haywood* (Washington, D.C.: University Press of America, 1982), p. 59.
23. Ibid., p. 60.
24. Ibid., p. 83.
25. Eliza Haywood, *Reflections on the Various Effects of Love, According to the Contrary Dispositions of the Persons on whom it operates*, by the author of *The Mercenary Lover* (London: N. Dobb, 1726), p. 12.
26. *Love Letters on All Occasions Lately passed between Persons of Distinction*. Collected by Eliza Haywood (London: Francis Cogan, 1730), pp. 13–14.
27. *The Life of Madam de Villesache* (London: For W. Feales and sold by J. Roberts, 1727), p. 59.
28. *The Perplex'd Dutchess*, ed. Schofield, p. 34.
29. Eliza Haywood, *Fruitless Inquiry* (London: J. Stephens, 1727), p. 255.
30. Ann Messenger identifies this theme as central to Haywood's work in "Educational Spectators: Richard Steele, Joseph Addison, and Eliza Haywood," in *His and Hers*, pp. 108–47.
31. Eliza Haywood, *The British Recluse; or, The Secret History of Cleomira, Supposed Dead* (London: D. Browne and S. Chapman, 1725), p. 114.
32. This change is recorded by Whicher, *Life*; Walter and Clare Jerrold, *Five Queer Women* (New York: Brentano's, 1929); Schofield in *Quiet Rebellion*; and Grieder, ed., *The Court of Caramania*, pp. 5–11.
33. Schofield, *Quiet Rebellion*, p. 87.
34. Spencer, *Woman Novelist*, pp. 152–53.
35. Eliza Haywood, *The Female Spectator* (London: T. Gardner, 1745), 1:74–75.
36. Eliza Haywood, *Epistles for Ladies* (London: T. Gardner, 1765), 3d ed., 1:232.
37. Catherine Trotter Cockburn, *Olinda's Adventures* (London: Samuel Briscoe, 1718; repr., ed. R. A. Day [Los Angeles: W. A. Clark Memorial Library, 1969] Augustan Reprint Society, no. 138), p. 176.
38. *The Adventures of Lindamira, A Lady of Quality*, ed. Benjamin Boyce (Minneapolis: University of Minnesota Press, 1949), p. 11.
39. Mary Davys, *The Reform'd Coquet; A Novel* (London: J. Stephens, 1724; repr., ed. Josephine Grieder [New York: Garland, 1973]), p. 123.
40. Mary Davys, *Familiar Letters Betwixt a Gentleman and a Lady, Works of Mrs. Davys* (London: P. H. Woodfall for the author, 1725; repr., ed. R. A. Day [Los Angeles: Clark Library, 1955] Augustan Library Reprint, no. 54), p. 302.
41. S. G., "To the Author," *Love Intrigues: Or, The History of the Amours of Bosvil and Galesia* (London: E. Curll and C. Crownfield, 1713; facsimile, ed. Josephine Grieder [New York: Garland, 1973]), Sig. Aᵛ.
42. Margaret A. Doody, "Jane Barker," *British Novelists, 1660–1800*, ed. Martin C. Battestin (Detroit, Mich.: Gale, 1985), pp. 27–28. For analysis of the dreams in *Love Intrigues*, see also Doody's "Deserts, Ruins and Troubled Waters: Female Dreams in Fiction and the Development of the Gothic Novel," *Genre* 10 (Winter 1977): 529–72.
43. Jane Barker, *Exilius or, the Banished Roman* (London: E. Curll, 1715; facsimile, ed. Josephine Grieder [New York: Garland, 1973]), Sig. A2–A2ᵛ.
44. Doody, "Barker," p. 26.

45. Jane Barker, *A Patch-Work Screen for the Ladies; or, Love and Virtue Recommended: In a Collection of Instructive Novels* (London: E. Curll, 1723; facsimile, ed. Josephine Grieder [New York: Garland, 1973]), pp. iv–v.

46. For an excellent account of Aubin's career and work, see Frans De Bruyn, "Penelope Aubin," in *British Novelists, 1660–1800*, pp. 10–17.

47. Penelope Aubin, *The Life of Charlotta DuPont* (London: A Bettesworth & C. Hitch, 1736), p. 281.

48. Penelope Aubin, *The Life of Madame De Beaumont* (London: E. Bell, J. Darby, F. Fayram, J. Pemberton, et al., 1721), p. vii.

49. Penelope Aubin, *The Illustrious French Lovers: Being the True Histories of the Amours of Several French Persons of Quality* (London: C. Dorey, A. Bettesworth, F. Fayram, et al., 1737), p. x.

50. See De Bruyn, "Aubin," pp. 14–15.

51. Spencer, *Woman Novelist*, p. 87.

52. Elizabeth Singer Rowe, *Friendship in Death in Twenty Letters from the Dead to the Living including Letters Moral and Entertaining*, 3d ed. (London: T. Worrall, 1733), p. 44.

53. *Letters Moral*, p. 1.

54. For an analysis of Stowe's spiritual and domestic vision, see Jane Tompkins, *Sensational Designs: The Cultural Work of American Fiction 1790–1860* (Oxford: Oxford University Press, 1985), pp. 142–46.

55. Ibid., p. 126.

56. John J. Richetti, "Mrs. Elizabeth Rowe: The Novel as Polemic," *PMLA* 82 (1967), 523.

Chapter Five

1. Patricia Higgins, "The Reactions of Women, with Special Reference to Women Petitioners," in *Politics, Religion, and the English Civil War*, ed. Brian Manning (London: Edward Arnold, 1973), p. 179.

2. See Higgins, and Ellen A. McArthur, "Women Petitioners and the Long Parliament," *English Historical Review* 24 (1909): 698–709; and Antonia Fraser, *The Weaker Vessel* (New York: Knopf, 1984), pp. 222–43.

3. Higgins, "Reactions," p. 221.

4. McArthur, "Petitioners," p. 705.

5. Higgins, "Reactions," p. 222.

6. Ibid., p. 185.

7. Aristophanes, *The Congresswomen*, trans. Douglas Parker, ed. William Arrowsmith (Ann Arbor: University of Michigan Press, 1967).

8. *The Parliament of Women* (London: J. O[kes], sold by J. Wright the Younger, 1640), n.p.

9. *The Parliament of Women* (London: For John Holford, 1684), p. 2.

10. *The History of Rivella*, in *The Novels of Mary Delariviere Manley*, ed. Patricia Koster (Gainesville, Fla.: Scholars Facsimiles and Reprints, 1971), 2:116. Also known as *The Adventures of Rivella*.

11. C. C. Mambretti, "Orinda on the Restoration Stage," *Comparative Literature* 37 (1985): 233–51.

12. Katherine Philips, *Poems By . . . The matchless ORINDA* (London: by J. M. for H. Herringman, 1667), p. 2.

13. Katherine Philips, *Letters from Orinda to Poliarchus* (London: by W. B. for Bernard Lintott, 1705), pp. 156–57.

14. Lady Mary Chudleigh, *Poems on Several Occasions* (London: Bernard Lintott, 1703), "To the Queen's Majesty."

15. Lady Mary Chudleigh, *Essays upon Several Subjects in Prose and Verse* (London: By T. H. for R. Bonwicke, W. Freeman et al., 1710), p. 5.

16. Sarah Fyge Field Egerton, *Poems on Several Occasions* (London: J. Nutt, n.d.). p. 18.

17. Anne Finch, countess of Winchilsea, "Manuscript of Poems," Wellesley College Library, p. 145.

18. *The Poems of Anne Countess of Winchilsea*, ed. Myra Reynolds (Chicago: University of Chicago Press, 1903), p. 90.
19. For Winchilsea's place in the country-house tradition, see Virginia C. Kenny, *The Country-House Ethos in English Literature, 1688–1750: Themes of Personal Retreat and National Expansion* (New York: St. Martins, 1984).
20. James G. Turner, *The Politics of Landscape: Rural Scenery and Society in English Poetry, 1630–1660* (Cambridge, Mass.: Harvard University Press, 1979), pp. 186–95.
21. *Poems on Several Occasions Written by Philomela* (London: John Dunton, 1696), p. 21.
22. Penelope Aubin, *The Stuarts: A Pindarique Ode* (London: John Morphew, 1707); *The Extasy: A Pindarique Ode to Her Majesty the Queen* (London: For the author, 1708); *The Welcome, A Poem to His Grace the Duke of Marlborough* (London: For John Morphew, 1708).
23. See Margaret A. Doody, "Jane Barker," in *British Novelists, 1660–1800*, ed. Martin C. Battestin (Detroit, Mich.: Gale, 1985), 39:30.
24. Mary Masters, *Poems on Several Occasions* (London: By T. Browne for the author, 1733), pp. 70–73.
25. Mary Barber, *Poems on Several Occasions* (London: C. Rivington, 1734), pp. lxiii–xiv.
26. Quoted in William H. McBurney, "Mrs. Penelope Aubin and the Early Eighteenth-Century English Novel," *Huntington Library Quarterly*, 20 (May 1957): 258.
27. Quoted in Angeline Goreau, *Reconstructing Aphra: A Social Biography of Aphra Behn* (New York: Dial Press, 1980), p. 236.
28. *The Works of Aphra Behn*, ed. Montague Summers (London: Heinemann, 1915), 2:107.
29. Goreau, *Aphra*, p. 275.
30. Aphra Behn, *A Pindarick on the Death of Our Late Sovereign With an Ancient Prophecy on His Present Majesty* (London: J. Playford for Henry Playford, 1685), p. 3.
31. Aphra Behn, *A Congratulatory Poem to her Sacred Majesty Queen Mary upon her Arrival in England* (London: R. Bently and W. Canning, 1689).
32. Maureen Duffy, *The Passionate Shepherdess* (London: Jonathan Cape, 1977).
33. Maureen Duffy, "Commentary: Of Loyalty, Money, and Power," *TLS*, 27 July 1984, p. 843.
34. George Guffey, "Aphra Behn's *Oroonoko*: Occasion and Accomplishment," in *Two English Novelists: Aphra Behn and Antony Trollope. Papers Read at a Clark Library Seminar, May 11, 1975* (Los Angeles: Clark Library, 1975), pp. 3–41.
35. Manley, *Rivella*, 2:116.
36. Gwendolyn Needham, "Mary de la Riviere Manley, Tory Defender," *Huntington Library Quarterly* 12 (1949): 253–54.
37. Delariviere Manley, *The Secret History of Queen Zarah, and the Zarazians* (London: J. Huggonson, 1743), p. 39.
38. Needham, "Tory Defender," p. 263.
39. Manley, *Rivella*, 2:113.
40. Needham, "Tory Defender," p. 267.
41. Manley, *Rivella*, 2:118.
42. *The Works of Jonathan Swift*, ed. Sir Walter Scott (London: Bickers, 1883), 2:140.
43. Manley, *Rivella*, 2:116.
44. F. P. Lock, *Susanna Centlivre* (Boston: Twayne, 1979), p. 22.
45. Ibid., p. 25.
46. *The Plays of Susanna Centlivre*, facsimile, ed. Richard C. Frushell (New York: Garland, 1982), 3:56.
47. Lock, *Centlivre*, pp. 100–03.
48. "A Monthly Packet of Advices from Parnassus" (London: For the author, sold by K. Nelthrop, 1723), p. 33.
49. For further description see Lock, *Centlivre*, pp. 127–30.
50. Susanna Centlivre, *A Woman's Case in an Epistle to Charles Joye* (London: E. Curll, 1720).
51. Catherine Trotter Cockburn, *The Revolution of Sweden A Tragedy* (London: James Knapton and George Strahan, 1706), Prologue, Sig. A.

Chapter Six

1. Hilda Smith, *Reason's Disciples: Seventeenth-Century English Feminists* (Urbana: University of Illinois Press, 1982), pp. 151–87.
2. See Harry Levin, *The Myth of the Golden Age in the Renaissance* (Bloomington: Indiana University Press, 1969).
3. Angeline Goreau, *Reconstructing Aphra: A Social Biography of Aphra Behn* (New York: Dial Press, 1980), pp. 271–73.
4. Sarah Fyge Field Egerton, *Poems on Several Occasions* (London: J. Nutt, n.d.), p. 11.
5. *Poems by Mrs Anne Killigrew* (1686), ed. Richard Morton, facsimile (Gainesville, Fla.: Scholars Facsimiles and Reprints, 1967), p. 68.
6. Elizabeth Singer Rowe, *Poems on several Occasions, as Philomela* (London: John Dunton, 1696), p. 51.
7. Katherine Philips, *Poems by . . . the Matchless ORINDA* (London: by J. M. for H. Herringman, 1667). p. 103.
8. Lady Mary Chudleigh, *Essays upon Subjects in Prose and Verse* (London: By T. H. for R. Bonwicke et al., 1710), Sig. A4ᵛ.
9. Mary Astell, *A Serious Proposal to the Ladies* (London: R. Wilkin, 1694), p. 67.
10. Jane Barker, *A Patch-Work Screen for the Ladies* (London: E. Curll, 1723), pp. 4–5.
11. Elizabeth Singer Rowe, *Letters Moral and Entertaining with Friendship in Death in Twenty Letters from the Dead to the Living,* 3d ed. (London: T. Worrall, 1733), pp. 131–38, 268–72.
12. *The Poetical Works of Mrs Elizabeth Rowe . . . with an Account of her Life and Writings,* ed. Theophilus Rowe (London: Sultaby et al., 1820), p. xxxvii.
13. See Ann Messenger, "Selected Nightingales," in *His and Hers,* pp. 71–83.
14. James G. Turner, *The Politics of Landscape: Rural Scenery and Society in English Poetry 1630–1660* (Cambridge, Mass.: Harvard University Press, 1979), pp. 1–7.

Conclusion

1. Virginia Woolf, *A Room of One's Own* (New York: Harcourt, Brace, 1929), p. 112.
2. Jane Spencer, *The Rise of the Woman Novelist from Aphra Behn to Jane Austen* (London: Basil Blackwell, 1986), pp. 81–90.
3. See *First Feminists: British Writers, 1578–1799,* ed. Moira Ferguson (Bloomington: Indiana University Press, 1985), pp. 349–67.
4. Spencer, *Woman Novelist,* pp. 3–5.
5. Doris Stenton, *The English Woman in History* (London: Allen and Unwin, 1957; repr., New York: Schocken Books, 1977), p. 296.
6. Janet Todd, "Introduction," *A Dictionary of British and American Women Writers, 1660–1800* (Totowa, N.J.: Rowman and Allanheld, 1985), p. 13.
7. *The Works of Anna Laetitia Barbauld with a Memoir by Lucy Aikin* (London: Longmans, Green, 1825), 1:xviii–xix.
8. Ruth Perry, "Introduction," *Memoirs of Several Ladies of Great Britain . . . by George Ballard* (Oxford: W. Jackson, 1752; repr. Detroit, Mich.: Wayne State University Press, 1985), p. 34.
9. Katherine E. Maus, "'Playhouse Flesh and Blood': Sexual Ideology and the Restoration Actress," *ELH* 46 (1979): 595–617.

Index

Marilyn L. Williamson is a professor of English at Wayne State University and also serves as the deputy provost of the University. She holds the M.A. degree from the University of Wisconsin and the Ph.D. degree from Duke University. In addition to numerous articles in scholarly journals, Dr. Williamson's recent publications include *The Patriarchy of Shakespeare's Comedies* and an edition of Frederic Rowton's *Female Poets of Great Britain*.

The manuscript was edited by Robert S. Demorest. The book was designed by Mary Primeau. The typeface for the text is Galliard. The display face is Windsor Elongated. The book is bound in Holliston Mills Roxite A Grade cloth.

Manufactured in the United States of America.